THE FLAG THAT CIRCLES TH[E]

The ship that
circles the world
S. S. SOUTHERN CROSS

TRAVEL SHAW SAVILL

COMPAGNIE DES MESSAGERIES MARITIMES

Incorporated in France.

Head Office in Australasia: 36 GROSVENOR STREET, SYDNEY
'Phone: BU 2654-9 (6 lines)

Agents in Australia:

Brisbane:
Nixon-Smith.

Newcastle:
Messrs. John Reid
Pty. Limited.

Townsville:
Samuel Allen and
Sons.

Melbourne:
Macdonald, Hamilton
& Co.

Adelaide:
Dalgety & Co.

Fremantle:
Dalgety & Co.

Hobart:
Wm. Crosby & Co.

Branch Offices:

New Caledonia:
Noumea:
Rue de Verdun

Tahiti:
Papeete:
Quai Bir Hakeim

Agents at:

Port-Vila,
Espiritu-Santo
Rabaul, Suva, etc.

Compagnie Des Messageries Maritimes Le Paquebot Polynesie.

Approved by I.A.T.A. as freight and booking Agents for all International Air Companies.
General Representatives in Australia of AIR FRANCE from Paris to Noumea, via Saigon and Brisbane, every four weeks.

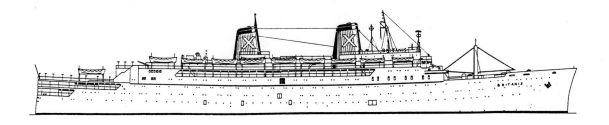

NEW AUSTRALIA AT CIRCULAR QUAY, SYDNEY

PASSENGER SHIPS TO AUSTRALIA
AND NEW ZEALAND 1945-1990

EMIGRANT SHIPS TO LUXURY LINERS

PETER PLOWMAN

NSW PRESS

Published by
NEW SOUTH WALES UNIVERSITY PRESS
PO Box 1, Kensington NSW Australia
Tel: (02) 398 8177
Fax: (02) 398 3408

© *Peter Plowman 1992*

First published 1992

National Library of Australia
Cataloguing-in-Publication entry:

Plowman, Peter.
  Emigrant Ships to Luxury Liners.

  Includes index.
  ISBN 0 86840 379 2.

  1. Passenger ships – Australia.   2. Passenger ships – New
  Zealand.   3. Shipping – Australasia – History.   I. Title.

  387.243099

Available in North America through:

International Specialized Book Services
5602 N.E. Hassalo St
Portland Oregon 97213 – 3640

Printed by Kyodo Printing, Singapore

CONTENTS

INTRODUCTION

This book includes all the ships that brought passengers to Australia from 1946 to 1990. These vessels range from humble migrant ships to some of the finest liners of the modern era. There is also a selection of the more interesting cruise ships to visit the area during the period under review. However, to keep this book within necessary bounds, I have not included those ships that carried less than 50 passengers, unless they were of particular interest or significance.

The logical starting point was 1946, as it was the first year in which regular voyages recommenced after the war, and also saw the start of the massive immigration and resettlement schemes that would have such an effect on the country. Between 1946 and 1977, millions of people were brought to Australia by ship, yet most of these vessels are almost forgotten today, except by those who travelled on them.

Immigration is nothing new for Australia, and in fact started as long ago as 1793, when the first group of 11 "free settlers" arrived in Sydney. For the next 130 years, the Australian population grew steadily, with almost all migrants being of British stock. In 1921 the country had a population of 5.5 million, and it was only then that the Federal Government introduced controls over migrant selection. Over the next decade some 30 000 non-British migrants were accepted, these being mainly from Italy, Greece, Yugoslavia and Germany. In the same period, 300 000 British migrants arrived, many under the assisted passage scheme.

The depression of the 1930s brought this flow of migration to a virtual halt, though the Empire Settlement Act resulted in some 3000 British migrants arriving during 1939. In the same year, Australia agreed to accept 15 000 political refugees, mostly Jews, from Germany and Austria, but only 7000 had arrived when war broke out.

It was during 1944 that the Australian Government began looking towards post-war migration, and in 1945 established the first Department of Immigration. Late that year, a Commonwealth Immigration Advisory Committee made a tour of Europe, seeking suitable migrants, and suggested that people be accepted from many European countries as well as Britain. In March 1946, an agreement was signed with the British Government regarding post-war migration by Britons, for which the Ministry of Transport initially supplied a number of old British liners, carrying large numbers of "assisted passage" migrants under austere conditions. The first departure under the new agreement was taken by *Ormonde* from Tilbury on 10 October 1947, with 1052 migrants.

On 21 July 1947, the Australian Government signed an agreement with the International Refugee Organisation in Geneva, under which 12 000 displaced persons per year would be able to migrate. This number was to be increased enormously in future years, to meet the huge demand from displaced persons wishing to make a new life for themselves in Australia. To transport these people, the IRO sought suitable tonnage, and chartered a large number of vessels of all ages, types and sizes. The first of these vessels to come to Australia was the American troopship, *General Stuart Heintzelman*, which departed Bremerhaven on 1 November 1947 with 843 Balts on board, who arrived in Fremantle on 28 November.

In 1947 the population of Australia was 7.5 million, of which 98 per cent came from British descent. Over the next few years, the numbers of migrants being accepted from European countries increased enormously, so that by 1961 the population had increased to 10.5 million, of which about 25 per cent were of non-British descent.

The peak years for British migration were 1949 to 1952. The actual numbers carried, as listed in the statistics issued by the Department of Immigration on a financial year basis, were as follows, with numbers of assisted migrants shown in brackets:-

1948–49	62 057	(33 579)
1949–50	68 746	(41 704)
1950–51	68 904	(43 198)
1951–52	73 082	(45 113)
1952–53	46 559	(26 250)
1053–54	37 977	(17 679)

As an indication of the demand for passages to Australia, over a four-day period in July 1949, 3646 British migrants departed on four ships, these being:-

26 July	*Asturias*	from Southampton	1340 migrants
28 July	*Ormonde*	from Tilbury	1030 migrants
29 July	*Chitral*	from Tilbury	734 migrants
29 July	*Dorsetshire*	from Liverpool	542 migrants

The number of non-British arrivals was even greater, and in December 1950 alone, 10 ships arrived in Australia carrying over 12 000 new settlers from Europe, these being:-

2 December at Melbourne from Naples	*Protea*	1096 migrants
6 December at Newcastle from Bremerhaven	*Roma*	949 migrants
8 December at Melbourne from Naples	*Skaugum*	1854 migrants
10 December at Melbourne from Naples	*Liguria*	930 migrants
10 December at Melbourne from Naples	*Castelbianco*	1003 migrants
16 December at Newcastle from Naples	*General Ballou*	1272 migrants
23 December at Sydney from Bremerhaven	*Nelly*	1570 migrants
29 December at Melbourne from Naples	*Anna Salen*	1570 migrants
31 December at Fremantle from Naples	*Hellenic Prince*	1000 migrants
31 December at Fremantle from Naples	*Goya*	900 migrants

The agreement with the IRO was terminated in 1952, and a new contract signed with the Intergovernmental Committee for European Migration (ICEM), while individual contracts were also signed with countries such as Finland, Denmark, Sweden, Norway and Switzerland. The ICEM ships were of a better calibre than the IRO ships, but each made only a few voyages to Australia. Demand for migrant passages from Europe declined rapidly during the 1950s, but the British continued to migrate in large numbers.

In 1957, the last of the old British Ministry of Transport vessels was phased out, and migrants were carried on newer liners making regular voyages between Britain and Australia. These included ships owned by British companies, P & O and the Orient Line, and also foreign flag vessels. For many years, the Sitmar company was the main carrier of British migrants to Australia, but in 1970 Chandris gained the contract. By then demand for passages by sea was declining, and on 19 December 1977, *Australis* arrived in Sydney with 650 assisted migrants, the last to be brought to Australia from Britain by ship.

During the 1950s, regular shipping trades had been re-established between Australia and the rest of the world, though the main destinations were still Britain and Europe. By the end of 1950s, the combined fleets of P & O and the Orient Line were offering weekly departures to Britain, as they had before the war. Foreign flag companies such as Messageries Maritimes, Lloyd Triestino, and Matson Line had re-established their services, but they were faced with competition from a number of post-war companies, such as Flotta Lauro, Cogedar, and Chandris.

The introduction of jet passenger aircraft in 1960, followed a decade later by the jumbo jet, brought about the eventual demise of passenger shipping on a regular basis from Australia to the rest of the world. During the 1970s, many companies went out of business altogether, while others transferred their ships to cruising in order to survive. By the start of the 1980s, it was virtually impossible to travel by sea to Britain and Europe, with at most two voyages each year.

Cruising became a major industry, and a number of new companies were formed locally to attract this market. Unfortunately, most did not prosper, due to deficiencies in planning and management. The few that did survive have done well for themselves. The potential market for cruising from Australia is quite large, yet only 7 per cent of the present population have actually made a cruise. Australia is also a magnet for cruise companies on the American market, who have been sending their ships here on long cruises for many years, probably the most notable being *Queen Elizabeth* II of Cunard Line, and the new *Royal Princess*, owned by Princess Cruises, a subsidiary of P & O.

All the ships included in this book are listed by the order in which they first arrived in Australia. As with my previous books, I have researched each at great length, but if anyone can supply further information, I will be most grateful to receive it.

ACKNOWLEDGEMENTS

While researching my first book, *Passenger Ships of Australia and New Zealand*, I made copious notes on other ships that attracted my attention, but were not to be included in that book. Those notes formed the nucleus of the text of this book, but it also required more lengthy research to compile the material I needed. More hours than I care to remember were spent in the New South Wales State Library, scanning newspapers, in particular *The Daily Commercial News*, *The Sydney Morning Herald*, *The Age* and *The West Australian*. Articles and shipping details extracted from these sources proved invaluable to the compilation of this book, especially with regard to the more obscure of the migrant ships. I was also grateful for an exchange of correspondence with Tom Stevens, of Melbourne, who was writing a series on migrant ships for the quarterly magazine, *The Log*, published by the Nautical Association of Australia.

No work of this scope or detail could be undertaken without the assistance of others, especially when it came to the selection of photographs to accompany the text. I possess quite an extensive collection of photographs, many taken by myself, but I have also purchased pictures whenever possible. As a result, many of the photographs in this book are from my collection, but I am also extremely grateful to various shipping friends for allowing me unlimited access to their photo collections.

In particular, Robert Tompkins provided me with a great deal of assistance, including photographs of many of the migrant ships, which were the most difficult to obtain. I would also like to take this opportunity to express my sincere thanks to other friends, without whose help this book would not have eventuated: Stephen Berry, the late Peter Britz, Dennis Brook, Ian Farquhar, David Finch, Jim Freeman, Ross Gillett and Fred Roderick, all of whom generously supplied me with photographs. In some cases, it is impossible to identify the actual photographer, as many of the pictures were uncredited.

Throughout the entire process of researching and writing this book I have had the unstinting support of my wife and children, who tolerated the many hours I spent at my desk and were supportive through the various problems and disappointments that arose during the period this book was being published.

I initially signed a contract with a publisher in 1988 and delivered the manuscript to them in August that year, but in September 1989 I was advised that the contract was being cancelled, for reasons I never really understood. I am most grateful to the New South Wales University Press for taking over this book and providing me with the opportunity to have it published, though it did require some additional writing to bring it up to date for a 1991 publication.

NESTOR

BUILT: *1913 by Workman, Clark & Co., Belfast*
TONNAGE: *14 501 gross*
DIMENSIONS: *580 × 68 ft (176.8 × 20.8 m)*
SERVICE SPEED: *14 knots*
PROPULSION: *Triple expansion/twin screws*

Nestor and her sister, *Ulysses*, were notable for their huge funnels, which rose 75 ft (22.9 m) above the boat deck. *Nestor* was launched on 7 December 1912, and departed Liverpool on 19 May 1913 on her maiden voyage to Australia, following the old sailing ship route around South Africa. For the first months of her career, *Nestor* was the largest vessel operating to both Australia and South Africa. As well as having a huge cargo capacity, she provided excellent accommodation for 275 first class passengers, which was soon increased to 338.

In September 1915, *Nestor* was converted into a troopship, being used to transport Australian troops to Britain. She later took part in the Gallipoli campaign. In 1917 *Nestor* returned to the Australian trade, though still under government control, as her huge cargo holds were desperately needed to carry supplies to Britain. She was not released from government control until the middle of 1919, when she was given a refit.

On 22 April 1920 *Nestor* left Glasgow on her first post-war commercial voyage to Australia, but after a few years the passenger trade began to decline. This was partly due to the route followed by the Blue Funnel ships around Africa, as most travellers preferred the shorter route through Suez. In 1926 the accommodation on *Nestor* was reduced to 250 first class, and she operated on a joint service with *Ulysses* and ships of the Aberdeen and White Star Line. In 1935 the accommodation on *Nestor* was reduced again, to 175 first class, by joining cabins on the boat deck to make suites, and altering some two-berth cabins to singles.

When war broke out again in 1939, *Nestor* along with *Ulysses* remained on the Australian trade, though their passenger accommodation was increased to 265 first class. *Nestor* was used to evacuate children from Britain to safety in Australia, and late in 1941 made a special voyage to the Far East. *Ulysses* also made a voyage to the Far East, being the last ship to leave Hong Kong before it fell to the Japanese. *Ulysses* was routed back to Britain through the Panama Canal, but sunk off the Florida coast on 11 April 1942.

Nestor survived the war, and continued on the Australian trade afterwards, her accommodation reduced again to 175 first class. Blue Funnel Line ordered four new passenger – cargo vessels for the Australian trade, the first entering service in November 1949. On 23 December 1949 *Nestor* left Liverpool on her final voyage to Australia, then was sold to shipbreakers. On 2 July 1950 she left Liverpool bound for Faslane, where she was scrapped.

BLUE FUNNEL LINER *NESTOR*

BRITISH INDIA LINERS

BUILT: *Madura 1921 by Barclay Curle & Co. Ltd, Glasgow*
   Mulbera 1922 by A. Stephen & Sons, Glasgow
TONNAGE: *9032 gross*
DIMENSIONS: *465 × 58 ft (141.7 × 17.4 m)*
SERVICE SPEED: *13 knots*
PROPULSION: *Geared turbines / twin screws*

At one time the British India Line was the largest shipping company in the world, but apart from a period during the last century, their vessels did not regularly visit Australia. During the immediate post-war years, there was a demand for passages from India to Australia, which resulted in *Madura* and *Mulbera* making a number of voyages on the route. This pair was the first and last built of six sister ships to operate from London to either India or East Africa. They had accommodation for 127 first class and 41 second class passengers, and capacious cargo holds.

When war broke out, all six vessels were left in commercial service for some time, but in 1940 *Madura* became a troopship. In December 1941 she was sent to Singapore, arriving on 15 January 1942. On 30 January, as the Japanese closed in, *Madura* was hit by several bombs during an air raid, though not extensively damaged. Four days later, with some 200 refugees aboard, *Madura* left for Java, only to be attacked again. One bomb hit the ship, causing five fatalities and considerable damage, but the ship managed to reach Java, later going on to Calcutta. Only one of the six ships was lost during the war, with the five survivors returning to British India Line service in 1945.

In October 1945, *Mulbera* left Calcutta bound for Australia, arriving in Melbourne on 19 November, and staying until 1 December loading cargo. On her second voyage departing in February 1946, *Mulbera* also visited Sydney, arriving on 8 March, and remaining in port for several weeks. This pattern was followed for a further five voyages over the next two years, though most of those commenced in Bombay. The vessel visited other ports during these voyages, calling regularly at Fremantle, and in December 1947 going to Newcastle.

Madura joined her sister on the service to Australia with a departure from Calcutta in early September 1946, being in Melbourne from 19 September to 5 October, then returning to Calcutta. *Madura* made a further three voyages to Australia in 1947, all of which terminated in Melbourne. In December 1947 the vessel also visited Geelong and Hobart to load cargo. Her final voyage was from Calcutta in March 1948, and took the ship to Sydney for a lengthy stay, as well as two calls at Melbourne.

Mulbera made her final voyage from Bombay in April 1948, also visiting Sydney, and Melbourne twice, her final departure being on 25 June. Both ships were then placed on Indian Ocean services. During 1953, *Madura* was sold to shipbreakers, while *Mulbera* met a similar end in 1954.

MULBERA IN SYDNEY COVE

THE 'VILLES'

BUILT: *1920/1924 by North of Ireland Shipbuilding Co., Londonderry*
TONNAGE: *7140 gross*
DIMENSIONS: *425 × 53 ft (129.5 × 16.1 m)*
SERVICE SPEED: *13 knots*
PROPULSION: *Triple expansion/single screw*

For several years after the war, Messageries Maritimes had to rely on a variety of older vessels to maintain their service between France and Australia. This pair, *Ville de Strasbourg* and *Ville d'Amiens*, were originally built for another French company, Cie. Havraise Peninsulaire, along with a third sister, *Ville de Verdun* of 1920. *Ville de Strasbourg* was launched on 20 August 1920, and chartered on completion to Messageries Maritimes, along with *Ville de Verdun*. They operated on various routes until *Ville de Strasbourg* left Marseilles on 9 September 1922, bound for Colombo, Australia and Noumea, being joined soon after by *Ville de Verdun*. *Ville d'Amiens* was launched on 9 April 1924, and chartered by Messageries Maritimes on completion, making her first departure for Australia on 10 March 1925 from Marseilles.

As built, this trio were primarily cargo carriers, with limited passenger accommodation. In 1928 Messageries Maritimes purchased them outright, and enlarged their accommodation to 40 first class and 50 second class. The ships remained on the Australian trade until 1935, when *Ville de Strasbourg* and *Ville d'Amiens* were transferred to the route through Panama to Tahiti and Noumea only,

while *Ville de Verdun* continued operating to Australia.

After the war started, these ships remained on their regular trades until the fall of France. In July 1940, *Ville d'Amiens* was taken over by the British at Papeete, and used as a troop transport under Clan Line management. *Ville de Strasbourg* was captured by British naval forces on 10 March 1941, and managed for the government by Union Castle Line. On 7 January 1943, she was torpedoed off Bougie, but was towed to Algiers, where she suffered further damage in an air raid. Following repairs, the vessel returned to service. *Ville de Verdun* was torpedoed and sunk on 17 October 1942.

After the war, *Ville de Strasbourg* and *Ville d'Amiens* were handed back to Messageries Maritimes, and returned to the Australian trade. The first sailing was taken by *Ville de Strasbourg* from Marseilles on 10 September 1945, with *Ville d'Amiens* joining her on 29 October. The ships had been given only a brief refit, and offered very basic accommodation. This pair managed to maintain a skeleton service over the next few years, and were joined in 1946 by the war-built standard cargo ships *Bir Hakeim* and *Monkay*, each of which provided austere accommodation for 36 passengers.

Messageries Maritimes ordered two new ships for the Australian trade, and the first of these, *Caledonien*, entered service in October 1952, joined by *Tahitien* in May 1953. This enabled the company to dispose of their older tonnage, so in September 1952, *Ville de Strasbourg* was sold to shipbreakers at Faslane. *Ville d'Amiens* went to shipbreakers at La Seyne in February 1953.

VILLE D'AMIENS

SAGITTAIRE

BUILT: *1929 by Bremer Vulkan, Vegesack*
TONNAGE: *8254 gross*
DIMENSIONS: *494 × 61 ft (150.5 × 18.6 m)*
SERVICE SPEED: *13 knots*
PROPULSION: *Diesel/single screw*

Messageries Maritimes employed *Sagittaire* to reopen their service to Sydney via the Panama Canal, her first departure from Marseilles being on 13 March 1948, with calls at Tahiti and Noumea before arriving in Sydney on 21 May. This vessel was originally named *Washington*, being built for Cie. Generale Transatlantique along with three sisters as German war reparations to France. This group was designed primarily as cargo carriers, but did provide accommodation for 37 passengers. They operated from French ports to the east coast of America via the Panama Canal. In 1936, *Washington* was entering Vancouver in fog when she struck a wharf, causing considerable damage to both herself and the wharf.

Early in 1938, *Washington* was transferred to the route from France to the Caribbean, but in September that year, Messageries Maritimes exchanged their vessel *Indochinois*, which was under construction, for the *Washington*, which was then renamed *Sagittaire*. The vessel was given an extensive refit, during which the original island bridge was joined to the main superstructure, and accommodation installed for 37 first class, 45 second class and 38 third class passengers. There were also facilities to transport up to 922 troops in temporary berths. *Sagittaire* joined *Ville de Strasbourg* and *Ville d'Amiens* on the trade from Marseilles through the Panama Canal to Tahiti and Noumea.

Sagittaire remained under the French flag throughout the war, maintaining a one-ship service to French possessions in the Pacific. Soon after the war ended, the vessel began trading to the eastern Mediterranean only, then in 1948 began operating to the South Pacific again, this time extending to Australia. Over the next two years, *Sagittaire* was a regular visitor, but unfortunately suffered from mechanical problems caused by her heavy workload during the war with insufficient maintenance. During 1950 the vessel was used to transport troops to Indochina, then resumed the Australian trade in 1951.

The delivery of the second of two new liners, *Caledonien* and *Tahitien*, in May 1953, meant that *Sagittaire* could be removed from passenger service. During February 1954, her passenger quarters were removed at Dunkirk, and then the vessel was offered for sale. On 27 May 1954 she was handed over to Cia. Maritime Asiatic Panamense, of Hong Kong, and renamed *Pacific Glory* under Panamanian registry. In 1956 she was transferred to Pacific Bulk Carriers Inc., without change of name. She remained active a further three years, then on 10 October 1959, arrived at Mihara, Japan, having been sold to shipbreakers there.

SAGITTAIRE

UNION CASTLE LINERS

DURBAN CASTLE

BUILT: *1938 by Harland & Wolff Ltd, Belfast*
TONNAGE: *17 382 gross*
DIMENSIONS: *594 × 76 ft (181.2 × 23.2 m)*
SERVICE SPEED: *18.5 knots*
PROPULSION: *B & W diesels/twin screws*

The vessels of the Union Castle Line were always associated with the service between Britain and South Africa, being famous for their lavender-grey hulls and red funnels with black top. However, in the period immediately following the end of World War II, ships of many companies were seconded for journeys far from their normal spheres of operation. It was in this manner that the trio described here made their visits to Australia, carrying war brides and their families, as well as emigrants.

The first of the Union Castle vessels to come to Australia in the post-war period was *Durban Castle*, which had been completed only eight months before war broke out. Designed for the round-Africa service, and providing accommodation for 550 passengers in two classes, *Durban Castle* became a troop transport in 1940, and later was converted into a landing ship. At the end of the war, the vessel was given rather austere accommodation, and on 20 December 1945 departed Southampton, bound for Australia. Passing through the Suez Canal, *Durban Castle* reached Fremantle on 18 January 1946, and Melbourne five days later. She then crossed to Wellington, being in port from 27 to 31 January, then on 4 February arrived in Sydney for a two-day stop. With a final call at Fremantle on 12 February, *Durban Castle* left Australian waters. Soon after the vessel began a refit that lasted until July 1947, when she once again joined the Union Castle Line round-Africa service. *Durban Castle* remained on this trade until 1962, when she was broken up in Hamburg.

The sisters *Athlone Castle* and *Stirling Castle* each made several voyages to Australia in the immediate post-war year, before they were refitted for the African trade. The Union Castle Line ships were noted for their fine looks, and this pair were amongst the smartest ever owned by that company. *Stirling Castle* was the first completed, in January 1936, while her sister joined her in May that year. With accommodation for about 750 passengers in two classes, this pair joined the express mail service between Southampton and Cape Town, *Stirling Castle* breaking the record for the route with a passage time of 13 days 9 hours in August 1936. In 1939,

ATHLONE CASTLE STIRLING CASTLE

BUILT: *1936 by Harland & Wolff Ltd, Belfast*
TONNAGE: *25 550 gross*
DIMENSIONS: *725 × 82 ft (221 × 25 m)*
SERVICE SPEED: *20 knots*
PROPULSION: *B & W diesels/twin screws*

both liners were requisitioned for service as troopships, and saw service in many parts of the world over the next six years.

The war was not long over when both liners were scheduled for trips to Australia, carrying families of servicemen and new settlers. The first of these trips was taken by *Athlone Castle*, which departed Southampton on 30 November 1945, voyaging via Bombay to reach Fremantle on 28 December, then on to Melbourne, and across the Tasman to be in Wellington from 10 to 17 January 1946. *Athlone Castle* then visited Sydney and Fremantle on the return voyage to Britain. *Stirling Castle* left Britain in January 1946 on her first voyage to Australia, following the same route as her sister, calling at Fremantle before reaching Melbourne on 21 February, then to Wellington and back to Sydney and Fremantle. *Athlone Castle* made a second voyage on the same route, departing Southampton on 21 March 1946, being in Wellington from 26 April to 8 May, and Sydney from 11 to 13 May. She passed through Fremantle on 21 May returning to Britain, and then went to be refitted.

Stirling Castle departed Southampton on 19 May 1946 on her second voyage, this time calling at Fremantle on 13 June, then proceeding direct to Sydney, arriving on 20 June. *Stirling Castle* called at Melbourne and Fremantle on her voyage back to Southampton. On 31 August, *Stirling Castle* commenced her third, and final voyage to Australia, calling at Fremantle and Melbourne before berthing in Sydney on 2 October, leaving seven days later for Melbourne, where she stayed from 11 to 20 October. With a final visit to Fremantle on 24 October, *Stirling Castle* returned to Southampton on 18 November, and was then taken in hand for refitting.

During 1947 both *Athlone Castle* and *Stirling Castle* returned to the express mail service between Southampton and Cape Town. In September 1965, *Athlone Castle* arrived in Kaohsiung to be broken up, while *Stirling Castle* was disposed of to Japanese shipbreakers in March 1966.

DURBAN CASTLE IN SYDNEY COVE FEBRUARY 1946

ATHLONE CASTLE IN SYDNEY HARBOUR IN 1946

SARPEDON

BUILT: *1923 by Cammell Laird & Co., Birkenhead*
TONNAGE: *11 321 gross*
DIMENSIONS: *530 × 62 ft (161.6 × 19 m)*
SERVICE SPEED: *15 knots*
PROPULSION: *Geared turbines / twin screws*

Sarpedon was built for the Far East trade of Blue Funnel Line, and transferred to the Australian trade after the end of the war, to partner *Nestor*. Launched on 2 February 1923, *Sarpedon* was the first of four sister ships. On 15 May she ran trials from Liverpool, this being a trip to St Kilda Island, where the islanders were in a distressed state, so food and other essentials were distributed as a gift from Blue Funnel Line. *Sarpedon* made her maiden departure from Liverpool on 9 June 1923, bound for the Far East and Japan, being joined over the next 18 months by her sisters, *Patroclus, Hector* and *Antenor*. *Sarpedon* and *Patroclus* were coal-fired, the other pair oil-fired, and each provided accommodation for 155 first class passengers.

Early in 1927 there were political uprisings around Shanghai, and *Sarpedon* was delegated to transport munitions and supplies to the British Army in China. When the cargo had been off-loaded in Shanghai, *Sarpedon* took the commander of the local defence force and his staff to Tientsin on survey, following which British troops were despatched to occupy the area.

Sarpedon was not requisitioned during the war, but served as a cargo ship on her regular route under government control. Her sisters all became armed merchant cruisers, and only *Antenor* survived the war, and returned to the Far East Trade. However, Blue Funnel Line had also lost the bulk of their fleet operating to Australia as well, so *Sarpedon* was transferred to partner *Nestor* on that trade. First she was converted to oil-firing, and fitted with accommodation for 48 first class passengers.

On 5 January 1946 *Sarpedon* left Liverpool on her first voyage to Australia, following the regular Blue Funnel Line route around South Africa. After calling at Durban on 6 February, she reached Fremantle on 24 February, Adelaide on 1 March, and Melbourne on 5 March. Four days later she left for Sydney, arriving on 11 March, and later called at Newcastle on her way to Brisbane. Homeward bound, there was some trouble among the crew, but this was quickly sorted out. On occasion *Sarpedon* made a regular outward voyage to Australia, but on leaving Brisbane headed north to Hong Kong, and then returned to Britain through the Suez Canal. After *Nestor* was withdrawn in 1949, *Sarpedon* worked with the four ships built for the Australian trade after the war.

In January 1953, *Sarpedon* left Liverpool on her final voyage, which included a call at Townsville. Returning via Brisbane, Sydney and Melbourne, the vessel cleared Fremantle on 7 April. Shortly after returning to Liverpool, *Sarpedon* was sold to J. Cashmore, arriving at their Newport yard on 5 June 1953 to be scrapped.

SARPEDON

ESPERANCE BAY

TOSCANA

NIEUW HOLLAND

CASTEL BIANCO

HIMALAYA

FAIRSEA

ORSOVA

MARIPOSA

TJIWANGI

GEORGE ANSON

FAIRSTAR

AUSTRALIS

CENTAUR

QUEEN ELIZABETH 2

ROYAL ODYSSEY

ROYAL VIKING SUN

ARAWA

BUILT: *1922 by Wm Beardmore & Co., Dalmuir*
TONNAGE: *14 491 gross*
DIMENSIONS: *552 × 68 ft (168.3 × 20.8 m)*
SERVICE SPEED: *15 knots*
PROPULSION: *Geared turbines/twin screws*

The Shaw Savill liner *Arawa* was originally built as *Esperance Bay*, one of five emigrant steamers ordered by the Australian Government after the end of World War One. The five vessels were delivered between December 1921 and September 1922, with *Esperance Bay* being the fourth. Launched on 15 December 1921, the vessel left London on her maiden voyage on 1 August 1922, joining *Moreton Bay*, *Largs Bay* and *Hobsons Bay*, followed by *Jervis Bay*. Accommodation was provided for 723 passengers in one class, and the ships were owned by the Commonwealth Government Line.

The service did not prosper, and in May 1928 all five ships were sold to Lord Kylsant, who established a new company, the Aberdeen & Commonwealth Line, to operate them to Australia. Their accommodation was reduced to 550 in one class, then in 1931 the Kylsant shipping empire crashed. Aberdeen & Commonwealth Line was bought jointly by P & O and Shaw Savill, who retained the ships on their previous trade.

In 1936, Shaw Savill retired their veteran liner, *Ionic*, and sought a suitable second-hand replacement, selecting *Esperance Bay*. Refitted by Harland & Wolff in Glasgow, she was altered to accommodate only 292 tourist class passengers, and renamed *Arawa*. On 22 January 1937, *Arawa* left Southampton on her first voyage to New Zealand, by way of the Panama Canal,

returning around South Africa.

In September 1939 she arrived in Wellington from Britain, and was immediately requisitioned by the British Government. Despatched to Sydney, she was converted into an armed merchant cruiser, commissioned into the Royal Navy on 17 October 1939, and ordered to join the China Station, based in Hong Kong. On an early patrol, *Arawa* stopped the Japanese liner *Asama Maru*, and removed some German nationals, a controversial action as Japan was still officially neutral at the time. In mid-1940, *Arawa* was transferred to the Atlantic, doing convoy escort duty.

During 1941, *Arawa* was converted at Birkenhead into a troopship, with a capacity of 1700 officers and men. She made several trips to South Africa, was present at the North African landings, and then transported American troops to Europe. In 1945, *Arawa* repatriated released prisoners-of-war from Black Sea ports and Istanbul to Marseilles, but by the end of the year she had been handed back to her owner.

Refitted at Newcastle-upon-Tyne to carry 274 tourist class passengers, *Arawa* left London on 7 February 1946 on her first post-war voyage to New Zealand, via Panama. From 1947, she was routed out and back via South Africa, with calls at Fremantle and Melbourne.

On 3 December 1954, *Arawa* left London on her final voyage to New Zealand, departing Wellington in March 1955, and returning to Britain two months later. By then, the vessel had been sold to shipbreakers, J. Cashmore of Newport in Wales, arriving at their yard under her own steam on 21 May 1955.

ARAWA

HIGHLAND PRINCESS

BUILT: *1930 by Harland & Wolff Ltd, Belfast*
TONNAGE: *14 128 gross*
DIMENSIONS: *544 × 69 ft (165.8 × 21.1 m)*
SERVICE SPEED: *15 knots*
PROPULSION: *B & W diesels/twin screws*

The ships of Royal Mail Line were not usually seen in the South Pacific, but in the post-war years, some became regular visitors. *Highland Princess* did not fall into this category, as she only made a single voyage. The last of five sister ships built for the Nelson Line, *Highland Princess* was launched on 11 April 1929, and entered service in March 1930 between London and the River Plate ports. Accommodation was provided for 135 first class, 66 second class and 500 third class passengers, the latter being mainly occupied by Spaniards. The vessel also had an enormous refrigerated cargo capacity, to bring meat to Britain.

The fourth unit of the class, *Highland Hope*, was wrecked within a year of entering service, so a sixth unit was then built, *Highland Patriot*. In 1932 the Nelson Line was taken over by Royal Mail Line, and the five "Highland" ships joined their fleet. During the war, they all served as transports, with *Highland Patriot* being sunk in October 1940. During 1945, two of the vessels made voyages to Australia, *Highland Brigade* and *Highland Chieftain*.

On 12 March 1946, *Highland Princess* departed Southampton on a voyage to Australia with the wives and children of service personnel. Passing through Fremantle on 9 April, she called at Melbourne on 14 April, then arrived in Sydney two days later. Leaving on 17 April, the liner crossed to Wellington, berthing on 21 April and remained in New Zealand waters for over five weeks, loading meat. *Highland Princess* then returned to Sydney on 3 June, and called again at Fremantle on 10 June on her way back to Britain.

In 1947 *Highland Princess* and her three surviving sisters returned to the River Plate trade, then in 1959 they were withdrawn from service. *Highland Monarch* went to shipbreakers, but the other three were sold for further trading. *Highland Princess*, along with *Highland Brigade*, was sold to the Greek shipowner, John S. Latsis, and renamed *Marianna*, her sister becoming *Henrietta*.

It was the intention of Latsis to refit the ships with one funnel, and place them on the emigrant trade to Australia from Genoa. *Henrietta* was altered, but *Marianna* was not, and in 1960 she was sold again, to the Czechoslovak Ocean Shipping and renamed *Slapy*. Within months, the vessel had changed hands again, being sold to China Ocean Shipping Co., and renamed *Guanghua*. Just to confuse matters, when Latsis sold *Marianna*, he then renamed *Henrietta*, and she served out the rest of her career as *Marianna*.

Guanghua operated along the coast of mainland China for many years, and from time to time was seen in Hong Kong. As was the case with Chinese ships at that time, very little was known of their operation or capacities. *Guanghua* is no longer seen, and has no doubt been broken up, but just when and where she finished her career is unknown.

HIGHLAND PRINCESS

ORBITA

BUILT: *1915 by Harland & Wolff Ltd, Belfast*
TONNAGE: *15 486 gross*
DIMENSIONS: *569 × 67 ft (173.4 × 20.5 m)*
SERVICE SPEED: *14 knots*
PROPULSION: *Triple expansion/triple screws*

The PSNC is one of the oldest British shipping companies, tracing its origins to 1839, when a service was commenced from Panama to ports in Chile. In 1868 the company was able to start operating ships from Britain to Chile, via the Magellan Strait. In 1910 the PSNC was bought outright by Royal Mail Line, but continued to operate as an individual entity. The pending completion of the Panama Canal in 1914 resulted in PSNC ordering three liners for the new route that would be opened, cutting 7200 miles off the voyage from Liverpool to Valparaiso.

Orbita was the second of this trio, being launched on 7 July 1914. Due to the outbreak of war, Orbita was completed as an auxiliary cruiser during April 1915, serving in this role until March 1919. She then returned to her builders yard to be refitted for commercial service, following which she entered the PSNC trade to Valparaiso, in September 1919. Accommodation was provided for 190 first class, 221 second class and 476 third class passengers.

In April 1921, Orbita and her sister Orduna were transferred to Royal Mail Line ownership, and placed in service from Hamburg and Southampton to New York, remaining on this route until 1927. At that time, Orbita

was converted to oil-firing, and her accommodation altered to cater for 230 first class, 180 second class and 400 third class passengers. The liner then resumed her place on the trade from Liverpool to Valparaiso, on which she served until February 1941. Orbita was then requisitioned for the second time in her career, this time being converted into a troop transport.

Orbita operated in many parts of the world over the next five years, but when the war ended, her owner did not wish to refit the old liner for commercial service again. Her accommodation was upgraded slightly, and the old liner was used to repatriate prisoners-of-war, and transport the wives and children of servicemen. It was in this role that Orbita voyaged to Australia. Departing Liverpool on 21 June 1946, the vessel travelled through the Mediterranean and Suez Canal, arriving in Fremantle on 25 July, Melbourne six days later, and then Sydney on 2 August. After an eight-day stay in port, she again went to Melbourne and Fremantle on the way back to Liverpool. Here she boarded a further complement of wives and children of servicemen, and on 19 October 1946 left Liverpool on her second voyage to Australia. Following the same route, Orbita reached Fremantle on 22 November, berthed in Melbourne five days later, and in Sydney on 29 November. Again she stayed eight days before departing for Liverpool, passing through Melbourne on 10 December and Fremantle six days later.

In 1950 the old liner was finally paid off, and sold to shipbreakers in Newport, Wales.

ORBITA IN SYDNEY COVE

THE 'MARINES'

BUILT: *1945 by Kaiser Co. Richmond, California*
TONNAGE: *12 420 gross*
DIMENSIONS: *523 × 71 ft (159.3 × 21.7 m)*
SERVICE SPEED: *17 knots*
PROPULSION: *Geared turbines/single screw*

Between July and November 1945, the United States Maritime Commission took delivery of 15 ships of the C4-S-A3 Class, all except one being given names prefixed "Marine". These ships were designed to carry 3485 troops, with a crew of 256, but saw only brief service in this role, as the war in the Pacific ended in August 1945. Instead, they were used to bring home American troops, and some were converted for civilian use by various American shipping companies.

Like most American companies, the Matson Line had ceased operations during the war. Before the war the company had operated a regular service to Australia from Californian ports, using *Mariposa* and *Monterey*, both of which were retained by the government until September 1946. Matson sought to charter a vessel from the government, and in April 1946 obtained *Marine Lynx*.

Launched on 17 July 1945, this vessel began service as a transport in December that year, being managed for the government by Moore–McCormack Line until being taken over by Matson. Refitted to carry 900 tourist class passengers in rather austere conditions, *Marine Lynx* departed San Francisco on 22 April 1946, arriving in Sydney on 5 May, and remaining in port nine days before commencing her return trip. On returning to San Francisco, *Marine Lynx* was handed back to the government. Transferred to the management of American President Line, *Marine Lynx* left San Francisco in April 1947 on a voyage for them

that took her round the world via the Mediterranean and New York, but on her return to San Francisco she was taken to Suisan Bay and laid up.

Matson Line then took over another vessel of the same class, *Marine Falcon*, which was also fitted out to carry 900 tourist class passengers. This vessel had been launched on 27 April 1945, entering service five months later as a transport. On 1 August 1946 *Marine Falcon* left San Francisco for Matson, passing through Auckland on 19 August to reach Sydney on 23 August. Three days later she left, calling at Suva and Papeete en route back to San Francisco, then was returned to the government in December. In April 1947, *Marine Falcon* was chartered by United States Line, and operated from New York to Southampton, Havre and Hamburg until March 1949, then was laid up in the Reserve Fleet.

The success of these two voyages resulted in Matson Line arranging to charter another vessel of the class for three voyages, so on 19 November 1946 they took over *Marine Phoenix*. The twelfth unit of the class to be built, this vessel was launched on 9 August 1945, and delivered to the US Maritime Commission on November 9. Placed under the management of Moore–McCormack Line, *Marine Phoenix* left Seattle on 12 December on her maiden voyage, to the Japanese port of Nagoya, departing again on 4 January 1946 to return to Seattle. In February she made a voyage to Inchon, Shanghai and Yokohama, and on 1 May 1946 left Seattle again bound for Guam and Saipan.

Following her transfer to Matson Line, *Marine Phoenix* was refitted to carry 520 passengers in one class, though the conditions were still rather austere. Two lounges and improved dining facilities were also installed. On 13 December 1946, *Marine Phoenix* left San Francisco, calling at Honolulu, Pago Pago and Suva

MARINE PHOENIX

MARINE FALCON IN SYDNEY, AUGUST 1946

before arriving in Auckland on 28 December, and reaching Sydney on 3 January 1947. Departing on 6 January, the ship retraced the route back to San Francisco. Her second voyage commenced on 31 January, and the third on 22 March, which was the last under the original charter arrangement. The ship was doing quite well, as there was no competition on the route, so Matson had the charter extended for a further five voyages. The last of these voyages departed San Francisco on 12 December 1947, but then the charter was extended into 1948 for a further four voyages.

During 1947 work on refitting *Mariposa* and *Monterey* for a return to the Australian trade had been halted, due to a sharp increase in the cost of the work above original estimates. Responding to requests from the governments of Australia and New Zealand, Matson Line agreed to maintain *Marine Phoenix* in service until *Aorangi* was refitted, and the vessel made four voyages in 1948. The last of these departed San Francisco on 6 July 1948, terminating in Sydney on 27 July, and departing three days later on the return trip, passing through Auckland on 3 August, and arriving back in San Francisco on August 17. On 26 August *Marine Phoenix* was handed back to the US Maritime Commission, and she was towed to Suisan Bay to be laid up in the Reserve Fleet.

The fourth member of the class to visit Australia was *Marine Jumper*, under charter to the International Refugee Organisation. Launched on 30 May 1945, *Marine Jumper* entered service as a transport in October that year. Converted to carry 850 tourist class passengers, the vessel was chartered by United States Line for their American Scantic service, departing New York in June 1947 bound for Havre, Copenhagen, Oslo and Gdynia. She then made one voyage for American Export Line from New York to Mediterranean ports in September 1947, reverting to United States Line until July 1949. *Marine Jumper* then went to Naples, where a

full complement of displaced persons was boarded and transported to Sydney, departing Naples on 11 August and arriving in Sydney on 7 September. On 9 September the vessel left for Manila, returning to Sydney with refugees from China on 9 October, then leaving two days later to return to Naples. Shortly afterwards, *Marine Jumper* joined the Reserve Fleet in lay up.

In July 1950, following the outbreak of the Korean War, *Marine Lynx* and *Marine Phoenix* were among a number of vessels reactivated to act as troop transports, remaining in service until 1958, when both were laid up again, on the Columbia River at Astoria in Washington. During the 1960s, the American Government decided to dispose of many of its laid up transports to commercial operators, and many were sold for conversion into cargo ships or container carriers.

In 1966 both *Marine Falcon* and *Marine Jumper* were sold to Litton Industries Leasing Corp., and rebuilt by Ingalls at Pascagoula as container ships. The bow and stern sections were retained, but new midbody sections were built, extending their length to 684 ft (208.5 m). *Marine Jumper* was renamed *Panama* while *Marine Falcon* became *Trenton*, then was renamed *Borinquen* in 1975. *Panama* was broken up in 1987.

Marine Lynx was sold in August 1967 to Hudson Waterways Corp., and rebuilt at Savannah as a heavy lift carrier, being renamed *Transcolumbia*. In March 1968, this vessel was altered for service as a car transporter at Newport News, entering service in this role in 1969. She was sold to Taiwanese shipbreakers in August 1988. *Marine Phoenix* was sold in April 1967 to Mohawk Shipping, and rebuilt at the Jacksonville Shipyard as a cargo ship. Renamed *Mohawk*, she entered service in April 1968, and served for 10 years in her new role. On 19 June 1980, *Mohawk* arrived in Kaohsiung, having been sold to a firm of shipbreakers there.

VOLENDAM

BUILT: *1922 by Harland & Wolff Ltd, Belfast*
TONNAGE: *15 434 gross*
DIMENSIONS: *472 × 67 ft (175.6 × 20.5 m)*
SERVICE SPEED: *15 knots*
PROPULSION: *Geared turbines/twin screws*

The vessels of Holland-America Line are not usually associated with the Australian trade, but several of their ships made such voyages in the post-war years.

Volendam was launched on 6 July 1922, and four months later left Rotterdam on her maiden voyage to New York, being joined six months later by her sister ship, *Veendam*. Initially they carried 263 first class, 436 second class and 1200 third class passengers, but the latter was changed to 484 tourist class in 1928. Through the thirties, *Volendam* often cruised from New York.

Volendam was on a regular voyage from New York to Rotterdam when Holland was invaded in May 1940, and instead went to Britain. Taken over by the British Government, and under Cunard Line management, though retaining her Dutch crew, she was first used to evacuate British children to Canada. On 30 August 1940, with 335 children and 271 adult passengers on board, she was torpedoed off the Irish coast. All aboard were put into lifeboats and rescued, while *Volendam*, heavily down at the bow, was towed to the Isle of Bute and beached. Later she was taken to the Mersey for repairs at the Cammell Laird shipyard, during which she was refitted to carry 3000 troops. She returned to

service as a troopship in July 1941, and in July 1945 was returned to Holland-America Line.

The Ministry of Transport then chartered the vessel for further service as a troopship, returning her to Holland-America Line in mid-1946. The Dutch Government then chartered the vessel, to make some trooping voyages to the Dutch East Indies, and also migrant voyages to Australia, her accommodation being refitted to carry 1682 persons in a single class. The first voyage by *Volendam* to Australia was really an extension of her first trooping trip to Batavia, leaving there in July 1946 and going first to Brisbane, then arriving in Sydney on 14 August for a 10-day stay. She then visited Melbourne and Fremantle before returning to Rotterdam.

During 1947, *Volendam* returned to the North Atlantic trade again, though offering very basic accommodation. She usually made one voyage each year to Australia, departing Rotterdam in December, and visiting Fremantle, Melbourne and Sydney. On her 1949 voyage, the liner left Sydney on 1 February 1950, bound for Noumea and then Jakarta on her return trip. On 17 October 1950, *Volendam* left Rotterdam on her final Australian voyage, being in Fremantle on 20 November and Melbourne six days later. Leaving Sydney on 2 December, she went to Jakarta again before returning to Rotterdam on 12 November. *Volendam* was then withdrawn from service, and laid up until sold to Dutch shipbreakers in February 1952.

VOLENDAM PASSING UNDER THE SYDNEY HARBOUR BRIDGE

HWA LIEN

BUILT: *1907 by Wm Denny & Bros, Dumbarton*
TONNAGE: *3399 gross*
DIMENSIONS: *350 × 47 ft (106.7 × 14.3 m)*
SERVICE SPEED: *17 knots*
PROPULSION: *Geared turbines/triple screws*

In January 1947 a small vessel named *Hwa Lien* arrived in Sydney at the end of a harrowing voyage from Shanghai. Although unfamiliar to Australians, this vessel was better known to New Zealanders as *Maori*, which operated on the Union Steam Ship Co. express ferry service between Wellington and Lyttelton for almost 40 years. *Maori* was launched on 11 November 1906, when she crashed into the opposite bank of the river, and on trials she ran aground, having to go into drydock for repairs. On her second trial runs, she collided with and sank a small coaster, with *Maori* going back into drydock for more repairs. At the start of her delivery voyage, the vessel ran aground again, this time without suffering damage, but by the time she arrived in New Zealand during November 1907, the Union Steam Ship Co. must have been wondering what sort of a jinx ship they had acquired.

With accommodation for 630 passengers in two classes, *Maori* gave her owner many years of excellent service on the overnight ferry service between the islands, and during a refit in 1923 was converted to oil-firing. In 1931 *Maori* became relief ship when *Rangatira*

entered service, then returned to full-time service during the war years. On 6 January 1944, *Maori* was laid up again in Wellington, and after two and a half years idle, was sold in June 1946 to the United Corporation of China Ltd, based in Shanghai, Renamed *Hwa Lien*, she left Wellington on 22 August, going first to Sydney, then to Shanghai.

She was intended to operate on the China coast, and the local populace considered her the last word in luxury. However, her first voyage was from Shanghai to Sydney, carrying 474 European Jews who had escaped as far as Shanghai, and been given permission to enter Australia. Leaving Shanghai in December 1946, *Hwa Lien* tried to make a direct voyage to Sydney, but on 10 January 1947, the ship radioed that it was running short of food and water, and had to divert to Darwin, arriving on 14 January. Restocked and replenished, the voyage continued, reaching Brisbane on 26 January, and finally berthing in Sydney on 28 January, where the passengers disembarked.

Hwa Lien then returned to Shanghai, but the advance of communist forces on Shanghai brought her coastal service to an end in 1948. She ferried Nationalist troops to Formosa, then in 1950 was laid up in Keelung Harbour. On 13 January 1951 the vessel sank at her moorings during a storm, being raised four months later and sold to shipbreakers. However, a section of the hull was converted into a barge and had a crane fitted, serving in Keelung Harbour for many more years.

HWA LIEN

JOHAN DE WITT

BUILT: *1920 by Netherland Shipbuilding Co., Amsterdam*
TONNAGE: *10 474 gross*
DIMENSIONS: *523 × 59 ft (159.4 × 18.1 m)*
SERVICE SPEED: *15 knots*
PROPULSION: *Triple expansion/twin screw*

This vessel had a long and varied career, mostly under the Dutch flag for the Nederland Line, which included one voyage to Australia with migrants. Launched on 2 May 1919, she entered service in July 1920 from Amsterdam to the Dutch East Indies, carrying 197 first class, 120 second class and 36 third class passengers. After a mere 10 years in service, *Johan de Witt* was laid up, having been replaced by newer vessels.

In November 1932, one of these vessels, *Pieter Corneliszoon Hooft*, was destroyed by fire in Amsterdam. *Johan de Witt* began a refit in April 1933, during which she was given a new Maierform bow, increasing her speed to 16 knots. In October 1933 she returned to service again, and was in the Dutch East Indies when Germany invaded Holland in May 1940. After a period laid up at Sourabaya, *Johan de Witt* steamed to Sydney, where she was fitted out as a troopship. For five years the vessel served the Allies, manned by her Dutch crew and managed by the Orient Line.

In 1945, *Johan de Witt* was handed back to the Nederland Line, who decided against refitting the vessel for commercial service, as she was twenty-five years old, and the political situation in the Dutch East Indies had changed. *Johan de Witt* was fitted out with austere accommodation, for the carriage of migrants and displaced persons. On 4 February 1947, the vessel left Ijmuiden on a voyage to Australia, calling at Batavia en route to Cairns, where she arrived on 13 March. *Johan de Witt* then proceeded to Sydney, berthing on 20 March, leaving three days later for Melbourne, and then Fremantle. She went back to Batavia before returning to Holland, and this was the only visit made by this vessel to Australia in peacetime.

On 15 December 1948, *Johan de Witt* was sold to the Goulandris Group, better known as the Greek Line, though registered in Panama under the ownership of Cia. Maritime del Este. During an extensive refit, one funnel was removed, and accommodation installed for 39 first class and 748 tourist class passengers. The vessel was renamed *Neptunia*, and in April 1951 entered service between Bremerhaven and New York. Four years later she began operating from Europe to Canada, partnered by two other vessels that had made one migrant voyage to Australia, *Columbia* and *Canberra*.

On 2 November 1957, *Neptunia* was entering Cóbh when she struck Daunt's Rock, and had to be run ashore with serious bottom damage. Abandoned as a total loss, the wreck was refloated four months later, and towed to Holland to be broken up.

JOHAN DE WITT

AKAROA

BUILT: *1914 by Harland & Wolff Ltd, Belfast*
TONNAGE: *15 320 gross*
DIMENSIONS: *570 × 67 ft (173.6 × 20.5 m)*
SERVICE SPEED: *15 knots*
PROPULSION: *Triple expansion/triple screws*

One of the oldest liners to be refitted for regular commercial service after the war was *Akaroa*, which made her first voyage to Australia just before the start of World War One. This vessel was launched on 29 January 1914 as *Euripides* for the Aberdeen Line, and departed London on 1 July bound for Australia on her maiden voyage. Arriving in Brisbane the following month, she was requisitioned by the Australian Government, and converted to transport 2340 troops and some horses. In June 1917 she came under the control of the British Government, but continued as a troopship until being handed back to her owners in February 1919.

Following a refit, she returned to commercial service in September 1920, carrying 140 first class and 334 third class, plus 750 migrants on outbound passages from London to Australia. In 1929 the Aberdeen Line ceased operation, and *Euripides* was controlled by White Star

Line within the Kylsant Group until 1932, when she was transferred to Shaw Savill Line. During an extensive refit, the vessel was converted from coal- to oil-firing, and given accommodation for just 200 cabin class passengers. She was then renamed *Akaroa*, and on 30 December 1932 left Southampton on her first voyage to New Zealand.

Akaroa remained on the New Zealand trade throughout the war years, though under the Shipping Controller, and made occasional trips to Australia during this period. In 1946 she went to Newcastle for a much-needed refit, emerging with accommodation for 190 cabin class passengers.

On 5 July 1947, *Akaroa* resumed her commercial career with a departure from London for Auckland and Wellington, then on to Melbourne and back to Britain around South Africa. She made a further four visits to Australia up to July 1950, but most of her voyages were to New Zealand and return, making three trips each year.

On 28 April 1954, *Akaroa* arrived at Southampton at the end of her final voyage, and was then sold. On 12 May 1954 the old liner arrived at the shipbreaking yard of J. de Smedt & Co., in Antwerp, where she was scrapped.

AKAROA

STRATHMORE AND STRATHEDEN

BUILT: *1935/1937 by Vickers–Armstrong Ltd, Barrow*
TONNAGE: *23 580/23 732 gross*
DIMENSIONS: *665 × 82 ft (202.7 × 25 m)*
SERVICE SPEED: *20 knots*
PROPULSION: *Geared turbines/twin screws*

Strathmore and *Stratheden* were the third and fourth units of the famous "Strath" liners built for P & O during the 1930s. The first pair, *Strathnaver* and *Strathaird*, had entered service in 1931 and 1932, having three funnels and turbo-electric machinery. When P & O ordered a third similar ship, she was slightly larger, but given only one funnel, and carried fewer passengers.

Strathmore was launched on 4 April 1935, being completed five months later with accommodation for 445 first class and 665 tourist class passengers. Her first commercial voyage was a cruise from London on 27 September to the Canary Islands, then on 26 October she departed on her maiden voyage to Bombay and Australia.

Despite the worsening Depression, P & O ordered a further two liners similar to *Strathmore*, the first being named *Stratheden* when launched on 10 June 1937. There were minor differences to *Strathmore*, in particular the accommodation, which was divided between 448 first class and 563 tourist class. This was to make her more suitable for cruising, though her maiden voyage was on the regular trade to Australia, departing Tilbury on 24 December 1937.

The fifth and final "Strath" liner was launched on 23 September 1937 as *Strathallan*, commencing her maiden voyage on 18 March 1938. All three ships spent a considerable time cruising, and were so engaged when war broke out in September 1939. *Stratheden* and *Strathmore* were immediately requisitioned as troopships, as was *Strathallan* when she returned to Britain. They saw service in many parts of the world, and on 28 November 1940, *Strathmore* and *Stratheden*, along with *Orion* and the Polish liner *Batory*, left Fremantle in convoy bound for Colombo and Egypt. This was their last visit to Australia for several years.

In November 1942, all five "Straths" were among the many vessels involved in the North African landings, *Strathnaver* in the first assault, the others in follow-up convoys. *Strathallan* was on her second voyage to the area when she was torpedoed on 21 December, sinking the next day off Oran.

Strathmore and *Stratheden* survived the war, and were then used to repatriate troops. *Strathmore* boarded New Zealand troops in Egypt and carried them to Wellington, arriving on 5 October 1945. From there she went to Melbourne, gathering several thousand Tasmanian troops disembarked from other troopships, and took them across Bass Strait to Burnie. In 1946 *Stratheden* was the first vessel to be returned to P & O.

STRATHEDEN

STRATHMORE

Following an extensive refit at her builder's yard, she left Tilbury in June 1947 on a voyage to Australia again, now having accommodation for 527 first class and 453 tourist class passengers.

Strathmore was retained by the government until 1948, then went to the Vickers–Armstrong yard in Newcastle for a refit. This should have been completed in June 1949, but it was 8 October before she left the shipyard. With accommodation for 497 first class and 487 tourist class, *Strathmore* left Tilbury on 26 October for Australia. The two ships were used only occasionally for cruises in the post-war years, spending almost all their time on the mail service from Britain. An unusual diversion for *Stratheden* was a charter to Cunard Line in 1950 to make four round trips across the Atlantic.

In 1954, *Strathnaver* and *Strathaird* had been converted into one-class liners, and when they were withdrawn in 1961, *Strathmore* and *Stratheden* were similarly converted, being given tourist class accommodation for 1200 passengers. However, the demand for assisted migrant passages was declining, and within two years both ships were withdrawn.

On 20 June 1963 *Strathmore* left Tilbury on her final voyage to Australia, departing Sydney on 29 July and

Fremantle on 7 August, then being laid up on her return to Britain. It was normal policy for P & O to sell their old liners to shipbreakers, so it was a surprise when *Strathmore* was sold to Greek shipowner, John S. Latsis, being delivered to him on 11 November 1963 at Piraeus.

Stratheden made her final departure from Tilbury on 7 August, leaving Sydney on 15 September and Fremantle on 23 September to return to Tilbury on 23 October. After a brief period laid up off Portland, *Stratheden* was chartered by the Travel Savings Association to make four cruises from Britain. After a further brief lay up, *Stratheden* was also sold to John S. Latsis.

Under the Greek flag, *Strathmore* was renamed *Marianna Latsi*, while *Stratheden* became *Henrietta Latsi*. They were used to transport pilgrims from Asiatic countries to Jedda for part of each year, and at other times were either laid up, or acted as floating hotels off Jedda. In a most confusing move, the names of the two ships were swapped in 1966, so *Strathmore* became *Henrietta Latsi* and her sister *Marianna Latsi*.

In 1969, both were sold to shipbreakers at La Spezia, the former *Stratheden* arriving there on 19 May, her sister on 27 May.

ORION

BUILT: *1935 by Vickers—Armstrong Ltd, Barrow*
TONNAGE: *23 696 gross*
DIMENSIONS: *665 × 82 ft (202.7 × 25 m)*
SERVICE SPEED: *20 knots*
PROPULSION: *Geared turbines/twin screws*

Orion was built to the same hull design as *Strathmore*, and at the same time, the Orient Line ship being yard number 697, the P & O ship number 698. However, she was given a different superstructure, and only one mast. Her appearance was so different from previous Orient Line vessels, she was also given a new colour scheme, introducing the corn hull and buff funnel. Her launching on 7 December 1934 was performed by the Duke of Gloucester. He was in Brisbane when he pressed a button that sent an electric signal around the world to Barrow, triggering the launching mechanism.

On completion, in August 1935, *Orion* was the first British ship to have air-conditioning, though it was confined to the dining rooms only. Accommodation was provided for 486 first class and 653 tourist class passengers, but was so designed that for cruises, 600 passengers could be carried in a single class. Cruises were be a major part of her schedule, and her first voyage was a cruise from Southampton on 14 August to Norway, followed by a second cruise to the Mediterranean.

On 29 September 1935, *Orion* left Tilbury on her maiden voyage to Australia, creating a favourable impression at every port of call. The only problem encountered was smuts falling on the after decks, and to

recify this, the funnel was heightened in October 1936. *Orion* alternated line voyages with cruises out of Britain and Australia, and in 1937 was joined by her sister ship, *Orcades*. Both liners were requisitioned within weeks of war breaking out in September 1939, and became troopships.

In December 1939 *Orion* was despatched to Wellington, leaving there on 6 January 1940 with the first convoy of New Zealand troops sent overseas. Meanwhile *Orcades* had been sent to Sydney, where she boarded Australian troops, and along with *Otranto*, *Orford* and *Strathnaver*, left on 10 January 1940, linking up with *Orion* and her consorts off Sydney Heads, and carrying their precious cargo to Egypt. *Orcades* went to New Zealand in August 1940 to transport New Zealand troops to Egypt, while in November 1940, *Orion* along with *Strathmore*, *Stratheden* and the Polish *Batory* departed Fremantle in convoy.

Orion was in the South Atlantic in a troop convoy bound for Singapore when, on 15 September 1941, she rammed the escorting battleship HMS *Revenge*. *Orion* had a large hole torn in her bow, but was able to limp into Cape Town for temporary repairs, then continue to Singapore, where repairs were completed. With the Japanese closing in on Singapore, *Orion* took aboard over 1000 civilians, and carried them to Australia.

Both *Orion* and *Orcades* were selected to carry troops during the landings in North Africa in November 1942. *Orcades* had to return to Britain from Egypt around South Africa, with 1000 troops aboard, but on 10 October 1942 she was torpedoed 300 miles west of the Cape of Good Hope, and sank. *Orion* played her part in

A FINE STERN VIEW OF *ORION*

ORION DEPARTING FROM THE PYRMONT WHARVES IN SYDNEY

the North African landings, making two trips with 5000 troops each time, and surviving several attacks by enemy bombers.

In 1943, the troop capacity of *Orion* was increased to 7000, and she operated subsequently in various parts of the world, escaping unscathed from intense air attacks while in Port Said in 1943. She had covered over 380 000 miles and carried over 175 000 persons by the time she was released from government service in April 1946.

Orion arrived back at her builder's yard for refitting on 1 May 1946. With accommodation for 546 first class and 706 tourist class passengers, she left Tilbury on 25 February 1947, being the first Orient Line vessel to resume the service to Australia. Over the next few years the liner made occasional cruises from Southampton and Sydney, but was mainly employed on line voyages. *Orion* was leaving Melbourne in strong winds on 23 February 1949 when a hawser wrapped around one of her propellers. She almost ran ashore at Port Melbourne, but after a four-hour struggle by tugs, the liner was safely returned to her berth. On 17 September 1954, *Orion* left Sydney on the first trans-Pacific voyage

operated by Orient Line, arriving in San Francisco on 11 October, then returning to Sydney. In 1955 she made two further voyages to the west coast of America.

During a refit in 1958, the accommodation of *Orion* was altered to 342 cabin class and 722 tourist class, and she began operating an independent schedule to the mail steamers. Most of her outbound passengers were assisted migrants, so in 1960 she became a one-class ship carrying 1691 persons. In the early 1960s the demand for migrant passages declined, so on 28 February 1963, *Orion* left Tilbury on her final voyage to Australia, which included a call at Piraeus. Leaving Sydney on 8 April, and Melbourne three days later, *Orion* departed Fremantle on 15 April, returning to Tilbury on 15 May flying a paying-off pennant.

Orion was then chartered for service as a floating hotel in Hamburg for the International Gardening Exhibition. With a capacity of 1150 guests, she lay alongside the Overseas Landing Stage from 23 May to 30 September 1963. On 1 October, *Orion* left Hamburg bound for Antwerp, where she was handed over to shipbreakers.

ATLANTIS

BUILT: *1913 by Harland & Wolff Ltd, Belfast*
TONNAGE: *15 363 gross*
DIMENSIONS: *589 × 67 ft (179.5 × 20.5 m)*
SERVICE SPEED: *17 knots*
PROPULSION: *Triple expansion/triple screws*

This beautiful liner had five distinct careers, first as a regular passenger liner under the name *Andes*, interrupted by several years as an armed merchant cruiser, then as the full-time cruise liner *Atlantis*. For seven years she became a hospital ship, and finally served as an emigrant carrier. Although the majority of her voyages in this final role were to New Zealand, the vessel also made several trips to Australia.

Between 1905 and 1915 the Royal Mail Line built a series of nine passenger liners. The seventh unit was intended for the subsidiary Pacific Steam Navigation Co., only to be transferred to Royal Mail while being built. Launched on 8 May 1913 as *Andes*, she made her maiden voyage in September from Liverpool to Valparaiso on behalf of the PSNC, then joined the Royal Mail service from Southampton to River Plate ports. *Andes* had accommodation for 380 first class, 250 second class and 700 third class, the latter intended for Spanish migrants.

When war broke out in 1914, *Andes* began operating from Liverpool, but in March 1915 she was requisitioned, and converted into an armed merchant cruiser, being armed with eight 6-inch guns. *Andes*

joined the 10th Cruiser Squadron, patrolling between Scotland and Norway, along with one of her sisters, *Alcantara*. On 29 February 1916, *Andes* sighted a suspicious vessel, and closed in for inspection. Just at this time, *Alcantara* also appeared on the scene, and stopped to lower a boat to board the suspicious vessel, which suddenly dropped her Norwegian disguise, hoisted a German ensign, and began firing on *Alcantara* at short range. *Alcantara* was soon sinking, as *Andes* rapidly closed in, shelling the German ship until it, too, sank. The German was later identified as the raider *Greif*, and *Andes* picked up survivors from both vessels.

Andes finished the war escorting Atlantic convoys, then made a voyage to Murmansk before being handed back to Royal Mail in January 1919. After being refitted at her builder's yard, *Andes* left Southampton on 4 November 1919 to resume her commercial career. However, as the 1920s progressed, demand for passages to South America, especially by migrants, declined considerably. In 1930 *Andes* was withdrawn from the trade, and went to Gladstone Dock in Liverpool to be refitted as a cruise liner.

Converted to oil-firing, and fitted out with luxurious accommodation for 450 first class passengers, she was painted all white and renamed *Atlantis*. Entering her new service in October 1930, *Atlantis* cruised to the Mediterranean, Norway, the West Indies, even as far as the Pacific. In 1933 she was further upgraded, and had an outdoor swimming pool installed. She took part in

ATLANTIS IN WELLINGTON, NEW ZEALAND

the 1935 Silver Jubilee naval review at Spithead in honour of King George V, and the Coronation Review for King George VI in 1937.

Late in August 1939, *Atlantis* was in Danzig on a cruise, when she was ordered to return to Britain, being one of the last British ships to pass through the Kiel Canal. On arriving in Southampton on 25 August, she was taken over by the government, and then bought outright by the Ministry of War Transport a few weeks later, with Royal Mail Line as her managers. Converted into HM Hospital Ship *No. 33*, with a medical staff numbering 129, she was sent to Alexandria. Returning to Britain in 1940, *Atlantis* made several trips to Norway, being bombed on 1 May and 5 May by German aircraft, despite her markings, but not suffering any damage. On 8 June she was in company with the Orient liner *Orama*, then a troopship, when the German heavy cruiser *Admiral Hipper* appeared. *Orama* was shelled and sunk, but *Atlantis* was allowed to proceed. For two years *Atlantis* carried wounded soldiers between Suez and Durban, later serving in the Atlantic and Mediterranean.

During her seven years as a hospital ship, *Atlantis* carried over 35 000 wounded, and voyaged over 280 000 miles. Her final voyage was from Britain to Australia with war brides in September 1946, on her return trip collecting the Italian brides of Polish soldiers at Naples, and transporting them to England. *Atlantis* was then refitted in London for further service, this time as an emigrant carrier. In contrast to her pre-war luxury, she was now fitted with austere accommodation for 900

persons, and repainted in her original Royal Mail Line colours, as they were still managing the ship for the Ministry of Transport.

On 3 September 1947, *Atlantis* left Southampton on her first emigrant trip, arriving in Fremantle on 1 October, then going directly to Wellington, berthing on 12 October, returning to Britain via Fremantle and Bombay. On 21 December she left Southampton, again bound for the same ports, and made several similar voyages early in 1948. *Atlantis* was then taken on a four-year charter by the New Zealand Government, leaving London on 30 November 1948 on her first voyage under this arrangement.

The vessel also made several voyages to Australia during this period, as on 26 November 1949 she left Southampton for Fremantle, arriving on 10 January 1950, then returning to London. On her next voyage, *Atlantis* left London on 31 March 1950 for New Zealand, with 870 single emigrants comprising 581 males and 289 females. By now the liner was nearly 40 years old, and her machinery was wearing out. The voyage scheduled to depart on 30 November 1950 was delayed by engine trouble, which continued to plague her through 1951.

On 16 August 1951, *Atlantis* left Southampton on her final voyage, passing through Fremantle on 19 September en route to Wellington. Departing there on 8 October, she called at Fremantle again on 21 October, and on her return to Britain, was laid up in the Clyde. Early in 1952, *Atlantis* was sold to shipbreakers at Faslane.

ATLANTIS DEPARTING SOUTHAMPTON ON HER LAST VOYAGE

SHAW SAVILL QUARTET

CORINTHIC

BUILT: *1947 by Cammell Laird & Co., Birkenhead*
TONNAGE: *15 682 gross*
DIMENSIONS: *560 × 71 ft (170.6 × 21.7 m)*
SERVICE SPEED: *17 knots*
PROPULSION: *Geared turbines/twin screws*

ATHENIC

BUILT: *1947 by Harland & Wolff Ltd, Belfast*
TONNAGE: *15 187 gross*
DIMENSIONS: *564 × 71 ft (171.8 × 21.7 m)*
SERVICE SPEED: *17 knots*
PROPULSION: *Geared turbines/twin screws*

GOTHIC

BUILT: *1948 by Swan, Hunter & Wigham Richardson, Newcastle*
TONNAGE: *15 902 gross*
DIMENSIONS: *561 × 72 ft (171 × 22 m)*
SERVICE SPEED: *17 knots*
PROPULSION: *Geared turbines/twin screws*

CERAMIC

BUILT: *1948 by Cammell Laird & Co., Birkenhead*
TONNAGE: *15 896 gross*
DIMENSIONS: *564 × 72 ft (171.9 × 22 m)*
SERVICE SPEED: *17 knots*
PROPULSION: *Geared turbines/twin screws*

As soon as possible after the war ended, Shaw Savill & Albion ordered a group of four passenger–cargo liners, for their service to New Zealand. They were given a large cargo capacity, and accommodation for 85 first class passengers only, in 53 cabins, of which 36 were single-berth, and 23 had private facilities. The order was divided between three British shipyards, and for this reason, there were minor differences between all the ships.

The first to be launched was *Corinthic*, on 30 May 1946. She should have been completed in February 1947, but on 4 January a fire broke out on the ship. Firemen pumped so much water on the blaze it was feared the vessel would capsize at her dock, but eventually the fire was extinguished, and the water pumped out. *Corinthic* was delivered to Shaw Savill in April 1947, and left Liverpool on her maiden voyage, which took her first to Cape Town, then on to Fremantle, Melbourne and Sydney, before arriving in Auckland on 7 June. The vessel returned via the Panama Canal to London, which was to be the base port for all four ships. On 26 November 1946, *Athenic* was launched, leaving London on her maiden voyage on 1 August 1947, following the regular route to New Zealand and back through the Panama Canal.

The second pair of ships were slightly wider, with

CERAMIC, WITH THE SYDNEY SKYLINE BEHIND

ATHENIC IN SYDNEY HARBOUR

Gothic being the first launched, on 12 December 1947, followed by *Ceramic* on 30 December. *Ceramic* was the first completed, departing Liverpool on 16 November 1948 for her maiden voyage to New Zealand, returning to London. *Gothic* also departed Liverpool on her maiden voyage, but it was on an unusual route, going first to Cape Town and then to Fremantle, Melbourne and Sydney, from where she returned by the same ports to London. *Gothic* then made her first voyage to New Zealand, so that all four ships were finally able to operate regular monthly departures on the route for which they were built.

At first the two pairs were indistinguishable, but after a short time in service, *Gothic* and *Ceramic* had Thorneycroft smoke deflectors fitted to the tops of their funnels, which gave them a distinctive appearance. In 1950 it was announced that King George VI would tour Australia and New Zealand in 1952, and that one of the new Shaw Savill vessels would be used as a Royal yacht for part of the journey. After reference to sailing schedules, *Ceramic* was selected, and during 1951 her hull was painted white in preparation for the voyage. However, a series of delays in New Zealand put the ship behind schedule, and as the time grew nearer it was decided to use *Gothic* instead.

In September 1951, *Gothic* went to the Cammell Laird shipyard to be converted for her special role, with furniture for the Royal suites coming from the old Royal Yacht, *Victoria & Albert*. At the same time, the funnel was heightened and a saluting platform erected over the wheelhouse. A full cargo was to be carried to New Zealand, so when the work was completed in December 1951, *Gothic* went to Southampton to load.

On 12 January 1952, *Gothic* left Southampton for Mombasa, where the King was due to join the ship on 7 February. However, the King was in poor health, and at the last minute it was decided that Princess Elizabeth would make the tour instead, going first to Ceylon, then Australia and New Zealand. *Gothic* was waiting in Mombasa when, on 6 February, King George VI died, and the tour was cancelled. *Gothic* continued to Australia to unload her cargo, then returned to Britain to have the Royal fittings removed, and resume her normal schedule.

The Royal Tour was rescheduled for 1953, and again *Gothic* was selected to serve as the Royal Yacht. On 3 September 1952 she arrived back at the Cammell Laird shipyard to have the Royal furniture installed once more, and be painted white again. Again a full cargo was loaded before the vessel left London in November 1953 for Kingston, Jamaica, where the new Queen boarded, having flown from London. After visits to Fiji and Tonga, the ship arrived in New Zealand in January 1954. *Gothic* discharged her cargo at various ports, while the Royal party toured the country, then rejoined the ship at Bluff. *Gothic* then crossed to Sydney, arriving on 3 February 1954. After their Australian tour, the Royal party rejoined *Gothic* at Fremantle on 1 April, and left for Aden. Here the Queen left *Gothic* and boarded the new Royal Yacht *Britannia* for the final stages of the tour. *Gothic* continued to London, to discharge cargo loaded in New Zealand and Australia, then was returned to her original state at the Cammell Laird yard.

Over the next decade, the four ships maintained a regular service to New Zealand, but in 1964 Shaw Savill decided to remove the passenger accommodation from *Corinthic* and *Athenic*. On 28 January 1965, *Athenic* made her final departure from London as a passenger carrier, followed by *Corinthic* on 18 February, and on their return both were relegated to carry cargo only. They operated in this state until 1969, when both were sold to Taiwanese shipbreakers. *Athenic* left London in August, bound for Philadelphia and Montreal, from where she voyaged to Kaohsiung, arriving on 25 October. *Corinthic* made a regular voyage to New Zealand, then crossed to Sydney, departing on 10 October and arriving at Kaohsiung on 23 October.

Ceramic and *Gothic* continued to carry passengers,

and on 28 July 1968 *Gothic* left Bluff, with six passengers and seventy-two crew on board. Five days out a fire broke out in the superstructure which destroyed the radio room before a message could be sent, and later burnt out the bridge. Four passengers and two crew lost their lives in the fire, which left the ship with no communications and few navigational aids. However, the master was able to bring the ship back to Wellington on 6 August.

Temporary repairs were effected, and the ship returned to Britain, arriving in Liverpool on 10 October. The damage was so great it was not fully repaired, and after one more round trip to New Zealand, *Gothic* was withdrawn. Soon after she was sold to Taiwanese shipbreakers, arriving in Kaohsiung on 13 August 1969.

Ceramic was left to maintain a lone service for three more years, then was also withdrawn. The day of the passenger–cargo liner was over, so the vessel was sold to shipbreakers, in this case Boel & Fils of Antwerp. *Ceramic* arrived at their yard on 13 June 1972.

GOTHIC

MISR AND AL SUDAN

BUILT: *1943/1944 by Consolidated Steel Corp.,*
Wilmington, California
TONNAGE: *7372 gross*
DIMENSIONS: *417 × 60 ft (127.1 × 18.2 m)*
SERVICE SPEED: *14 knots*
PROPULSION: *Geared turbines/single screw*

This pair of Egyptian vessels made several voyages to Australia with migrants. They were laid down as standard C1 type cargo ships, *Misr* being launched on 8 September 1943, as *Cape St Roque*, while her sister was named *Cape St Vincent* when launched on 16 November 1943. Both were completed as landing ships infantry (large), being fitted out with extensive accommodation for troops. They were then handed over to the British Government under the lend-lease scheme. Initially they were renamed *Empire Mace* and *Empire Arquebus* respectively, then were transferred to the Royal Navy and became HMS *Galteemore* and HMS *Cicero*. They took part in the Normandy landings, and later served in the Pacific. During 1946 both ships were handed back to the Ministry of Transport, regaining their "Empire" names briefly before being handed back to the Americans, and once again resuming their original "Cape" names.

The Americans had no use for the pair, and in 1947 they were sold to Soc. Misr de Nav. Maritime S.A.E., of Alexandria, who renamed them *Misr* and *Al Sudan*. The Egyptians retained the troop accommodation, and placed the vessels on the pilgrim trade to Jedda for part of each year, offering them for charter at other times. They could carry about 770 persons, so were ideal for transporting migrants, or displaced persons on behalf of the IRO.

On 10 March 1947, *Misr* departed from Haifa, called at Mombasa on 24 March, and then voyaged to Fremantle, arriving on 14 April, then Melbourne on 20 April. Leaving on 6 May, she again stopped at Fremantle before crossing to Durban, and back to Egypt. On 1 December 1947, *Misr* departed Alexandria on her second voyage to Australia, calling at Fremantle before arriving in Melbourne on 31 December. *Al Sudan* left Alexandria on 20 December 1947 for the same two ports, being in Fremantle on 27 February and Melbourne from 3 March for nine days loading cargo before returning to Egypt via Singapore. *Misr* returned to Genoa, departing there on 15 March 1948 on another voyage to Melbourne, arriving on 28 April, and departing on 12 May for Genoa and Marseilles. *Misr* made a further four voyages to Australia at irregular intervals up to 1951, but it seems that *Al Sudan* made only the one trip.

Subsequently the accommodation on these ships was altered to 54 first and 117 second class, but on pilgrim voyages they would carry up to 1143 persons, using temporary quarters installed in the cargo holds. In the late 1950s, Soc. Misr de Nav. Maritime amalgamated with the Alexandria Nav. Co. to form Soc. Generale Pour la Navigation Maritime S.A.E., but in the early 1960s all Egyptian shipping companies were nationalised into a single entity, United Arab Maritime Co. Throughout all these changes, *Misr* and *Al Sudan* remained on their usual trades.

In 1980 both ships were laid up, and offered for sale. *Al Sudan* was sold to shipbreakers in Suez, where she arrived on 20 October 1980, but work did not commence on dismantling her until July 1984. *Misr* was sold to Millwala Sons Ltd of Pakistan, and arrived at their shipbreaking location on Gadani Beach on 30 January 1982.

THE EGYPTIAN MIGRANT SHIP *MISR*

THE 'GENERALS'

BUILT: *1944–45 by Kaiser Co., Richmond, California*
TONNAGE: *10 645 gross*
DIMENSIONS: *523 × 71 ft (159.3 × 21.7 m)*
SERVICE SPEED: *17 knots*
PROPULSION: *Geared turbines / single screw*

The International Refugee Organisation was faced with the problem of moving huge numbers of displaced persons from Europe when the war ended. To facilitate this, a motley collection of vessels was chartered by the IRO, including a group of 10 American troopships.

During the war, the Americans had greatly expanded their troopship fleet, including a group of thirty vessels classified as Class C4–S–A1, all built in California between 1943 and 1945. The first of these ships was launched on 11 November 1942 and named *General G. O. Squier*, and the rest were launched at almost monthly intervals. Fitting out usually took about a year, but on completion these ships could carry up to 3000 troops in quite comfortable conditions, with a crew numbering 256 men. The first of the series was completed and entered service in October 1943, with a further 16 being completed during 1944, and the last of the series, *General Stuart Heintzelmann*, entering service in October 1945. All 30 ships served primarily in the Pacific, and all survived the war. During 1946, five of the vessels were laid up in the US Reserve Fleet, while the other 25 were transferred to the US Army. For some time all these vessels were kept busy repatriating American soldiers from the various theatres of the war. A few of the class visited Australia in these years, the

first being *General J. H. McRae* in January 1945, while others to visit included *General A. W. Greely*, *General C. G. Morten*, *General Le Roy Eltinge*, *General R. E. Callan*, and *General W. F. Hase*.

By the end of 1947, there was less demand on these ships in their trooping role, and some were placed at the disposal of the International Refugee Organisation to assist in the transportation of displaced persons. The usual departure point for IRO ships was Naples, though some voyages did commence at either Genoa or Bremerhaven. The first of the "General" class ships to voyage to Australia under IRO auspices was *General Stuart Heintzelmann*, which arrived in Fremantle in November 1947 with 843 persons on board.

In order to suit these vessels for their civilian role, separated quarters for males and females were required, and no more than 1000 were carried on each trip. Whilst the accommodation was somewhat austere, it was a great improvement on the rather squalid conditions endured in the various camps that housed these unfortunate people until they left for their new homeland. The American crewmen took great care of their passengers, especially the children, and for most, these voyages introduced them to such previously unknown delights as ice cream and motion pictures.

During September and October 1947, authorities from the Australian Government visited camps in Germany housing displaced Balts, people from Lithuania, Latvia and Estonia, whose homelands were now under communist control. A total of 843 adults were selected to be taken to Australia as migrants, and this group was taken to Bremerhaven to board the

GENERAL STUART HEINTZELMANN IN DARLING HARBOUR, SYDNEY

GENERAL A. W. GREELY

Heintzelmann. The vessel then made a fast passage to Fremantle, arriving there on 28 November 1947. The final destination of the Balts was Melbourne, but they were taken ashore in Fremantle, apart from four who were refused entry and returned to Europe. The day after the *Heintzelmann* arrived, *Kanimbla* arrived in Fremantle with a full complement of internees and prisoners–of–war being repatriated to Europe. These people were transferred from *Kanimbla* to *Heintzelmann*, which then left for Bremerhaven again, while the Balts were taken from their overnight camp to *Kanimbla*, and completed their journey to Melbourne.

In January 1948, a second group of selected displaced persons arrived at Fremantle on the second of the troopships to be used, *General M. B. Stewart*, which then left for Bombay. The third voyage was taken by *General W. M. Black*, also from Bremerhaven, and going to Melbourne, where she arrived on 27 April, departing on 2 May bound for New York. The final voyage by these ships for 1948 was taken by *General S. D. Sturgis*, her departure point being Venice on April 16. This ship was the first of the class to bring new settlers to Sydney, where she arrived on 20 May, departing the next day, also bound for New York.

There was then a gap of almost a year before further voyages were made for the IRO by these ships. In April 1949, *Stewart* and *Heintzelmann* each made their second voyages to Australia, and this was to herald the start of a frequent schedule of voyages by a number of the vessels until the end of 1950. In June 1949, *Black* made her second voyage while *General W. C. Langfitt* made her first, as did *General Harry Taylor* and *General Omar*

Bundy in July, this being the only voyage by *Bundy*. Also that month, *Stewart* arrived for the third time. In September *Langfitt* arrived for the second time, while in October *General R. M. Blatchford* made her first voyage. November saw two more new ships on the service, *General W. G. Haan* and *General A. W. Greely*, plus a third visit by *Heintzelmann*, while in December *General M. L. Hersey* and *General R. L. Howze* made initial voyages, with *Black* making her third trip to round out the year with a total of 15 voyages by the various ships of the class, all departing from either Bremerhaven or Naples.

During 1950 the number of voyages would increase to 17 by these ships. In January *Stewart* arrived for her fourth visit, and *Langfitt* for her third, while February saw the second, and final, visits by both *Haan* and *Blatchford*. During March *General C. H. Muir* made a first visit to Australia, while *Heintzelmann* made her fourth and last trip. The only voyage for the year not to commence in either Naples or Bremerhaven was that taken by *General C. C. Ballou*, which left from Piraeus on 6 February, arriving in Sydney on 28 March, and then returning to Bremerhaven. April 1950 saw six of these vessels arrive in Australia, *Hersey* for the second time, *Taylor, Howze* and *Sturgis* for their second and final visits, while *Black* made her fourth and last trip also during the month. *Stewart* departed Naples on 22 March on her fifth voyage, going to Sydney, and this was also her final trip. In May, only *Greely* arrived, and on departing Melbourne on 15 May, went to Jakarta to collect Dutch nationals wishing to return to Holland.

There was then a five-month break before *Muir* arrived in October for the second time, followed in November by *Hersey*, which only went to Fremantle. The demand for IRO ships was now on the decrease, so in November the departure of *Ballou* from Naples bound for Newcastle, where she arrived on 16 December 1950, brought to an end this phase of the connection between the "General" ships and Australia.

During 1950, all the active members of the class had been transferred back to navy control from the army, but they continued to operate as troopships for several more years after the end of their IRO work. On 4 November 1951, *General Hersey* collided with and sank the brand new Argentine liner *Maipu* in the mouth of the Elbe River, fortunately with no loss of life. Over the next few years the ships were kept busy on government business, but in 1957, two of the class once again made voyages to Australia with new settlers.

On 17 May 1957, *General Langfitt* departed Genoa bound for Australia, arriving in Fremantle on 8 June, and going on to call at Melbourne and Sydney, departing on 15 June for New York. Meanwhile, *General Taylor* made a departure from Marseilles on 28 May, reaching Fremantle on 19 June, then sailing directly to Sydney, where she arrived on 24 June, leaving the next day bound for New York.

Both *Langfitt* and *Taylor* were laid up in the Reserve Fleet during 1958, along with *Howze, Sturgis, Stewart* and *Haan*, and over the next 10 years all other members of the class were withdrawn from active service. Subsequently, many of these ships would be sold, and converted for commercial service. *Howze* and *Greely* were sold to Pacific Far East Line during 1968, and rebuilt as container ships, being renamed *Guam Bear* and *Hawaii Bear*, though in 1975 the former was renamed *New Zealand Bear*. In 1976 both were sold to Farrell Lines, and as *Austral Glen* and *Austral Glade* were frequent visitors to Australian ports in their new guise for the next three years. In 1979 they were again renamed, *Pacific Endeavour* and *Pacific Enterprise*. The first of the pair was sold to shipbreakers in 1980, but *Pacific Enterprise* was laid up in San Francisco on 2 October 1980. During 1981 the vessel returned to service as *Caribe Enterprise*, only to be laid up in New York with machinery damage in 1983. She left under

tow on 26 May 1986 bound for the breaker's yard in Taiwan, but sank in the Pacific on 25 July.

General Bundy was converted into the cargo ship *Portmar* in 1965. In 1976 her name was shortened to *Port*, and then changed to *Poet* during 1979. On 24 October 1980, she left Philadelphia with a cargo of corn, bound for Port Said, but disappeared in the Atlantic. *General Black* became the cargo ship *Green Forest* in 1967, while *General Sturgis* was renamed *Green Port*, and both were sold to shipbreakers in Taiwan during January 1980. *General Langfitt* entered commercial service in December 1969 as *Transindiana*, being scrapped during 1983, while *General Haan* became *Transoregon* in 1969 for the same owners. She was sold to Puerto Rico in 1975, and renamed *Mayaguez*, then in 1982 became *Amco Trader*, being scrapped during 1987. *General Blatchford* was rebuilt as the container ship *Stonewall Jackson* in 1970, being renamed *Alex Stephens* in 1973, and going to shipbreakers in Taiwan in April 1980.

Four of the ships were purchased by Sea Land Services Inc., *General Ballou, General Heintzelmann, General Muir* and *General Hersey*. The first became *Brooklyn*, and the second *Mobile*, while the latter pair were cut in half, and a new, longer bow section fitted, increasing their length to 695 ft (211.8 m). *Muir* was renamed *Chicago* while *Hersey* became *St Louis*. *Mobile* was scrapped in 1984, and the *St Louis* in 1987. The other two were sold to Puerto Rico in 1975, *Brooklyn* being renamed *Humacao*, then becoming *Eastern Light* in 1981, only to be scrapped the same year. *Chicago* was renamed *San Juan*, and broken up in 1989.

Two of the ships had most unusual conversions. *General Stewart* was initially rebuilt as a cargo ship, *Albany*, entering service in December 1968. In 1974 she was purchased by Avondale Shipyards, and converted into a drilling barge, being renamed *Mission Viking*. She served in this capacity until being broken up in July 1987. *General Taylor* was rebuilt as a satellite tracking ship by the Bethlehem Steel Corporation during 1962–63. Having previously been operated by both the US Navy and US Army, the vessel was transferred to the US Air Force and commissioned on 18 July 1963 as *General Hoyt S. Vandenberg*. However, a year later the vessel was handed back to the navy, without change of name, and is believed to be still in existence.

TALMA

BUILT: *1923 by Hawthorn, Leslie & Co., Newcastle*
TONNAGE: *10 004 gross*
DIMENSIONS: *471 × 59 ft (143.6 × 18.1 m)*
SERVICE SPEED: *13 knots*
PROPULSION: *Quadruple expansion/single screw*

The British India Line placed one of their passenger–cargo ships on a service to Australia from India at the end of 1945, adding a second similar vessel a year later. Early in 1948, they despatched one of their larger passenger vessels to Australia, though she was also at the end of her career.

Talma had been launched on 14 June 1923, and when completed in September the same year, she was sent out to India, to operate on the service from Calcutta to Japan. Quite an imposing looking vessel, with a large superstructure and two small funnels close together, she was joined the following year by a sister ship, *Tilawa*. They provided cabin accommodation for 135 passengers divided between first and second class, and in addition could carry about 1000 Asiatic steerage class passengers. This standard of travel was very basic, passengers being provided only with an area on the deck in which to sleep, having to furnish their own bedding. As most Asiatic people slept on the floor anyway, this was not a great hardship for them, and enabled them to travel very cheaply. *Talma* could also carry a large amount of cargo, and was typical of the vessels operating in Eastern waters prior to the war.

Talma remained on her regular trade after the war in Europe started, but as soon as Japan entered the conflict, she was placed on a coastal service around India with her sister. Later both ships began operating from Bombay to East Africa, and on 23 November 1942 *Tilawa* was torpedoed by a Japanese submarine. The steerage passengers began to panic, and 280 lives were lost as the lifeboats were lowered. When it appeared that the ship would not sink, the submarine fired a second torpedo, and *Tilawa* quickly went to the bottom.

Despite this incident, *Talma* remained in service across the Indian Ocean for the remainder of the war, which passed for her without incident. When peace was restored, *Talma* was used on a variety of Indian Ocean routes, until leaving Calcutta on 29 January 1948, bound for Australia.

Talma went first to Fremantle, arriving on 29 February, after a very slow voyage, and then to Melbourne, berthing on 7 March for a 10-day stay. The vessel arrived in Sydney on 20 March, and spent some weeks anchored in the harbour, before leaving on 4 May bound for Suva. Leaving Fiji she voyaged to Singapore, and then Rangoon before arriving back in Calcutta.

On 4 August 1948, *Talma* left Calcutta on her second voyage to Australia, calling at Fremantle and Adelaide before reaching Melbourne on 3 September. A week later she left for Sydney, being in port from 12 September to 7 October. After returning to Melbourne for a three-day stop, and Adelaide, *Talma* passed through Fremantle on 28 October, then voyaged to Mauritius and East Africa. From there the old vessel made her way back to Bombay.

Early in 1949, *Talma* was withdrawn from service, and sold to British shipbreakers. On 14 April 1949, she was towed out of Bombay by the salvage tug *Twyford*, and on 29 May arrived at Inverkeithing, where she was scrapped.

TALMA ANCHORED IN SYDNEY HARBOUR

STRATHNAVER AND STRATHAIRD

BUILT: *1931/32 by Vickers-Armstrong Ltd, Barrow*
TONNAGE: *22 568 gross*
DIMENSIONS: *664 × 80 ft (202.4 × 24.4 m)*
SERVICE SPEED: *20 knots*
PROPULSION: *Turbo-electric/twin screws*

This pair were built with three funnels, but after the war returned to the Australian trade with only a single funnel. The first vessel was named in honour of Lord Inchcape of Strathnaver, who had been chairman of the company for many years. The ships were given a modern colour scheme, white hull and yellow funnels, which was applied to all future P & O liners. The first and third funnels were dummies, but the paint on the middle funnel used to peel and darken at the top. They were also much higher powered than previous liners, to operate a combined mail schedule from London to Bombay and Australia.

Strathnaver was launched on 5 February 1931, handed over to P & O on 2 September, and left Tilbury on her maiden voyage on 2 October 1931. *Strathaird* was launched on 18 July 1931, being delivered to P & O on 10 January 1932, and made her maiden departure on 12 February. They provided excellent accommodation for 498 first class and 668 tourist class.

On 23 December 1932, *Strathaird* became the first P & O liner to operate a cruise from Australia, departing Sydney on a five-day jaunt to Norfolk Island. Both vessels had made occasional cruises from Britain, and

would continue to do so throughout the 1930s. However, their main employment was on the mail service from Britain to Australia, on which they were joined over the years by *Strathmore*, *Stratheden* and *Strathallan*. This ended in September 1939, when both ships were requisitioned as troopships.

No sooner had they been converted for their new role, and painted all black, than they returned to familiar waters, *Strathnaver* arriving in Sydney while *Strathaird* went to Wellington. They carried troops in the first convoy to depart for the Middle East, in January 1940, with *Strathaird* returning to Melbourne in April to take part in the second convoy as well. She then went to Liverpool for a refit, but this was interrupted when *Strathaird* was sent to Brest to evacuate British troops. She boarded 6000 persons, both military and civilian, and carried them to safety in Plymouth, then resumed her refit. On 24 March 1941, all five "Straths" were included in the largest troop convoy to depart Britain during the war, some 23 vessels leaving Liverpool and Glasgow to link up, and proceed to Cape Town.

Both ships carried troops to the North African landings in November 1942, with *Strathnaver* being in the first convoy, and surviving several attacks by German bombers. *Strathaird* was in the second convoy, and did not undergo a similar ordeal. *Strathnaver* then spent some time in the Red Sea as a training ship for the invasion of Italy, in which she later took part. Both vessels completed the war doing general trooping duties.

STRATHAIRD WAS BUILT WITH THREE FUNNELS

POST-WAR APPEARANCE OF *STRATHNAVER*

Strathaird was handed back to P & O at the end of 1946, having carried 128 961 persons and covered 387 745 miles during the war. She went back to her builder's yard for refitting, which was completed in January 1948, with only a single, taller funnel, and accommodation for 573 first class and 496 tourist class passengers. On 22 January *Strathaird* left Tilbury bound for Bombay and Australia once again.

Strathnaver was retained by the British Government until October 1948, by which time she had carried 128 792 persons while travelling 352 443 miles since 1939. On 5 November 1948 she arrived at the Harland & Wolff shipyard in Belfast to be refitted in an identical manner to her sister. She was the last of the P & O liners that survived the war to return to service, making her first departure from Tilbury on 5 January 1950.

Both liners were mainly involved in the mail service from Britain to Australia, but also made occasional cruises. As P & O proceeded with a programme of new buildings, their importance in the fleet declined. However, in June 1953, *Strathnaver* was selected to carry official guests to the Coronation Naval Review off Spithead. During 1954, *Arcadia* and *Iberia* were delivered, with the result that *Strathnaver* and *Strathaird* were refitted as one-class liners for 1252 passengers in tourist class. *Strathaird* left Tilbury in this guise for the first time on 8 April 1954, followed by *Strathnaver* on 29 July, and they operated to an independent schedule.

They were now the oldest units in the P & O fleet, and the bulk of their passengers from Britain were assisted migrants. They were not air-conditioned or fitted with stabilizers. *Strathaird* also began suffering engine problems, having to return to Fremantle in December 1955, being delayed in Port Said in August 1957, and delayed again in Sydney in September 1959.

In 1957 plans were drawn up for the construction of a giant new liner that would replace both *Strathaird* and *Strathnaver*, which entered service in 1961 as *Canberra*. *Strathaird* left Tilbury for her final voyage on 28 March 1961, leaving Sydney on 9 May for the homeward journey. Having been sold to shipbreakers in Hong Kong, she left Tilbury on 17 June, and on arrival in Hong Kong on 24 July was delivered for demolition.

This left *Strathnaver* to make her final voyage from Tilbury on 7 December 1961, departing Sydney on 17 January 1962 and arriving back in Tilbury on 23 February. Sold to the same shipbreakers as *Strathaird*, she made the long voyage to Hong Kong, arriving in April 1962.

A Panama Canal Veteran

BUILT: *1902 by Maryland Steel Corp., Sparrows' Point*
TONNAGE: *10 005 gross*
DIMENSIONS: *489 × 58 ft (149.1 × 17.7 m)*
SERVICE SPEED: *13 knots*
PROPULSION: *Triple expansion/twin screws*

Some migrant ships had unexpected claims to fame, and this vessel made the first official transit of the Panama Canal. Built as a large freighter for the Boston Steamship Co., she was launched on 19 December 1901 as *Shawmut*, with a sister named *Tremont*, and operated from California to Japan. In 1908, both ships were sold to the Panama Railroad Steamship Co. to carry building materials to the canal construction areas, *Shawmut* being renamed *Ancon*, while her sister became *Cristobal*.

On 3 August 1914, *Cristobal* became the first ship to traverse the entire canal, with a trip from the Pacific to the Atlantic. However, it was *Ancon* that was selected to carry 300 guests for the first official transit, on 15 August, from Cristobal to Balboa.

Ancon continued to operate to the canal until 1917, when she was used to transport nitrates, and later became a supply ship for the US Army. At the end of the war, *Ancon* made two voyages from Europe to America, carrying 6112 American soldiers home.

Returned to her owners, she again became a cargo ship, then in 1924 was rebuilt, along with *Cristobal*, with accommodation for 200 passengers. *Ancon* and *Cristobal* operated from New York to Haiti and the Panama Canal zone, and in 1939 were withdrawn.

Ancon was renamed *Exancon*, and laid up pending disposal. However, she was reactivated on 15 August 1939 to make a passage through the Panama Canal to mark the twenty-fifth anniversary of her first transit. She was sold in October 1940 to the Permanente Steamship Co., of San Francisco, and renamed *Permanente*, being used to carry cement. She later served as a supply ship in the Pacific and in 1946 carried war brides from Australia to America. Later that year she was sold to Tidewater Commercial Co., and renamed *Tidewater* under Panamanian registry.

Refitted at Genoa with accommodation for about 350 persons, on 9 September 1947, *Tidewater* left Marseilles with 353 migrants and a cargo of phosphate, arriving in Fremantle on 5 November, Melbourne on 13 November, and Sydney on 18 November, then crossing to Auckland to berth on 26 November, where the phosphate was unloaded. She then went to Cairns and Melbourne to load cargo for the return trip.

Shortly after, *Tidewater* was chartered to Arnold Bernstein Shipping Co., and renamed *Continental*. She left New York on 3 June 1948 for the first of four voyages to Plymouth, Antwerp and Rotterdam, the last departing New York on 13 September, following which the ship was returned to her owners.

The name *Continental* was retained, and on 12 January 1949 she left Genoa bound for Australia again. She made two further voyages to Australia from Genoa during 1949, departing on 2 June and 15 September, each time calling at Fremantle, Melbourne and Sydney. On 20 January 1950, *Continental* left Genoa on her final voyage to Australia, but after leaving Melbourne on 5 March, bound for Alexandria, was in Fremantle from 13 March until 10 April. On 26 October 1950 she arrived at a Savona shipbreaking yard.

CONTINENTAL

ORMONDE

BUILT: *1918 by John Brown & Co., Clydebank*
TONNAGE: *15 047 gross*
DIMENSIONS: *600 × 66 ft (182.9 × 20.3 m)*
SERVICE SPEED: *18 knots*
PROPULSION: *Geared turbines/twin screws*

During the war, the Orient Line lost their newest ship, *Oreades*, which was less than five years old, yet their oldest liner, *Ormonde*, survived her second global conflict. Laid down in May 1913, her construction was halted when war broke out in 1914. Late in 1916 work recommenced, and she was launched without ceremony in February 1917, then completed in June 1918 as a troopship. She made a voyage to China via South Africa, then was handed over to the Orient Line, and fitted out with accommodation for 278 first class, 195 second class and 1000 third class passengers.

On 15 November 1919, *Ormonde* left London on her maiden voyage to Australia, being the first new liner to enter the trade after the war, and the first vessel with geared turbines to operate to Australia. She was also the first Orient liner to have a cruiser stern, but was coal-fired until July 1923, when she was converted to oil-firing. In 1933 her accommodation was remodelled to carry 777 tourist class only, and *Ormonde* joined the veteran *Orsova* on a secondary service to Australia.

In September 1939, *Ormonde* was requisitioned for her second war, again being used as a troopship, though in April 1940 she was returned to Orient Line to make one return trip to Australia. *Ormonde* made numerous voyages across the Atlantic, and five trips to North Africa following the landings there. She spent the latter part of the war on voyages to and around Africa, then went to Madras late in 1945 to collect troops for the Pacific war, but the Japanese surrendered before she arrived.

In 1946 *Ormonde* was released from government service, but the Orient Line did not wish to refit her for regular service again. Instead she was chartered by the British Ministry of Transport, and arrived at the Birkenhead shipyard of Cammell Laird in April 1947 to be refitted to carry 1070 persons. On 10 October 1947 *Ormonde* left London with 1052 migrants on board, becoming the first vessel to make a voyage under the joint agreement between the British and Australian governments to transport migrants on chartered ships.

On her return trips, *Ormonde* carried a limited number of fare-paying passengers on her owner's account. Over a five-year period, she made 17 voyages, bringing some 17 500 British migrants to Australia. Her final voyage departed London on 21 August 1952, and on her return to Britain, the old vessel was sold to shipbreakers. On 1 December 1952, *Ormonde* left London bound for the breaker's yard at Dalmuir. During her entire peacetime career, *Ormonde* completed 75 round trips between Britain and Australia.

ORMONDE

RADNIK

BUILT: *1908 by Newport News Shipbuilding & Drydock Co., Newport News*
TONNAGE: *6665 gross*
DIMENSIONS: *437 × 53 ft (133.3 × 16.1 m)*
SERVICE SPEED: *11 knots*
PROPULSION: *Triple expansion/single screw*

One of the more unusual looking migrant ships to visit Australia was *Radnik*, owned by the Yugoslav shipping company, Jugoslavenska Linijska Plovidba. She was a vessel with a most interesting history, having been launched on 11 January 1908 as *Lurline* for the Matson Line. She was the first vessel built to the order of that company, which at the time had a large fleet of sailing ships, and only a few steamers. *Lurline* was fitted out with accommodation for 64 passengers, and also had a large cargo capacity.

On 8 June 1908 *Lurline* departed San Francisco on her maiden voyage to Hawaii, serving on this route until 29 October 1917, when she was taken over by the US Shipping Board. After nine trips to Honolulu and three to Manila she was returned to Matson Line on 31 January 1919. *Lurline* spent the next nine years plying to Hawaii again, and had completed 218 voyages for Matson by the time she was sold to the Alaska Packers Association, and renamed *Chirikof*. She operated as a cargo ship, bringing Alaskan salmon to ports on the west coast of America.

In July 1940, *Chirikof* was bareboat chartered to the US Government, for a cargo service from Seattle to Alaskan ports, being handed back in April 1941. In June 1942 the ship was taken over by the government, and accommodation for 1290 troops installed, as well as heavy left gear, and for the first time the bridge was enclosed. She mainly operated to Alaska in this role, but also made a voyage to Honolulu. When handed back to Alaska Packers on 6 February 1946, they had no use for the ship, which was offered for sale.

After a period laid up, *Chirikof* was purchased by the Yugoslavs, and renamed *Radnik*. It was their intention to utilise the vessel on the migrant trade, using the former troop spaces, though a reduced number of passengers would be carried. The first voyage by *Radnik* to Australia was from Malta on 4 December 1947. It was a slow passage, as the ship did not reach Fremantle until 25 January 1948, and Melbourne on 2 February. *Radnik* then crossed the Tasman to Auckland, arriving on 7 February and staying in port for a week. On 20 February *Radnik* arrived in Sydney, where cargo was loaded, and she then departed for the Middle East, with another call at Fremantle on 2 March.

Over the next three years *Radnik* was used on a variety of services, making several more voyages to Australia at varying intervals. On 15 January 1951, *Radnik* departed Rijeka on her final voyage to Australia, calling at Fremantle on 26 February, Melbourne on 7 March, and terminating in Sydney on 11 March. Several days later the vessel departed for Adelaide, where she berthed on 24 March, and after loading of cargo departed for Rijeka. In June 1952 *Radnik* was laid up in Split, and sold to a local shipbreaking firm in August 1953.

RADNIK

PARTIZANKA

BUILT: *1927 by Newport News Shipbuilding & Drydock Co., Newport News*
TONNAGE: *6267 gross*
DIMENSIONS: *395 × 62 ft (120.4 × 18.9 m)*
SERVICE SPEED: *17 knots*
PROPULSION: *Geared turbines/twin screws*

Another very interesting Yugoslav flag vessel to make emigrant voyages to Australia was *Partizanka*. Like *Radnik*, she was a former American ship, having been built for the Clyde Line to operate along the east coast of America from New York. Launched on 18 April 1927, she was named *Shawnee*, and provided comfortable accommodation for 600 passengers. Clyde Line later merged with the Mallory SS Co., to form Clyde–Mallory Lines, and in 1934 they amalgamated with the New York and Porto Rico SS Co. to form the Atlantic, Gulf & West Indies SS Co.

With her sister ship, *Iroquois*, *Shawnee* operated from New York to Miami most of the year, apart from cruises to Bermuda and Havana.

As war broke out in Europe, *Shawnee* was chartered by the US Government, and on 13 September 1939 left New York on a trans-Atlantic voyage to Bordeaux, where she collected stranded American citizens. She then returned to the coastal trade until December 1941, when she was taken over by the government for conversion into a troopship. At the Todd–Johnson shipyard in New Orleans, the interior of the ship was gutted and accommodation for 1589 troops installed.

For some time *Shawnee* operated out of New York to the Caribbean, or Chile and Peru, then in January

1943 she crossed the Atlantic again, taking troops to North Africa. She spent the remainder of the year on the Atlantic ferry to both British and African ports. Early in 1944 *Shawnee* passed through the Panama Canal, and began operating from San Francisco to the South Pacific, making several visits to Brisbane and Townsville, as well as ports in New Guinea. In January 1946 *Shawnee* returned to New York, and on 4 March 1946 was handed back to AGWI Lines.

Shawnee was laid up in Norfolk, and purchased in October 1946 by Iberian Star Line, registered in Panama but owned in Portugal. Renamed *City of Lisbon*, she was badly damaged in a collision with the cargo ship *Virgolin* on 28 May 1947, when some 150 miles from Lisbon. Her owners decided to sell the ship for scrap, but instead she was purchased in July 1947 by Jugoslavenska Linijska Plovidba, and renamed *Partizanka*.

During a refit at Rijeka, accommodation for about 800 persons was installed, but externally the ship was not altered at all. On 15 December 1947, *Partizanka* left Malta on her first voyage to Australia, arriving in Fremantle on 9 January 1948. From there she went directly to Sydney, berthing on 15 January, and leaving four days later bound for the Middle East, with another call at Fremantle. For most of 1948 *Partizanka* operated from Rijeka to South America.

On 12 August 1949, while the ship was still in drydock, a fire broke out, leaving her 70 per cent destroyed. She was declared a total loss on 13 September, and the hulk was sold to local shipbreakers in 1950. However, the lower part of the hull was rebuilt as a barge, and used in the Split area for several years.

PARTIZANKA

The Bays

Moreton Bay and Esperance Bay

Built: *1921/22 by Vickers Ltd, Barrow*
Tonnage: *14 343 gross*
Dimensions: *549 × 68 ft (167.2 × 20.8 m)*
Service Speed: *15 knots*
Propulsion: *Geared turbines/twin screws*

Largs Bay

Built: *1921 by Wm Beardmore & Co. Ltd, Glasgow*
Tonnage: *14 362 gross*
Dimensions: *552 × 68 ft (168.3 × 20.8 m)*
Service Speed: *15 knots*
Propulsion: *Geared turbines/twin screws*

Shortly after World War One ended, the Australian Government decided to become directly involved in the emigrant trade. Five new vessels were ordered on behalf of the Commonwealth Government Line of Steamers, from two British yards. Three came from Vickers Ltd at Barrow, being named *Moreton Bay, Hobsons Bay* and *Jervis Bay*, while *Largs Bay* and *Esperance Bay* were built by Wm Beardmore at Dalmuir. All five entered service between December 1921 and September 1922, offering rather basic accommodation for 723 passengers in one class.

The Commonwealth Government Line was not well run, and also suffered considerable disruption to operations from strikes by seamen, so early in 1928 it was decided to dispose of the five "Bay" vessels. Soon after they were sold to Lord Kylsant, who then controlled a major shipping empire. Managed by Geo. Thompson & Co., who had previously operated ships to Australia as the Aberdeen Line, the five ships were run as the Aberdeen & Commonwealth Line, with deep green hulls. Apart from a reduction to 635 in their passenger capacity, the ships were not altered, and continued to serve Australia as before.

In 1931 the Kylsant empire collapsed, and in April 1933 the Aberdeen & Commonwealth Line was jointly purchased by P & O and Shaw Savill, the latter being the majority shareholder, and manager of the ships. Still maintaining their Aberdeen Line colours, they remained on the Australian emigrant trade, operating an independent schedule. During 1936, *Esperance Bay* was transferred to Shaw Savill and renamed *Arawa*, and soon after the name of *Hobsons Bay* was changed to *Esperance Bay*. The four remaining ships maintained a six-weekly schedule until September 1939, when *Moreton Bay, Esperance Bay* and *Jervis Bay* were requisitioned and converted into armed merchant cruisers.

On 5 November 1940, *Jervis Bay* was escorting a convoy of 38 fully laden merchant ships in the North Atlantic, when the German pocket battleship *Admiral Scheer* was sighted. Despite the hopeless odds, *Jervis Bay* turned toward the enemy while the convoy scattered, but within an hour the gallant armed merchantman had been battered to a hulk and sunk. As a result of her sacrifice, all but six of the convoy escaped destruction as well.

Largs Bay had continued to operate to Australia until August 1941, when she was converted into a troopship. Also during 1941, both *Moreton Bay* and *Esperance Bay* were converted into troopships, and all three served the remainder of the war in this capacity. On 2 January 1944, *Largs Bay* was damaged by a mine off Naples, and out of action for several months. All three surviving "Bays" were released from government service during 1947, and refitted for the Australian trade again, with accommodation for 514 tourist class passengers. By the end of 1948, the trio were back in service for the Aberdeen & Commonwealth Line, offering a two-monthly schedule of departures. Up to 1951, Aberdeen & Commonwealth Line remained in the joint ownership of P & O and Shaw Savill, but during that year Shaw Savill purchased the P & O shareholding.

During the 1950s, new ships began to appear for the Australian trade, and the older steamers found it harder to survive in the competitive market. In April 1955, *Esperance Bay*, the former *Hobsons Bay*, left London on her final voyage to Australia. On her return, the ship was sold to Shipbreaking Industries, arriving at their Faslane yard on 6 July 1955. The service continued with two ships for 18 months, then on 30 November 1956, *Moreton Bay* left London on her final voyage. Returning to Britain three months later, she disembarked her final passengers at Southampton, then went on to Hull and London to off-load cargo. By then *Moreton Bay* had been sold to T. W. Ward of Barrow, and so went back to the place of her construction to be broken up, arriving on 13 April 1957.

By then, *Largs Bay* was on her final voyage, having left London on 11 January 1957. Departing Sydney on 27 April, and Melbourne three days later, *Largs Bay* was also sold to T. W. Ward on her arrival back in Britain, and arrived at their Barrow scrap yard on 22 August 1957. With the withdrawal of these ships, the Aberdeen & Commonwealth Line also ceased to exist.

ESPERANCE BAY

MORETON BAY DRESSES UP FOR HER LAST VOYAGE

KOMNINOS

BUILT: *1911 by John Brown & Co. Clydebank*
TONNAGE: *931 gross*
DIMENSIONS: *254 × 31 ft (78.1 × 9.5 m)*
SERVICE SPEED: *12 knots*
PROPULSION: *Triple expansion/twin screws*

Quite a smart looking vessel, *Komninos* was not really suited for a long voyage to Australia, having been designed as the luxury private yacht *Jeanette* for a British millionaire.

In 1910, the John Brown shipyard completed a private yacht named *Doris* for Solomon B. Joel. Sir Harry Livesay was so impressed by *Doris*, he tried to have John Brown build him a copy, but without reference to the designers, G. L. Watson & Co. John Brown refused, so Livesay went to Watson's, and they designed a vessel in which minor changes from *Doris* were incorporated.

Sir Harry Livesay owned *Jeanette* from 1911 to 1936, when she was sold to William Lancaster, but in 1938 he sold the vessel to John Gretton. Within three months of the war starting in 1939, *Jeanette* had been taken over by the British Admiralty, and converted into an anti-submarine vessel. Renamed *St Modwen*, pennant No. FY025, she was fitted out with depth charges, and later also carried one or two small guns. She was returned to her owner in 1945, and once again named *Jeanette*, but in 1946 was offered for sale.

Purchased by Cia. de Nav. Dio Adelphi S.A., registered in Panama, the vessel was renamed *Komninos*, and is shown in Lloyds as a cargo ship. A number of changes were effected, the most noticeable being the removal of the original clipper bow, which was replaced by a straight stem. The accommodation must have been greatly enlarged, as when *Komninos* left Marseilles bound for Australia in February 1948, there were 217 migrants aboard, consisting of 132 Greeks, 29 Palestinians, and smaller numbers of Lebanese, Poles, Italians and Britons.

No sooner had *Komninos* arrived in Fremantle, than a delegation of passengers complained that the ship had been horribly overcrowded, the meals monotonous, and conditions on board generally dirty. Some bed linen had not been changed throughout the voyage, and water had been rationed on the longer sectors between ports. It was claimed that only seven lavatories were provided, of which two were unusable, while only one of the two shower baths had been in service. The only public room for passengers was a smoke room, but this could seat only 25 persons. There were three dining rooms, which the stewards had to sleep in as they had no other quarters provided for them. For exercise, there was only a single narrow promenade deck.

This story was given considerable prominence in the Perth newspapers, and the Britons also complained about the lack of personal hygiene practised by some of the others on board. Two days later, a letter was published, signed by a group of Italian passengers, refuting some of the earlier claims. They said that the captain had done all he could to make the voyage tolerable, the meals had been plain, but food was plentiful, and in fact some twenty lavatories and ten shower baths had been available. *Komninos* remained four days in Fremantle, departing on 24 April bound for Batavia.

Later in 1948, *Komninos* was sold to an Israeli company, Ships and Vessels Ltd, and renamed *Eilath*. In 1950 she was laid up in Haifa, where it was reported on 27 December 1950 that she was being broken up.

THE CONVERTED YACHT *KOMNINOS* OFF FREMANTLE

MAETSUYCKER

BUILT: *1937 by Netherlands Dock Co., Amsterdam*
TONNAGE: *4272 gross*
DIMENSIONS: *376 × 52 ft (114.6 × 15.8 m)*
SERVICE SPEED: *14.5 knots*
PROPULSION: *Werkspoor diesel/single screw*

This attractive little ship operated between Fremantle and Singapore for 12 years in the post-war period, but before the war she visited ports on the east coast of Australia and New Zealand. Named after a seventeenth century Dutch governor-general of Batavia, *Maetsuycker* was built for the Dutch KPM company, who operated a network of services from the Dutch East Indies.

Maetsuycker looked like a private yacht, having a white hull and superstructure with a yellow funnel, and operated from ports in South-East Asia and the Dutch East Indies to New Guinea, Noumea and New Zealand, returning via the east coast of Australia with visits to Sydney and Brisbane. Excellent accommodation was provided for 55 first class passengers, and on short segments in the islands, a large number of deck passengers could also be carried.

When Holland was attacked by Germany, *Maetsuycker* was handed over to the Allies. Still manned by her Dutch crew, and based in Australia, the vessel operated as a troop transport in the South Pacific. During 1942 she carried supplies to Allied forces at Milne Bay, being the first ship to berth at the wharf constructed there. Late in 1942, *Maetsuycker* was converted into a hospital ship, and saw out the remainder of the war in this role.

Early in 1947, *Maetsuycker* was handed back to her owners, and made the long trip back to Holland to be refitted, arriving in Amsterdam in July 1947. At that time the Dutch shipping activities in eastern waters were being reorganised. KPM retained local services around the Dutch East Indies, while a new company was formed to operate the international routes, Royal Interocean Line. *Maetsuycker* was transferred to this company, and repainted in its colours prior to leaving Holland for the last time, in January 1948.

Still providing accommodation for 55 first class passengers, *Maetsuycker* was placed on a new service between Singapore and Fremantle, with calls at Penang and Port Swettenham on most voyages. Initially a call was also made at Jakarta, and sometimes Geraldton was included in the itinerary. Southbound the vessel carried general cargo, returning with a mixture of cargo and livestock, being able to carry 2500 head of sheep.

On 17 May 1960, *Maetsuycker* left Fremantle for the last time, completing 156 round trips from Singapore, and Royal Interocean Line then abandoned the route. *Maetsuycker* was soon sold to Kie Hock Shipping Co. Ltd, a Hong Kong based firm. Renamed *Tong Han*, she operated in the South China Seas on a variety of routes.

In 1964 the vessel was renamed *Gavina* by Kie Hock, but the following year she was sold to Cia. Naviera Thompson, another Hong Kong firm. Renamed *Paceco*, she was placed in service between Hong Kong and Malaysia. After only a few months, her name was changed to *Gambela*, then in 1970 this was changed again to *Gamsolo*. In 1971 her name was changed again, to *Hysan*, which she retained for the next three years. Early in 1974 the vessel was sold to shipbreakers in Taiwan, demolition beginning at their Kaohsiung yard on 7 June 1974.

MAETSUYCKER

GORGON AND CHARON

BUILT: *1933/36 by Caledon Shipbuilding & Engineering Co., Dundee*
TONNAGE: *3678/3964 gross*
DIMENSIONS: *336 × 51 ft (102.4 × 15.5 m)*
SERVICE SPEED: *13.5 knots*
PROPULSION: *B & W diesels/single screw*

Alfred Holt & Co., better known as the Blue Funnel Line, operated a diverse pattern of shipping services, including one between Singapore and Fremantle, which commenced in 1890. Up to 1936 this service was operated jointly with the West Australian Steam Navigation Co. In 1933 when *Gorgon* was built, she was owned jointly by the two companies, though painted in Blue Funnel colours.

Gorgon joined *Centaur* and *Minderoo* on the Singapore route, with the latter ship being withdrawn when the joint service ended in 1936. Blue Funnel Line acquired full title to *Gorgon*, and built a sister ship, which was delivered in 1936 as *Charon*. *Gorgon* and *Charon* provided accommodation for 84 first class passengers, while temporary berths for an additional 60 passengers could be provided when necessary.

Charon and *Gorgon*, along with *Centaur*, operated to Fremantle until December 1941, when all three were requisitioned. *Gorgon* was sent to Singapore, arriving as the Japanese closed in on the island. On 11 February 1942, she left, overloaded with evacuees, and safely negotiated Banka Strait to return to Australia. *Charon* was despatched to Singapore from Fremantle on 30 January 1942, but was rerouted to the Dutch East Indies when Singapore fell. *Charon* returned to Australia, and was converted into a victualling stores issue ship, serving in this capacity in the Pacific for the remainder of the war.

Gorgon became a transport, and on 14 April 1943 was in Milne Bay when it was attacked by Japanese bombers. *Gorgon* was struck by several bombs, being set on fire and disabled, and having 6 crew members killed, with a further 28 wounded. After the fires were put out, an unexploded bomb was found in a hold filled with ammunition, and when this was defused, the vessel left under tow, bound for Australia. Following repairs, *Gorgon* resumed her transport role.

Centaur became a hospital ship, and was sunk by a Japanese submarine off the Australian east coast in March 1943, but *Gorgon* and *Charon* survived the conflict, and were returned to Blue Funnel Line. During their refits, *Gorgon* was given accommodation for 72 passengers, while *Charon* could carry 88. Now operating a two-ship service between Singapore and Fremantle, Blue Funnel Line offered two departures a month, but in November 1949 *Gorgon* suffered serious engine problems, and was out of service four months.

Gorgon and *Charon* remained on the Singapore service until 1964, when a new *Centaur* entered service, to replace both of the older ships. On 10 May 1964, *Charon* left Fremantle for the last time, arriving in Singapore on 18 May. *Gorgon* made the final sailing of the pair from Fremantle on 21 July 1964, and on arrival in Singapore had completed 294 round trips in peacetime. Soon after, *Gorgon* was sold to shipbreakers in Hong Kong, arriving at their yard on 10 August 1964.

Charon was sold to Singapore shipbreakers, in a deal largely financed by the Singapore Government to provide local employment. The contract stated the ship must be broken up, but the shipbreakers resold *Charon* to Chan Kai Kit, a Panama registered concern, who renamed her *Seng Kong No. 1*. In June 1964 the ship was arrested by the Singapore Government, lay idle in the port for a year while the matter was settled in court, then was sold to local shipbreakers in August 1965.

GORGON

CHARON

MATAROA AND TAMAROA

BUILT: *1922 by Harland & Wolff Ltd, Belfast*
TONNAGE: *12 375 gross*
DIMENSIONS: *519 × 63 ft (158.1 × 19.3 m)*
SERVICE SPEED: *13 knots*
PROPULSION: *Geared turbines/twin screws*

This pair were the last vessels built for the Aberdeen Line, *Tamaroa* being launched on 22 September 1921 as *Sophocles*, while her sister was named *Diogenes* when launched on 2 March 1922. They had accommodation for 131 first class and 422 third class passengers, and a large cargo capacity. *Sophocles* departed London on her maiden voyage to Australia on 1 March 1922, with *Diogenes* making her first sailing on 16 August. They followed the old sailing ship route around South Africa, but the 1920s saw a rapid decline in demand for passages to Australia.

In 1926 the New Zealand Government, in conjunction with Shaw Savill Line, began offering subsidised fares to British migrants. To transport these people, Shaw Savill chartered *Sophocles* and *Diogenes* from the Aberdeen Line. They were repainted in Shaw Savill colours, converted to oil-firing, and refitted to carry 135 first class and 570 third class passengers, the latter being for the assisted migrants. *Sophocles* was then renamed *Tamaroa*, while her sister became *Mataroa*, and they began operating from Southampton through the Panama Canal to New Zealand.

The government subsidy scheme ended in 1931, but the two ships remained under charter to Shaw Savill, though their accommodation was reduced to only 130 cabin class. In 1932, Aberdeen Line was wound up, and Shaw Savill Line bought *Mataroa* and *Tamaroa* outright. Their accommodation was then increased to 158 cabin class, and they continued to operate from Southampton to New Zealand via Panama.

Both ships remained on the New Zealand trade during the early part of the war, with occasional diversions to other duties. *Tamaroa* was used to evacuate British children to safety in Canada early in 1940. Both vessels became troop transports in November 1940, with a capacity of 1900 men. *Mataroa* spent most of the war carrying troops to South Africa, then crossing the South Atlantic to the River Plate ports to load meat, which was transported to Britain. *Tamaroa* was in a convoy attacked by the German cruiser *Admiral Hipper* on 25 December 1940, but escaped unscathed. She saw service in several theatres of the war, including the landings in North Africa in November 1942.

Both ships were handed back to Shaw Savill during 1947, and refitted to carry 372 tourist class passengers. On 30 April 1948 *Mataroa* left London on her first post-war voyage to New Zealand via Panama. On her second voyage the vessel went to Melbourne as well in July 1948 to collect cargo. *Tamaroa* made her first post-war departure on 27 August 1948 from London to Wellington, then crossed to Melbourne and Tasmanian ports to collect cargo.

In New Zealand both ships spent several weeks going to several ports to load dairy goods and meat for Britain. This reduced their effectiveness as passenger carriers, as they were subject to frequent delays due to industrial problems.

On 24 October 1956, *Tamaroa* left London on her final voyage, with *Mataroa* making her final departure on 21 November, returning to London on 19 February 1957, having completed 82 round trips to New Zealand. Both ships were sold to British shipbreakers, with *Tamaroa* arriving at Blyth on 5 March 1957, and *Mataroa* at Faslane on 29 March.

MATAROA

NIEUW HOLLAND

BUILT: *1928 by Netherlands Dock Co., Amsterdam*
TONNAGE: *11 215 gross*
DIMENSIONS: *527 × 62 ft (160.6 × 19 m)*
SERVICE SPEED: *15 knots*
PROPULSION: *Geared turbines/twin screws*

Nieuw Holland was one of the most graceful liners to operate to Australia before the war, with her sister *Nieuw Zeeland*. Built for Koninklijke Paketvaart Mij., better known as KPM, *Nieuw Holland* was launched on 17 December 1927, and completed in April 1928. She voyaged out to the East to commence service from ports in Malaya, Singapore, and the Dutch East Indies to Brisbane, Sydney and Melbourne. Accommodation was provided for 123 first class and 50 third class, with 199 crew.

Nieuw Holland looked very smart, having a white hull with a graceful counter stern, and a pair of yellow funnels. With *Nieuw Zeeland*, she maintained a regular service to Australian ports until the German invasion of Holland in May 1940. Both ships were then offered to the Allies by the Dutch Government in exile. *Nieuw Holland* was taken over by the Australians on her arrival in Melbourne on 9 August 1940, and converted into a troopship with space for over 1000 men. *Nieuw Zeeland* was similarly converted in Singapore. Both ships were operated by the Dutch crews, and joined convoys carrying troops to Europe and the Middle East.

Nieuw Holland served in the Mediterranean for some time, and then in the Indian Ocean. Late in 1941 the vessel voyaged via South Africa to England, where her trooping capacity was doubled to 2000, requiring additional galleys and toilet blocks to be constructed. In November 1942, *Nieuw Holland* and *Nieuw Zeeland* were involved in the invasion of North Africa, with *Nieuw Zeeland* being sunk on 11 November after landing her troops.

Nieuw Holland later took part in the Normandy landings, carrying over 27 000 troops across the English Channel between July and November 1944. She was then sent to the Pacific war zone, and when Singapore was recaptured, repatriated British prisoners-of-war. *Nieuw Holland* was then handed back to the Dutch Government, and made several trips between Holland and the Dutch East Indies before being released in March 1948, going to Hong Kong to be refitted.

In 1947 the operations of KPM were rationalised, the original company keeping the local services in the Dutch East Indies, while a new company, Royal Interocean Lines, was formed to operate international routes. *Nieuw Holland* was transferred to Royal Interocean, and repainted in its dark colours. Her accommodation was altered to carry 155 first class only, and she was placed in service from Singapore and Indonesia to Brisbane, Sydney and Melbourne. Later her route was extended to include Ceylon, India and Pakistan on some voyages.

In December 1958, the Indonesians seized all Dutch possessions in the islands, and the same month *Nieuw Holland* commenced her final voyage. Calling at Brisbane on 19 January, and Sydney two days later, the vessel spent five days in Melbourne, sailing on 28 January for Adelaide, then Fremantle, from where the voyaged to Malaya and India, then back to Singapore. On 6 March 1959, *Nieuw Holland* arrived in Hong Kong, having been sold to shipbreakers there.

NIEUW HOLLAND

LAKEMBA AND LEVUKA

Built: *Lakemba 1945 by Burrard Drydock Co., North Vancouver*

Levuka 1945 by West Coast Shipbuilders, Vancouver

Tonnage: *7459 gross*

Dimensions: *441 × 57 ft (134.4 × 17.3 m)*

Service Speed: *12 knots*

Propulsion: *Triple expansion / single screw*

Pacific Shipowners Ltd, of Fiji, had the distinction of operating the only British flag passenger vessel across the Pacific on a regular basis for a number of years. This was *Lakemba*, one of a pair of ships purchased by the company in 1947. Originally laid down as standard "Fort" class cargo ships, they had been redesigned as maintenance vessels for the Royal Navy, but were completed too late to be used in the war. The first was launched on 3 March 1945 as HMS *Dungeness*, while her sister was launched on 8 June as HMS *Spurn Point*. Both ships were subsequently delivered to the Royal Navy, HMS *Spurn Point* on 21 December 1945, but were laid up in Vancouver, and in 1947 were offered for sale.

Pacific Shipowners purchased both ships, and they were sent to a shipyard in Vancouver to be rebuilt as passenger–cargo liners. HMS *Spurn Point* was renamed *Lakemba*. Her sister became *Levuka* and was the first to be completed, in January 1948, having accommodation for 60 passengers. *Levuka* went to Coos Bay in British Columbia to load cargo, leaving there on 16 February 1948 for Victoria, from where she sailed on 25 February to Vancouver, to board passengers.

Departing Vancouver on 26 February, *Levuka* arrived in Sydney on 24 March, and Melbourne on 26 March. This was the only voyage she would make for Pacific Shipowners, as a few weeks later *Levuka* was sold to the British Phosphate Commission, and renamed *Triadic*. On 17 May 1948 she left Melbourne bound for Ocean Island, her accommodation in future being used only by company personnel.

Lakemba was given accommodation for 98 passengers, all in two-berth cabins, and also full air-conditioning. Completed in April 1948, she went first to New Westminster to load cargo, leaving there on 17 April for Crofton, in British Columbia, from where she sailed on 28 April back to Vancouver to board passengers. On 30 April *Lakemba* left Vancouver, and after calling at Suva on 21 May, arrived in Sydney on 28 May, and Melbourne two days later.

Managed by W. R. Carpenter & Co. Ltd, of Sydney, *Lakemba* maintained a regular schedule across the Pacific, with a departure about every 14 weeks. Her hull was originally grey, but in the 1960s it was repainted black. When *Aorangi* was withdrawn from the Pacific trade in 1953, *Lakemba* was the sole British flag ship operating regularly across the Pacific from Australia, until P & O and the Orient Line introduced Pacific sailings.

In the middle of 1967 it was announced that *Lakemba* was to be withdrawn from service in October that year. By the time she left Vancouver on her final voyage on 14 September, a sale to shipbreakers had been finalised. On 5 October *Lakemba* was travelling from Lautoka to Suva when she ran hard aground on a reef off Vatulele Island. The 56 passengers and most of the 55 crew members were taken off the same day by the cable repair ship *Retriever*, and the few crew who remained on board were later removed by a tug sent to refloat the vessel, after several attempts had failed. When the tug returned to the scene of the grounding four days later, *Lakemba* had disappeared, apparently sinking after slipping off the reef.

Her former sister, *Triadic*, survived a further decade operating for the British Phosphate Commission. On 4 February 1977, *Triadic* left New Plymouth in New Zealand bound for Shanghai, where she arrived on 6 March, and was handed over to shipbreakers there.

LAKEMBA

SITMAR 'VICTORY' SHIPS

BUILT: Castelbianco *1945 by Bethlehem Fairfield Shipyard, Baltimore*
Castelverde *1945 by California Shipbuilding Corp., Los Angeles*
TONNAGE: *7604 gross*
DIMENSIONS: *455 × 62 ft (138.7 × 18.9 m)*
SERVICE SPEED: *15 knots*
PROPULSION: *Geared turbines/single screw*

The "Victory" ship was a mass produced successor to the famous "Liberty" ship in World War Two. The first were built in 1943, and after the war hundreds were sold for commercial service. The Vlasov Group bought four "Victory" ships at an auction in 1947, but two were sold within a year. The two that were retained had been built as *Wooster Victory* and *Vassar Victory*, and were amongst the last of the type built.

Wooster Victory was launched in April 1945, and *Vassar Victory* on 3 May 1945, both being completed as troopships, along with some 100 other "Victory" ships. Multi-tiered bunks for 1597 men were fitted in cargo holds and 'tween decks, shower and toilet blocks installed, along with galleys and messes, hospital facilities and a few public rooms. By the time the ships were completed, the war was almost over, but they saw some service in the Pacific. *Wooster Victory* paid a brief visit to Melbourne in May 1945, but in 1946 both ships were laid up.

In 1947, these two ships were bought by Alexandre Vlasov, with *Wooster Victory* being allocated without a change of name to Cia. Argentina de Nav. de Ultramar,

registered in Panama. *Vassar Victory* was assigned to Sitmar Line, and renamed *Castelbianco*. In Geneva on 21 July 1947, the Mass Resettlement Scheme began with the signing of a contract by the International Refugee Organisation for a number of ships to transport displaced persons from Europe to countries that would accept them. Among the ships included in this original contract were *Wooster Victory* and *Castelbianco*, and both were refitted for the job. The troop quarters were upgraded, to allow for some 900 persons to be carried in segregated areas. A single deck of superstructure was added aft of the existing central island, and four sets of double-banked lifeboats installed.

The first voyage to Australia by one of these ships was that of *Castelbianco*, which arrived in Sydney on 23 April 1948 from Europe and Madras. On 19 October that year, *Castelbianco* left Genoa on her second voyage to Australia, arriving in Sydney on 19 November. In October 1948, *Wooster Victory* made her first departure for Australia, landing 892 persons in Melbourne the following month.

Both ships made trips to Australia on an irregular basis over the next few years. In 1950, *Wooster Victory* was transferred to the Italian flag under Sitmar ownership, and renamed *Castelverde*. It was also at this time that the hulls of both vessels were repainted white. The pattern of their operation was to transport migrants and displaced persons from Europe, and return empty. They were most frequently voyaging to Australia at this time, so in February 1952, Sitmar opened an office in Sydney, and began offering passages to Europe.

WOOSTER VICTORY PASSES UNDER THE SYDNEY HARBOUR BRIDGE

CASTEL BIANCO AFTER REBUILDING

CASTEL VERDE AFTER REBUILDING

With the end of the IRO contract, Sitmar decided to rebuild the two vessels for the regular passenger trade. During 1952 *Castelbianco* went to the Monfalcone shipyard of Cant. Riuniti dell'Adriatico for a major reconstruction. An entirely new superstructure, two decks high, was added, the original masts and funnel replaced, and accommodation installed for 1200 tourist class passengers. Her tonnage was increased to 10 139 gross, and prior to resuming service in 1953, her name was amended to *Castel Bianco*, and she began operating from Genoa to Australia. Later in 1953, her European terminal was changed to Bremerhaven. *Castelverde* was then sent to the same shipyard, but her rebuilding was not as extensive. She was given only one deck of superstructure, which increased her tonnage to 9008 gross, and accommodation for 800 tourist class passengers. Her name was amended to *Castel Verde*, and she returned to service with a departure from Bremerhaven on 10 June 1953.

Castel Verde made a further four voyages to Australia up to October 1954, but from 1955 both ships were mainly used on the service from Italian ports to Central and South America. *Castel Bianco* also made some trans-Atlantic voyages, two in September 1953 from Bremen to Quebec, and one in December 1956 from Bremen and Southampton to St John. Just prior to this voyage, *Castel Bianco* had made her final trip to Australia, leaving Sydney on 15 November.

In 1957 Sitmar decided to abandon their service to Central and South America, with the result that *Castel Bianco* and *Castel Verde* were both offered for sale. They were quickly purchased by Cia. Transatlantica Espanola, otherwise known as the Spanish Line. *Castel Bianco* was renamed *Begona*, while her sister became *Montserrat*, but the only other change was repainting the funnel plain black.

Begona was immediately despatched on a voyage to Australia in May 1957, arriving in Sydney on 20 June, and returning to Genoa on 19 July. The ship was then refitted to carry 830 tourist class passengers, while *Montserrat* was altered to carry 708 tourist class. In May 1958, *Begona* inaugurated a service from Southampton and Spanish ports to the West Indies and Venezuela, being joined by *Montserrat* in August.

On 6 May 1959, *Montserrat* departed Naples bound for Australia, but was delayed 14 days in Colombo with engine trouble. Arriving in Fremantle on 29 June, local inspectors found her lifesaving gear to be faulty, in particular several lifeboats, which had holes in them. Refused permission to sail further, all passengers were off-loaded and forced to make their own way to their destinations. *Montserrat* remained in Fremantle until she passed inspection, and on 8 July left for Spain.

For the next 10 years, *Begona* and *Montserrat* remained on the Venezuela service, then on 11 August 1970, *Montserrat* broke down in mid-Atlantic, with 660 persons on board. *Begona* was nearby, and rescued all the passengers from *Montserrat*, meaning she had 1530 persons aboard. Fearful that her food supplies would run out, *Begona* headed for port, leaving *Montserrat* adrift. Four days later a tug arrived, and towed her to port. After repairs, *Montserrat* returned to service until February 1973, when she was sold to Spanish shipbreakers.

Begona also suffered a mid-Atlantic breakdown, on 10 October 1974, when she had 800 passengers on board. After several days adrift she was towed in to Bridgetown in Barbados on 17 October, and her passengers were flown to their destination. It was decided her engines were not worth repairing, so *Begona* was towed back to Spain, arriving at Castellon on 24 December 1974, having been sold to shipbreakers there.

BEGONA IN SYDNEY COVE

SKAUGUM

BUILT: *1949 by Germaniawerft, Kiel and Howaldtswerke, Kiel*
TONNAGE: *11 626 gross*
DIMENSIONS: *552 × 66 ft (168.1 × 20.2 m)*
SERVICE SPEED: *15 knots*
PROPULSION: *Diesel electric/twin screws*

In the late 1930s, Hamburg–America Line ordered a pair of large cargo ships from the Germaniawerft shipyard in Kiel. The first of these was completed in 1938 as *Steiermark*, but when war broke out she was converted into the commerce raider *Kormoran*. During 1941, *Kormoran* ventured into the Pacific, and at the end of the year was in the Indian Ocean. She encountered HMAS *Sydney* off the coast of Western Australia on 19 November 1941, and in the ensuing battle, both ships were sunk.

The second ship was launched on 17 January 1940, and named *Ostmark*, having been hurriedly completed to clear the slipway for naval work. *Ostmark* was towed to a quiet backwater and laid up in this incomplete state for the duration of the war. When the Allies entered Kiel in May 1945, the British claimed *Ostmark* as a prize of war, and she was placed under the control of the Ministry of Transport. However, no further work was done on the ship, which remained idle in Kiel.

In 1948, the Ministry of Transport sold *Ostmark* to the Norwegian shipowner, Isak M. Skaugen, who owned a number of freighters and tankers. His original intention was to have her completed as a cargo ship, but he then obtained an 18 month contract from the International Refugee Organisation to transport displaced persons. Not having a suitable ship at the time, he decided to have *Ostmark* completed as a passenger carrier. The work was done in Kiel by the Howaldtswerke yard, where an extra deck was built along the full length of the hull, though the original small central superstructure was retained, as were the two masts, but four pairs of kingposts were added. Austere quarters for up to 1700 persons was installed in the holds, consisting of large dormitories, with numerous toilet and washing blocks, and a large number of lifeboats fitted along each side. Conditions must have been very cramped, but no worse than many other vessels doing similar work at the time.

When the work was completed, in April 1949, the vessel was renamed *Skaugum*, and nine years after being launched she prepared to make her maiden voyage. On outward bound trips she would carry full loads of displaced persons, but under the contract terms had to return to Europe empty. *Skaugum* went to Naples, from where she departed on 1 May 1949 on a voyage to Melbourne, followed by a second voyage from Naples on 4 July, also to Melbourne, and a third voyage in September. In November *Skaugum* left Naples again, with 1700 persons on board, and went directly to Newcastle, where they all disembarked on 29 November.

In December 1949, *Skaugum* was crossing the Indian Ocean returning to Europe empty, when another IRO ship, *Anna Salen*, developed engine trouble while outward bound with 1600 persons on board. *Anna Salen* had to return to Aden, and *Skaugum* was also directed there, to take on board the displaced persons from *Anna Salen* and carry them to their destinations in Australia.

During 1950 *Skaugum* made four voyages to Australia, the first from Naples to Melbourne in March, but on her return trip called at Tandjung Priok to board Dutch nationals returning to Holland. The second voyage was from Bremerhaven in June to Fremantle only, and such was the demand for passages that she arrived on 18 July 1950 with 1854 persons on board. Her third voyage, in August, was also from Bremerhaven to Fremantle, and when she departed on 29 September, again went to Indonesia to collect more Dutch evacuees. Her fourth voyage for the year was from Naples in November to Melbourne.

Skaugum continued to operate from Naples and Bremerhaven until the IRO contract ended, and then remained trading to Australia carrying migrants. During the early 1950s the four pairs of kingposts were removed, giving her a less cluttered outline, but she still gave the appearance of a cargo ship. In March 1951, *Skaugum* was joined by *Skaubryn*, another former cargo ship, but more extensively converted. This pair maintained a regular service to Australia until 1957, when *Skaugum* was withdrawn.

Returning to the Howaldtswerke shipyard at Kiel, *Skaugum* was rebuilt as a cargo ship, and also given new diesel engines. For the next seven years she operated in this capacity for I. M. Skaugen, then in 1964 was sold to Ocean Shipping & Enterprises, and renamed *Ocean Builder* under the Liberian flag.

Under her new name the vessel continued to operate as a tramp cargo ship, and in May 1970 returned to Australian waters again for a brief visit. This was her last time in these parts, as on 25 August 1972 she arrived in Kaohsiung, having been sold to a shipbreaking firm there.

ORIGINAL APPEARANCE OF *SKAUGUM*

SKAUGUM AFTER THE KING POSTS WERE REMOVED

Blue Funnel Line Quartet

HELENUS, HECTOR AND IXION

BUILT: *1949/50/51 by Harland & Wolff Ltd, Belfast*
TONNAGE: *10 125 gross*
DIMENSIONS: *522 × 69 ft (159.2 × 21.1 m)*
SERVICE SPEED: *18 knots*
PROPULSION: *Geared turbines/single screw*

Prior to World War One, Blue Funnel Line owned the largest passenger ship operating to Australia. The fleet was primarily composed of passenger–cargo liners, many of which were lost during the war. Having re-established the Australian service with two old vessels, Blue Funnel Line ordered a class of four passenger–cargo liners for the trade.

The first of the new ships to be launched was *Helenus*, on 13 April 1949, soon followed by *Jason* on 9 June and *Hector* on 27 July. *Helenus* entered service first, departing Liverpool on 14 November 1949 on her maiden voyage via Cape Town to Fremantle, Adelaide, Melbourne, Sydney and Brisbane. *Jason* followed on 18 February 1950, then *Hector* on 5 April 1950, but it was not until 28 July 1950 that the last of the group, *Ixion* was launched. She joined the others with a maiden departure from Liverpool on 24 January 1951. It was an indication of the changing conditions that accommodation was limited to only 30 first class, whereas before the war the Blue Funnel vessels had carried several hundred passengers.

Up to 1956 the vessels followed the long established Blue Funnel route to Australia around Africa, but then they were re-routed through Suez, with calls at Port

JASON

BUILT: *1950 by Swan, Hunter & Wigham Richardson Ltd, Newcastle*
TONNAGE: *10 160 gross*
DIMENSIONS: *522 × 69 ft (159.2 × 21.1 m)*
SERVICE SPEED: *18 knots*
PROPULSION: *Geared turbines/single screw*

Said and Aden. The closure of the Canal later that year meant a return to the old route for some months, until Suez was reopened in 1957. Passengers were only carried as far as Sydney, with an occasional call also made at Newcastle.

For passengers, a regular schedule had to be maintained, but industrial problems on the waterfront disrupted the working of cargo quite frequently, and the ships were often thrown off their schedule. Since they were primarily cargo carriers, in 1964 Blue Funnel decided to close down the passenger quarters on all four ships. On 28 February 1964, *Helenus* made her final departure from Liverpool with passengers, followed by *Hector* on 9 April and *Jason* on 7 May, leaving *Ixion* to make the final Blue Funnel Line voyage with passengers to Australia, departing Liverpool on 23 June 1964.

All four vessels continued to operate to Australia for another eight years, carrying cargo only, but during 1972 they were withdrawn, and sold to shipbreakers. *Ixion* was the first to go, arriving at a shipbreaker's yard in Barcelona on 13 February 1972, while the other three were all sold to Taiwanese breakers. *Jason* arrived in Kaohsiung in May, while *Hector* arrived on 2 July and *Helenus* five days later.

HECTOR

MOOLTON AND MALOJA

BUILT: *1923 by Harland & Wolff Ltd, Belfast*
TONNAGE: *21 039 gross*
DIMENSIONS: *625 × 73 ft (190.5 × 22.3 m)*
SERVICE SPEED: *17 knots*
PROPULSION: *Quadruple expansion/twin screws*

The first P & O liners to exceed 20 000 tons, this pair were constructed on adjoining slipways, and spent most of their careers operating together. *Mooltan* was launched on 15 February 1923 and *Maloja* on 19 April. They were fitted out to carry 327 first class and 329 second class passengers, and looked very powerful. However, they were rather underpowered with their outdated quadruple expansion machinery and could only manage 16 knots.

Designed for the mail service from Britain to Australia, on completion both ships made a return voyage to Bombay, *Mooltan* in September 1923, *Maloja* two months later. *Mooltan* made her maiden departure for Australia from Tilbury on 21 December 1923, being joined by *Maloja* on 18 January 1924.

In 1929, P & O reorganised their services, combining the Indian and Australian routes on an accelerated schedule. To attain the higher speed required, *Mooltan* and *Maloja* had exhaust turbines fitted, increasing their speed by one knot. This pair had been painted in very drab colours, black hulls and funnels and dark brown upperworks, but when the new "Strath" liners entered service with their white hulls, the upperworks of *Maloja* and *Mooltan* were repainted a light stone colour. At the same time their accommodation was altered to 346 first class and 336 tourist class.

On the day war broke out, *Maloja* was in the Red Sea, outbound to Australia. The voyage was terminated at Bombay, where she was converted into an armed merchant cruiser. This included removal of the mainmast and the top half of the aft funnel. Eight 6-inch guns were also fitted, and *Maloja* was sent off to patrol the Indian Ocean. *Mooltan* was requisitioned in Britain, and converted in a similar manner, then sent to the South Atlantic. In March 1940, *Mooltan* joined the Northern Patrol, operating near the Faroe Islands.

In 1941 both vessels became troopships, later taking part in the landings in North Africa, Sicily and the Italian mainland. After the war they repatriated troops, *Mooltan* arriving in Australian waters again in August 1945. Both vessels were returned to P & O in July 1947, and refitted by Harland & Wolff, *Mooltan* in Belfast, *Maloja* in London. They were given austere accommodation for 1030 tourist class passengers only. The aft funnel was rebuilt, but no mainmast was fitted, and they were repainted in their pre-war colours.

Relying heavily on assisted migrants to fill the ships, *Maloja* left Tilbury on 10 June 1948, followed by *Mooltan* on 26 August. They sailed independently of the mail ships, calling at Aden and Colombo en route to Fremantle and other major Australian ports. On the return trip, fare-paying passengers were carried, and extra ports included. For some time they regularly called at Bombay, to collect British officials and their families returning home.

The demand for migrant passages declined, so on 30 September 1953, *Mooltan* left Tilbury on her final voyage to Australia, departing Sydney on 24 November and Melbourne four days later to return to London on 7 January 1954. *Maloja* made her final departure on 5 November 1953, leaving Sydney on 2 January 1954. After several days in Melbourne, she sailed on 9 January for Adelaide and then Fremantle, departing on 16 January to reach Tilbury for the last time on 18 March.

Both liners had completed 80 round trips in peacetime to Australia. They were sold to British Iron and Steel for scrapping, *Mooltan* at Faslane and *Maloja* at Inverkeithing.

MOOLTAN

NAPOLI

BUILT: *1940 by Harland & Wolff Ltd, Belfast*
TONNAGE: *8082 gross*
DIMENSIONS: *451 × 57 ft (137.5 × 17.3 m)*
SERVICE SPEED: *14 knots*
PROPULSION: *Diesel/single screw*

Flotta Lauro was founded in Naples during 1923 by Achille Lauro, and over the next sixteen years he built up a fleet of over fifty ships. With the return of peace, Achille Lauro set out once again to build up a fleet. Amongst the ships bought by Lauro in 1946 was the wreck of the *Araybank*, which had been abandoned in 1941.

Araybank was to have been the first of a series of ships built by Harland & Wolff for the Bank Line, for service on their various cargo routes. Launched on 6 June 1940, she was immediately requisitioned by the British Government, and completed as a supply ship during October 1940.

Araybank carried a contingent of Australian and New Zealand troops on her maiden voyage from Britain to Greece, then was used to transport provisions from Alexandria to the Greek islands. While lying in Suda Bay in Crete on 3 May 1941, *Araybank* was severely damaged during an attack by German aircraft, and had to be run aground to prevent her sinking. It was hoped that the vessel could be repaired, but on 16 May the Luftwaffe mounted a series of attacks on Allied shipping as the Germans invaded the island of Crete, and *Araybank* was abandoned by her crew, ablaze and sinking in shallow water. During 1944, the Germans salvaged the wreck, and towed it to Trieste for rebuilding, only to abandon the ship as the Allies

advanced in 1945. Seized by the British, the ship was not wanted back by the Bank Line, and instead was bought by Achille Lauro.

Patched up, the vessel was renamed *Napoli*, and taken to Genoa for rebuilding in 1946. *Napoli* was rebuilt as an emigrant ship to carry 656 persons, 176 in cabins and 480 in dormitories. The accommodation was quite austere, and the ship still resembled a freighter on completion of the rebuilding in August 1948.

Napoli departed Marseilles on her maiden voyage on 15 September 1948, bound for Australia, reaching Melbourne on 21 October and berthing in Sydney four days later. She did not embark any passengers in Australia for the return trip, but instead proceeded to Java to take on board Dutch nationals wishing to return home, and also visited Singapore on her way back to Europe. Subsequent voyages by *Napoli* to Australia were from Genoa and Naples, and initially no passengers were carried on the return voyage.

Napoli made a total of 15 round trips to Australia, on a schedule of four voyages per year, up to 1951. During that year, Flotta Lauro introduced two new ships to the Australian trade, *Roma* and *Sydney*. *Napoli* was transferred to another route, from Italy to ports in South America. This trade also relied heavily on emigrants, for which there was considerable competition between several Italian companies. Towards the end of 1952, *Napoli* was withdrawn from the South American trade. Her passenger accommodation was then removed, and the ship resumed service as a cargo carrier only.

In this guise, *Napoli* served in the Flotta Lauro fleet for almost 20 years. In April 1971 the vessel was withdrawn, and sold to shipbreakers at La Spezia.

NAPOLI

RANCHI

BUILT: *1925 by Hawthorn Leslie & Co., Newcastle*
TONNAGE: *16 974 gross*
DIMENSIONS: *570 × 71 ft (173.7 × 21.7 m)*
SERVICE SPEED: *17 knots*
PROPULSION: *Quadruple expansion/twin screw*

Ranchi was the second of four sisterships delivered to P & O during 1925 for their service from London to India, the others being *Ranpura*, *Rawalpindi* and *Rajputana*. Launched on 24 January 1925, *Ranchi* made her maiden voyage in August the same year. She could carry 308 first and 282 second class passengers, and remained on the Indian trade until October 1939, when she was requisitioned at Bombay.

Converted into an armed merchant cruiser, with her aft funnel removed, she served in this capacity until late 1942, then was refitted in Southampton as a troopship. *Ranchi* returned to service in this capacity in March 1943, and was in a Mediterranean convoy in November 1944 when it was attacked by German bombers. One bomb aimed at *Ranchi* was deflected by a wire over the forecastle head, and passed through the side of the ship without exploding. Had it not been deflected, the bomb would have struck the bridge and caused extensive damage. As a troopship, *Ranchi* steamed 85 977 miles, and carried 54 711 personnel, and after the war ended, she was used to repatriate troops and prisoners-of-war, eventually being handed back to P & O in July 1947. Of

her sisters, *Rawalpindi* and *Rajputana* were sunk, while *Ranpura* had been sold to the British Admiralty in 1942, and converted into a repair ship.

Being a lone ship, and over 20 years old, she was not worth refitting for regular service again, but P & O accepted an offer from the British Ministry of Transport to charter *Ranchi* as an emigrant ship to Australia. Refitted by Harland & Wolff in Belfast, accommodation for 940 persons in 8-, 10- and 12-berth cabins was installed, and the ship repainted in the P & O pre-war colours, black hull and funnel with stone upperworks.

On 17 June 1948, *Ranchi* left London on her first voyage to Australia, being in Fremantle on 17 July, Melbourne on 22 July, and reaching Sydney on 27 July. Returning to Britain, *Ranchi* carried a limited number of fare-paying passengers on her owner's account. On several occasions in 1950 and 1951, *Ranchi* left Sydney empty, and in Indonesian ports boarded Dutch nationals returning home.

The four year charter ended during 1952, and the ship also suffered some damage during a boiler fire off the Cocos Islands on 7 March that year. When the migrant charter was not renewed, P & O decided to dispose of *Ranchi*. On 6 October 1952 she left London on her final voyage, departing Sydney on 3 November. On her return to London, she was immediately sold to shipbreakers, and arrived at their yard in Newport, Monmouthshire, during January 1953.

RANCHI

Svalbard and Goya

BUILT: *1938/39 by Bremer Vulkan, Vegesack*
TONNAGE: *6789/6996 gross*
DIMENSIONS: *438 × 58 ft (133.8 × 18 m)*
SERVICE SPEED: *15 knots*
PROPULSION: *Diesel engine/single screw*

Although not under the same ownership when they came to Australia with migrants, this pair were ordered by the Woermann Line as *Togo* and *Kamerun*, fast cargo ships with accommodation for 12 passengers only. *Kamerun* was launched on 17 May 1938 and delivered to her owner on 28 June, while *Togo* was launched on 13 August that year, and delivered on 22 September. Both were employed from Hamburg to West Africa.

When war broke out, *Kamerun* was in Hamburg, and on 13 November 1939 was taken over by the German Navy for conversion into a repair ship, in which capacity she served throughout the war. *Togo* was at sea when the war began, but in November 1939 managed to elude the British blockade and return to Germany. She was taken over by the Navy in March 1940, and in August that year began serving as a minelayer. In 1941 *Togo* went to the Wilton Fijenoord shipyard in occupied Holland, and was fitted out as a commerce raider. The conversion was completed at the Oder Werke shipyard in Stettin, by which time she was armed with six 5.9 inch guns, anti-aircraft guns, four torpedo tubes and three seaplanes. Her fuel capacity was greatly increased, allowing for a cruising endurance of 36 000 miles at 10 knots. Accommodation was installed for 16 officers and 331 crew.

In December 1942 the ship was renamed *Coronel*, otherwise known as *Schiff 14*, her raider number. Hoping to break out into the Atlantic through the English Channel, in early February 1943 *Coronel* began her dangerous voyage, but on 13 February was attacked and damaged by Allied aircraft off Gravelines, and had to put in to Boulogne the next day. After further air attacks while in Boulogne, the break out attempt was abandoned, and on 2 March *Coronel* returned to Kiel. This was the last attempt by the German Navy to get a commerce raider past the British blockade. Renamed *Togo* again, the vessel was altered for duty as a night fighter direction ship, and served in this capacity in Baltic waters until the end of the war.

In May 1945 *Kamerun* was ceded to the Norwegians as war reparations, while *Togo* was taken by the British three months later. However, in 1946 *Togo* was also handed over to the Norwegians, being retained by the Norwegian Government and renamed *Svalbard*. In 1947 *Kamerun* was allocated to L. Mowinckels Rederi, and renamed *Goya*, being fitted out initially as a cargo ship.

Since *Svalbard* still retained considerable accommodation areas from her wartime rebuilding, it was natural that she should be selected to transport migrants, though her capacity was increased to about

SVALBARD IN FLENSBURG, AUGUST 1949

THE EMIGRANT SHIP *GOYA*

900 persons. On 26 May 1948 she left Southampton for Australia, going only to Melbourne where she berthed on 29 June. *Svalbard* then obtained an IRO charter to transport displaced persons, and on 20 September 1948 she left Bremerhaven on her first voyage in this capacity, arriving in Fremantle on 23 October, then proceeding directly to Sydney where she berthed on 29 October. The vessel returned empty to Genoa, from where she sailed again on 13 December for Australia. During 1949 *Svalbard* made a further three voyages to Australia from Italian ports, being in Melbourne on 20 April, 27 June and finally on 8 October. Following this voyage, *Svalbard* passed into the Norwegian Navy.

It was also during 1949 that Mowinckels obtained a contract from the IRO, and decided to convert *Goya*. She was fitted out with basic quarters for 900 persons, and in March 1949 left Genoa on her first voyage to Australia. This was followed by four voyages from Naples to Australia, then on 17 April 1950, *Goya* left Bremerhaven for the first time bound for Australia. On her return voyage she stopped in Indonesia to board Dutch refugees. *Goya* made two further trips to Australia from Bremerhaven in 1950, the last in October, departing Melbourne on 7 November. This was her last visit to Australia, but in March 1951 she left Piraeus on a voyage to Wellington. She made two more trips to New Zealand, but only carried 505 passengers on the last one.

This marked the end of her career as a migrant ship,

as in 1953 *Goya* reverted to being a cargo ship again. In 1961 she was sold to T. J. Skogland and renamed *Reina*, but the following year was sold again, to T. Matland Jr and renamed *Svanholm*. In 1963 she changed hands again, being renamed *Hilde* when bought by Skibs A/S Hilde, then in 1964 finally left the Norwegian flag when sold to Meldaf Shipping Co. of Greece, being given her final name, *Melina*. She served under this name for five years, then was sold to shipbreakers in Taiwan in 1969, arriving in Kaohsiung on 19 July for demolition.

Svalbard remained in the Norwegian Navy until 1954, then was sold to A/S Tilthorn and renamed *Tilthorn*, though this was soon after changed to *Stella Marina*. In an unusual occurence, in 1956 she was sold to Deutsche–Afrika Linien, and regained her original name of *Togo*, returning to the route for which she was built.

Togo remained under the German flag again for 12 years, then in 1968 was sold to Taboga Enterprises Inc., and renamed *Lacasielle* under the Panamanian flag. This phase of her career lasted eight years, then in 1976 the vessel changed hands for the last time, going to Caribbean Real Estate S.A., also a Panamanian concern, and being renamed *Topeka*. She operated along the South American coast for Linea Argomar of Columbia, but when on a voyage from Tampico to Barranquilla she ran aground off Coatzacoalcos on 24 November 1984 when her anchors dragged during a storm, and became a total loss.

CHANGTE AND TAIPING

BUILT: *1925/26 by Hong Kong & Whampoa Dock Co. Ltd, Hong Kong*
TONNAGE: *4324 gross*
DIMENSIONS: *368 × 48 ft (112.1 × 14.6 m)*
SERVICE SPEED: *12 knots*
PROPULSION: *Triple expansion/single screw*

Australian–Oriental Line was formed in Australia in 1912, to take over the service operated by China Navigation, and two of their ships, the clipper-bowed *Taiyuan* and *Changsha*, built in 1886. This pair continued in service until 1925, when two new vessels were ordered as replacements.

Changte was launched in March 1925, and departed Hong Kong on 30 September for her maiden voyage to Australia, arriving in Sydney on 20 October. On this trip she did not visit Melbourne, but on subsequent voyages went on to the Victorian port. *Taiping* was launched on 11 June 1925, and left Hong Kong for the first time on 22 January 1926.

Both ships had been fitted out with comfortable cabin accommodation for 40 first class and 30 second class passengers, with separate quarters for 26 Chinese passengers. A large number of deck passengers could also be carried on short sectors in the Orient. Their route took the ships from Melbourne, Sydney and Brisbane to Townsville, Cairns, Thursday Island, Manila and Hong Kong.

On 27 August 1939, *Changte* was requisitioned and converted into a victualling stores issue ship, for service with the Royal Navy, being based on Trincomalee for several years, then moving into the Pacific as the war drew to a close. *Taiping* remained on her regular trade, and was one of the last ships to leave Manila in December 1941, crowded with women and children being evacuated ahead of the advancing Japanese forces. *Taiping* was the target of several air raids while she lay in Manila Bay, but got away safely and returned to Sydney. Taken over by the Royal Navy, *Taiping* also became a victualling stores issue ship, and saw service in numerous theatres of the war, including Egypt, Malta, South Africa, the Persian Gulf, and finally in the Pacific.

Changte was released from government service at the end of 1946, and returned to Sydney on 11 February 1947 to undergo a long conversion at the Poole & Steele shipyard in Balmain. *Changte* departed Sydney again on 21 April 1948, on her original route. *Taiping* arrived in Sydney on 30 June 1947 to commence her reconversion, which was done at Mort's Dock, and she eventually returned to commercial service in September 1949. Both ships were provided with accommodation for 91 first class passengers and 100 third class in dormitories, this being popular with Chinese, students and for a few years, White Russian immigrants.

In 1949, China Navigation returned to the Australian trade with a new *Taiyuan* and *Changsha*, to operate a joint service with the veterans of Australian–Oriental Line. Despite their advancing years and small size, *Taiping* and *Changte* remained popular with travellers through the 1950s and maintained a regular service. By the start of the 1960s, the pair were totally outdated, and well past their prime, so it was no surprise when they were sold to shipbreakers in 1961. *Changte* departed Sydney for the last time on 23 June, and the last sailing by Australian–Oriental Line was taken by *Taiping* from Sydney on 15 August, terminating in Hong Kong on 3 October. Both ships were broken up in Hong Kong.

CHANGTE

RIMUTAKA

BUILT: *1922 by Armstrong Whitworth Ltd, Newcastle*
TONNAGE: *16 596 gross*
DIMENSIONS: *568 × 72 ft (173.2 × 21.9 m)*
SERVICE SPEED: *16 knots*
PROPULSION: *Geared turbines/twin screws*

This ship had a long career, having been built for P & O as *Mongolia*, for their service to Australia. Launched on 24 August 1922, she left Tilbury on 11 May 1923 on her maiden voyage, joining her sister *Moldavia*. Accommodation was provided for 230 first class and 180 second class passengers, and there was also a large cargo capacity. *Mongolia* was a mixture of old and new, having an outdated counter stern, yet modern machinery.

In 1928, her second class quarters were regraded third class, and *Mongolia* was placed on an independent schedule. In 1930 *Moldavia* was given a second funnel, but not *Mongolia*, and the next year both vessels were refitted to carry 830 tourist class passengers only. On 20 August 1937, *Mongolia* left Tilbury on her final voyage to Australia, then was laid up. *Moldavia* was also laid up at the same time, then sold to shipbreakers in 1938. *Mongolia* was saved from a similar fate by being transferred to the New Zealand Shipping Co., a member of the P & O Group.

Refitted to carry 272 tourist class passengers and renamed *Rimutaka*, she left London on 8 December 1938 on her first voyage through the Panama Canal to Wellington, but within a year had been taken over for service as an armed merchant cruiser. However, it was decided her cargo capacity was too valuable, so she was returned to the New Zealand Shipping Co., and spent the war operating on her regular route, though her accommodation was controlled by the British government, and she often carried troops or government officials.

These controls were lifted in 1948, when *Rimutaka* was refitted, and resumed the New Zealand trade, until new ships were completed. On 11 October 1949, she left London on her final voyage to New Zealand, then in February 1950 was sold to Incres Line.

Renamed *Europa*, she operated briefly between New York and Antwerp, then in 1951 was renamed *Nassau*, and began cruising from New York to the Bahamas, carrying 617 first class passengers. This lasted a decade, as in 1961 she was sold to Cia. Nav. Turistica Mexicana, renamed *Acapulco*, and modernised for a cruise service from Californian ports to Mexico. This service never eventuated, and the ship then served as a floating hotel during the Seattle World Fair in 1962. She was sold to Japanese shipbreakers in 1964.

RIMUTAKA

AORANGI

BUILT: *1924 by Fairfield Shipbuilding & Engineering Co., Glasgow*

TONNAGE: *17 491 gross*

DIMENSIONS: *600 × 72 ft (182.9 × 22 m)*

SERVICE SPEED: *17.5 knots*

PROPULSION: *Sulzer diesels/quadruple screws*

During the inter-war years, the prestige service operated by the Union Steam Ship Co. of New Zealand was between Sydney and Vancouver via Auckland. It had been maintained by two liners, *Niagara* and *Aorangi*, for most of this period, but required subsidies from the governments of Australia, New Zealand and Canada to remain viable. Up to 1931, the service was totally a Union Line operation, but in July that year a half share in the route was acquired by Canadian Pacific. A new company was formed, Canadian–Australasian Line Ltd, which was incorporated in Canada, though management of the ships remained with the Union Line.

Niagara had been completed in 1913, and an improved version of this ship was ordered for delivery in 1915. Unfortunately, on completion this vessel, named *Aotearoa*, was taken over by the British Government, converted into an armed merchant cruiser, and sunk in 1916. In 1922 a replacement vessel was ordered, being named *Aorangi* when launched on 17 June 1924. Completed in December 1924, the new liner was much larger than both her predecessors, providing accommodation for 436 first class, 284 second class and 227 third class passengers. Three quarters of the cabins were for no more than two persons, and the eight suites were each decorated in a different period style. On trials, a top speed of 18.5 knots was attained.

Aorangi went to Southampton to take on passengers for her first voyage, to Vancouver via the Panama Canal. On 6 February 1925, she left the Canadian port on her maiden voyage to Australia, calling at Honolulu en route to Auckland and Sydney, where she arrived on 3 March. At that time, *Aorangi* was the largest and fastest motorship in the world, and the first diesel engined vessel in the Union Line fleet, as well as being their only quadruple screw ship. Despite all these claims to fame, *Aorangi* was never a ship that made money for her owners, even though the service with *Niagara* was a popular one. Without government subsidies it would have folded.

Aorangi and *Niagara* remained on their regular trade after war broke out in 1939, and *Niagara* was mined and sunk in June 1940 off the New Zealand north coast. *Awatea* then joined *Aorangi* on the route until she was requisitioned, and in July 1941 *Aorangi* was also taken over by the British Government and converted into a troopship. In May 1944, *Aorangi* was transformed into a depot ship for small craft, and in this capacity was stationed in the Solent during the Normandy invasion. From July 1944 to March 1945, the vessel was on the Clyde, being rebuilt as a submarine depot ship, then was sent to Ceylon, but arrived too late to be used. *Aorangi* subsequently served as the commodore's ship in the fleet train of the British Pacific fleet until May 1946, when she was handed back to her owner.

Work on refitting *Aorangi* for commercial service again was done in Sydney at Mort's Dock, and lasted two years. It was 19 August 1948 before the vessel left Sydney on her first post-war voyage to Vancouver. Her accommodation had been reduced to 212 first class, 170 cabin class and 104 third class, reflecting the decreased demand for passages on the route. For the first two round trips, *Aorangi* had a white hull with a dark green band, but this was then altered back to the former dark green hull with yellow band of her pre-war days. Also, her port of registry was changed from London to Wellington, making her the largest liner ever registered in New Zealand.

Only the Australian Government was forthcoming with a subsidy for the service, which attracted good passenger loadings but little cargo, and being a one ship operation, there was a long gap between sailings. In December 1950, Canadian–Australasian Line announced that the vessel would be withdrawn from service on her return to Sydney in January 1951. This action prompted the Canadian and New Zealand Governments to offer a subsidy to keep the ship operating, so in April 1951 *Aorangi* returned to service again.

The two year subsidy agreement ran out in April 1953, and over this period the financial returns continued to be very poor. The various governments decided not to renew their subsidies, which effectively killed the service. On 14 May 1953, *Aorangi* left Vancouver for the last time, and her arrival in Sydney on 8 June brought the Canadian–Australasian Line operation to an end.

Aorangi had already been sold to shipbreakers by the time she completed her last trip across the Pacific, and left Sydney on 18 June bound for Britain. She was handed over to British Iron & Steel Corporation at their Dalmuir shipbreaking yard on 25 July 1953.

ABOVE AND BELOW — TWO VIEWS OF *AORANGI* AT ANCHOR IN SYDNEY HARBOUR

A Former War Prize

BUILT: *1917 by Bremer Vulkan, Vegesack*
TONNAGE: *5751 gross*
DIMENSIONS: *436 × 56 ft (132.9 × 17.1 m)*
SERVICE SPEED: *11 knots*
PROPULSION: *Triple expansion/single screw*

This vessel made two voyages to Australia under different names, the first as *Derna* in 1948, the second as *Assimina* in 1951. She was ordered in 1914, prior to the outbreak of war, by Deutsche Ost Afrika Linie for their service from Germany to East Africa. Launched on 27 July 1915 and named *Kagera*, she entered service on 17 November 1917, but nothing is known of her wartime activities. She was designed as a cargo ship, with accommodation for 9 passengers.

On 30 March 1919 *Kagera* was seized by the victorious Allied forces as a prize of war, and allocated to France. Initially operated by the French Government, the vessel was purchased from them in 1922 by Cie. Generale Transatlantique, better known as the French Line. Renamed *Indiana*, she was placed on a cargo service between French ports and the Gulf of Mexico, and remained in this trade for almost 20 years. Shortly after the fall of France in 1940, *Indiana* was seized by the Americans, and laid up. In 1942 she was taken over by the United States War Shipping Administration, and used as a transport.

In 1945, *Indiana* was handed back to the French Line, and they retained her for the next three years. In 1948, *Indiana* was sold to Dos Oceanos Cia. de Nav., a Panamanian registered concern, and renamed *Derna*. It was at this time that the vessel was converted to carry displaced persons, with rather austere facilities being installed in the holds. On 30 August 1948, *Derna* departed Marseilles bound for Australia, voyaging to Melbourne where she berthed on 5 November. The vessel remained in the port for six weeks, loading cargo for the return trip, then sailed on 16 December bound for Le Havre.

During 1949 the vessel was renamed *Assimina* by her owner, but did not make a voyage to Australia under that name for almost two years. Departing Genoa on 29 December 1950, *Assimina* arrived in Fremantle on 5 February 1951, then proceeded to Melbourne, berthing on 13 February, and finally arrived in Sydney on 19 February. After another lengthy stay in port loading cargo, *Assimina* left Sydney on 7 March, returning to Genoa. The vessel was due to make another voyage to Australia, departing Genoa in May 1951, but this did not eventuate.

Late in 1952, *Assimina* was sold to Hughes Bolckow Ltd, and arrived at their shipbreaking yard in Blyth on 12 December 1952.

DERNA IN MELBOURNE, NOVEMBER 1948

CHARLTON SOVEREIGN

BUILT: *1930 by Cammell Laird & Co. Ltd, Birkenhead*
TONNAGE: *5516 gross*
DIMENSIONS: *366 × 57 ft (110.5 × 17.3 m)*
SERVICE SPEED: *20 knots*
PROPULSION: *Geared turbines/twin screws*

Charlton Sovereign was another of the vessels to make but a single voyage to Australia after the war with migrants. Her appearance in local waters was very different from her original design, as she was the last of a trio of three-funnelled vessels built for Canadian National Railways. Her original name was *Prince Robert*, her sisters being *Prince Henry* and *Prince David*, and they were splendid ships, designed for the highly competitive service between Seattle and Vancouver. Accommodation was provided for 334 first class and 70 third class passengers.

Despite all this, they failed dismally in competition with the vessels of Canadian Pacific on the same route, so in 1931 *Prince Henry* and *Prince David* were transferred to the east coast of Canada, while *Prince Robert* was laid up until the summer of 1935, when she began a summer cruise service to Alaska. On 26 November 1939, *Prince Robert* was taken over by the Royal Canadian Navy, and rebuilt as an armed merchant cruiser. The two forward funnels were trunked into one, and two decks of superstructure removed, completely altering her appearance.

On 5 February 1940, *Prince Robert* was bought by the Royal Canadian Navy, and initially served in the Pacific. In 1943 she was converted into an auxiliary anti-aircraft cruiser, seeing action in the Mediterranean, and later taking part in the Normandy landings. She finished the war back in the Pacific, and was in Sydney when the Japanese surrendered. Her final task was the repatriation of released Canadian prisoners-of-war from Hong Kong, then late in 1945 *Prince Robert* was paid off, and offered for sale.

In October 1946 *Prince Robert* was bought by the Charlton Steam Shipping Co. Ltd, along with *Prince David*. They were refitted as emigrant carriers in Belgium, with austere accommodation for 750 persons. *Prince Robert* was renamed *Charlton Sovereign* and her sister *Charlton Monarch*, and both were chartered by the IRO in March 1948. On 4 August 1948, *Charlton Sovereign* departed Bremerhaven for Australia, but was delayed almost a month at Gibraltar by boiler problems. After visiting Colombo, she was held up 10 days in Batavia with further engine trouble, then stopped at Cairns before arriving in Sydney on 29 October, after a voyage lasting 86 days. She remained in Sydney for two weeks undergoing further repairs, then left on 15 November for Britain, where further extensive repairs were completed. *Charlton Sovereign* made five further voyages for the IRO, three to South America, one to Central America and one to Halifax, followed by a pilgrim voyage from North Africa to Jedda, all of which were delayed by engine problems.

In April 1951, the vessel was sold to Fratelli Grimaldi, and rebuilt as a passenger liner. New engines were installed, a full superstructure added topped by two funnels, a raked bow fitted, and accommodation provided for 80 first class, 80 intermediate, and 560 third class passengers. Renamed *Lucania*, and looking very smart and modern, the vessel entered service in July 1953 operating between Italy and South America. In 1962 she was withdrawn, and sold to shipbreakers in Italy, to end a very varied career.

CHARLTON SOVEREIGN

A 'HOG ISLANDER'

BUILT: *1920 by American International Shipbuilding Corp., Hog Island*
TONNAGE: *7783 gross*
DIMENSIONS: *448 × 58 ft (136.6 × 17.6 m)*
SERVICE SPEED: *16 knots*
PROPULSION: *Steam turbines/single screw*

Designed as a standard "Hog Island–A" type transport ship, this name deriving from the site at which they were built, Hog Island in Pennsylvania. A total of 110 basic "Hog Islanders" were built there, followed by a dozen of this type, and they were very plain ships, with no sheer or camber. This vessel was launched on 27 October 1919, and named *Cantigny*, being owned by the US Shipping Board. Between 1920 and 1923 she served as a troopship, then in 1924, along with four sisters, was transferred to the newly formed American Merchant Line.

Renamed *American Banker*, she operated on a cargo service between New York and London, carrying only 12 passengers. During 1926 her accommodation was enlarged to carry 80 tourist class passengers. In October 1931, American Merchant Line was absorbed into United States Line, but *American Banker* remained on her regular route. On 8 November 1939 the vessel arrived in New York from London for the last time.

In February 1940, *American Banker* was among eight ships transferred by the US Government to a new Belgian company, Soc. Maritime Anveroise, though under management of United States Line. Renamed *Ville d'Anvers*, she left New York on 9 March 1940 for Liverpool, as it was too dangerous for her to try and reach Antwerp. When the Germans overran Belgium in May 1940, all eight ships were taken over by the Allies, and the other seven were sunk.

Ville d'Anvers was returned to the United States Line in February 1946, but was not needed, so in July 1946 she was transferred to Isbrantsen Line. They also had no use for the ship, and in October 1946 sold her to Cia. di Vapores Mediterranea, who renamed the ship *City of Athens* under the Honduran flag. Refitted to carry 200 tourist class passengers, and managed by T. J. Stevenson & Co. of New York, *City of Athens* left New York on 11 November 1946 for Istanbul. Following a second trip to Istanbul, the vessel made a voyage to Piraeus, returning to Baltimore on 12 July 1947, and being laid up. On 13 August 1947, she was sold to Panamanian Lines, a forerunner of Home Lines.

Renamed *Protea*, the vessel was despatched to Genoa for an extensive refit, during which her passenger capacity was increased to 965 in one class. *Protea* entered service in April 1948 with two voyages with migrants from Italy to South America, then on 20 August 1948 departed Genoa bound for Australia. After calling at Melbourne on 23 September, the voyage terminated in Sydney on 29 September, and was followed by another departure from Genoa in November to the same ports.

It was not until 2 November 1950 that *Protea* left Naples on her third voyage to Australia, calling only at Melbourne. During 1951 she made a further two trips, the second leaving Genoa on 19 May and reaching Melbourne on 22 June, followed by her arrival in Sydney, on 3 July. On returning from this voyage, *Protea* was sold by Panamanian Lines in August 1951 to Cia. Internacional Transportadora, a new company owned in Switzerland, but registered in Panama.

At first *Protea* was not renamed, and made a trooping voyage to Haiphong for the French Government, followed by two trans-Atlantic voyages under charter to Incres Line. In January 1952 she arrived in Bremen for an extensive refit, during which her accommodation was altered to 46 first and 919 tourist class. The ship was then renamed *Arosa Kulm*, and her owner adopted the name Arosa Line. On 18 March 1952, *Arosa Kulm* left Bremerhaven, opening a new service to Canada.

On 21 December 1954, *Arosa Kulm* left Bremerhaven bound for Australia, reaching Fremantle on 27 January 1955, Melbourne on 3 February and Sydney two days later. On her return voyage the vessel called at Saigon, to carry French settlers back to Europe. The vessel returned to her Canadian service until 29 October 1955, when she left Bremerhaven on a second voyage to Australia, visiting the same three ports, leaving Sydney on 11 December bound for Trieste. It was from that port that she sailed on 18 January 1956, going only to Fremantle and Melbourne, leaving there on 20 February for Saigon again.

The fourth voyage to Australia made by *Arosa Kulm* was also her last, departing Genoa on 2 April 1956, and she arrived in Fremantle on 5 May. The next day her lifesaving equipment was inspected and found to be faulty, delaying her five days before she could continue to Melbourne, from where she sailed on 16 May for Auckland, arriving on 20 May. *Arosa Kulm* then crossed the Pacific, going to Boston and on to Europe.

Arosa Line was encountering financial difficulties, and on 6 December 1958 *Arosa Kulm* was arrested at Plymouth while returning from a voyage to the West Indies from Bremerhaven. The same month the three other liners owned by Arosa Line were also arrested, and on 10 April 1959 the company was declared bankrupt. All four ships were put up for auction, but *Arosa Kulm* was of interest only to shipbreakers. She was sold to the Belgian firm, Van Heyghen Freres, and on 7 May 1959 arrived at their yard in Bruges.

PROTEA

AROSA KULM

LUCIANO MANARA

BUILT: *1941 by Ansaldo S.A., Genoa*
TONNAGE: *7121 gross*
DIMENSIONS: *472 × 62 ft (143.8 × 18.9 m)*
SERVICE SPEED: *14 knots*
PROPULSION: *Fiat diesel/single screw*

Many of the ships that carried new settlers to Australia in the late 1940s are virtually unknown, and forgotten by all but those who travelled on them. *Luciano Manara* is one such ship, as she only served in a passenger carrying capacity for a very brief period, and her facilities were extremely basic.

During 1941, the Garibaldi Group of Italy took delivery of three new cargo ships, named *Augistino Bertani*, *Nino Bixio* and *Luciano Manara*. They were placed under the ownership of a subsidiary company, Soc. Anon. Co-operativa di Navigazione, which already owned a dozen dry cargo ships and four tankers. The Italian merchant navy was decimated by the war, yet all three of these new ships managed to survive, though nothing is known of their activities during the conflict.

The Garibaldi Group set about rebuilding its fleet, and then saw the possibility of joining the booming migrant trade. It was for this purpose that *Luciano Manara* was converted, being given very austere accommodation for about 700 persons. This entailed the enlarging of the superstructure, additional lifeboats, and the installation of basic facilities in the holds. It was in this guise that *Luciano Manara* made two voyages to Australia from Italy.

Her first voyage departed Italy in September 1948, and the vessel was in Melbourne on 21 October, and then continued on to Sydney. Her second voyage commenced in April 1949, and again the vessel called at Melbourne, on 15 May, before continuing to Sydney. On each of these voyages she only carried about 350 persons. It appears that *Luciano Manara* was not a success as a migrant carrier, and her passengers must have had some very uncomfortable voyages.

Soon after her second Australian voyage, *Luciano Manara* reverted to being a cargo ship again, with her superstructure reduced and extra lifeboats removed. In 1953 she was renamed *Giuseppe Canepa* by her owner, and served under this name in the fleet for two years.

In 1955 the vessel was sold to Polish Ocean Lines and renamed *Malgorzata Fornalska*, then in 1965 passed to the flag of the People's Republic of China, being sold to China Ocean Shipping Co. and renamed *Chung Ming*. In 1977 her name was changed to *Hong Qi 144*, being registered in Guangzhou, and as far as is known she is still active under that name.

LUCIANO MANARA

TOSCANA

BUILT: *1923 by AG Weser, Bremen*
TONNAGE: *9584 gross*
DIMENSIONS: *480 × 62 ft (146.3 × 18.9 m)*
SERVICE SPEED: *13 knots*
PROPULSION: *Triple expansion/twin screws*

Toscana was a most unusual looking vessel, having a corrugated hull and a bulbous sponson down each side. These were intended to reduce the rolling of the ship, and were quite unsightly.

This vessel had been built for North German Lloyd as the *Saarbrücken*, with accommodation for 98 first and 142 second class passengers. She operated from Bremen to the Far East until 1935, when she was purchased by the Italian Government, and renamed *Toscana*. Initially allocated to Italia Line for their South American service, she was transferred to Lloyd Triestino in 1937. Fitted out with austere accommodation for up to 2000 passengers, she was used on the service from Italy to East and South Africa, at this time having a thin, upright funnel and being painted white. When Italy came into the war, *Toscana* was converted into a hospital ship, and was one of the few Italian flag vessels to survive the conflict. Initially taken over by the Allies, she was handed back to Italy in 1947, and restored to Lloyd Triestino.

Refitted with accommodation for 136 saloon class and 690 third class passengers, and sporting a much

larger funnel and a black hull, *Toscana* returned to service with several voyages to South Africa, then on 19 October 1948 departed Genoa on the first post-war voyage by a Lloyd Triestino vessel to Australia, going first to Melbourne, where she berthed on 30 November, then Sydney on 2 December. In 1949 she was joined by *Sebastiano Caboto* and *Ugolino Vivaldi*, and this trio maintained the Lloyd Triestino presence on the Australian trade for the next two years.

During 1951 the new liners *Australia, Neptunia* and *Oceania* entered service, so *Toscana* was altered to carry 819 third class only. Outbound she carried migrants to Australia, returning with her six holds filled with cargo. In this way the old vessel was able to maintain her place on the Australian trade for a further 10 years. On 3 June 1952, *Toscana* lost both her anchors in heavy weather off Portsea, while waiting for the seas to moderate so she could enter Port Phillip Bay, and had to remain in Melbourne until new anchors were fitted. A more serious accident was a collision on 7 March 1953 with the US Navy oiler *Cowanesque* in Suez Roads, in which one passenger on *Toscana* was killed. On 7 May 1956, her lifesaving gear was found to be faulty during an inspection in Australia, and the owner was fined.

Despite these incidents, *Toscana* gave good service to Lloyd Triestino. During 1960 she was withdrawn and laid up, then sold to a Genoa shipbreaking firm, arriving at their yard on 21 February 1962.

TOSCANA, SHOWING THE BULBOUS SPONSON

CAMERONIA

BUILT: *1921 by W. Beardmore & Co. Ltd, Glasgow*
TONNAGE: *16 584 gross*
DIMENSIONS: *578 × 70 ft (176.3 × 21.4 m)*
SERVICE SPEED: *16 knots*
PROPULSION: *Geared turbines / twin screws*

The keel of *Cameronia* was laid on 7 March 1919, the first British passenger liner laid down after the end of World War One. She was launched on 23 December 1919, but it was May 1921 before *Cameronia* entered service. She was the first of four similar vessels built jointly for Cunard and the Anchor Line.

Cameronia provided accommodation for 265 first class, 370 second class and 1150 third class passengers, but proved to be a very unsatisfactory sea-boat. In November 1928 the lower section of the bow back to the bridge was removed, and rebuilt to a new design.

In September 1935 *Cameronia* was chartered by the British Government to carry troops. Between April and July 1936 the liner was out of service again, being refitted, then on 10 July she left Glasgow again bound for New York. *Cameronia* remained on the Atlantic trade until November 1940, when she was requisitioned as a troopship.

Fitted out to carry 3000 men, she entered her new service in January 1941. In December 1942, while on her second voyage to the North African landings, *Cameronia* was hit by a torpedo dropped from an aircraft, but was able to limp into Bone, then return to Gibraltar. She took part in several landings, including D-day, then was handed back to Anchor Line in May 1945. They did not intend to resume their Atlantic

service, so the ship was laid up.

In 1947, *Cameronia* was chartered by the British Government to carry troops to Palestine, following which the Ministry of Transport decided to use the ship on the Australian migrant trade. In July 1948, *Cameronia* arrived at the shipyard of Barclay, Curle & Co., for an extensive refit. Four of her six boilers were replaced, the machinery overhauled, a shorter funnel fitted, while the gap between the boat deck and the bridge was filled in. Accommodation for 1266 persons was installed in cabins with up to six berths. She was managed for the Ministry of Transport by Anchor Line and painted in its colours.

On 1 November 1948, *Cameronia* left Glasgow on her first voyage to Australia, and over the next four years was to make a further 11 voyages from the Scottish port. The only unfortunate incident to mar her career occurred in June 1950, when the starboard engine broke down shortly after leaving Glasgow, and the ship had to spend several days being repaired. On most voyages she returned empty, but in August 1950 she stopped off in Indonesia to collect Dutch nationals and return them home.

In October 1952, *Cameronia* departed Glasgow on her final voyage to Australia, departing Melbourne on 6 November to return to Britain. In January 1953, the liner was bought from the Anchor Line by the Ministry of Transport, and renamed *Empire Clyde*. Repainted in troopship colours, all white with a yellow funnel and coloured ribband, she served a further four years under her new name. In September 1957, *Empire Clyde* was sold to shipbreakers, and on 22 October arrived at their Newport yard.

CAMERONIA

RENA

BUILT: *1904 by John Brown & Co., Clydebank*
TONNAGE: *1619 gross*
DIMENSIONS: *279 × 36 ft (85 × 10.9 m)*
SERVICE SPEED: *16 knots*
PROPULSION: *Triple expansion/single screw*

Migrant ships came in all sizes after the war, and one of the smallest was *Rena*, a former British ferry. She was originally named *Woodcock*, having been built for G. & J. Burns Ltd to operate the overnight service across the Irish Sea between Ardrossan and Belfast. This was a high density service, and the vessel could carry over 1200 passengers, mostly travelling in lounges or on deck, and also had a large cargo capacity. As was usual on this route, there were also spaces for live cattle.

From 1914 to 1919 she served as the armed boarding ship HMS *Woodnut*, being armed with three 12-pounder guns. In 1920, following a refit, she returned to the Irish Sea trade again under her original name.

In 1922, following the merger of two Irish Sea shipping companies, *Woodcock* became part of the Burns & Laird fleet, and in 1923 her passenger capacity was shown as 1133. In 1929 she was renamed *Lairdswood*, when a new naming system was adopted. However, the following year the vessel was sold to the Aberdeen Steam Navigation Co. Ltd, being renamed *Lochnager*. With her passenger capacity reduced to 450, most in berths, she operated the long service along the east coast of Britain from Aberdeen to London.

When war broke out in September 1939, *Lochnager* was laid up in Aberdeen, then in April 1940 was requisitioned by the Admiralty. Soon after, she was sent to Molde in Norway, being attacked by German bombers as she made her way up the fjord, but escaping damage. Going on to Alesund, she suffered slight damage during a bombing raid there, then returned to Scapa Flow. *Lochnager* then spent the rest of the war operating between Aberdeen and Lerwick, apart from three trips to Iceland to ferry personnel around the island. At the end of 1945, *Lochnager* was returned to her owners, and resumed the coastal trade.

In October 1946, the vessel was sold to Rena Cia. de Nav. S.A., of Panama, and renamed *Rena*. The new owner converted her from coal to oil-firing, and added a new deckhouse behind the mainmast. *Rena* was used to carry displaced persons, and in October 1948 left Europe with 360 persons aboard, bound for Melbourne, where she arrived six weeks later, on 29 November. *Rena* remained in Melbourne for two months, until a cargo was obtained for the return trip. On 16 January 1949 she was struck by the cargo ship *Citos*, which had broken adrift during a storm, causing some minor damage. On 22 January *Rena* finally left Melbourne, bound for Alexandria.

Rena remained in active service a further three years, and early in 1952 was renamed *Blue Star*. Shortly afterwards she was sold to shipbreakers, arriving on 26 April 1952 at their La Spezia yard.

RENA IN MELBOURNE, DECEMBER 1948

DOMINION MONARCH

BUILT: *1939 by Swan, Hunter & Wigham Richardson Ltd, Newcastle*
TONNAGE: *26 463 gross*
DIMENSIONS: *682 × 84 ft (207.8 × 25.8 m)*
SERVICE SPEED: *19 knots*
PROPULSION: *Doxford diesels/quadruple screws*

During 1937 Shaw Savill Line decided to inaugurate a service from Britain to New Zealand via Cape Town and Australian ports, and consequently ordered a new liner. During construction extensive use was made of welding for the hull and superstructure, saving considerable weight. Launched on 27 July 1938, fitting out took six months. In January 1939, *Dominion Monarch* ran trials, reaching 21.5 knots, being at the time the most powerful British motorship, developing 32 000 bhp from her four Doxford diesels.

Despite her size, *Dominion Monarch* was designed as much as a cargo carrier as a passenger liner. She had six holds with a capacity of 12 800 tons of frozen cargo and 3600 tons of general cargo. Accommodation was provided for 517 passengers, all first class, but only the dining room was air-conditioned, and amenities included several lounges, a playroom for children, swimming pool and gymnasium. *Dominion Monarch* was the largest ship trading to South Africa as well as Australia and New Zealand, though not as long as the veteran *Ceramic*.

In early February 1939, *Dominion Monarch* went to London, berthing in the King George V Dock to load cargo, departing on her maiden voyage on 16 February. The next day she berthed in Southampton to take on her passengers, then left for Teneriffe and on to Cape Town and Durban. Crossing the Indian Ocean she averaged 19.86 knots to Fremantle, arriving on 13 March. Following visits to Melbourne and Sydney, the vessel crossed the Tasman Sea to Wellington. The maiden voyage was a triumphant passage, with *Dominion Monarch* creating enormous interest at every port of call.

Once her passengers had disembarked in Wellington, the liner went on to Napier, becoming the largest vessel to visit the port, but had to anchor out. She also called at Lyttelton, then went back to Wellington to board passengers, returning to Britain on the reverse route, the entire round trip lasting about 15 weeks.

Dominion Monarch departed on her second voyage to New Zealand in late June 1939, and was berthed in Lyttelton working cargo when war broke out on 3 September. She was immediately sent to Sydney, arriving on 7 September, where some armaments were fitted, then voyaged back to England around South Africa as usual. Arriving at the mouth of the Thames at

the same time the first magnetic mines were found there, she reached her berth safely.

The vessel was inspected with a view to being converted into a troopship, but it was decided that her existing accommodation would not carry enough troops to warrant the change, and her enormous capacity for frozen cargo was more valuable. As a result, *Dominion Monarch* remained in commercial operation to Australia and New Zealand until August 1940. Then, with the war situation getting worse, she was requisitioned by the British Government, and sent to Liverpool for conversion into a troopship.

Only some of her passenger fittings were removed, as accommodation for 142 officers and 1340 other ranks was installed, using tiered bunks. It was still hoped to make use of her cargo spaces, so on her first trooping voyage she was sent around South Africa to Egypt, and then went to Australia and New Zealand to load a full cargo of frozen foodstuffs and carry them back to Liverpool. Her next voyage was back to New Zealand, where she collected 1550 men and carried them to Singapore, then returned to Britain again.

Leaving Britain in September 1941, *Dominion Monarch* voyaged around South Africa to Singapore again, arriving as the Japanese were advancing on the island and air raids were a daily occurrence. Despite this, the vessel was put into drydock there, and her engines dismantled for overhaul, so she was totally helpless when the Japanese made their final thrust on Singapore. In an incredible feat of skill, her own engineering crew were able to rebuild the engines themselves in a matter of days, and the ship escaped only a matter of days before the island fell to the Japanese.

Returning to Liverpool, further conversion work resulted in the removal of all her remaining fittings, as her trooping capacity was increased to 3556 men. *Dominion Monarch* was then despatched to Egypt in convoy, but came into collision with *Highland Chieftain* off the coast of West Africa, and had to put into Freetown for repairs, then voyaged unescorted to Cape Town to rejoin the convoy.

During 1943 *Dominion Monarch* made a voyage that lasted almost nine months, taking her first from Britain to India via Cape Town, then on to Australia and New Zealand where a full cargo was loaded. She then returned to Cape Town, where 1900 wounded and sick men from the campaign in North Africa were taken aboard, and carried back to Britain. On her next voyage, 3600 troops were carried to Egypt, returning with a similar number of 8th Army veterans.

Going into 1944, *Dominion Monarch* joined the Atlantic troop run, bringing thousands of American

DOMINION MONARCH

soldiers to Europe, and she also made a trip to Iceland. By the time the war ended, *Dominion Monarch* had carried over 90 000 troops and over 70 000 tons of cargo while travelling some 350 000 miles.

After the war ended, *Dominion Monarch* made several voyages repatriating troops to Australia and New Zealand, then in July 1947 was finally handed back to her owner. She returned to her builder's yard for an extensive refit that lasted 15 months, in which her accommodation was rebuilt for 508 first class passengers. On 17 December 1948, *Dominion Monarch* left London on her first post-war commercial voyage, following her pre-war route. For some time Wellington was her only port of call in New Zealand, but later Auckland and Lyttelton were added.

Dominion Monarch relied heavily on cargo to make her operation viable, but due to frequent waterfront strikes in both Australia and New Zealand, her schedule was constantly disrupted, which made her unpopular with passengers. A lone ship service is seldom a commercial success, so in 1955, Shaw Savill introduced *Southern Cross*, which carried no cargo at all, and such was her success that a second ship of similar type was ordered, to replace *Dominion Monarch*.

As *Northern Star* neared completion, *Dominion Monarch* departed London on 30 December 1961 on her final voyage, departing Wellington on 15 March 1962 to return to Britain. By the time she reached London, a sale to the Mitsui Group of Japan had been finalised, and it then chartered the liner to an American consortium for service as a floating hotel in Seattle during the World Fair from June to November 1962. She was renamed *Dominion Monarch Maru* for the voyage from Seattle to Osaka, where she arrived on 25 November 1962, at the Mitsui shipbreaking yard.

BIBBY LINE TWINS

BUILT: *1920/21 by Harland & Wolff Ltd, Belfast*
TONNAGE: *9787 gross*
DIMENSIONS: *468 × 57 ft (142.6 × 17.4 m)*
SERVICE SPEED: *12 knots*
PROPULSION: *B & W diesels/twin screws*

The Bibby Line had been engaged in the trade between Britain and Burma since 1890, operating a fleet of very distinctive passenger ships, all with four masts and a single tall funnel, of which the *Oxfordshire*, described elsewhere in this book, was a typical example. However, shortly after the end of World War One Bibby Line ordered two cargo ships, the first in their fleet, intended to carry lead ore from the Namtu mines in Burma to Britain.

The first of the pair was launched on 22 April 1920 and named *Dorsetshire*, being delivered in August the same year, while her sister was named *Somersetshire* when launched on 24 February 1921, being delivered three months later. Unfortunately, by the time this pair were in service, the mine company had built a smelter at Namtu, so the two ships were not needed. Instead, *Dorsetshire* and *Somersetshire* were chartered out, with *Somersetshire* operating for Royal Mail Line on their service to the west coast of America, and later both ships saw service with the Brocklebank Line, operating to India.

In 1921, Bibby Line won a British Government contract to transport troops, and at first used their old liner *Derbyshire* on this trade. When the contract was renewed in 1927 for a further five years, *Dorsetshire* and *Somersetshire* were sent to the Vickers-Armstrong shipyard at Barrow, and rebuilt as troopships. A new superstructure was built aft of the bridge, but the long foredeck retained to be used by the troops for parades. Accommodation was installed for 1450 troops, 108 troop dependants, 58 warrant officers and 112 officers. The ships were painted white with a yellow funnel, and a wide coloured ribband around the hull. Both ships began operating as troopers in October 1927, mainly between Britain and India, which was a seasonal service from October to April. For the rest of the year they would be laid up in the River Dart. On occasions they also made trips to China.

Both vessels served as troopers until war broke out in 1939, and then, surprisingly, they were converted into hospital ships. It was in this role that *Somersetshire* visited Melbourne during April 1941. The ship had been involved in the withdrawal from Narvik in 1940, and on 7 April 1942 was struck by a torpedo in the Mediterranean, but managed to reach Alexandria safely on one engine. *Dorsetshire* also saw action in the Mediterranean, being subjected to intense air attack for two days late in January 1943 off Tobruk, escaping with minor damage. On 12 July 1943 she was again damaged in an air attack, off the coast of Sicily.

From 1946 both ships reverted to their trooping roles, and were used in the repatriation of prisoners-of-war and other duties. *Somersetshire* was released from government service in February 1948, and *Dorsetshire* the following month. Bibby Line had no need of the pair, and were very pleased to obtain a contract from the Ministry of Transport to carry migrants to Australia. Both ships were sent to Liverpool and converted for their new role by Harland & Wolff, being given basic accommodation for 550 persons. For the first time since they were rebuilt in 1927, they were painted in Bibby Line colours.

Somersetshire was the first to enter service, departing Liverpool on 12 November 1948 for Australia, followed by *Dorsetshire*, which departed Liverpool on 10 December. Despite their slow speed and unusual appearance, the two ships were highly successful as emigrant carriers, making four round trips per year. At times they were routed via Indonesia on the homeward voyage, to collect Dutch evacuees. In August 1952, *Somersetshire* suffered engine problems in the Mediterranean while returning to Britain, but was able to limp back to port where repairs were effected.

Both ships were withdrawn from the Australian migrant trade during 1952, with *Dorsetshire* departing Melbourne for the last time on 13 July, while *Somersetshire* made her final departure from Melbourne on 6 November.

Somersetshire remained under charter to the Ministry of Transport, but from February 1953 operated once again as a troopship, carrying British troops to Kenya. *Dorsetshire* was sent to Aden in November 1952 to serve as an accommodation ship for workers building an oil refinery there. On 1 March 1953 she was released from that static duty, and joined her sister again as a troopship to East Africa. *Dorsetshire* only served in this capacity for six months, as on 9 November 1953 she arrived at Liverpool for the last time, and was laid up. *Somersetshire* remained active until her arrival at Liverpool on 26 January 1954, when she was also offered for sale.

Dorsetshire was purchased by John Cashmore Ltd, and arrived at their Newport shipbreaking yard on 1 February 1954. *Somersetshire* was disposed of to British Iron & Steel, and arrived at the Barrow shipbreaking yard of T. W. Ward on 4 March 1954.

DORSETSHIRE IN SYDNEY COVE

SOMERSETSHIRE

CHITRAL

BUILT: *1925 by A. Stephen & Sons Ltd, Glasgow*
TONNAGE: *15 555 gross*
DIMENSIONS: *548 × 70 ft (167 × 21.4 m)*
SERVICE SPEED: *16 knots*
PROPULSION: *Quadruple expansion/twin screws*

Chitral was the sole survivor of a group of three ships built for P & O in 1925 to operate between Britain and Australia. The first two, *Cathay* and *Comorin*, were launched at the Barclay, Curle shipyard on the same day, 31 October 1924, while *Chitral* followed on 27 January 1925. She made her maiden departure from London on 3 July 1925, and provided accommodation for 200 first and 135 second class passengers.

All three sisters served on the Australian route until 1931, when *Chitral* and *Comorin* were transferred to operate from Britain to India and the Far East. In July 1936, while anchored off Gibraltar, *Chitral* was narrowly missed by bombs from a Spanish aircraft. All three sisters were requisitioned for conversion into armed merchant cruisers in September and October 1939.

Cathay was converted in Bombay, and patrolled the Indian Ocean. *Chitral* and *Comorin* were altered in Britain, *Chitral* being armed with seven 6-inch guns and three 4-inch anti-aircraft guns. Both were posted to the Northern Patrol, and on 20 November 1939, *Chitral* intercepted the German vessel *Bertha Fisser*, which was scuttled by her crew to avoid capture. In April 1941,

Comorin caught fire in the North Atlantic, and was subsequently sunk by British destroyers, while *Cathay* was bombed and sunk during the North African landings in November 1942. In April 1944 *Chitral* arrived in Baltimore to be converted into a troopship, returning to service in September. She served in this capacity until released in September 1947.

Instead of refurbishing the ship to her pre-war condition, P & O elected to have her refitted for the Australian emigrant trade. The work was done in London, where accommodation for 738 persons was installed, mostly comprising cabins with between six and twelve berths, and only nine two-berth cabins. One concession to comfort was the inclusion of two outdoor swimming pools. *Chitral* was painted in the old P & O colours, and on 30 December 1948 left London on her first post-war voyage to Australia. Outbound she carried assisted migrants, while on the return trip she carried fare-paying passengers on behalf of P & O. On a few occasions, *Chitral* was diverted to Indonesia on her homeward voyage, to collect Dutch nationals.

Chitral served four years as an emigrant ship, making four return trips each year. On 19 December 1952, she left London on her final voyage to Australia, departing Sydney for the last time on 4 February 1953, arriving back in London on 18 March. By that time a sale had been finalised to shipbreakers at Dalmuir, with *Chitral* arriving on 1 April 1953 at their yard.

CHITRAL AS AN EMIGRANT SHIP

ERIDAN

BUILT: *1929 by Soc. Provencale de Constructions Navales,*
   La Ciotat
TONNAGE: *9928 gross*
DIMENSIONS: *475 × 61 ft (144.7 × 18.6 m)*
SERVICE SPEED: *14.5 knots*
PROPULSION: *Sulzer diesels/twin screws*

Messageries Maritimes began a programme of building new passenger liners with the construction of *Eridan* in 1929, followed by five liners of increasing size up to 1933. The unique feature of all these vessels was their square funnels with "mushroom" tops.

Apart from her funnels, *Eridan* had a number of other unusual features, with the forward well deck being decked over and used by third class passengers as a covered promenade area. *Eridan* was launched on 3 June 1928, and when completed was the largest motor ship built in France to that time. Accommodation was provided for 60 first, 90 second and 420 third class passengers, the latter being mostly emigrants.

On 19 November 1929, *Eridan* departed Marseilles on her maiden voyage, a shakedown trip to Alexandria, Haifa and Beirut. On 10 January 1930 the vessel left Marseilles again on a voyage to the Far East, which would be her main route for the next six years. However, in 1935 she was transferred to the Pacific trades, operating from Marseilles through the Panama Canal to Papeete and Noumea.

On 8 March 1939, *Eridan* collided with the Canadian Pacific liner *Empress of Australia* in Algiers. She returned to the Pacific trade after repairs, then in 1940 came under Vichy control following the fall of France. *Eridan* was captured by Allied ships off North Africa on 8 November 1942, being despatched first to Arzew and then Oran, where she was officially taken over by the Allies. Managed by British India Line for the Ministry of War Transport, *Eridan* served as a troopship in the Indian Ocean and Far East. On 29 December 1945, an engine room fire caused serious damage when *Eridan* was in Saigon, but she was able to return to Marseilles to be handed back to her owners in March 1946. Once repairs had been effected, *Eridan* was briefly used for trooping in the Mediterranean, then began a major refit that lasted well into 1947. Now fitted with accommodation for 95 first class and 102 second class passengers, plus 900 troops, *Eridan* began operating to Madagascar, Reunion and Mauritius.

On 19 November 1948, *Eridan* departed Marseilles on her first voyage to Australia passing through the Panama Canal and proceeding direct to Noumea, arriving on 13 January. Four days later, *Eridan* entered Sydney Harbour, berthing at No. 5 Circular Quay, where she remained until 2 February. On leaving Sydney, *Eridan* returned to Noumea, and then back to Marseilles.

In 1951 *Eridan* returned to her builder's yard for a refit, during which a new large, single funnel was fitted, which quite changed her appearance. After a further spell on the Madagascar trade, *Eridan* carried troops to Haiphong in 1953, then returned to the Noumea route. Her last voyage ended in Marseilles in January 1956, and in March she was sold to local shipbreakers.

ERIDAN, SHOWING THE UNIQUE FUNNELS

ORCADES

BUILT: *1948 by Vickers–Armstrong Ltd, Barrow*
TONNAGE: *28 164 gross*
DIMENSIONS: *709 × 60 ft (216 × 27.6 m)*
SERVICE SPEED: *22 knots*
PROPULSION: *Geared turbines/twin screws*

The first brand new liner to arrive in Australia after the war was *Orcades*, built for the Orient Line to replace a liner of the same name sunk during the war. Launched on 14 October 1947, *Orcades* achieved 24.74 knots on trials, and departed Tilbury on 14 December 1948 on her maiden voyage, arriving in Fremantle on 6 January 1949, then going on to Melbourne and Sydney, where she berthed on 13 January. *Orcades* introduced a new look to the Orient Line, with her bridge amidships, and just a tripod signal mast. The hull of *Orcades* was identical to that of *Himalaya*, but the pair had different superstructures. Accommodation was provided for 773 first class and 772 tourist class.

For the first six years of her career, *Orcades* plied only between Britain and Australia through the Suez Canal. On 7 May 1952 she grounded in Port Phillip Bay while leaving Melbourne in strong winds, but was pulled free later the same day. On 17 December 1954, she left Sydney on her first voyage across the Pacific, arriving in San Francisco on 6 January 1955, then returning to Sydney. On 22 August 1955, *Orcades* left Southampton on her first voyage to Australia through the Panama Canal. For the rest of her career, the vessel would make frequent crossings of the Pacific, and also

was used for cruising. During November 1956, *Orcades* spent two weeks berthed in Melbourne, serving as a floating hotel during the Olympic Games.

Early in 1959, *Orcades* was given an extensive refit by Harland & Wolff at Belfast, during which air-conditioning was installed and a new swimming pool installed for first class, the old one then being allocated to tourist class. Following the integration of the Orient Line into P & O in 1960, *Orcades* retained her corn-coloured hull a further four years, then it was repainted white during a refit in 1964. At the same time, her accommodation was altered for 1635 passengers in one class. She made her first voyage in this configuration from Tilbury in May 1964, but in subsequent years was used more for cruising than line voyages.

On 17 April 1972, *Orcades* was in Hong Kong on a cruise from Sydney when fire damaged the boiler room. *Iberia* was laid up at the time in Southampton, so replacement parts were removed from her, and flown to Hong Kong to be installed in *Orcades*. The liner was now at the end of her career, as on 3 June 1972 she left Sydney for the last time, bound for Britain.

Orcades made a short series of cruises from Southampton, the last returning on 13 October, following which the vessel was laid up. In January 1973, with only a skeleton crew on board, *Orcades* left Southampton bound for Taiwan, arriving in Kaohsiung on 6 February 1973 and being handed over to shipbreakers there. On 15 March 1973, work began on scrapping the liner.

ORCADES AFTER 1964 REPAINTING

NEA HELLAS

BUILT: *1922 by Fairfield Shipbuilding & Engineering Co.,*
  Glasgow
TONNAGE: *16 991 gross*
DIMENSIONS: *580 × 70 ft (176.8 × 21.4 m)*
SERVICE SPEED: *16 knots*
PROPULSION: *Geared turbines / twin screws*

The Greek liner *Nea Hellas* made a single voyage to
Australia in 1949, bringing over 1500 displaced persons,
respresenting eight nations, and one stowaway to
Melbourne. She was the third of four liners ordered by
the Anchor Line for their trans-Atlantic services. The
first of this group, *Cameronia*, made many trips to
Australia after the war with migrants, while the second
was transferred while building to the Cunard Line.
Launched as *Tyrrhenia*, she was later renamed *Lancastria*,
and sunk with great loss of life at St Nazaire in June
1940. The fourth unit, *California*, was also lost in the
war.

This vessel was launched on 4 October 1921 as
Tuscania, and made her maiden voyage in September
1922 from Glasgow in New York. She provided
accommodation for 240 first class, 377 second class and
1818 third class passengers. After a mere four years
service, she was surplus to Anchor Line requirements,
and put up for sale, but when no buyers were
forthcoming, was employed in a variety of ways.

From May 1926 to October 1930, she spent the
summer months operating from London to New York
under charter to the Cunard Line, and was laid up in
winter. From August 1931, *Tuscania* operated on the
Anchor Line service to India in winter, and spent the
summer either trooping under charter, or cruising from

British ports. By 1935 her accommodation had been
reduced to 206 cabin, 439 tourist and 431 third class, and
in 1937 she was laid up, and again offered for sale.

In April 1939, the General Steam Navigation Co. of
Greece, better known as the Greek Line, bought
Tuscania, and renamed her *Nea Hellas*. On 19 May 1939,
she left Piraeus on her first voyage to New York under
the Greek flag, but within months the service was
abandoned due to the war. *Nea Hellas* was taken over by
the British in 1941, and used as a troopship, being
managed for the Ministry of War Transport by the
Anchor Line. In January 1947, *Nea Hellas* was returned
to her owner, and after a refit, returned to the
New York trade from Piraeus in August, with
accommodation for 1430 passengers in three classes.

Nea Hellas was also available for charters, and on
24 January 1949 she left Genoa bound for Australia on
behalf of the IRO, arriving in Melbourne on the
afternoon of 23 February, berthing at Station Pier. Her
passengers were disembarked, but the Australian
Seamens Union placed a ban on the ship, involving
tugboat crews, over the actions of the Greek
Government in the detention and subsequent death of a
Greek trade union leader. This delayed the departure of
Nea Hellas to 26 February, when she left for Piraeus.

Nea Hellas returned to the New York trade, and at
the end of 1954 was given an extensive refit, emerging
with accommodation for 70 first class and 1369 tourist
class passengers, and a new name, *New York*. In March
1955 she began operating from Bremerhaven to New
York, until September 1959, when she made one
voyage from Piraeus to Quebec, and then was laid up.
New York was sold to Japanese shipbreakers, arriving in
Onomichi on 12 October 1961.

THE GREEK LINER *NEA HELLAS*

OXFORDSHIRE

BUILT: *1912 by Harland & Wolff Ltd, Belfast*
TONNAGE: *8624 gross*
DIMENSIONS: *474 × 55 ft (144.5 × 16.8 m)*
SERVICE SPEED: *15 knots*
PROPULSION: *Triple expansion/twin screw*

Designed for service from Britain to Burma, *Oxfordshire* was fitted with accommodation for 276 first class passengers only, and had a large cargo capacity.

On the outbreak of war in 1914, *Oxfordshire* was converted into the first British army hospital ship. She spent six months operating across the English Channel, then took part in the disastrous Gallipoli landings, looking after many wounded soldiers from Australia and New Zealand. The ship saw active service in other parts of the world before being handed back to the Bibby Line on 24 March 1918. After a quick refit, she resumed her pre-war trade to Rangoon.

In 1919 *Oxfordshire* was converted to oil-firing, then spent the next 20 years plying between Britain and Burma.

On 3 September 1939, *Oxfordshire* was requisitioned for her second war, again being converted into a naval hospital ship. Initially she was despatched to Freetown, where she lay at anchor for almost three years as the local base hospital. *Oxfordshire* then joined the invasion fleet for North Africa in November 1942, and served in the Mediterranean over the next two years.

Oxfordshire finished the war in the Pacific then repatriated released prisoners-of-war, making her first visits to Australia in this role. On 10 July 1948, *Oxfordshire* was released from government service, and handed back to the Bibby Line.

Being 36 years old, she was not worth reconditioning for regular service, but instead was chartered to the Ministry of Transport. With austere accommodation for 400 persons, *Oxfordshire* left Liverpool in April 1949 on her first voyage to Australia. The vessel made a further two voyages to Australia from Liverpool in 1949, then in February 1950 departed Naples on a voyage to Fremantle. She returned to Bremerhaven, from where she sailed on 17 April 1950, again bound for Fremantle. This was followed by two more voyages from Liverpool, the last departing in August 1950.

In October 1950 *Oxfordshire* began to carry troops between Trieste and Port Said. In February 1951 the vessel returned to Britain again, and was offered for sale.

The Pan-Islamic Steamship Co., of Karachi, bought *Oxfordshire*, which was renamed *Safina-E-Arab*, and refitted to carry 101 first class, 46 second class and 1085 third class passengers. From June to October the liner carried pilgrims to Jedda, and the rest of the year traded from Karachi to ports in the Indian Ocean. After six years under the Pakistani flag, the old liner was sold to shipbreakers in Karachi early in 1958.

OXFORDSHIRE

RANGITIKI AND RANGITATA

BUILT: *1929 by John Brown & Co., Clydebank*
TONNAGE: *16 985 gross*
DIMENSIONS: *553 × 70 ft (168.5 × 21.4 m)*
SERVICE SPEED: *17 knots*
PROPULSION: *Doxford diesels / twin screws*

In 1925 the New Zealand Shipping Co. ordered three new liners, but delayed their construction until 1927, and the first was launched on 29 August 1928 as *Rangitiki*. She departed Southampton on 15 February 1929 for her maiden voyage to New Zealand. On 26 March 1929 the second ship was launched as *Rangitata*, followed on 27 May by *Rangitane*, both of which joined *Rangitiki* by the end of the year.

They were the first NZSC vessels to have two funnels, and their first motorships. Each was fitted out to carry 100 first class, 85 second class and 410 third class passengers, as well as a large amount of cargo, which was worked in London, passengers being embarked at Southampton. *Rangitata* was registered under the ownership of the Federal Steam Navigation Co., a subsidiary of the NZSC, but never wore their colours.

When war broke out in 1939, these liners were left on their regular trade, often travelling in convoys for safety. However, in January 1940, *Rangitata* was temporarily taken over to transport New Zealand troops to Egypt, calling at Melbourne on the way to join a convoy that left there on 12 January. On 5 November 1940, *Rangitiki* was in a convoy attacked by the pocket battleship *Admiral Scheer*, but managed to escape when the armed merchant cruiser *Jervis Bay* engaged the warship, only to be blown to bits in an heroic action. Just three weeks later, *Rangitane* was not to be so fortunate, as on 26 November, two days after leaving Auckland, she was spotted by two German commerce raiders, *Komet* and *Orion*, who opened fire on the unarmed merchantman. Ten persons were killed and the ship set on fire, with the survivors being rescued by the German ships, and then *Rangitane* was sunk by a boarding party.

In December 1941 *Rangitiki* was requisitioned, and converted to carry 2600 troops, while *Rangitata* was also taken in February 1941, and similarly converted. They took part in the North African landings in November 1942, and trooping voyages to the Mediterranean. In April 1945, they resumed voyages to New Zealand, though still under government control. *Rangitiki* was released in 1947, but *Rangitata* was retained until 1948. Both were sent to their builders' yard for refitting, during which their original Sulzer diesels were replaced by Doxford diesels. Accommodation was installed for 123 first class and 288 tourist class passengers.

Rangitiki resumed service with a departure from London on 24 September 1948, with *Rangitata* making her first sailing a year later, on 23 September 1949. The pair gave sterling service over the next fourteen years, with only one major incident to mar their record. In September 1958, *Rangitiki* grounded on the Goodwin Sands shortly after leaving London, but refloated without damage on the next high tide. On 12 January 1962, *Rangitata* left London on her final voyage to New Zealand, while *Rangitiki* made her last departure on 16 March. On their return to London, both ships were laid up, having each completed 87 round trips to New Zealand in peacetime.

Rangitata was sold to Dutch shipbreakers in May 1962, but was then resold to the Yugoslav firm, Brodospas, arriving at its Split shipbreaking yard on 21 July 1962, having made the journey from London under the name *Rang*. *Rangitiki* was sold to Spanish shipbreakers, and arrived at Santander on 26 July 1962.

RANGITIKI

THE NAVIGATORS

BUILT: *1948/1947/1947 by S. A. Ansaldo, Genoa*
TONNAGE: *8967 gross*
DIMENSIONS: *485 × 62 ft (149.2 × 19 m)*
SERVICE SPEED: *15 knots*
PROPULSION: *Fiat diesel/single screw*

In 1940 Italia Line had ordered a class of six cargo ships to be built for their South American trade, the first three of which were launched in 1942. Construction of the second trio was held up during the war, but all three were eventually launched in 1945, being named *Paolo Toscanelli, Ferruccio Buonapace* and *Mario Visentini*. During fitting out the names of two of the ships were changed, *Ferruccio Buonapace* becoming *Ugolino Vivaldi*, while *Mario Visentini* was renamed *Sebastiano Caboto*. Due to the great shortage of passenger berths in the immediate post-war years, each of these ships was completed with an enlarged superstructure and accommodation for 90 cabin class and 530 third class passengers.

During November 1947, *Sebastiano Caboto* reopened the Italia Line service from Genoa and Naples to Central America, and through the Panama Canal to ports on the west coast of South America as far as Valpariso, being joined on this trade by both *Ugolino Vivaldi* and *Paolo Toscanelli*. Meanwhile, work on completing the trio of ships launched in 1942 proceeded, and they entered service in 1948 and 1949, also having been fitted out with passenger accommodation, and named *Marco Polo, Amerigo Vespucci* and *Antoniotto Usodimare*. The addition of these ships resulted in a surplus of berths on the route, so Italia Line were able to charter two of the ships to Lloyd Triestino to help them on the Australian trade. The two selected were *Sebastiano Caboto* and *Ugolino Vivaldi*, refitted first to carry 100 cabin class and 735 third class passengers, most in dormitories.

The first sailing was taken by *Ugolino Vivaldi*, departing Genoa on 12 January 1949 to reach Fremantle on 5 February, Melbourne five days later, and Sydney on 14 February. *Sebastiano Caboto* did not make her first departure for Australia from Genoa until 7 July 1949. Outbound the vessels carried a combination of paying passengers and emigrants, but for the return voyage loaded their six holds full of Australian goods and only carried a minimal number of passengers. This pair and *Toscana* enabled Lloyd Triestino to operate a regular service once again, though much of the accommodation was somewhat austere.

In 1949, Lloyd Triestino placed orders for the construction of three new passenger liners in Italy, the first of which entered service in April 1951 as *Australia*.

Later in the year she was joined by *Oceania* and *Neptunia*, and their entry into service led to the withdrawal from the Australian trade of both *Ugolino Vivaldi* and *Sebastiano Caboto* during 1951. They were handed back to Italia Line, and once again placed on the route to Central and South America.

Four years later a third unit of the "Navigatori" class would make several voyages to Australia, this being *Paolo Toscanelli*. The demand for berths from Italy to Australia could not be met by the regular vessels on the route, so in March 1955 *Paolo Toscanelli* was chartered from Italia Line and made the first of five voyages to Australia, being in Melbourne on 17 April and Sydney two days later. Over the next year, this vessel made a further four voyages to Australia, the last departing Genoa in April 1956, arriving in Sydney on 27 May. On returning to Italy from this voyage, *Paolo Toscanelli* was handed back to Italia Line, and resumed her place on the trade to Central and South America.

In 1958, Italia Line decided to reduce their service on this route to only three ships, which resulted in the withdrawal of the three ships that had operated to Australia at various times. All were reduced to cargo ship status, retaining accommodation for only 12 passengers. *Paolo Toscanelli* remained with Italia Line, but *Sebastiano Caboto* and *Ugolino Vivaldi* were transferred to Lloyd Triestino, and placed on a service from Italy to East and South Africa. In 1963 the remaining trio of the "Navigatori" class were also reduced to 12-passenger cargo ships, and transferred to Lloyd Triestino to join the other pair on the South African trade. In June 1968, *Sebastiano Caboto* made a voyage to Australia as a cargo ship.

During the 1970s, the Italian Government sought to rationalise the services run by the various government supported shipping lines, and this led to the withdrawal from service of all six of the "Navigatori" class ships. First to go was the only unit to be retained by Italia Line, *Paolo Toscanelli*, which was laid up at Naples on 20 October 1972. Sold to shipbreakers, the vessel arrived at La Spezia in tow on 6 February 1973. Lloyd Triestino operated the other five units until 1978, when all were disposed of within a matter of months.

Ugolino Vivaldi was laid up in Trieste on 9 February 1978, then sold to a local firm of shipbreakers in August that year. *Sebastiano Caboto* was also withdrawn during the early part of 1978, and sold later in the year to Hikma Shipping Pte Ltd, of Singapore. They did not rename the ship, but instead sold her almost immediately to shipbreakers in Taiwan, the vessel arriving at Kaohsiung on 15 February 1979.

PAOLO TOSCANELLI IN PORT ADELAIDE

UGOLINO VIVALDI IN SYDNEY COVE

GEORGIC

BUILT: *1932 by Harland & Wolff Ltd, Belfast*
TONNAGE: *27 469 gross*
DIMENSIONS: *711 × 82 ft (216.7 × 25.1 m)*
SERVICE SPEED: *18 knots*
PROPULSION: *B & W diesels/twin screws*

Georgic was the last ship to be built for White Star Line, being preceded by her sister, *Britannic*, in 1930. Laid down in November 1929, *Georgic* was launched on 12 November 1931. Fitted out with accommodation for 479 cabin class, 557 tourist class and 506 third class passengers, *Georgic* departed Liverpool on 25 June 1932 for her maiden voyage to New York. White Star Line encountered serious economic problems and in 1934 a merger with Cunard was finalised, forming Cunard–White Star Line. *Georgic* and *Britannic* retained their White Star funnel colours, but operated in conjunction with the Cunard fleet.

Both former White Star liners were transferred to a new route from London to New York, *Georgic* making her first departure on 3 May 1935. During the winter months, *Georgic* was used for cruises from New York to the Caribbean. When war broke out in September 1939, *Georgic* made a further five round trips from London to New York, then in March 1940 was converted on the Clyde into a troop transport.

Georgic was involved in the evacuations of British troops from Norway and France, and made trooping voyages across the Atlantic, and also to the Middle East. On 3 June 1941, she left Glasgow on her second voyage to the Middle East, by way of Cape Town, arriving at Port Tewfik in the Suez Canal on 7 July. The troops were disembarked, and over 1000 civilians and internees were taken aboard over the next few days. On 14 July, German bombers attacked Port Tewfik, and singled out *Georgic* for special attention.

A near miss caused considerable hull damage and flooding through cracked plates, then a bomb exploded in No. 5 hold, starting a huge fire. Ruptured fuel tanks fed the blaze, and then one of the magazines exploded, enveloping the after end of the vessel in flames. Despite all this, the engineers were able to start the engines, and *Georgic* was nursed slowly out of the main shipping channel. After colliding with another ship she was run aground on a sandbar, then abandoned until the fires had burned themselves out.

Georgic was reduced to a blackened mess, gutted by the fires, with many cracked and buckled plates causing flooding and a list to port. Under normal circumstances the vessel would have been abandoned as a total loss, but after inspection it was decided she could be repaired and returned to service. Temporary repairs to the hull were effected, and on 27 October the vessel was refloated, and kept afloat by pumps until permanent patches could be placed over holes in the bottom.

On 29 December 1941, *Georgic* left Port Tewfik under tow of two cargo ships, *Clan Campbell* and *City of Sydney*, bound for Port Sudan, where she arrived 13 days later, listing and leaking. Following further repairs, *Georgic* left Port Sudan on 5 March 1942 bound

GEORGIC AS BUILT

GEORGIC IN WOOLLOOMOOLOO BAY, SYDNEY, AS AN EMIGRANT SHIP

for Karachi, being towed by the cableship *Recorder* and tug *St Sampson*. In bad weather, the tug was sunk, so the cargo ship *Haresfield* and tug *Pauline Moller* were called in to assist. Eventually the tow arrived on 31 March in Karachi, where the engines were repaired.

On 11 December 1942, *Georgic* left Karachi under her own power for Bombay, where she was drydocked for further repairs to the hull, leaving there on 20 January 1943, to arrive safely back in Liverpool on 1 March. *Georgic* was then sent to the Harland & Wolff shipyard in Belfast to be rebuilt as a troopship. The dummy forward funnel and the mainmast were removed, but the buckles in her hull caused by the fires remained. During this rebuilding, *Georgic* was sold by Cunard–White Star to the British Ministry of War Transport, with the former owners acting as managers. On 12 December 1944, *Georgic* was handed over by the shipyard, and returned to active service again.

Georgic served as a troopship until September 1948, when she was one of several older British liners selected for conversion into migrant carriers, to meet the demand for assisted passages from Britain to Australia. The work on *Georgic* was done by Palmer, Hebburn Ltd on the Tyne, where basic accommodation for 1962 persons was installed, and the ship repainted in the old White Star Line colours. She still had only one funnel and no mainmast, as well as a shortened foremast, giving an unusual appearance.

The first departure by *Georgic* on the migrant trade was from Liverpool on 11 January 1949, carrying 1529 adults and 465 children. She passed through Fremantle on 6 February, and was in Melbourne on 12 February before reaching Sydney on 14 February, then returning empty to Liverpool. Her second voyage departed Liverpool on 8 April 1949, but then *Georgic* was taken

off the run for a trooping voyage to Hong Kong, departing Liverpool on 8 July. During her third voyage to Australia, a propeller was damaged, and *Georgic* entered the Captain Cook drydock in Sydney for it to be changed, becoming the largest merchant vessel to be drydocked in Australia up to that time. On her fourth voyage, *Georgic* left Sydney on 20 February 1950, but went to Jakarta to collect Dutch nationals, and return them to Europe.

After one further round trip to Australia, *Georgic* was chartered to Cunard Line, to make six round trips with "tourist third" class passengers to New York from Liverpool, the first departing on 4 May. The vessel then returned to the migrant trade, but on 8 January 1951 was quarantined when she arrived in Sydney with 49 cases of smallpox on board. Leaving Sydney on 15 January, *Georgic* returned to Britain, and made some trooping voyages before once again being chartered by Cunard Line for seven round voyages between Southampton, Havré, Cóbh and New York during the peak summer months. In 1953, *Georgic* made seven round trips on this service, and a further seven during 1954, the last departing New York on 19 October.

On 16 April 1955, *Georgic* arrived in Liverpool on a trooping voyage from Japan, and was scheduled to be withdrawn, but instead she returned to the Australian migrant trade. Departing Sydney on 23 June, the vessel went to Saigon to pick up French refugees and return them home, then on 24 August 1955, *Georgic* left Liverpool on her final voyage. Passing through Fremantle on 29 September, she was in Melbourne on 4 October, and Sydney two days later, then went on to Brisbane before returning to Liverpool on 19 November. The old ship was then sold, and arrived in Faslane on 1 February 1956 to be broken up.

DUNDALK BAY

BUILT: *1936 by Bremer Vulkan, Vegesack*
TONNAGE: *7105 gross*
DIMENSIONS: *452 × 56 ft (137.8 × 17 m)*
SERVICE SPEED: *15 knots*
PROPULSION: *Diesel engine/single screw*

Dundalk Bay was the only Irish-owned vessel to transport migrants to Australia, and developed a reputation as one of the worst ships to travel on. The vessel was built for North German Lloyd as the *Nürnberg*, having four sisters, *Dresden, Leipzig, München* and *Osnabrück*. All five ships operated on a cargo service from Bremen to the west coast of America, and could carry 12 passengers.

Shortly after the war broke out, *Nürnberg* was taken over by the German Navy, and converted into a minelayer. Later in the war she was altered again for service as a depot ship, and sent to Copenhagen. It was here that the ship was found by the Allies in May 1945, in good condition, and immediately seized as a war prize. In 1947 she was allocated to Britain, and used briefly by the Royal Navy as a depot ship, but then offered for sale.

In 1948 the vessel was sold to H. P. Leneghan & Sons Ltd, of Belfast, who operated as the Irish Bay Line, and renamed *Dundalk Bay*. Having obtained an IRO contract for the carriage of displaced persons, they sent the ship to Trieste, where she was completely rebuilt as an emigrant carrier. Very austere quarters for 1025 persons was installed in the former cargo spaces, but the superstructure was only slightly enlarged.

On 15 March 1949, *Dundalk Bay* departed Trieste on her first voyage, bringing some 1000 displaced persons to Australia. On her second voyage, *Dundalk Bay* carried the first consignment of displaced persons to be sent to New Zealand after the war. She departed from Trieste, passing through Australia en route to Wellington, where she berthed on 26 June with 941 persons aboard. Her next two voyages departed Trieste on 12 August and 20 October, going only to Fremantle and Melbourne.

In 1950 the European base for *Dundalk Bay* was changed to Naples, from where she made two sailings, the first in January to Melbourne, the second in March to Fremantle only. Returning from this trip, *Dundalk Bay* proceeded to Rotterdam, then to Bremerhaven, departing there in May on her final voyage to Australia. Passing through Fremantle on 18 June, she went directly to Sydney, arriving on 25 June, and the next day proceeded up the coast to Newcastle, where she stayed four days. With a final call at Fremantle on 14 July, *Dundalk Bay* returned to Bremerhaven.

In mid-1951, *Dundalk Bay* was refitted as a cargo ship again, and used on general tramping by Irish Bay Lines. In 1953 she was sold to Duff, Herbert & Mitchell, of London, but her name was not changed until 1957, when she became *Westbay*. Under this name she spent a further five years as a tramp cargo ship. On 2 September 1962, *Westbay* arrived at the Hamburg shipbreaking yard of Eisen und Metall A.G., who had purchased the ship the previous month.

DUNDALK BAY

CYRENIA

BUILT: 1911 by Fairfield Shipbuilding & Engineering Co., Glasgow
TONNAGE: 7527 gross
DIMENSIONS: 447 × 56 ft (136.2 × 17 m)
SERVICE SPEED: 14 knots
PROPULSION: Quadruple expansion/twin screws

By the time the Greek liner *Cyrenia* entered the Australian emigrant trade in 1949, she was almost 40 years old, but was an old friend as a unit of the Union Steam Ship Company of New Zealand. Originally named *Maunganui*, she had been delivered to her owners in December 1911, and in February 1912 entered the famous "horseshoe service" of the Union Line, between Australia and New Zealand. *Maunganui* could accommodate 244 first class, 175 second class and 80 third class passengers.

In August 1914 *Maunganui* was requisitioned as a troopship, voyaging all over the world. Handed back to her owners late in 1919, it was the middle of 1922 before she returned to commercial service, having been converted from coal- to oil-firing. *Maunganui* then began operating from Australia and New Zealand to San Francisco, until 1925 when she reverted to the trans-Tasman trade again. Over the next seven years, *Maunganui* made occasional relief sailings to Vancouver and San Francisco, then in 1932 returned permanently to the San Francisco route until it was abandoned by the Union Line in 1936. She was then used as a relief ship on the Tasman routes, or for South Pacific cruises.

Maunganui was requisitioned in January 1941 and converted into a hospital ship. Over the next four years she voyaged to Egypt, South Africa and India, and then joined the British Pacific Fleet during the final assault on Japan. In 1946 she carried the official New Zealand contingent to the victory celebrations in London, and on her return to Wellington was handed back to the Union Line. Having steamed 2 184 081 miles so far in her career, she was offered for sale.

Surprisingly, *Maunganui* was sold for further trading, to Cia. Nav. del Atlantico, a Panamanian concern. Leaving Wellington on 12 February 1947, she went to Greece to be refitted with rather austere accommodation for 840 passengers, having obtained an IRO contract. Renamed *Cyrenia*, she was placed under the management of Hellenic Mediterranean Lines, and painted in their colours. On 6 March 1949 *Cyrenia* departed Genoa on her first voyage to Australia, arriving in Fremantle on 2 April and terminating at Melbourne on 8 April. Her second voyage commenced in Genoa on 1 June, and included a call at Malta three days later, again terminating in Melbourne.

During 1950, Hellenic Mediterranean Lines bought *Cyrenia* outright, and placed her under the Greek flag, but she continued to operate from Genoa to Fremantle and Melbourne. Departing Melbourne on 16 August 1950, *Cyrenia* called at Saigon to board French nationals fleeing the war-torn area. In June 1952, *Cyrenia* was taken out of service and laid up, due to a decline in the number of displaced persons seeking passages.

Cyrenia returned to service in May 1954, now operating from Piraeus to Melbourne with migrants, returning with fare-paying passengers. In December 1955 she paid her only visit to Sydney, and on 1 November 1956, *Cyrenia* left Melbourne for the last time. The old vessel was sold to shipbreakers and arrived at their Savona yard on 6 February 1957.

CYRENIA

SURRIENTO

BUILT: *1928 by Furness Shipbuilding Co., Haverton*
TONNAGE: *10 699 gross*
DIMENSIONS: *498 × 64 ft (151.8 × 19.5 m)*
SERVICE SPEED: *17 knots*
PROPULSION: *Sulzer diesels/twin screws*

Surriento had an unusual claim to fame, as she and her sister were built in Britain for the Grace Line of America, two of the very few American-owned ships to have been built in another country. Launched on 15 August 1927, she was named *Santa Maria*, and on completion in April 1928, crossed the Atlantic to New York. Her sister ship was named *Santa Barbara*, and completed in August 1928. The two ships were placed in service from New York to Central America and through the Panama Canal to the west coast of South America as far as Valparíso. *Santa Maria* and her sister had a very boxy appearance, with straight bows and a very square superstructure topped by two squat funnels, the forward one being a dummy. Accommodation was provided for 157 passengers, all first class, which was increased to 172 after a few years. *Santa Maria* remained on the South American route until August 1940, then was sold to the US Navy.

Renamed USS *Barnett*, the vessel was refitted to transport 1800 troops, and for protection given a single 5-inch gun and three 3-inch guns, plus some anti-aircraft weapons. *Barnett* served as a troopship until the end of 1942, when she was converted into an attack transport. Returning to service on 1 February 1943, *Barnett* took part in several of the Allied landings in Europe, and was hit by a bomb off Sicily on 11 July 1943, when seven men on board were killed. In July 1946 *Barnett* was withdrawn from service, and laid up in the James River. Her sister served as the transport *McCawley* in the war, but was sunk in June 1943.

During 1948 the US Government held a series of auctions to dispose of many ships it no longer required, and *Barnett* was purchased at one such auction in March 1948 by the Italian shipowner, Achille Lauro. The vessel was given a brief refit in Baltimore, then voyaged to Genoa, where she arrived in July, and over the next nine months was rebuilt. The alterations were quite radical, as a new raked bow was fitted, and the superstructure greatly extended both fore and aft, topped by two new, low funnels with raked tops. The interior of the ship was completely gutted, and new accommodation installed for 187 first class and 868 tourist class passengers. When the work was completed in May 1949, the vessel was renamed *Surriento*.

Surriento departed Genoa on 22 May 1949 on her first voyage for Flotta Lauro, going to Fremantle, Melbourne and Sydney, which she departed on 28 June bound for Singapore and Colombo on her return voyage. Her second voyage departed Genoa on 12 August, and a third in October 1949, each time returning via Singapore and Colombo, and also calling at Naples and Marseilles. On leaving Sydney on 26 July 1950, *Surriento* went to Brisbane, leaving on 29 July for Jakarta to collect Dutch nationals, who she carried to Genoa.

During 1951 Lauro placed two more passenger ships on the Australian trade, *Roma* and *Sydney*, which enabled them to withdraw *Surriento*, and transfer her to a new service from Naples to Venezuela. In 1952 *Surriento* was refitted during which her accommodation was altered to 119 first class and 994 tourist class. On 19 March 1953 the vessel departed Genoa bound for Australia once again, replacing *Roma*, which had been placed on a new service from the Mediterranean to New York. Over the next three years *Surriento* partnered *Sydney* on the route, then on 30 August 1956, the vessel left Genoa on what was destined to be her final voyage to Australia. Arriving in Fremantle on 22 September, *Surriento* was inspected by local authorities, who declared that many of the lifesaving facilities on board were defective, and levied a heavy fine on Flotta Lauro. Once the defects were rectified, *Surriento* continued to Melbourne, ariving on 28 September, and Sydney, where she berthed on 3 October, departing the next day on her return voyage to Genoa. *Roma* then returned to the Australian route, and *Surriento* reverted to the Central American service again.

During 1959, *Surriento* was given another major refit, during which her superstructure was further enlarged and streamlined, two outdoor swimming pools added, and a single modern funnel fitted in place of the former pair. Internally the accommodation was altered to carry 1080 passengers in a single class, and air-conditioning extended throughout the ship. These changes completely altered the appearance of the ship when she returned to the Central American trade in 1960, serving there for a further five years.

In 1965 *Surriento* was withdrawn, and chartered to Zim Lines for their service from Haifa to Marseilles, replacing another former Australian emigrant ship, *Flaminia*. When that charter expired in the middle of 1966, Flotta Lauro had added *Achille Lauro* and *Angelina Lauro* to the Australian service, and transferred *Roma* and *Sydney* to the Central American service, leaving no employment for *Surriento*. The old liner was laid up, then sold to shipbreakers, arriving at their La Spezia yard on 30 September 1966.

SANTA MARIA OF THE GRACE LINE

THE SAME SHIP AS *SURRIENTO*

A CONVERTED AIRCRAFT CARRIER

BUILT: 1940 by Sun Shipbuilding & Drydock Co., Chester
TONNAGE: 11 672 gross
DIMENSIONS: 494 × 69 ft (150.5 × 21.1 m)
SERVICE SPEED: 17 knots
PROPULSION: Busch–Sulzer diesels/single screw

Laid down as a standard C3 type cargo ship for Moore–McCormack Line, and launched on 14 December 1939 as *Mormacland*, fitting out was almost complete when the US Government requisitioned the vessel for conversion into an auxiliary aircraft carrier, originally for the US Navy. Before the conversion work was finished, the lend-lease agreement had been finalised, and this vessel was handed over to the Royal Navy at Norfolk, Virginia on 17 November 1941. Renamed HMS *Archer*, she was the second auxiliary aircraft carrier transferred to Britain.

During trials, *Archer* suffered numerous engine problems, and on the night of 12 January 1942, collided with and sank the Peruvian steamer *Brazos* some 200 miles off the South Carolina coast. *Archer* had a huge hole in her bow and serious flooding, so headed for safety stern first, her single propeller half out of the water. The stricken vessel arrived in Charleston on 21 January to be repaired.

On 18 March 1942, HMS *Archer* departed for active service, being based at Freetown in Sierra Leone, but was still plagued by machinery defects for some time, and also had other misfortunes. In June 1942 a bomb stored on the flight deck exploded, so the vessel went to Cape Town to collect a fortune in gold ingots, which she carried to New York, arriving on 15 July. Here her machinery was finally fixed, and *Archer* gave good service for the remainder of the war.

In 1945 HMS *Archer* was transferred to the Ministry of War Transport, rebuilt as a cargo ship and renamed *Empire Lagan*, under Blue Funnel Line management. On 8 January 1946, she was handed back to the Americans, and laid up pending disposal. During 1948 the US Government auctioned many of their surplus ships, and this vessel was purchased by Sven Salen, a noted Swedish shipowner. Renamed *Anna Salen*, she was registered under the ownership of Rederie A/S Pulp, a Salen subsidiary company. She was sent to the Bethlehem Shipyard at Baltimore for reconstruction as a bulk carrier, but when the job was almost finished, Salen obtained a contract from the IRO to transport displaced persons. *Anna Salen* loaded coal in America and carried it to Italy, and there was converted as a passenger carrier, with quarters for 600 persons built into the hold, numerous toilet and washing blocks, and a few public rooms.

On 22 May 1949, *Anna Salen* departed Naples on her first IRO voyage, going to Melbourne and Sydney,

where she arrived on 21 June. Her second voyage was only to Fremantle, while her third voyage was to Melbourne. On 1 December 1949, *Anna Salen* left Naples on her fourth voyage, but in the Indian Ocean was afflicted by engine trouble, and had to return to Aden. Her passengers were transferred to *Skaugum*, while *Anna Salen* limped back to Europe for repairs, which lasted six months. On 20 June 1950, the vessel returned to service, departing Bremerhaven on a voyage to Melbourne. From there she went to Tientsin, China, to collect refugees and carry them to Europe.

During 1951, *Anna Salen* made several trips to Canada with refugees, so it was 21 February 1952 before she again left Bremerhaven bound for Australia, by way of Cape Town. When the Olympic Games were held in Helsinki during the summer of 1952, *Anna Salen* operated a ferry service from Stockholm, her capacity being increased to 2500 passengers.

Over the next two years, *Anna Salen* made further voyages to Australia and Canada, but also made several summer voyages across the North Atlantic, carrying students. During 1955, she called at Saigon and also ports in mainland China during some of her return voyages to Europe from Australia. In the middle of 1955, *Anna Salen* was withdrawn from service, and sold to Hellenic Mediterranean Lines, being renamed *Tasmania*.

Apart from repainting, the ship was not altered, and returned to the Australian trade, departing Piraeus on 23 August 1955 on her first voyage as *Tasmania*, arriving in Melbourne on 23 September. On the return trip, the vessel was again sent to Saigon, where French troops were boarded and returned home. Entering Port Phillip Bay on 3 April 1956, *Tasmania* ran aground and suffered some bottom damage, which delayed her departure by eleven days. On 15 October 1956, *Tasmania* left Melbourne for the last time, as on her return to Greece, the passenger accommodation was removed, and she reverted to being a cargo ship.

Early in 1961, *Tasmania* was sold to China Union Lines, of Taipei, and renamed *Union Reliance*. Placed on a regular cargo service to American ports, the vessel was passing down the Houston Ship Canal on 7 November 1961, when she collided with the Norwegian tanker, *Berean*. An explosion was followed by a fireball that rapidly engulfed both vessels, with *Union Reliance* having to be beached and left to burn out. Totally gutted, the vessel was refloated four days later, and towed to Galveston, where the wreck was offered for sale, and bought by a New Orleans shipbreaking firm. She arrived at their yard on 28 January 1962, but while in the early stages of demolition, on 19 February 1962, the vessel was swept by a second fire and totally destroyed.

ANNA SALEN

TASMANIA

CHESHIRE

BUILT: *1927 by Fairfield Shipbuilding & Engineering Co., Glasgow*
TONNAGE: *10 623 gross*
DIMENSIONS: *502 × 60 ft (153 × 18.4 m)*
SERVICE SPEED: *15 knots*
PROPULSION: *Sulzer diesels/twin screws*

Cheshire was launched on 20 April 1927, and completed three months later, having been built for service between Liverpool and Rangoon. She had a typical Bibby Line appearance, four lofty masts and a tall, thin funnel, despite being a motorship. Accommodation was provided for 275 first class passengers only, along with a large cargo capacity.

On the outbreak of war in September 1939, *Cheshire* was in the Indian Ocean, so was diverted to Calcutta, where she was converted into an armed merchant cruiser. Six 6-inch guns were installed along with anti-aircraft weapons, and she was ballasted with pig iron and sand, then commissioned at Calcutta on 30 October 1939. After initial service in the Indian Ocean, *Cheshire* was transferred to the North Atlantic in 1940.

On 14 October 1940, *Cheshire* was torpedoed in No. 2 hold by *U137*, off the north west-coast of Ireland. She was towed into Belfast Lough and beached near Carrickfergus, and after basic repairs, refloated and towed to Liverpool, entering the Gladstone dock on 1 December 1940. In April 1941, *Cheshire* returned to

service, but on 18 August 1942, she was torpedoed for a second time, this time in mid-Atlantic, by *U214*. Again, *Cheshire* was able to reach safety, and during repairs, was converted into a troopship. Entering service in this role in May 1943, she later took part in the Normandy landings. *Cheshire* spent some time after the war repatriating troops and civilians, then on 5 October 1948, was handed back to her owners.

Bibby Line did not wish to restore *Cheshire* to her pre-war condition and route, so instead they chartered her to the Ministry of Transport. She was refitted for the emigrant trade, with accommodation for 434 sponsored migrants and about 200 fare-paying passengers. She emerged from her refit with only a foremast, forward and aft well decks plated in, and an extended boat deck. On 9 August 1949, *Cheshire* left Liverpool on her first voyage to Australia, passing through Suez to reach Fremantle on 12 September, and terminating the voyage in Melbourne on 18 September. *Cheshire* made a further 10 voyages to Melbourne, and Sydney, until the beginning of 1953, when she was taken for trooping in connection with the Korean War.

On 5 February 1953, *Cheshire* left Liverpool bound for Singapore, and served four years as a troopship. On 10 February 1957, she arrived in Liverpool, and was then laid up in Langton Dock. Sold to British Iron & Steel Corp., she left Liverpool on 10 July 1957 for Newport, where she arrived the next day, and was broken up by John Cashmore & Son Ltd.

CHESHIRE

HAVEN

BUILT: *1911 by Clyde Shipbuilding & Engineering Co., Glasgow*
TONNAGE: *4088 gross*
DIMENSIONS: *361 × 47 ft (109 × 14.4 m)*
SERVICE SPEED: *12 knots*
PROPULSION: *Triple expansion/single screw*

Of all the names given to ships that carried displaced persons to new lives in Australia, *Haven* must be the most appropriate, though she made only a single journey. Unlike most ships, which came from Europe, *Haven* carried 341 White Russians to Sydney from Shanghai. The vessel was actually well known to Australians, having been built as *Montoro* for Burns Philp, and operating for over thirty years from east coast ports.

Montoro left Sydney on 2 March 1912 on her first voyage to Singapore, with calls at Darwin and Batavia en route. She had accommodation for 100 first class and 40 second class passengers. *Montoro* remained on the Singapore trade throughout World War One. In October 1923 she spent four days aground on a reef near Thursday Island, but was refloated with little damage. In 1926 she began operating from Sydney to New Guinea, and was due to be disposed of in 1939.

The outbreak of war brought a reprieve, and she remained on the island trade. In 1940 *Montoro* sank in Sydney while taking on coal, but was quickly refloated

and returned to service. On 9 February 1942, *Montoro* left Darwin with 203 evacuees, bound for Sydney, and later was used to transport troops.

Returned to her owners in 1946, she resumed the New Guinea trade until August 1948, when she was sold to Wah Sing Shang Steamship Co. of Singapore. They renamed her *Haven*, and she began operating in Asian waters. Early in 1949 the Nationalist forces in China were pushed back to Shanghai by the Communists, and the city was under siege. *Haven* made a voyage from Shanghai to Manila with over 400 refugees, mostly White Russians. She then returned to Shanghai, where the Nationalists tried to commandeer the ship to carry their own men to Formosa. For six days *Haven* was held in Shanghai, before escaping with a further 400 refugees aboard, being the last ship to leave the port before it fell to the Communists.

Again *Haven* carried her passengers to Manila, where they disembarked, and then 341 of the White Russians who had been on the first voyage were taken back on board, and the ship left Manila in late May, bound for Australia. She arrived in Sydney on 12 June, and disembarked her passengers, remaining in port for nine days loading cargo. Leaving on 21 June, she made a brief call at Newcastle for bunkers, then voyaged to Hong Kong.

Haven continued to operate in Asian waters for a further six years. During 1955, the vessel was sold to shipbreakers in Japan.

THE BURNS PHILP LINER *MONTORO* WAS RENAMED *HAVEN*

OTRANTO AND ORONTES

OTRANTO

BUILT: *1925 by Vickers–Armstrong Ltd, Barrow*
TONNAGE: *20051 gross*
DIMENSIONS: *659 × 75 ft (200.6 × 22.9 m)*
SERVICE SPEED: *20 knots*
PROPULSION: *Geared turbines/twin screws*

ORONTES

BUILT: *1929 by Vickers–Armstrong Ltd, Barrow*
TONNAGE: *20186 gross*
DIMENSIONS: *664 × 75 ft (202.3 × 22.9 m)*
SERVICE SPEED: *20 knots*
PROPULSION: *Geared turbines/twin screws*

During the 1920s the Orient Line took delivery of five new liners for the Australian trade, which were built in two groups, the first consisting of three vessels, *Orama*, completed in 1924, with *Oronsay* and *Otranto* entering service the following year. They were followed by *Orford* in 1928 and finally *Orontes* in 1929.

Otranto was launched on 9 June 1925, and completed six months later, with accommodation for 572 first class and 1114 third class passengers, which was slightly less than her earlier sisters. On 9 January 1926, *Otranto* departed Tilbury on her maiden voyage to Australia. On returning from this voyage, *Otranto* made a cruise to the Mediterranean, and on 11 May 1926, struck rocks off Cape Matapán, incurring severe bow damage, and having to limp back to Britain for repairs.

It was not until 26 February 1929 that the last of the group was launched, as *Orontes*. Completed in July 1929, *Orontes* made a series of cruises from Britain before leaving Tilbury on 26 October on her maiden voyage to Australia. *Orontes* was slightly different to the earlier ships, having a raked bow that gave her extra length, and a smaller number of passengers, 460 first class and 1112 third class. When cruising, all ships carried a maximum of 550 passengers in a single class.

It was not until the end of 1932 that Orient Line made their first cruise from an Australian port. On 24 December, *Oronsay* departed Sydney on a trip to Noumea, and subsequently all five ships made cruises from Australia. By 1933 the third class accommodation on all these ships had been upgraded, and reduced to about 500 tourist class.

The outbreak of war brought the Orient Line services to a swift halt. By the beginning of 1940, all five sisters were operating as troopships, and it was not long before some became casualties. On 1 June 1940, *Orford*

was bombed by German aircraft off Marseilles, having to be beached to burn out, becoming a total loss. Only eight days later, *Orama* was caught by the German heavy cruiser *Admiral Hipper* off Norway, and sunk. *Oronsay* very nearly became a third victim in June 1940, being attacked by German bombers while evacuating troops from St Nazaire, and suffering serious damage. *Oronsay* had only a brief reprieve, as on 9 October 1942 she was sunk by an Italian submarine in the South Atlantic.

Otranto made several trips to the Middle East and India, then in 1942 was converted into a landing ship, for the North African landings. *Orontes* was also involved in these landings, and later both ships were involved in the landings in Sicily and at Salerno. During this period, each ship survived several intense attacks by German aircraft, *Orontes* once being straddled by five bombs, but not suffering any damage.

In 1945 *Otranto* carried New Zealand troops home, while *Orontes* arrived in Australia in June 1945. *Orontes* was retained by the government until 1947, then went to the Thorneycroft shipyard at Southampton to be reconditioned. With accommodation for 502 first class and 610 tourist class passengers, she left Tilbury on 17 June 1948 to resume her service to Australia.

Otranto was not released by the government until August 1948, and was refitted by Cammell Laird at Birkenhead, being given accommodation for 1416 tourist class passengers only. She was also fitted with two outdoor swimming pools, and a large playroom for children. On 14 July 1949, *Otranto* left Tilbury, arriving in Sydney on 19 August. She operated to an independent schedule, and mainly carried assisted migrants from Britain. Both these ships had been repainted in their former colours, instead of the new Orient Line colours, and looked very dated. In 1953, *Orontes* was refitted to carry 1410 tourist class passengers, and joined *Otranto* on the schedule independent of the mail steamers.

In February 1957, *Otranto* was delayed at Tilbury by engine problems, then left on 13 February, voyaging around South Africa, as the Suez Canal was closed. The engine problems recurred in Adelaide a month later, so it was not surprising that on her return to Tilbury, she was withdrawn from service. Having completed 64 round trips to Australia in peacetime, *Otranto* was sold to shipbreakers, leaving Tilbury on 12 June 1957 bound for the Faslane yard of Shipbreaking Industries.

Orontes continued to serve a further four years, but on 25 November 1961 she left Tilbury on her final voyage to Australia, departing Sydney on 12 January 1962 on the return leg. On 5 March 1962 she arrived in Valencia, and was broken up.

OTRANTO

ORONTES LEAVING SYDNEY ON 12 JANUARY 1962

ASTURIAS

BUILT: *1926 by Harland & Wolff Ltd, Belfast*
TONNAGE: *22 445 gross*
DIMENSIONS: *666 × 78 ft (203 × 23.9 m)*
SERVICE SPEED: *18 knots*
PROPULSION: *Geared turbines/twin screws*

Asturias was so badly damaged during the war, she was written off as a total loss, but was eventually repaired and gave several years good service as a migrant ship. When she arrived in Australian waters, she had a single funnel and mast, and geared turbine engines, but when built was quite different. The first of two liners built for Royal Mail Line, she was launched on 7 July 1925, and left Southampton on her maiden voyage to South America on 27 February 1926. The following year she was joined by her sister, *Alcantara*, and they were, for a short time, the largest motor liners in the world, being powered by Burmeister & Wain diesels. Unfortunately, these engines caused excessive vibration at cruising speed, so in 1934 *Asturias* and her sister returned to their builder's yard, where geared turbine machinery was installed. At the same time, the vessel was lengthened 10 ft (3.2 m), and her two funnels raised. On returning to service in September 1924, *Asturias* had accommodation for 330 first, 220 second and 768 third class passengers.

Asturias had been frequently used for cruises in the first eight years of her career, and continued to combine cruising with regular voyages to South America until September 1939. Being in Southampton when war broke out, she was immediately requisitioned, and

returned once more to the Harland & Wolff shipyard at Belfast, this time to be converted into an armed merchant cruiser. All her internal fittings were removed and placed in storage in Southampton, but in November 1940 they were destroyed during an air raid. Eight old 6-inch guns, relics of the previous war, were fitted, and at the same time the dummy forward funnel was removed.

The conversion work was completed at the end of September, when *Asturias* was sent north to join the North Atlantic Patrol, based on Scapa Flow. This lasted until late in 1941, when *Asturias* was sent to the Newport News shipyard in America to be refitted. An aircraft hangar and catapult were installed, which necessitated the removal of the mainmast and the after part of the superstructure, and new guns were fitted. Early in 1942, *Asturias* returned to service, being sent to Freetown to patrol in the South Atlantic.

In mid-1942, the Admiralty purchased a wooden floating dock from America, and *Asturias* was selected to escort it being towed across the Atlantic, but the dock sank en route. *Asturias* returned to patrol duty, then in June 1943 was sent to escort a steel floating dock the Admiralty had purchased in Montevideo. *Asturias* met up with the tug *Roode Zee* and the dock off the coast of Brazil, heading for Freetown.

Asturias followed a zigzag course ahead of the dock, with smaller escorts on each side. When the convoy was 400 miles from Freetown, *Asturias* was hit by a torpedo, fired by the Italian submarine *Ammiraglio Cagni*, just

ASTURIAS AS BUILT WITH TWO SQUAT FUNNELS

EMIGRANT SHIP *ASTURIAS* IN SYDNEY COVE

before midnight on 24 July 1943. Exploding in the port engine room, and killing four men, the ship was disabled by the hit. The dock continued on its way, and two small vessels stayed with *Asturias* until 26 July, when the tug *Zwartze Zee* arrived, at that time the most powerful tug in the world.

Asturias was towed to Freetown, arriving on 1 August, and beached with her midships open to the sea. She was left in this state for 18 months, and eventually declared a total loss. However, in February 1945 the hulk was purchased by the Royal Navy, and a concrete patch fitted over the hole in her side. *Zwartze Zee* and another tug, *Thames*, towed her to Gibraltar for drydocking and further repairs, which lasted three months, and then the two tugs towed her back to Belfast, for rebuilding by Harland & Wolff, as a troopship. The work was delayed by a fire on board, but in mid-1946 *Asturias* was ready for service once again, managed by Royal Mail Line on behalf of the Ministry of Transport.

On 12 October 1946, *Asturias* left Southampton for Cape Town, then went on to Australia, berthing in Fremantle on 12 November, Melbourne on 17 November and being in Sydney from 19 to 26 November before returning to Britain. During 1947 *Asturias* made two voyages to Fremantle, the first from Southampton on 29 August, arriving on 21 September, the second from the same British port on 9 November. Her career as a troopship continued through 1948, but in 1949 she was allocated by the Ministry of Transport for the Australian migrant trade.

Asturias was refitted yet again, to carry 160 first class, 113 third class and 1134 dormitory passengers on the Australian trade, though on her return trips she would be empty. Still painted in her troopship colours, grey hull and upperworks, with a yellow funnel, *Asturias* departed Southampton on 26 July 1949, with 1340 migrants on board, and voyaged to Fremantle, Melbourne and Sydney. On her second voyage, *Asturias* left Sydney on 10 December 1949 and went to Jakarta to board Dutch nationals and carry them back to Rotterdam.

The third voyage by *Asturias* departed Southampton on 8 February 1950, and on her return, the liner was repainted in the colours of her former owners, Royal Mail Line. Her first departure from Southampton in this guise was on 10 May, and after leaving Sydney on 19 June, she called at Fremantle on 25 June, then went back to Jakarta again on 29 June. *Asturias* remained on the Australian migrant trade until 1953, when she was withdrawn and returned to trooping duties.

Repainted in peacetime troopship colours, all white with a coloured ribband around the hull and a yellow funnel, *Asturias* began transporting British troops to the Korean war zone, a role she continued to fill for the next four years. On 14 September 1957, the old liner arrived at Faslane, to be broken up. Before this happened, though, she was used for deck scenes during the filming of 'A Night to Remember', the story of the *Titanic* disaster.

THE LONE AUSTRALIAN

BUILT: *1936 by Harland & Wolff Ltd, Belfast*
TONNAGE: *11 004 gross*
DIMENSIONS: *484 × 66 ft (147.6 × 20.2 m)*
SERVICE SPEED: *17 knots*
PROPULSION: *H & W diesels/twin screws*

Kanimbla was the only Australian-owned ship to make a voyage to Australia with migrants. Built for McIlwraith McEacharn Ltd, she was launched on 12 December 1935, running trials in April 1936, and arriving in Sydney on 1 June at the end of her delivery voyage. *Kanimbla* was destined to be the largest, and last liner to be built for the interstate trade from Sydney to Fremantle. She provided fine accommodation for 203 first class and 198 second class passengers.

Kanimbla operated from Sydney to Melbourne, Adelaide and Fremantle during the summer months, while in winter she ran from Melbourne and Sydney to northern Queensland as far as Cairns. Only three years after entering service, the liner was taken over by the Royal Australian Navy on 27 August 1939, and converted in Sydney to an armed merchant cruiser, sporting seven 6-inch guns and two 3-inch guns. Commissioned on 6 October 1939, though still in her peacetime colours, *Kanimbla* was posted to the China Station, based on Hong Kong. In June 1941 she

transferred to the East Indies Station at Colombo, and spent some time in the Persian Gulf.

Later *Kanimbla* returned to Australia, and patrolled in the South West Pacific until 1943, when she arrived at Garden Island in Sydney for conversion into a Landing Ship, Infantry. Carrying 26 landing barges, she spent several months training along the east coast, then went to New Guinea. Her first landing was at Hollandia on 22 April 1944, followed by similar operations at Morotai, Humboldt Bay and Leyte Gulf, then returned to Brisbane for a refit.

Kanimbla later took part in the landings at Brunei Bay and Balikpapan, being in Subic Bay when the Japanese surrendered. *Kanimbla* was then used to repatriate released prisoners-of-war to Australia, and later carried troops home. This duty kept her active for the next three years, then in June 1949 the vessel left Sydney with the crew designated to bring the new Australian aircraft carrier, HMAS *Sydney*, from Britain to Australia.

On her return voyage, *Kanimbla* took aboard a number of British recruits for the Royal Australian Navy. She then proceeded to Genoa, where 432 male migrants were embarked and brought to Sydney, arriving in September 1949.

Kanimbla was then released from government

KANIMBLA

ORIENTAL QUEEN

service, and given an extensive refit. She was given accommodation for 231 first class and 125 second class passengers, and resumed her coastal service again in December 1950. On 14 June 1952 she ran aground in Moreton Bay, suffering serious bottom damage, and being out of service for three months. Over the next few years, the demand for coastal passages declined, so in September 1958, *Kanimbla* made a cruise to Hong Kong and Japan. She made two similar cruises in both 1959 and 1960.

During 1960, *Kanimbla* was offered for sale, and purchased in January 1961 by Pacific Transport Co. Inc., of Liberia. Renamed *Oriental Queen*, she was placed on the pilgrim trade from Indonesia to Jedda for three years, then early in 1964 the Japanese firm, Toyo Yusen Kaisha, chartered the vessel.

Repainted in their colours, *Oriental Queen* was sent to Australia in May 1964, to serve as a cruise ship, being based in Sydney. Providing accommodation for 350 passengers in one class, she operated a mixture of short Pacific cruises interspersed with longer trips to Japan and the Far East, and some trans-Tasman voyages as well. In January 1967, Toyo Yusen Kaisha bought *Oriental Queen* outright, but at the same time withdrew her from the Australian cruise trade. On 13 January 1967, the liner arrived in Sydney at the end of a trans-Tasman voyage, leaving the following day for Hong Kong and Japan.

Oriental Queen operated a cruise service from Yokohama to Guam, and in 1968 made five voyages under charter to Honolulu and Los Angeles. After the charter finished, *Oriental Queen* returned to the Guam trade for a further five years, until arriving in Yokohama on 6 October 1973 at the end of her final voyage. She was then sold to Taiwanese shipbreakers, arriving in Kaohsiung on 7 December 1973.

CANBERRA

BUILT: *1913 by A. Stephen & Sons, Glasgow*
TONNAGE: *7707 gross*
DIMENSIONS: *426 × 57 ft (129.8 × 17.3 m)*
SERVICE SPEED: *15 knots*
PROPULSION: *Quadruple expansion/twin screws*

During the latter part of 1949, two vessels that had spent many years on the Australian coastal trade, returned with migrants. The first of them was *Canberra*, which had been owned by Howard Smith Ltd. Launched on 9 November 1912, *Canberra* arrived in Australian waters for the first time in April 1913, and was placed in service along the east coast from Melbourne to Cairns. She provided accommodation for 170 first class, 180 second class and 60 third class passengers.

In October 1917, *Canberra* was requisitioned and became a troopship, carrying 800 men to Egypt. She later formed part of a convoy to transport troops from Alexandria to Marseilles, and made a voyage from Britain to India and back. *Canberra* returned to Australia in September 1919, and in May 1920 resumed her coastal service. In February 1925 she was laid up in Sydney, then reactivated in June. In the early morning of 27 June a fire broke out and quickly spread through the ship. *Canberra* was taken to Mort's Dock in Sydney for repairs, and did not return to service until May 1926.

In July 1941, *Canberra* came under the Shipping Controller, but remained on the coastal trade, though often carrying troops. In August 1947 she was returned to her owners, being in need of an extensive refit. Howard Smith did not consider this to be worthwhile, so the ship was offered for sale, and quickly purchased by Singapore based Chinese interests. On 5 September, *Canberra* was towed out of Sydney by the tug *Roumania*, arriving in Singapore 53 days later. By then, *Canberra* had been resold to the Goulandris Group, better known as the Greek Line. Registered under the ownership of Cia. Maritima del Este S.A., Panama, *Canberra* went to Greece to be refitted, and without change of name, began operating from Europe to South America.

On 31 August 1949, *Canberra* departed Naples bound for Australia with a full complement of migrants. She berthed in Sydney on 5 October, and three days later left, returning to Naples on 15 November. She was then extensively remodelled, with accommodation for 52 first class and 752 tourist class passengers, and for five years operated between Europe and Canada. In 1954 *Canberra* was sold to the Dominican Republic, and renamed *España*. She voyaged between the West Indies and Spain carrying migrants and sugar until 1959, when she was sold to shipbreakers.

CANBERRA ARRIVING IN SYDNEY, 5 OCTOBER 1949

COLUMBIA

BUILT: *1913 by Harland & Wolff Ltd, Belfast*
TONNAGE: *9424 gross*
DIMENSIONS: *468 × 60 ft (142.6 × 18.2 m)*
SERVICE SPEED: *15 knots*
PROPULSION: *Triple expansion/triple screws*

The second former Australian coastal liner to return to local waters in 1949 was *Columbia*, better remembered as *Katoomba* of McIlwraith McEacharn Ltd. *Katoomba* was launched on 10 April 1913, and completed three months later. She was given accommodation for 209 first class, 192 second class and 156 third class passengers, and arrived in Australia for the first time in September 1913.

On 2 June 1918, *Katoomba* left Melboune with troops bound for New York via the Panama Canal, then made two Atlantic crossings before being sent into the Mediterranean. She returned to Sydney with a full load of troops in September 1919, and was then refitted, resuming her coastal trade in March 1920.

Katoomba spent most of the next 20 years operating between Sydney and Fremantle. In March 1941 she was requisitioned for her second war, carrying troops to New Guinea. She later carried troops to Colombo, returning in April 1942, and then resuming her coastal service again. Later in 1942, *Katoomba* was again taken over, and transported troops around the South Pacific. When handed back to McIlwraith McEacharn in

February 1946 she was offered for sale. In July 1946 she was purchased by the Goulandris Group and registered under their subsidiary company, Cia. Maritima del Este S.A., of Panama.

Katoomba was taken to Genoa for a refit, and on 31 December 1946 made the first Greek Line post-war sailing, from Genoa to New York. The following year she began a two year charter to French Line, operating to the West Indies. In April 1949, *Katoomba* was given another refit, during which she was converted to oil-firing, and given accommodation for 52 first class and 752 tourist class passengers. She was also painted white, and renamed *Columbia*.

Her first voyage as *Columbia* was to Australia, departing Genoa on 25 November. Arriving in Fremantle on 17 December, she left the next day for Sydney, berthing on 26 December. *Columbia* left Sydney on 30 December, returning to Naples on 29 January 1950.

Columbia was then placed on the regular Greek Line service to Canada, making two voyages from Naples, then being based at Bremerhaven. In April 1957 she began operating from Liverpool to Quebec. On 21 October 1957, *Columbia* left Quebec bound for Bremerhaven, where she was laid up. In March 1958 she was moved to Piraeus, but remained idle until August 1959, when she left for Japan, arriving on 29 September 1959 in Nagasaki, having been sold to shipbreakers there.

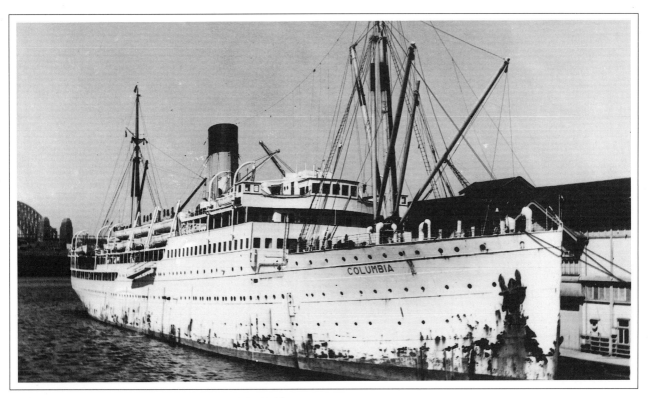

COLUMBIA IN SYDNEY, DECEMBER 1949

RANGITOTO AND RANGITANE

BUILT: Rangitoto *1949 by Vickers–Armstrong Ltd,*
  Newcastle
Rangitane *1949 by John Brown & Co., Clydebank*
TONNAGE: *21 809 gross*
DIMENSIONS: *609 × 78 ft (185.6 × 23.8 m)*
SERVICE SPEED: *17 knots*
PROPULSION: *Doxford diesels / twin screws*

The New Zealand Shipping Co. lost two liners during
the war, and two of the survivors were at the end of
their careers, so orders were placed as soon as possible
for new liners. In order to have them delivered as
quickly as possible, the order was divided between two
shipyards. The first to be launched was *Rangitoto*, on
12 January 1949, making her maiden departure from
London on 25 August 1949, bound for Wellington
through the Panama Canal. *Rangitane*, which
perpetuated the name of a liner lost in the war, was
launched on 30 June 1949, being completed six months
later. Her first departure from London was on 27
January 1950, joining *Rangitata* and *Rangitiki*.

Unlike their predecessors, *Rangitoto* and *Rangitane*
carried 416 passengers in a single class, and also had a
large cargo capacity. In 1951 they were joined by the
similar *Ruahine*, enabling a four-weekly schedule to be
maintained. Cargo was worked in London, and
passengers embarked there, but on the return trip
passengers disembarked at Southampton, following
which the ships went on to London, usually berthing in
the King George V Dock.

Both ships gave excellent service through the 1950s,
though *Rangitane* had a couple of mishaps. In February
1956, she was delayed by engine trouble near Panama
while returning to London, and went to Glasgow for
repairs. In October 1957, while transiting the Panama
Canal, the American freighter, *Hawaiian Tourist*,
collided with *Rangitane*, causing damage to some stern
plates, which took four days to repair. Over the years,
extra ports were added to the itinerary, including
Madeira, Kingston and Tahiti southbound, Miami and
Bermuda northbound, to attract more passengers.

In 1965, both *Rangitoto* and *Rangitane* were given
extensive refits, during which the accommodation was
increased to 460 in one class, and the mainmast
removed. At the same time, the New Zealand Shipping
Co. adopted the colours of the associated Federal Steam
Navigation Co. Both ships had their funnels repainted
prior to returning to service, which was then operated
only by *Rangitoto, Rangitane* and *Ruahine*, but was
struggling to survive. In 1968, New Zealand Shipping
Co. decided to abandon their passenger service, and all
three ships were withdrawn.

Rangitane was the first to go, arriving in Wellington
for the last time on 19 February 1968. After loading
cargo at various ports, she left Auckland on 30 March to
return to London in May, having completed 47 round
trips. After two months laid up, the vessel was sold to
Astroguardo Cia. Nav., and renamed *Jan*. She then
loaded cargo for a voyage to Australia, being delayed in
Melbourne in August with engine trouble, then going
on to Sydney. The vessel then left for Taiwan, having
been sold to shipbreakers there, arriving in Kaohsiung
in September 1968.

Shortly after, *Jan* was sold by the shipbreakers to
Oriental Latin American Lines, part of the C. Y. Tung
Group, who already owned the former *Ruahine*. The
former *Rangitane* was renamed *Oriental Esmerelda*,
refitted to carry 350 passengers in one class and had her
foremast removed, then crossed to San Diego. On 4
June 1969, she left on the first voyage of a new round-
the-world service, operating under the banner of Orient
Overseas Line.

Rangitoto remained on the New Zealand trade until
21 July 1969, when she berthed in London at the end of
her final voyage. She was also purchased by the Tung
Group, and placed under the same subsidiary as her
sister, being renamed *Oriental Carnaval*. She was refitted
in Hong Kong in a similar manner to *Oriental Esmerelda*,
then joined her on the round-the-world service from
San Diego, so the three ships were operating together
again.

The world energy crisis of the early 1970s brought
their careers to a sudden end. *Oriental Carnaval*
terminated a voyage in Port Everglades, picked up a
cargo in South America and went back to Hong Kong.
For a year both ships made cruises from San Diego and
Los Angeles to Mexico, and some voyages to the Far
East. However, on 7 March 1975, *Oriental Carnaval* was
laid up in Hong Kong, and eventually sold to local
shipbreakers, who began work on her in February 1976.

Oriental Esmerelda remained active a year longer, but
on 10 February 1976, she was laid up in Hong Kong,
and sold the following month to Taiwanese
shipbreakers. This time there would be no reprieve, and
she arrived in Kaohsiung for the second time on 2 April
1976, where demolition work began shortly after.

RANGITANE

RANGITOTO IN FEDERAL LINE COLOURS

HIMALAYA

BUILT: *1949 by Vickers–Armstrong Ltd, Barrow*
TONNAGE: *27 955 gross*
DIMENSIONS: *709 × 90 ft (216 × 27.6 m)*
SERVICE SPEED: *22 knots*
PROPULSION: *Geared turbines/twin screws*

Himalaya became one of the most popular liners to operate to Australia in the post-war era. She was the first new liner built for P & O after the war, being launched on 5 October 1948, and ran trials off Arran on 24 August 1949, reaching 25.13 knots. After a delivery voyage from Glasgow to Southampton with several hundred guests aboard, *Himalaya* was officially handed over to P & O on 1 September. She then went to Tilbury, from where she departed on her maiden voyage on 6 October 1949, reaching Sydney on 7 November.

Himalaya had an identical hull to *Orcades*, but a different superstructure, being a more attractive ship. Her accommodation was also very different, being for 758 first class and 401 tourist class. After only two round trips to Australia, *Himalaya* made two cruises from Southampton to the Mediterranean, and throughout her career she would be frequently used for cruising. One problem to affect the ship was smuts from the funnel falling on the afterdecks, so in 1953 a Thorneycroft top was fitted, which further enhanced her appearance. While passing through the Mediterranean on 30 August 1956, an explosion in the refrigeration plant killed four crewmen and injured twelve, causing a diversion to Malta for repairs.

Orient Line had begun operating across the Pacific in 1954, but it was not until 1958 that P & O followed them. *Himalaya* made the first voyage, departing Tilbury on a four-month journey that took her first to Australia, then from Sydney to the west coast of America and back to Sydney, returning to Tilbury on 2 June. Following her next voyage to Australia, *Himalaya* made a series of eight cruises from Sydney between 25 July and 5 November, then returned to Britain. In March 1959 she left Sydney on a trans-Pacific voyage, but on the return trip made the first ever P & O crossing from America to Japan, then came back to Sydney.

Himalaya had to enter the Garden Island drydock in Sydney on 18 August 1959 for replacement of a propeller which had been damaged in the Suez Canal, causing her to be 15 days late into Sydney. On her return to Britain she was drydocked again, in Rotterdam, this time to have air-conditioning installed. In 1963 *Himalaya* was converted into a one-class liner, with tourist class accommodation for 1416 passengers. She left Tilbury in this guise for the first time on 1 November 1963, and over the next 10 years was used increasingly for cruising, with very few line voyages. On 10 October 1969, *Himalaya* was the last P & O vessel to depart from Tilbury, as the company then moved their base to Southampton, which had been their cruise port for many years.

In the 1970s, *Himalaya* was used almost exclusively for cruising. From May to October she would cruise from Southampton, then make a line voyage to Sydney, cruising from there between November and April. On 9 April 1970 she became the first ship to berth at the new Kōbe passenger terminal. At the end of her 1973–74 Australian season, *Himalaya* voyaged back to Britain, but then left Southampton again on 16 May to return to Australia. She then made another series of cruises from Sydney.

On 18 October 1974, *Himalaya* moved slowly down Sydney Harbour for the last time, surrounded by small boats, and watched by thousands from the shore. Two days later there were similar scenes in Brisbane, as she swept majestically down the river to the sea, heading for Hong Kong. Here the full complement of passengers disembarked, and many of her fittings were removed. *Himalaya* then made the short passage to Kaohsiung in Taiwan, arriving on 28 November 1974, and being handed over to shipbreakers.

HIMALAYA

HIMALAYA AFTER ALTERATIONS TO THE FUNNEL

HELLENIC PRINCE

BUILT: *1929 by Cockatoo Island Dockyard, Sydney*
TONNAGE: *6558 gross*
DIMENSIONS: *444 × 61 ft (135.3 × 18.5 m)*
SERVICE SPEED: *20 knots*
PROPULSION: *Geared turbines/twin screws*

The only vessel built in Australia to bring migrants to the country was *Hellenic Prince*, which was also one of the most unusual looking ships converted for this purpose. In 1924, the Royal Australian Navy ordered a seaplane carrier, the first to be built for them. Laid down in April 1926, it was launched on 21 February 1928, completed on 21 December that year, and commissioned into the RAN on 23 January 1929 as HMAS *Albatross*. With a complement of 450 officers and ratings, she could carry six seaplanes, which were stored in a hangar forward, and lowered into the water by a large crane aft.

Unfortunately, by the time the ship was completed, seaplanes were almost obsolete in the Navy, so over the next four years HMAS *Albatross* made a few coastal voyages, then on 26 April 1933 was decommissioned. She remained idle in Sydney until 1938, then was transferred to the Royal Navy in part payment for the cruiser HMS *Amphion*, which was transferred to the RAN in October 1938 as HMAS *Perth*. HMAS *Albatross* voyaged to Britain, only to be laid up in Plymouth on 15 December 1938, as HMS *Albatross*, since the Royal Navy had no use for the ship either.

In August 1939 she was recommissioned, and converted into a aircraft repair ship, then sent to South Atlantic Station. Early in 1942 she was refitted in America, then joined the British Eastern Fleet, remaining with them until the end of 1943, when she returned to Britain. HMS *Albatross* was then converted to do ship repairs, and recommissioned in time to take part in the Normandy landings. She was stationed off the beaches, and repaired 132 damaged vessels over a period of several months. She was also attacked by enemy aircraft on numerous occasions, and on 11 August 1944 was hit by a torpedo. This caused the ship to return to Portsmouth for repairs, but these stopped in 1945 when the war ended. HMS *Albatross* was laid up at Portsmouth, then moved to Falmouth.

Offered for sale, she was purchased on 19 August 1946 by the South Western Steam Navigation Co., who intended to convert her for the Australian emigrant trade. Conversion work began at Chatham Dockyard, then the owners changed their minds after a

considerable amount of work had been done, and early in 1947 the vessel was towed to Torbay. Renamed *Pride of Torquay*, she spent several months serving as a storage hulk, but in late 1947 was towed to Plymouth and laid up, being offered for sale. When no buyers were forthcoming, an auction was organised for 19 October 1948, but a few days before that date, the ship was sold to China Hellenic Lines Ltd, of Hong Kong.

Renamed *Hellenic Prince*, she arrived on 20 December 1948 at the C. H. Bailey Ltd shipyard at Barry in Wales, to be converted for the Australian emigrant trade. The work involved the original hangar being divided into two decks, and accommodation installed for 1000 persons. Amenities provided included a 560 seat dining room, three hospitals and a cinema. The work was due to be completed at the end of March 1949, and an IRO contract was obtained for the ship to operate between Naples and Australia at 17 knots, for voyages of between 25 and 28 days, beginning in April 1949. Unfortunately, the work took much longer than anticipated, and it was 17 October 1949 before *Hellenic Prince* left Barry for Naples.

On 7 November 1949, *Hellenic Prince* left Naples on her first voyage to Australia, calling at Fremantle on 28 November, then going directly to Sydney, arriving on 5 December, returning empty to Naples. Her second voyage departed on 11 January 1950, but was quite protracted, as she lost an anchor off Sicily while boarding more passengers, then was held up three days at Port Said. Crossing the Indian Ocean the vessel was forced to stop engines due to boiler problems, and drifted for two days, eventually reaching Melbourne on 13 February. On her third trip, *Hellenic Prince* returned by way of Indonesia, picking up Dutch nationals who were taken to Bremerhaven. This became her European terminal port for future voyages, her first departure from there being on 25 June 1950.

In September 1950, *Hellenic Prince* made her second departure from Bremerhaven, but after calling at Fremantle in 10 October, she went to Wellington, arriving on 16 October, then returned to Fremantle on 2 November, and called at Jakarta on her return trip to Bremerhaven. *Hellenic Prince* remained on the Australian emigrant trade until 1952, when she was chartered by the British Government to transport troops to Kenya. On 12 November 1953, the vessel was laid up in Hong Kong, and on 28 August 1954 was sold to local shipbreakers, Pacific Salvage Co. Ltd, to end a varied career.

HMAS ALBATROSS, FIRST AUSTRALIAN AIRCRAFT CARRIER

HELLENIC PRINCE

A FORMER TROOPSHIP

BUILT: *1925 by Fairfield Shipbuilding & Engineering Co., Glasgow*
TONNAGE: *13 475 gross*
DIMENSIONS: *538 × 66 ft (164 × 20.2 m)*
SERVICE SPEED: *15 knots*
PROPULSION: *Geared turbines / twin screws*

This ship was well known in Australia as *Empire Brent* in the immediate post-war years, and through the 1950s as the New Zealand emigrant liner *Captain Cook*. Her original name was *Letitia*, built for the Donaldson Line to operate between Glasgow and Montreal. Launched on 14 October 1924, she entered service in April 1925, providing accommodation for 516 cabin and 1023 third class passengers. Her sister was named *Athenia*, and is best remembered as the first passenger vessel to be sunk by a German submarine in World War Two, within hours of hostilities commencing on 3 September 1939.

In October 1939, *Letitia* was requisitioned and converted into an armed merchant cruiser, joining the Northern Patrol in the stormy waters off the north of Scotland. Later the vessel was used as a troopship, and in 1944 she was transferred to the Canadian Government and converted into a hospital ship, capable of handling about 1000 casualties. Initially she operated between Europe and Canada, and then was ordered to the Pacific, but the Japanese surrendered before she

arrived. Following a period repatriating Canadian troops, *Letitia* was bought outright by the Ministry of Transport from Donaldson Line, who were retained as managers of the ship, and also provided the crew.

Renamed *Empire Brent*, she was used until the end of 1947 to carry the wives and families of Canadian servicemen who had married in Britain to their new homeland. It was while outbound on such a voyage that *Empire Brent* collided with and sank the small coaster *Stormont* in the Mersey on 20 November 1946. *Empire Brent* suffered severe bow damage, and had to be drydocked for repairs.

In December 1947, *Empire Brent* went to the Clyde for a refit, then on 31 March 1948 departed Glasgow for Australia, again with the families of servicemen aboard. She arrived in Fremantle on 2 May, Melbourne on 7 May and was in Sydney from 10 to 16 May, returning via Bombay to Glasgow. A second voyage to Australia departed Glasgow on 13 July 1948, but on her return to Britain, *Empire Brent* was sent to the Barclay, Curle shipyard on the Clyde to be refitted for the emigrant trade, with accommodation for 965 persons.

Still managed by Donaldson Line, *Empire Brent* left Glasgow on 30 November 1949 on her first migrant voyage, calling at Fremantle and Melbourne before reaching Sydney on 7 January 1950. Her second voyage departed Glasgow on 6 April 1950, but on leaving

DONALDSON LINER *LETITIA*

Sydney on 22 May, she went to Indonesia to collect Dutch nationals wishing to return home. After one more voyage to Australia, *Empire Brent* arrived back in Glasgow on 6 December 1950, and then was laid up pending a decision on her future.

Early in 1951, the New Zealand Government was seeking a replacement for the aging *Atlantis*, and accepted the offer of *Empire Brent*. The vessel returned to the Barclay, Curle shipyard for another refit, during which the accommodation was increased to 1088 in two-, four- and six-berth cabins. Still managed by Donaldson Line, she was renamed *Captain Cook*, and by a strange coincidence, her master was also Captain James Cook, who had been in command of the ship for several years, and stayed with her until 1954.

Captain Cook left Glasgow on 5 February 1952 on her first voyage to New Zealand, voyaging by way of the Panama Canal to Wellington, where she berthed on 10 March. Her schedule called for four migrant trips each year, returning to Britain empty. However, on some return voyages she was directed to the Far East to collect British troops and carry them home. In June 1953, *Captain Cook* was present for the Coronation Naval Review at Spithead.

The Donaldson Line had not renewed their passenger services after the war, but in 1955 they chartered *Captain Cook* for a series of seven return trips between Glasgow and Montreal, the first departing on 20 April, the last on 11 September. The results were disappointing, and marked the end of Donaldson Line

passenger operations, though they remained as a cargo line for some years. *Captain Cook* returned to the New Zealand migrant trade, only to be taken for trooping duties between August and December 1956 when the Suez crisis erupted.

In March 1957 the vessel was delayed at Glasgow with boiler problems, but eventually departed for Wellington. While berthed there on 29 April, an arsonist set fires in 10 cabins, but the outbreaks were extinguished quickly. In December 1957, *Captain Cook* was chartered by the Dutch Government for one voyage, to collect evacuees from Jararta and return them to Holland.

Over her years of service to New Zealand, the government had been purchasing *Captain Cook* by installments, and by 1959 they owned the ship outright. It was at this time that her hull was repainted white, but she was due for survey at the end of 1959, and would need considerable upgrading to pass. *Captain Cook* left Glasgow on 11 September 1959 on her twenty-fifth voyage to New Zealand, and after discharging her migrants, went to Malaya to collect the New Zealand battalion and return them to Wellington and Lyttelton, her only visit to that port. She then returned to Britain empty, arriving in Glasgow on 10 February 1960. After destoring, the old liner was laid up at Falmouth until being sold to T. W. Ward Ltd, and arrived at their Inverkeithing shipbreaking yard under tow on 29 April 1960.

CAPTAIN COOK

A PACIFIC WAR VETERAN

BUILT: *1941 by Sun Shipbuilding & Drydock Co., Chester*
TONNAGE: *11 086 gross*
DIMENSIONS: *492 × 69 ft (150 × 21.2 m)*
SERVICE SPEED: *16 knots*
PROPULSION: *Busch–Sulzer diesel/single screw*

Nelly was another emigrant ship that served during the war as an auxiliary aircraft carrier. Laid down as a standard design C3 cargo ship, she was launched on 11 January 1940 as *Mormacmail*. Her sister was *Mormacland*, which later also became an emigrant ship, the *Anna Salen*. Work on completing the ship proceeded very slowly, then on 6 March 1941 she was taken over by the US Navy, and converted into an auxiliary aircraft carrier at the Newport News shipyard.

Commissioned as USS *Long Island* on 2 June 1941, she could carry 21 aircraft, and was armed with one 5-inch gun and a pair of 3-inch guns. USS *Long Island* served in the Pacific zone throughout the rest of the war, with her aircraft capacity being increased as demand for aircraft grew. When the battle for Guadalcanal was being fought, USS *Long Island* was sent to the area, and on 20 August 1942 flew off 19 Wildcat fighters and 12 Dauntless dive-bombers from a position 210 miles away. These were the first combat planes to land at Henderson Field on Guadalcanal, only three days after the airstrip was completed, and thirteen days after the Americans had captured the area.

On 26 March 1946, *Long Island* was decommissioned, and laid up pending disposal. She remained idle for two years, then on 12 March 1948 was bought at auction by Caribbean Land & Shipping Corp., a Swiss based organisation. Renamed *Nelly*, and registered in Panama, she was rebuilt for the emigrant trade, being given rather basic accommodation for 1300 passengers. When completed she looked similar to *Anna Salen*, with a long, low superstructure.

Nelly made her first voyage from Naples to Australia in June 1949, being in Melbourne on 17 July. Her second voyage departed Naples in September, and her third on 15 December, going as far as Sydney where she arrived on 15 January 1950. On her fourth voyage to Australia, *Nelly* left Sydney on 26 March 1950 and went to Jakarta to collect Dutch nationals returning home. *Nelly* made regular trips to Australia from various European ports over a four-year period, and also made some migrant voyages to Canada. In January 1953 she left Southampton on her final voyage as *Nelly*, going only to Melbourne and being in port three days from 24 February. On her return to Bremerhaven, the vessel was withdrawn for an extensive refit.

The accommodation was extensively altered to cater for 20 first class and 987 tourist class passengers, and the bridgehouse enlarged. She was then renamed *Seven Seas*, and on 9 May 1953 left Bremerhaven for Australia once more, arriving in Fremantle on 8 June, and terminating in Melbourne on 12 June. On her return to Bremerhaven, *Seven Seas* was chartered by Europe–Canada Line, which was jointly owned by Holland–America Line and Royal Rotterdam Lloyd.

Europe–Canada Line was formed to provide cheap travel across the Atlantic, mainly for students, and *Seven Seas* began operating from Bremerhaven, Le Havre and Southampton to Quebec and Montreal. Towards the end of 1955, *Seven Seas* was bought outright by Europe–Canada Line, and registered in West Germany. Her service remained unchanged however, for the next five years.

On 30 October 1960, *Seven Seas* departed Southampton under charter to Royal Rotterdam Lloyd, visiting Fremantle, Melbourne and Sydney, then going on to Wellington and Auckland, where she berthed on 18 December.

Seven Seas returned to the Canadian trade until April 1963, when she began operating from Bremerhaven to New York. At the end of her 1963 season, *Seven Seas* was chartered by Chapman College to undertake study cruises for their University of the Seven Seas, visiting many countries. When this ended, she went to Amsterdam, and on behalf of Holland–America Line, departed there in March 1964 for Australia, passing through Fremantle on 28 April on her way to Melbourne and Sydney, from where she sailed on 6 May across the Pacific to New York. Following another season as a floating university, in March 1965 the vessel made another voyage to Australia on behalf of Holland–America Line.

She then resumed her Atlantic service for the summer months, and on 18 July 1965 was disabled by an engine room fire when some 500 miles from St John, to where she was towed for repairs, and then returned to service. *Seven Seas* made her final visit to Australia when, in her role as a floating university, she departed Los Angeles on 10 February 1966, being in Sydney for two days from 8 March, then going to Fremantle and on to the Middle East, and back to New York.

Following one more season on the Atlantic, *Seven Seas* was withdrawn in September 1966, and sold to Verolme Shipyards for duty as a floating hostel for workers at their Parkhaven yard in Rotterdam. She served in this static role for the next 10 years, until being sold to shipbreakers in April 1977. On 4 May *Seven Seas* was towed away from Parkhaven and arrived at the Ghent yard of Van Heyghen Freres the following day.

NELLY

SEVEN SEAS

CHANGSHA AND TAIYUAN

BUILT: *1949 by Scotts Shipbuilding & Engineering Co., Greenock*

TONNAGE: *7472 gross*

DIMENSIONS: *440 × 57 ft (134.1 × 17.3 m)*

SERVICE SPEED: *15 knots*

PROPULSION: *Doxford diesel / single screw*

China Navigation Co. had operated a regular service from Chinese ports to Australia from 1883 to 1912, but then concentrated their attention on the Far Eastern coastal and river trades. After the end of World War Two, the company ordered ten cargo/passenger ships, which were intended to re-establish the pre-war trades, but the Communist takeover of mainland China prevented this happening. Instead, China Navigation had to seek new routes, and at various times all 10 of the cargo/passenger ships operated to Australia, though the largest pair, *Changchow* and *Chungking* were under charter to other operators at the time.

Changsha was launched on 2 November 1948, and after running trials on 3 May 1949, went to Liverpool to load cargo. Departing on 17 May, *Changsha* came through the Suez Canal to Adelaide, Melbourne and Brisbane, then returned to Melbourne to commence her regular trade. Leaving on 23 July 1949, *Changsha* spent five days at Sydney, then went to Brisbane before going on to Hong Kong and Japan.

Taiyuan was launched on 13 May 1949, and departed Liverpool on her delivery voyage on 15 November, passing through Cape Town on 7 December to reach Melbourne on 21 December. Five days later she departed to follow the same route as *Changsha*, operated in conjunction with *Changte* and *Taiping* of Australian–Oriental Line, on a three-weekly schedule.

Changsha and *Taiyuan* were fitted out with accommodation for 84 first class and 72 third class passengers, with some cabins and public rooms being air-conditioned. They enjoyed many years of successful service, though *Changsha* was twice in trouble in Japanese waters. On 27 March 1956, she ran aground in Tokyo Bay, and was not refloated until 9 April. Three years later the vessel was fortunate not to be wrecked, when she was caught in typhoon Vera on 26 September 1959 off Yokkaichi, and was one of 18 ships driven ashore. *Changsha* ended up high and dry on a sandy beach, with a 20° list to port. Sand had to be excavated from around the hull, and a channel dug from the ship to the sea, so it was 15 December before *Changsha* was pulled into deep water. Towed into Yokkaichi for repairs, further damage was caused two days later by a fire, then the vessel was towed to Yokohama for drydocking. It was March 1960 before *Changsha* was

able to return to service. That was not the end of her troubles though, as on 18 December 1960, damage to a propeller shaft bearing caused the engine to stop off the coast of Victoria. *Changsha* drifted 14 hours while repairs were effected, and she was then able to reach Melbourne safely under her own power.

During 1961, *Taiping* and *Changte* were withdrawn, so China Navigation brought in *Anking* and *Anshun* to maintain their frequency of departures. However, during the early 1960s, passenger numbers declined, and in 1965 *Anking* and *Anshun* were withdrawn, while *Taiyuan* and *Changsha* were placed on a shorter route from east coast ports to Port Moresby, Manila and Hong Kong only. There was also increased competition, with both Dominion Line and E & A Line placing larger ships on a similar route.

On 20 May 1969, *Changsha* left Sydney on her final voyage, and was sold to Pacific International Lines, of Singapore. Renamed *Kota Panjang*, she began operating from Singapore to Hong Kong and Canton, a route China Navigation had once dominated. *Taiyuan* was left to maintain a lone-ship service to Hong Kong, until the route was abandoned by China Navigation at the end of 1970. *Taiyuan* was then given an extensive refit in Hong Kong, the third class being removed and first class upgraded to carry 86 passengers. An outdoor swimming pool and a playroom for children were added, then *Taiyuan* returned to Sydney in July 1971 to commence a new service to Fiji.

Operated as Fiji Australia Line, *Taiyuan* offered a departure from Sydney every third Saturday to Noumea, Lautoka and Suva, with a call at Brisbane on the return trip. Advertised as a cruise, the venture was not a success, as on 10 July 1972 *Taiyuan* left Sydney to return to Hong Kong. She was then also sold to Pacific International Lines, being renamed *Kota Sahabat*, and joined her sister on the service to Canton and Hong Kong, both ships having white hulls.

Several years later, *Kota Sahabat* was refitted to carry livestock, and on several occasions returned to Australia. Late in 1978 she was held up for several weeks off Newcastle by an industrial dispute, then loaded 12 000 sheep. In September 1979, *Kota Sahabat* was bound for Hobart when she lost radio contact, and was the subject of a major search off the south coast of Tasmania. She arrived safely in Hobart on 16 September, reporting a fault in her radio, and loaded more sheep. Shortly afterwards, *Kota Sahabat* was laid up, and in February 1980 left Singapore bound for the breaker's yard in Taiwan. *Kota Panjang* remained in service as a cargo/passenger ship until June 1981, when she was sold to shipbreakers in Karachi.

CHANGSHA

TAIYUAN

FAIRSEA

BUILT: *1942 by Sun Shipbuilding & Drydock Co., Chester*
TONNAGE: *11 678 gross*
DIMENSIONS: *492 × 69 ft (150 × 21.1 m)*
SERVICE SPEED: *16 knots*
PROPULSION: *Doxford diesels / single screw*

Fairsea was another of the converted aircraft carriers to see service in the Australian emigrant trade for many years. Although generally thought of as a Sitmar ship, *Fairsea* spent most of her career under the Panamanian flag, but had been built for service under the American flag as *Rio de la Plata*.

In February 1939, an American shipping company, Moore–McCormick Line, ordered four ships, with accommodation for about 70 passengers, to operate from New York to the east coast of South America. They were to be the first American passenger vessels to be fitted with diesel machinery, in this case two 6-cylinder Doxford diesels geared to a single shaft.

Launched on 1 March 1941, *Rio de la Plata* was taken over by the government in October that year, and completed as an escort carrier. Handed over to the Royal Navy under the lend-lease scheme, she was commissioned as HMS *Charger* on 3 March 1942. Later in 1942, the vessel was returned to the Americans, and as USS *Charger* saw considerable service in the Pacific.

USS *Charger* was released from naval service on 15 March 1946, and placed under the management of Moore–McCormick Line. The flight deck was removed, and the ship converted to carry troops, in which guise she saw brief service, then was laid up and offered for sale. In 1949, the vessel was bought by Alexandre Vlasov, and joined his Alvion Steam Ship Corporation as *Fairsea*. She was rebuilt as a passenger ship, while Vlasov obtained a contract from the IRO for her to transport displaced persons and refugees.

With rather austere accommodation for 1800 persons, *Fairsea* departed Genoa on 3 December 1949, bound for Australia, reaching Sydney on 30 December. Over the next three years, *Fairsea* voyaged regularly from Italy to Australia, but under the terms of the IRO contract, had to return to Europe empty. In February 1952, Vlasov opened an office in Sydney, and began offering passages to Italy on his ships.

In April 1953, *Fairsea* was taken off the Australian trade, to make six round trips between Bremerhaven and Quebec, offering accommodation for 40 first class and 1400 tourist class passengers. In September 1953, *Fairsea* made her first departure from Bremerhaven to Australia, a route she maintained for the next two years. While berthing in Melbourne in November 1953, a fire broke out in the engine room of *Fairsea*, but the

FAIRSEA AS FIRST REBUILT

FAIRSEA AFTER ALTERATIONS IN 1957

engineers were able to extinguish the blaze quickly, though the engine room was flooded.

When *Georgic* was withdrawn from service in 1955, *Fairsea* was chartered to carry British migrants. The first non-British ship to be allocated to this service, she left Southampton for the first time on 6 December 1955, and served in this role for the next 18 months. It was then decided to use *Fairsea* on a round-the-world route from Britain to Australia.

In February 1957, *Fairsea* crossed the Tasman for the first time to visit New Zealand, then crossed the Pacific for her first transit of the Panama Canal. In July 1957, *Fairsea* made the first of three round trips from Bremerhaven to New York, then was withdrawn for six months to undergo an extensive refit. The appearance of the ship was changed considerably, as the superstructure was raised one deck, and the forward section plated in. Internally, full air-conditioning was installed, the accommodation improved, and new public rooms added in a deckhouse forward. Emerging in April 1958, her tonnage had been increased to 13 432 gross. *Fairsea* offered accommodation for 1460 tourist class passengers, and she was transferred from Panamanian to Italian registry, and the ownership of Sitmar Line. *Fairsea* continued to carry British migrants to Australia under a government contract.

Fairsea voyaged regularly between Britain and Australia, and in 1961 was given another extensive refit, during which the accommodation was further

upgraded, and capacity reduced to 1212 in one class. On 7 July 1966, *Fairsea* departed Sydney on her first cruise, visiting Hayman Island, Brisbane and Melbourne, immediately followed by her second cruise, to Cairns, Hayman Island and Melbourne. At that time, Sitmar were not heavily involved in cruising, and *Fairsea* made very few such trips. In 1968, *Fairsea* reverted to Panamanian registry again, her registered owners being Passenger Liner Services Inc. She still operated as a unit of the Sitmar fleet, but was due to be withdrawn in 1970.

On 14 January 1969, *Fairsea* left Sydney for New Zealand and Britain, with 986 passengers on board. On 29 January, an engine room fire disabled the vessel when she was midway between Tahiti and Panama. The freighter *Louise Lykes* arrived on the scene, and towed *Fairsea* to Balboa, where she arrived on 3 February, with her passengers still on board. They were all flown to their destinations from Panama, while *Fairsea* was inspected to decide her future. Being one of a very few ships to have been fitted with Doxford geared diesels, spare parts were no longer available, and it would have been necessary to have new parts designed and manufactured to repair the damage. This was considered to be uneconomic, so she was sold to shipbreakers in Italy. On 9 July 1969, *Fairsea* left Panama under tow of the tug *Vortice*, arriving on 6 August 1969 at La Spezia.

INDIAN PASSENGER SHIPS

BUILT: *1947/48 by Lithgows Ltd, Port Glasgow*
TONNAGE: *7026 gross*
DIMENSIONS: *451 × 60 ft (137.5 × 18.3 m)*
SERVICE SPEED: *14.5 knots*
PROPULSION: *Triple expansion/single screw*

One of the more unusual episodes in the story of post-war emigration to Australia concerned the voyages made by two Indian owned vessels, which were renamed for the outbound voyage only. Built in Scotland, they were delivered as *Mohammedi* in 1947 and *Mozaffari* in 1948 to the Mogul Line, which was a subsidiary of P & O between 1913 and 1960. The company operated a mixed fleet, mostly cargo ships, but a few vessels capable of carrying passengers, or pilgrims. This pair were given cabin accommodation for ten deluxe and 52 first class passengers, and operated from Bombay to the Red Sea. During the pilgrim season, they could also carry 1390 passengers in the 'tween decks and cargo holds.

Early in 1950, both ships were chartered to make a single voyage to Australia from Malta with migrants. Although the reason is not clear, they had to be renamed for the outward voyage, the change being effected at Aden as the ships were en route to Malta to collect their passengers. *Mozaffari* was renamed *Ocean Victory*, and departed Malta on 24 February 1950, calling at Port Said four days later. It must have been a long voyage to Fremantle, which was reached on 24 March, then on to Melboune, arriving on 30 March. The voyage terminated in Sydney on 2 April, where all the emigrants disembarked. Next day, the name of the ship was changed back to *Mozaffari*, as which she left Sydney on 5 April bound for Port Lincoln. A cargo of wheat was loaded, and on 22 April *Mozaffari* left for India.

Mohammedi followed her sister to Malta, being renamed *Ocean Triumph*. She left Malta on 23 March 1950, arriving in Fremantle on 22 April, and Melbourne on 28 April, before terminating in Sydney on 1 May. As soon as the migrants were disembarked, her name was changed back to *Mohammedi*, and she remained in port loading cargo until 25 May, then departed for Calcutta.

At the time of these voyages, both ships had white hulls, but these were later repainted black. The pair spent the rest of their careers in the services for which they were built. *Mozaffari* was laid up in Bombay on 11 February 1977, and sold to local shipbreakers six months later. *Mohammedi* arrived in Bombay for the last time on 24 February 1978, and was also laid up. In July 1978 she was sold to the local shipbreakers.

OCEAN VICTORY IN MELBOURNE

SONTAY

BUILT: *1921 by Bremer Vulkan, Vegesack*
TONNAGE: *8917 gross*
DIMENSIONS: *469 × 58 ft (144.3 × 17.8 m)*
SERVICE SPEED: *13 knots*
PROPULSION: *Triple expansion/single screw*

Messageries Maritimes were operating a rather sporadic schedule on their Australian service for several years after the war, relying on some of their older vessels assisted by chartered tonnage. Several of their ships made only a single voyage to Australia, one of which was *Sontay*.

This vessel was built to the order of Hamburg America Line, being launched on 2 June 1921 as the *Bayern*. Along with a sister ship, *Wuttemberg*, she was designed as a supplementary liner for the lucrative migrant trade between Germany and America. Permanent cabin accommodation was provided for 16 cabin class passengers, with austere quarters for 750 third class set up in the holds for the westbound voyage. On the return trip, the temporary berths would be removed to make way for cargo. *Bayern* departed Hamburg on 13 September 1921 on her maiden voyage to New York, but only served on this route until December 1923.

Early in 1924, *Bayern* and *Wuttemberg* were transferred to another major Hamburg America Line route, from Germany to South America. *Bayern* spent the rest of her career under the German flag on this route. During 1930, a low pressure turbine was added to the existing machinery, to increase speed and economy.

On 8 December 1936, *Bayern* was sold by Hamburg America Line to Messageries Maritimes, and hoisted the French flag as *Sontay*, joining the main Messageries Maritimes trade from Marseilles to French colonies in South East Asia. Her passenger arrangements were not altered, though the third class was often used by troops. From 1940 to 1945, *Sontay* operated under Allied control, being managed by Union Castle Line. On being handed back to Messageries Maritimes, *Sontay* resumed her pre-war trade to South East Asia.

On 5 August 1950, *Sontay* departed Marseilles on her first and only voyage to Australia, stopping at Malta to collect further migrants. *Sontay* arrived in Fremantle on 9 September, then proceeded directly to Sydney, berthing at No. 1 Circular Quay on 19 September. All her migrant passengers were disembarked in Sydney during a five day layover, then on 24 September *Sontay* left, bound for Haiphong.

Sontay spent the remainder of her career under the French flag on the trade to South East Asia. In February 1955, she was sold to a Panamanian company, Wheelock Marden & Co., though not handed over until 5 June. Renamed *Sunlock*, she operated as a general cargo ship until 1959, then was sold to shipbreakers in Japan.

SONTAY

A FORMER HOSPITAL SHIP

BUILT: *1920 by W. Denny & Sons Ltd, Dumbarton*
TONNAGE: *8173 gross*
DIMENSIONS: *484 × 59 ft (147.6 × 18 m)*
SERVICE SPEED: *13 knots*
PROPULSION: *Triple expansion/single screw*

This vessel was built as *Amarapoora* for The British & Burmese Steam Nav. Co., otherise known as P. Henderson & Co., a Glasgow based firm that traded to Burma. In her original guise she had seven holds, and provided accommodation for 146 first class passengers only. Her boilers were designed to burn either oil or coal, but in 1929 two boilers were converted to burn pulverised pellets in an experiment on behalf of Yarrows Ltd, who hoped to utilise this form of fuel in future ships. Unfortunately the tests were unsuccessful, and the ship even suffered a serious backfire whilst on a voyage to Rangoon, and reverted to oil-firing.

In 1935, *Amarapoora* was given an extensive refit, during which the passenger accommodation was upgraded, and capacity reduced to 124, still first class, by introducing more single and twin berth cabins. At the same time, all the public rooms were also refurbished and upgraded, and the forward end of the promenade deck was glassed in. Similar alterations were made at the same time to her sister ship, *Pegu*, but that vessel was wrecked at the mouth of the Mersey in November 1939.

In September 1939, *Amarapoora* was requisitioned and converted into a hospital ship, attached to the Royal Navy. She was based at Scapa Flow until October 1942, when she went to Gibraltar, and later to Salerno after the landings there. In July 1944, following a refit, *Amarapoora* was sent to Ceylon, and finished the war based at Trincomalee.

Handed back to Henderson's early in 1946, they did not wish to return the ship to their service, and instead sold her to the Ministry of Transport in June 1946. Henderson's continued to provide crew for the ship, and managed her on behalf of the government. Still retaining her hospital fittings, *Amarapoora* became a "mercy ship", and among her duties during this period of her career, brought French soldiers home from Saigon to Toulon and repatriated German prisoners-of-war. Her hospital ship role finally ended in 1948, when

all the fittings were removed on the Clyde, and *Amarapoora* was reconditioned to carry displaced persons under an IRO charter. Austere quarters for 617 persons was installed, and on 1 August 1950 *Amarapoora* left Genoa on her first voyage to Australia. This phase of her career lasted two years, when the IRO charter ended, and *Amarapoora* left Australia for the last time.

The Ministry of Transport offered the ship to the New Zealand Government to transport British migrants. The offer was accepted, but first *Amarapoora* was sent to the Glasgow shipyard of Alex Stephen & Sons for an extensive upgrading and refit. Accommodation for 584 persons was installed, and when the work was completed, the ship was renamed *Captain Hobson*. Still managed and crewed by Henderson's, she left Glasgow on 15 July 1952 on her first voyage to New Zealand, voyaging through the Panama Canal to Wellington.

In August 1953, *Captain Hobson* was diverted to Hong Kong to collect British troops and return them to Britain. She made several more trooping voyages from the Far East over the next two years, and in January 1955 ran aground when leaving Singapore while en route from Japan to Britain. In July 1955, *Captain Hobson* was back on the New Zealand emigrant trade again, only to return to trooping duties in August 1956 at the time of the Suez crisis.

In December 1956, *Captain Hobson* returned to the New Zealand migrant service. In April 1957 she left Glasgow with 590 migrants aboard, but on 12 June, when two days out from Wellington, was disabled when the high pressure cylinder of her main engine fractured. The Port Line freighter *Port Macquarie* was close by, and connected a line to *Captain Hobson*, towing her to Auckland, where they arrived on 18 June. Temporary repairs were effected, and then the vessel limped back to Britain, where a new cylinder was fitted.

In May 1958, *Captain Hobson* left Glasow on her twelfth and final voyage to New Zealand, arriving in Wellington on 19 July. Once her migrants had disembarked, the vessel was sent to Bombay and laid up. In December 1958, *Captain Hobson* was sold to P. D. Marchessini & Co., but they resold her several weeks later to Japanese shipbreakers, Okushogi & Co., and she arrived at their Osaka yard on 18 March 1959.

A PRE-WAR PICTURE OF *AMARAPOORA*

AMARAPOORA AS AN EMIGRANT SHIP

SIBAJAK

BUILT: *1928 by Kon. Maats. de Schelde, Flushing*
TONNAGE: *12 226 gross*
DIMENSIONS: *530 × 62 ft (161.5 × 19.1 m)*
SERVICE SPEED: *17 knots*
PROPULSION: *Sulzer diesels / twin screws*

The Dutch Government encouraged emigration in the post-war years which resulted in a number of vessels built for the Dutch East Indies trade coming to Australia, one of them being *Sibajak*, which had been built for Rotterdam Lloyd.

Sibajak was launched on 2 April 1927, and entered service in February 1928. As built she carried 200 first, 196 second, 68 third and 34 fourth class passengers, but in 1935 was modernised, and altered to cater for 200 first, 250 second and 75 third class. *Sibajak* remained on the Dutch East Indies trade until Germany invaded Holland in May 1940. She was taken over by the British, under management of P & O Line, but still with her Dutch crew, as a troopship. In September 1946 the vessel visited Fremantle, Melbourne, Sydney and Brisbane, then returned to Rotterdam.

By this time the situation in the Dutch East Indies had changed, and there was little demand for passages from Holland. As a result, *Sibajak* was refitted to carry 956 passengers in one class, and then chartered to the Dutch Government to transport migrants to Australia.

On 15 April 1950 *Sibajak* left Rotterdam on her first post-war voyage as a passenger ship, going to Melbourne, from where she sailed on 22 May to Indonesia and back to Holland. Her second voyage departed Rotterdam in July, passing through Fremantle on 18 August, Melbourne on 24 August and arriving in Sydney two days later, returning again via Indonesia. This pattern was followed by the vessel for the next two years, which made four round trips each year.

In January 1952, *Sibajak* left Rotterdam on her first voyage to New Zealand, disembarking her migrants at Wellington. Over the next few years she would make a further six voyages to New Zealand, but was mainly used on the service to Australia. Between 1952 and 1955 *Sibajak* also made nine voyages across the Atlantic, again under charter to the Dutch Government. The first of these was in April 1952, from Rotterdam to Quebec, and later she visited Halifax and New York.

Sibajak remained in the migrant trade throughout the 1950s, but by 1959 demand for such passages was declining. In 1958 a round-the-world service was started jointly by Royal Rotterdam Lloyd and Nederland Line, in which *Sibajak* participated briefly, but she was now wearing out. On 23 June 1959 she left Rotterdam on her final voyage to New Zealand and Australia, terminating in Melbourne. On 8 August she left Melbourne bound for Hong Kong, where she arrived on 25 August and was handed over to shipbreakers.

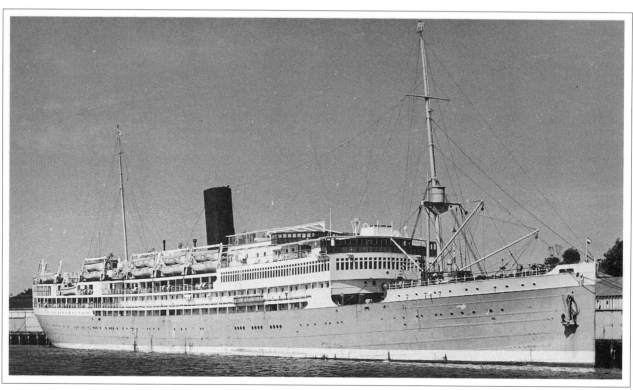

SIBAJAK

NEW AUSTRALIA

BUILT: *1931 by Vickers–Armstrong Ltd, Newcastle*
TONNAGE: *20 256 gross*
DIMENSIONS: *579 × 76 ft (176.6 × 23.3 m)*
SERVICE SPEED: *19 knots*
PROPULSION: *Turbo-electric/quadruple screws*

One of the best remembered of the migrant ships must be *New Australia*, which made 25 trips to Australia between August 1950 and September 1957. She was a most unusual looking vessel, yet started life as one of the most luxurious liners in the world.

She was launched as *Monarch of Bermuda* on 17 March 1931, and completed in November the same year, to the order of Furness Withy & Co., for the luxury service between New York and Bermuda. She was an outstanding ship, with three funnels, the last being a dummy, high superstructure, and accommodation for 830 first class passengers only, all in cabins with private facilities. In 1933 she was joined by a sister, *Queen of Bermuda*, and they were known as the "millionaire ships" during the 1930s. In September 1934, *Monarch of Bermuda* rushed to the rescue of the burning American liner, *Morro Castle*, off the New Jersey coast, rescuing 71 people.

In September 1939, *Monarch of Bermuda* was laid up in New York, then in November began service as a troopship. She collected 962 troops in Halifax and carried them to Gourock, then went to Liverpool where her luxury fittings were removed, and quarters for 1385 men installed. Early in 1940, *Monarch of Bermuda* was delegated to transport the bulk of bullion of the British Government, valued at some 690 million pounds. Departing the Clyde with a destroyer and cruiser escort, the convoy ran into very heavy weather, and eventually *Monarch of Bermuda* lost her escorts, and sped on alone. On the fourth day out, violent avoiding action was taken when two torpedoes were sighted coming towards the ship, but she reached Halifax safely, followed some days later by her battered escorts.

Monarch of Bermuda carried troops to Norway, being attacked by enemy bombers but escaping undamaged, and also carried children from Britain to Canada. In 1941 her trooping capacity was increased to 3250, and in August 1942 she was altered to carry landing craft, then took part in the North African landings, making three voyages with troops. She later took part in the landings on Sicily, and in 1943 had her troop capacity increased again, to 4050, though 5560 men could be carried by double berthing in some of the three-tiered bunks.

Monarch of Bermuda finished the war carrying troops

MONARCH OF BERMUDA

NEW AUSTRALIA

to the Pacific war, and returning with released prisoners-of-war. In July 1946 the liner was released from government service, having travelled 450 512 miles and carried 164 840 persons during her military career. She was sent to the Palmer shipyard at Hebburn-on-Tyne to be refitted for a return to her pre-war service. The work was well in hand when, on 24 March 1947, a fire broke out which completely gutted the ship. Furness Withy decided she was a total loss, and the hulk was towed away to Rosyth. The Argentine Government made a bid for the vessel, intending to rebuild her as a passenger ship, but the British Government refused to sanction the sale, and instead purchased the hulk on behalf of the Ministry of Transport early in 1948, after trials had shown her engines were still in working order.

The British and Australian Governments came to an agreement to use the ship to transport migrants. In April 1948 she arrived at the Southampton yard of John I. Thorneycroft & Co., to be rebuilt, the cost being shared equally between the British and Australian Governments. A new superstructure was constructed, not as high as the original, while the first and third funnels were not replaced. Instead a single large funnel was placed amidships, with a bipod mast erected where the forward funnel had been, which also served this function. Accommodation for 1600 persons was installed, with a large number of six-berth cabins, and also some four-berth and eight-berth cabins. All

contained two-tier metal bunks and wardrobes, but did not have washbasins, there being a large number of communal facilities throughout the ship. From being one of the most luxurious liners ever built, she was now the epitome of austerity. One concession to her former identity was the retention of the outdoor swimming pool aft.

In July 1949 the vessel was renamed *New Australia*, but her rebuilding was longer and more expensive than anticipated, so it was 18 July 1950 before she ran trials, only to have a steam pipe burst, scalding nine people. Two days later she achieved full power, and was accepted by the Ministry of Transport. She had been placed under the management of Shaw Savill Line, and her funnel was painted in their colours. Her first voyage departed Southampton on 15 August 1950, passing through Suez to reach Fremantle on 9 September, Adelaide on 13 September, Melbourne on 15 September and Sydney on 18 September. From there she went to Jakarta to board Dutch nationals and return them home.

The original plan was for the vessel to make three voyages to Australia each year with assisted migrants, returning empty, while in the northern summer she would ply the Atlantic. The Atlantic operation was abandoned, and instead the vessel was scheduled to make four return trips each year, and carry some fare-paying passengers on the return voyage.

In September 1953, *New Australia* was taken off the run, and carried British troops to Korea until April

ARKADIA

1954, when she resumed the emigrant service. She was diverted again in 1956, leaving Sydney on 8 March for the Far East, going to Kure and Inchon before returning to Sydney, then making her regular voyage back to Britain.

On 21 September 1957, the migrant charter terminated, and was not renewed. *New Australia* had left Southampton on 16 August on her final voyage to Australia, and on leaving Sydney went to Singapore, where she stayed 10 days, then returned to Sydney again on 31 October. Leaving on 2 November, she bypassed Melbourne, but stopped at Adelaide on 4 November, and departed Fremantle on 8 November, bound for Southampton, where she was laid up.

In January 1958 *New Australia* was sold to the Greek Line, and renamed *Arkadia*. She was sent to the Blohm & Voss shipyard in Hamburg for refitting, during which the superstructure was streamlined and a new, raked bow fitted. The accommodation was completely rebuilt to carry 150 first class and 1150 tourist class passengers. Repainted white, and looking very smart, *Arkadia* left Bremerhaven on 22 May 1958 on her first voyage, to Quebec and Montreal. This remained her basic trade, but in 1959 she made some cruises out of

New York, and in 1960 began cruising from Southampton. At the end of that year she returned to Blohm & Voss and was altered to carry only 50 first class, and 1337 tourist class, and the after end of the superstructure was glassed-in.

Arkadia alternated between Atlantic voyages and cruises until 1963, when she departed Bremerhaven on 23 October, and Tilbury two days later, bound for Australia. She arrived in Fremantle on 18 November, Melbourne five days later, and Sydney on 25 November, leaving next day to return to Europe. Whilst *Arkadia* was on this voyage, Greek Line suffered the loss of *Lakonia*, the former *Johan van Oldenbarnevelt*, so on her return *Arkadia* was put on the cruise service from Southampton in her place.

In May 1965 *Arkadia* suffered mechanical problems that kept her out of service until 3 July, and she spent most of 1966 cruising. On 21 November 1966 the vessel was withdrawn from service, and laid up in the River Fal. On 9 December she was sold to Spanish shipbreakers, arriving at their Valencia yard on 18 December. By a strange twist of fate, her former sister, *Queen of Bermuda*, was also sold to shipbreakers that month.

JOHAN VAN OLDENBARNEVELT

BUILT: *1930 by Nederland Shipbuilding Co., Amsterdam*
TONNAGE: *19 787 gross*
DIMENSIONS: *608 × 74 ft (185.4 × 22.8 m)*
SERVICE SPEED: *17 knots*
PROPULSION: *Sulzer diesels/twin screws*

During the years following the end of the war, there was considerable upheaval in the Dutch East Indies, as the local population fought for independence from their Dutch masters. Eventually they would win, and rename their country Indonesia, and it was this chain of events that resulted in *Johan van Oldenbarnevelt* becoming a familiar sight in Australian and New Zealand ports over a 12-year period.

This liner was built for the Nederland Line service from Holland to the Dutch East Indies. Launched on 3 August 1929, *Johan van Oldenbarnevelt* was named in honour of a sixteenth-century Dutchman executed by his political enemies. The vessel provided accommodation for 366 first, 280 second, 64 third and 60 fourth class passengers, and had 360 crew. On 7 May 1930 the liner left Amsterdam for Batavia, but while passing through the North Sea Canal came into collision with the small Dutch coaster *Reggestroom*, and had to return to port for repairs, sailing again several days later. In October 1930, she was joined by her sister ship, *Marnix van St Aldegonde*.

For the next nine years these ships operated regularly to the Dutch East Indies, but as war clouds gathered, *Johan van Oldenbarnevelt* was chartered by Holland America Line for a single return trip to New York, departing Amsterdam on 30 August 1939. She then made a return trip to Batavia, and was outward bound again when Holland was invaded. Both *Johan van Oldenbarnevelt* and her sister were taken over by the British as troopships, the former being converted by Harland & Wolff at Belfast. Both ships retained their Dutch crews, and on 6 November 1943, *Marnix van St Aldegonde* was torpedoed and sunk off Algeria. *Johan van Oldenbarnevelt* visited Australia several times during the war, to carry troops overseas, and in October 1945 was handed back to Nederland Line.

Refitted at Amsterdam, she returned to her pre-war service from Holland to Batavia in July 1946. As the revolt against Dutch rule intensified, demand for passages out to the area declined rapidly, so in 1950 Nederland Line withdrew *Johan van Oldenbarnevelt* from the route. Chartered by the Dutch Government to carry new settlers, the liner departed Amsterdam on 5 September 1950 on her first commercial voyage to Australia, calling at Malta en route, and arriving in Fremantle on 5 October, Melbourne on 10 October and Sydney two days later, leaving on 14 October for Jakarta, where she boarded Dutch nationals returning home. On 19 December she left Amsterdam on her second voyage, departing Sydney on 23 January 1951

ORIGINAL APPEARANCE OF *JOHAN VAN OLDENBARNEVELT*

for Surabaya, and then back to Amsterdam.

Johan van Oldenbarnevelt was then taken out of service for an extensive refit, to better suit her for the Australian migrant trade, being completely altered internally to carry 1414 passengers in a single class. On 23 January 1952, the liner departed Amsterdam bound for Australia again, and after leaving Sydney called at Surabaya on the return trip. She remained on the emigrant trade to Australia for the next seven years, though from 1954 to 1958 she was used for occasional voyages across the North Atlantic, making eleven trips in all to New York or Montreal.

In August 1958 the Dutch Government terminated their charter of *Johan van Oldenbarnevelt* at the end of her final Atlantic voyage, and Nederland Line decided to place her on a new round-the-world service. First she was sent back to her builder's yard for another refit, during which her accommodation was altered to cater for 1210 tourist class passengers. This consisted of 247 two-berth cabins, 90 three-berth, 81 four-berth, 6 five-berth and 5 large dormitories. The biggest alteration, though, was to the external appearance of the liner, as her original squat funnels were heightened and given round tops, the mainmast removed and the foremast shortened, and a new signal mast installed behind the bridge. Her hull, which had always been black, was repainted light grey, and all these changes increased her to 20 314 gross tons.

On 3 April 1959, *Johan van Oldenbarnevelt* left Amsterdam on her first voyage on the new route, calling first at Southampton, then through Suez to Fremantle on 30 April, Melbourne on 5 May and Sydney on 8 May, leaving next day for Wellington, where she arrived on 13 May. The liner then continued across the Pacific to the Panama Canal and back to Amsterdam, with calls at Port Everglades and New

York. Her schedule called for four trips per year, but unfortunately this new service was not a success, despite the addition of extra ports of call along the way. Nederland Line persevered with the route for three years, but then decided to withdraw *Johan van Oldenbarnevelt* from service.

Her final round-the-world voyage departed Amsterdam on 30 June 1962, then on 29 September she left for Australia and New Zealand. On reaching Wellington, *Johan van Oldenbarnevelt* turned back to Sydney, and then went to Fremantle, serving as a floating hotel during the Commonwealth Games in Perth. Leaving Fremantle on 2 December, she returned to Sydney, and made two cruises to New Zealand, departing on 9 December and 23 December. Two return trips between Sydney and Wellington followed. *Johan van Oldenbarnevelt* had been sold to the Greek Line by the time she berthed in Sydney for the last time on 3 February 1963, and she left empty the same day bound for Genoa.

Handed over to her new owners on 8 March, she was renamed *Lakonia*, and given a quick refit at Genoa, being repainted white, but work on the interior was still in progress when she arrived at Southampton to begin her new career as a cruise liner. Her first cruise departed on 24 April, going to Madeira, Teneriffe and Las Palmas.

Lakonia was on her eighteenth cruise out of Southampton when, on 22 December 1963, a fire broke out and quickly spread through the liner, which was 200 miles from Madeira. Her calls for assistance were quickly answered, but of her 1028 passengers, 128 lost their lives. On 24 December the Dutch salvage tug *Herkules* took *Lakonia* in tow, but on 29 December 1963 the liner sank some 250 miles west of Gibraltar.

IN 1959 THE SHIP WAS GIVEN A LIGHT GREY HULL

BRASIL

BUILT: *1905 by A. Stephen & Sons Ltd, Glasgow*
TONNAGE: *11 182 gross*
DIMENSIONS: *538 × 60 ft (164 × 18.4 m)*
SERVICE SPEED: *17 knots*
PROPULSION: *Geared turbines/triple screws*

Brasil was the second of a pair of sisters built for the Allan Line that made maritime history, being the first large liners to be fitted with geared turbine engines. The first ship was named *Victorian*, while the second was launched on 22 December 1904 as *Virginian*. Completed in March 1905, she departed Liverpool on her maiden voyage to Canada, providing accommodation for 426 first class, 286 second class and 940 third class passengers.

In August 1914, *Virginian* was requisitioned by the British Government and became a troopship, but three months later was converted into an armed merchant cruiser, serving with the 10th Cruiser Squadron. In October 1915, the Allan line was bought by Canadian Pacific, to whom *Virginian* was handed when released from government service in January 1920. The following month the liner was sold to Swedish America Line, and renamed *Drottningholm*.

In 1922 *Drottningholm* was refitted to carry 532 cabin class and 854 third class, and also given new De Laval geared turbine machinery. The liner served on the New York trade for 20 years, then served during the war under the auspices of the International Red Cross. *Drottningholm* became famous as a "mercy ship", transporting over 25 000 prisoners-of-war and civilian internees being exchanged by the belligerent powers. In March 1946, *Drottningholm* returned to the Gothenburg–New York trade, making the first post-war trans-Atlantic sailing by any company from Europe. In 1948, the vessel was sold to Home Line, registered in Panama, and renamed *Brasil*, for service from Genoa to South America. During 1950, *Brasil* was transferred to operate between Naples and New York.

On 12 October 1950, under charter to the IRO, *Brasil* boarded 1172 displaced persons in Bremerhaven, to bring to Australia. After calling at Fremantle on 12 November, *Brasil* proceeded directly to Sydney, where she berthed at 13 Pyrmont on 18 November. *Brasil* left empty on 22 November, passing through Fremantle again on 28 November, and returning to Italy. The vessel was then extensively refitted, to carry 96 first class and 846 tourist class passengers.

Renamed *Homeland*, she operated from Hamburg and Southampton to New York between June 1951 and March 1952, when she returned to the Genoa–New York trade. Her final voyage was to South America, returning to Genoa in February 1955, then on 29 March 1955 the old liner arrived in Trieste to be broken up.

BRASIL

ROMA

BUILT: *1914 by Newport News Shipbuilding & Drydock Co., Newport News*
TONNAGE: *6530 gross*
DIMENSIONS: *410 × 54 ft (125 × 16.4 m)*
SERVICE SPEED: *15 knots*
PROPULSION: *Triple expansion/single screw*

Roma made only a single voyage to Australia, but has a place in maritime history due to the length of her career, which spans three-quarters of a century. She was launched on 22 August 1914 as the cargo ship *Medina*, for the Mallory Steamship Co., an American coastal line. Her sister, *Neches*, was also built in 1914, but sunk four years later. *Medina* was designed for service along the west coast of America, but on completion made a couple of trips across the Atlantic.

Medina remained in the coastal trade between the wars, her owners becoming Clyde–Mallory Line after a merger in 1932, and then AGWI Lines after a further amalgamation in 1934. *Medina* remained on the coastal trades throughout World War Two, though under government control, then was offered for sale when returned to her owners.

In 1948 the vessel was purchased by Cia. San Miguel S. A. of Panama, and sent to La Spezia to be converted into a passenger carrier. The original small central superstructure and tall, thin funnel were removed, being replaced by a new, much larger superstructure, topped by a squat funnel, and a raked bow added. Internally, the cargo holds were converted into accommodation for 950 persons.

Renamed *Roma*, she was one of several ships chartered by the International Catholic Travel Committee to carry pilgrims from America to Europe for the Holy Year celebrations in Rome. Her first voyage was from New York on 19 June 1950 to Cherbourg, followed by two further trips under the charter. *Roma* then returned to Bremerhaven to undertake a voyage to Australia, leaving on 31 October 1950. She arrived in Fremantle on 9 December after a slow voyage, then went directly to Newcastle, where she berthed on 18 December, and disembarked her 950 passengers. On returning to Europe, *Roma* was laid up and offered for sale.

Her engines were now worn out after forty years service, but in 1952 the vessel was bought by Giacamo Costa fu Andrea, known as the Costa Line. They had her re-engined with Fiat diesels, and renamed her *Franca C*. The vessel was placed on a regular service from Italy to South America, carrying 925 passengers in three classes, but in 1953 she was withdrawn and given an extensive refit. The superstructure was streamlined, and luxury accommodation for 370 passengers installed, with all cabins having private facilities, and the entire ship being fully air-conditioned. *Franca C* then became one of the first permanent cruise liners. She operated in the Mediterranean most of the year, and was highly successful.

In 1970, despite her hull being over fifty years old, *Franca C* was given another new set of Fiat diesels, and she remained as a cruise ship in the Costa fleet until 1977. She was then offered for sale, and amazingly was bought for further trading by Operation Mobilisation, who took over the ship on 4 November 1977. Renamed *Doulos*, which is Greek for servant, she has since been used as a floating book display. *Doulos* has visited ports throughout the world, and in 1989 called at seven ports in Australia: Devonport, Melbourne, Adelaide, Sydney, Newcastle, Brisbane and Townsville.

ROMA

RAVELLO

BUILT: *1941 by Cant. Nav. Riuniti, Genoa*
TONNAGE: *8452 gross*
DIMENSIONS: *473 × 63 ft (145.5 × 19.4 m)*
SERVICE SPEED: *13 knots*
PROPULSION: *Fiat diesel/single screw*

Flotta Lauro were the owners of a fleet of over 50 cargo ships and tankers when Italy came into the war on the Axis side in June 1940. At that time they had a vessel under construction in Genoa, which was completed in 1941 as *Ravello*. A cargo ship, she was immediately placed under Italian Government control, and would be one of the very few Italian ships to survive the war years unscathed. The Flotta Lauro fleet was decimated during the war, so the company was very grateful to have *Ravello* returned to them. To rebuild his company, Achille Lauro purchased second-hand vessels, even wrecks, and refitted them to suit his purposes.

During 1948, Flotta Lauro rebuilt the wreck of a British freighter into the emigrant ship *Napoli*, which was placed on a service to Australia. Meanwhile, *Ravello* was operating as a cargo ship, but the results from *Napoli* were so good that in 1949 *Ravello* was taken in hand for rebuilding as an emigrant ship as well. The original superstructure was extended aft, and dormitory accommodation installed for some 480 persons. Although the facilities provided were extremely austere, the displaced persons who comprised most of the passengers found it better than the camps in which they had existed for many years.

At the end of November 1950, *Ravello* departed Genoa on her first voyage to Australia with passengers, arriving at Fremantle on 4 January after a slow voyage. After a week in port, *Ravello* left for Melbourne, being there on 15 January, and eventually arrived in Sydney on 17 January. Having disembarked her passengers, *Ravello* then took on cargo, and several days later proceeded to Port Lincoln to complete loading, departing on 30 January for Genoa. In April 1951, the vessel departed Genoa on her second voyage to Australia, calling again at Fremantle, Melbourne and Sydney, from where she departed on 1 June bound for Genoa with a full cargo.

On 4 August 1951, *Ravello* left Genoa on what was to be her final voyage to Australia with passengers, calling at the same ports again, and loading cargo in Sydney before leaving on 9 October to return to Genoa. By this time Flotta Lauro had introduced two further ships to their Australian service, *Sydney* and *Roma*, which could adequately cater to the passenger trade. *Ravello* was therefore transferred to the service from Italy to ports in Central and South America.

This phase of her career lasted only a short while, before *Ravello* was again rebuilt. Her passenger accommodation was all removed, and the ship reverted to cargo status again. *Ravello* served in the Flotta Lauro fleet in this capacity until she was laid up at La Spezia on 28 May 1971. In August that year the vessel was sold to local shipbreakers.

RAVELLO

A FORMER BURNS PHILP LINER

BUILT: *1917 by Reiherstieg Co., Hamburg*
TONNAGE: *7474 gross*
DIMENSIONS: *442 × 55 ft (134.7 × 16.7 m)*
SERVICE SPEED: *14 knots*
PROPULSION: *Quadruple expansion/twin screws*

This vessel made two voyages to Australia with migrants, but prior to the war had been well known in local waters as the *Marella*, operated by Burns Philp. She was ordered by the Woermann Line for a service between Germany and South Africa, and launched on 6 June 1914 as *Hilda Woermann*. Completion was delayed by the war, and in 1917 the vessel was renamed *Wahehe*, only to be claimed by the British as a prize in 1918. Placed under Shaw Savill management, she made three voyages to Australia between May 1919 and June 1920, as a troopship. Burns Philp purchased *Wahehe* from the British Government in November 1920, and she was refitted in Sydney and renamed *Marella*.

Under this name, the vessel operated between Sydney and Singapore for the next 20 years, having accommodation for 165 first and 75 second class passengers. In 1941, *Marella* again became a troopship, and spent the war in the South Pacific. Late in 1946 she was returned to Burns Philp, and resumed the trade to Singapore, until leaving Sydney for the last time on 2 November 1948, having been sold.

In Singapore *Marella* was handed over to Cia. Nav. Baru, a Panama concern, and renamed *Captain Marcos*. Sent to Italy for refitting, all cargo spaces were converted into passenger accommodation, increasing her capacity to 929 persons. She made a voyage from Genoa to Valparaiso in October 1949, then was renamed *Liguria*, and used in the summer of 1950 to carry pilgrims from America to Italy.

On 19 November 1950, *Liguria* left Bremerhaven with 950 persons aboard, bound for Australia. It was a slow voyage, and on 15 January 1951 the vessel suffered serious engine problems when 200 miles from Fremantle, and had to be towed to port by the British India Line cargo ship *Chandpara*, arriving on 17 January. *Liguria* spent eight months in Fremantle being repaired, her passengers having to find their own way to their destinations. After a dispute over payment for the repairs was settled, *Liguria* left Fremantle on 18 August.

Her name was then changed to *Corsica*, though still under the same ownership and on 17 December 1951 she left Limassol in Cyprus for Australia again, arriving in Fremantle on 25 January 1952, and Melbourne on 4 February, where she was arrested three days later. Two weeks later *Corsica* departed, and called at Adelaide on 24 February on her voyage back to Europe.

In August 1952, *Corsica* was laid up at Casablanca, and remained idle until October 1954, when she was sold to Belgian shipbreakers. On 14 November, the old liner arrived at their Ghent yard under tow.

LIGURIA

FLORENTIA

BUILT: *1914 by W. Denny & Bros. Ltd, Dumbarton*
TONNAGE: *7821 gross*
DIMENSIONS: *484 × 58 ft (147.6 × 17.6 m)*
SERVICE SPEED: *13 knots*
PROPULSION: *Triple expansion/single screw*

Florentia was completed in November 1914 as the *Burma* for P. Henderson & Co., otherwise known as the British & Burmese Steam Navigation Co. Ltd, being coal-fired, and providing accommodation for 120 passengers. Nothing is known of the war service of *Burma*, but it is likely she was taken over by the British Government at some stage. In the early 1920s, the vessel was converted to oil-firing, and partnered by *Amarapoora* and her sister, *Pegu*, on the trade from Glasgow to Rangoon.

It was an unspectacular career until 1940, when *Burma* was requisitioned by the government and converted into a troopship. She was employed mainly in the Indian Ocean, running troops between Suez and India, but also made some trips to East Africa and South Africa. On 23 December 1943 *Burma* ran aground off Mombasa, and was not refloated until 10 April 1944. Following repairs, she returned to her trooping duties, and was retained in this capacity until 1948.

When her requisition was terminated, *Burma* was handed back to Henderson's, but they had no desire to use the ship again, as she was 34 years old, and the post-war trade to Burma was not as strong as in the pre-war years. *Burma* was offered for sale, and early in 1949 purchased by Cia. Nav. Florencia, a Panamanian

concern. Renamed *Florentia*, she was fitted out to transport displaced persons under an IRO contract, with austere accommodation.

On 15 December 1950, *Florentia* departed Malta on her first voyage to Australia, reaching Fremantle on 14 January 1951, then visiting Melbourne. Arriving in Sydney on 26 January, the vessel remained in port for three weeks loading cargo, which she carried to Port Sudan, then went on to Haifa before returning to Genoa. For this voyage, *Florentia* had a black hull, but during 1951 she was repainted white when transferred to the ownership of Cia. Florentina de Nav., and placed under the Italian flag.

In this guise, *Florentia* made two voyages to Australia, both from Genoa. The first departed in April, visiting Fremantle, Melbourne and Sydney, from where she departed on 11 June. *Florentia* departed Genoa on her third and final voyage to Australia on 18 August, calling at Fremantle on 22 September and Melbourne on 28 September before arriving in Sydney on 7 October. From there the vessel went to Port Thevenard in South Australia to load cargo, departing on 27 October bound for Cyprus.

Although she made no further voyages to Australia, *Florentia* continued to serve under that name until 1953, when she was sold to the Pan-Islamic Steamship Co., a Pakistani firm who were building up a fleet of old passenger vessels for the pilgrim trade to Jeddah. Renamed *Safina-E-Nusrat*, she served a further four years, then was sold to shipbreakers in Karachi in September 1957.

FLORENTIA

JENNY

BUILT: *1918 by Workman, Clark & Co. Ltd, Belfast*
TONNAGE: *7914 gross*
DIMENSIONS: *465 × 58 ft (141.7 × 17.7 m)*
SERVICE SPEED: *14 knots*
PROPULSION: *Triple expansion/twin screws*

During World War One, there were several series of ships built as replacements for losses. *Jenny* had her beginnings as a "G" class British standard ship, of which 22 were ordered by the shipping controller, being designed as fast refrigerated cargo liners. However, none of these ships were completed by the end of the war, as the first, named *War Argus*, only ran trials on 12 December 1918.

War Argus remained under government control through 1919, but then the British Government began disposing of such tonnage to enable shipping companies to rebuild their depleted fleets. *War Argus* was sold in January 1920 to the famous White Star Line, best known for their passenger liners. However, White Star also operated a large cargo fleet, and they renamed their new acquisition *Gallic*, placing her on their cargo service between Britain and Australia.

When White Star Line ceased to exist as a separate entity, their ships and services were either taken over by other companies, or sold. In the case of *Gallic*, she was sold in 1933 to another famous British company, Clan Line, and renamed *Clan Colquhoun*. Under this name she operated a variety of cargo services, and remained in commercial operation throughout World War Two. In 1947, the vessel was sold again, to Zarata Steamship

Co., of Panama, which was part of the Greek Livanos Group, and the ship was renamed *Ioannis Livanos*. This lasted only a brief time, as in 1948 she was transferred within the Livanos Group to the ownership of Dos Oceanos Cia. de Nav. SA, also a Panamanian company, and renamed *Jenny*.

It was at this time that the vessel was refitted to carry passengers. Very basic temporary facilities were installed in the holds for about 290 persons, and the original three island deckhouses joined together to form a low superstructure. Just how many voyages with displaced persons or migrants this ship made is uncertain, but it is known that she made a single voyage to Australia. This departed Genoa on 20 January 1951, and it was a very slow trip, as *Jenny* did not reach Fremantle until 26 February, then arrived in Melbourne on 7 March. After a lengthy stay, the vessel continued on to Sydney, berthing on 20 March for another long stay. After her passengers were disembarked, the vessel loaded cargo, and did not depart until 17 April, bound for Egypt.

In 1952 *Jenny* was sold to Djarkarta Lloyd and renamed *Imam Bobdjol*, which was soon changed to *Djatinegra*. After three years of further service, she was sold to Japanese shipbreakers late in 1955, and left Jakarta under tow of the tug *Golden Cape* bound for Osaka. However, on 1 December *Djatinegra* sprang a leak, and had to be beached at Lingayen. Refloated on 21 February 1956, she was towed first to Manila, and then to Hong Kong, where she was broken up during June 1956.

JENNY

CHARTERED BY THE FRENCH

BUILT: *1950/1951 by Scotts Shipbuilding & Engineering Co., Greenock*
TONNAGE: *9393/9403 gross*
DIMENSIONS: *477 × 62 ft (145.3 × 18.9 m)*
SERVICE SPEED: *15 knots*
PROPULSION: *Scotts diesel/single screw*

These two ships were ordered soon after the war ended by China Navigation Co., of Hong Kong, to replace war losses on their major trade along the coast of China and on to the Malay peninsula. First to be launched was *Chungking*, on 19 January 1950, while *Changchow* was launched on 31 July the same year. They were fitted out with accommodation for about 180 passengers in two classes.

These two ships were ordered in the expectation that the pre-war trade would be revived, but the rapidly changing political situation in China, and the eventual Communist victory, was to prevent this occurring. China Navigation thus found themselves in a peculiar position, having no need for two brand-new ships at a time when many companies were still desperately short of modern tonnage. One such company was Messageries Maritimes, who were struggling to re-establish their vast network of routes, having only aging ships at their disposal. Messageries Maritimes were able to charter *Chungking* and *Changchow* when they were completed, and placed them on their service from France to the South Pacific.

Chungking was the first to enter service, departing Marseilles late in December 1950. After passing through the Panama Canal, the vessel called at Tahiti and Noumea before arriving in Sydney on 8 February 1951, departing eight days later for the return voyage. *Changchow* departed Marseilles on 6 March 1951, following the same route to arrive in Sydney for the first time on 30 April.

This pair would form the backbone of the Messageries Maritimes service to Australia for two years. In 1951, *Chungking* made three trips, while *Changchow* made two, and both ships made two trips in 1952. On 1 September 1952, *Chungking* arrived in Sydney for the fifth and last time, and on her return to France was handed back to China Navigation. She was replaced by the new *Caledonien*.

China Navigation still had no service on which to operate *Chungking*, and in December 1952 the vessel was sold to the British Admiralty, for eventual conversion into a fleet replenishment ship. Renamed *Retainer*, she was chartered out by the Admiralty to Buries Marks until July 1954, when she arrived at the Palmers shipyard on the Tyne. Her conversion into a storeship was completed in April 1955.

Changchow remained on the Messageries Maritime service, but in April 1953 she too was bought by the

CHUNGKING

CHANGCHOW

Admiralty for future conversion into a fleet replenishment ship. *Changchow* had left Sydney on 3 January 1953, and on 25 April she was renamed *Resurgent*, then placed under the management of British India Line. However, the charter to Messageries Maritimes continued, and the ship arrived in Sydney as *Resurgent* for the first time on 11 August. *Resurgent* followed a pattern of alternate voyages to Sydney, every second voyage terminating in Noumea.

On 31 October 1956, *Resurgent* departed Marseilles on her final voyage to Australia, leaving Sydney on 24 December. On her return to Marseilles, the vessel was handed back to her owner, and replaced on the Australian trade by another chartered ship, *Melanesien*. *Resurgent* also went to the Palmer shipyard for conversion into an armament stores issuing ship, in which capacity she joined the Far East Fleet of the Royal Navy, based on Hong Kong.

The conversion did not extensively alter the external appearance of either ship, which were painted warship grey, and had a thick black band around the top of their funnels. On 29 October 1966, *Resurgent* arrived in Sydney again, as part of a Royal Navy flotilla led by HMS *Victorious* which came for joint exercises with the Royal Australian Navy.

Resurgent eventually returned to British waters, where *Retainer* had spent most of her career. In April 1978, *Retainer* was decommissioned, and laid up at Rosyth, being joined there in June 1979 by *Resurgent*, and both ships were offered for sale. On 24 September 1979, *Retainer* was sold to Spanish shipbreakers, leaving Rosyth under tow on 29 October, and arriving in Barcelona on 19 November 1979. *Resurgent* was idle longer, until sold on 18 March 1981 to Asturamerican Shipping Co. Inc., a Panamanian concern. They immediately resold the ship to Spanish shipbreakers, and *Resurgent* left Rosyth under tow on 5 May 1981. She arrived in Avilez on 13 March, where some superstructure was removed to enable her to be towed up the river to Gijon, where the final dismantling of the ship was completed.

STELLA POLARIS

BUILT: *1927 by Gotaverken, Gothenburg*
TONNAGE: *5209 gross*
DIMENSIONS: *416 × 51 ft (126.8 × 15.5 m)*
SERVICE SPEED: *16 knots*
PROPULSION: *B & W diesels/twin screws*

Stella Polaris was built as a luxury cruising yacht for the Bergen Line, a Norwegian company. Her career was interrupted when the Germans invaded Norway in 1940. *Stella Polaris* was recovered by her owner when the war ended, but was in a very poor condition.

Sent back to her builder's yard for reconditioning, with accommodation for 165 passengers in what was considered the height of luxury for that era. In June 1946, *Stella Polaris* returned to cruise service, being used for world cruises on occasion.

It was in the course of her third world cruise that *Stella Polaris* called at Darwin, being in port on 19 February 1951, the ninth anniversary of the Japanese air raids on the town, in 1942.

The Darwin Town Management Board were concerned as to how the American tourists aboard *Stella Polaris* would find enough to see and do in the town, so decided to arrange a corroboree, to be performed at one of the Aboriginal settlements outside the town.

Transporting the passengers from the ship to the settlement then posed a problem, so advertisements appeared in the local newspaper requesting people with cars to volunteer their services to drive the American tourists to and from the corroboree.

A further problem arose with the early arrival of the north west monsoon, which brought torrential rain for the two weeks preceding the arrival of *Stella Polaris*, causing major flooding. Despite this, the corroboree went on as planned, and by all accounts was a great success.

One person who did not find the *Stella Polaris* to his liking was a Norwegian seaman, who jumped ship, and gave himself up to the police an hour after the cruise ship left harbour. Hoping to be allowed to stay in Australia, he was instead deported back to his native Norway.

So ended the only visit to Australia of *Stella Polaris*. In October 1951, Bergen Line sold her to the Clipper Line, of Sweden. For the next 18 years she continued to operate year-round cruises, but *Stella Polaris* was withdrawn from service in 1969. Instead of being doomed to the scrap yard, she was purchased by a Japanese firm. Renamed *Scandinavia*, the beautiful vessel was taken to Shizoura, a resort area near Tokyo, where she is still in service today as a floating hotel.

STELLA POLARIS

CARONIA

BUILT: *1949 by John Brown & Co., Clydebank*
TONNAGE: *34 183 gross*
DIMENSIONS: *715 × 91 ft (217.9 × 27.8 m)*
SERVICE SPEED: *22 knots*
PROPULSION: *Geared turbines/twin screws*

Caronia was the first major passenger vessel to be built after the war, being launched on 30 October 1947 by Princess Elizabeth. When completed in January 1949, she was painted in three shades of green, and had one of the largest funnels ever fitted to a passenger liner.

Caronia was designed for a dual-purpose role, making Atlantic crossings to New York in the peak summer months, carrying 581 first class and 351 tourist class passengers, and at other times being a luxury cruise ship for about 600 passengers in one class.

On 22 December 1950, *Caronia* left New York on a 111 day cruise that took her to the South Pacific for the first time. She called at Auckland on 8 February, Wellington two days later, then arrived in Sydney on 13 February, staying in port four days.

On 23 January 1954, *Caronia* left New York for the South Pacific once again, this time including a visit to Melbourne, on 4 March, then coming to Sydney for a three-day stopover. Leaving on 8 March, *Caronia* headed north to Japan, becoming the first British cruise ship to visit that country since the war.

Over the next 12 years, *Caronia* made several more visits to Australia and New Zealand during her long cruises. Surprisingly, her accommodation was not fully air-conditioned until 1956. During 1965, *Caronia* was extensively refitted again, having a new lido deck added aft.

The final visit to the South Pacific by *Caronia* was in March 1967, by which time Cunard Line were considering withdrawing her from service. A sale to Yugoslav interests early in 1968 fell through, but in May that year she was sold to Universal Line, of Panama.

Renamed *Columbia*, she went to Piraeus for an extensive refit, and when the work was completed in December 1968, the vessel was renamed *Caribia*. She began cruising from New York, but was disabled by an engine room explosion on 11 March 1969, during a West Indies cruise. She managed to limp back to New York, arriving on 25 March, and was then laid up.

In January 1974, after five years idle, *Caribia* was sold to Taiwanese shipbreakers. Leaving New York under tow on 27 April, *Caribia* began taking water off Honolulu, but pumps were able to contain the situation Nearing Guam, the tow encountered very bad weather, and the tug suffered engine problems. On 12 August, *Caribia* was cut adrift, and the empty liner was blown onto the breakwater at the entrance to Apra Harbour in Guam, then broke into three pieces and sank.

CARONIA

Dutch 'Victory' Ships

GROOTE BEER

BUILT: 1944 by Permanente, Richmond, California
TONNAGE: 9190 gross
DIMENSIONS: 455 × 62 ft (138.7 × 18.9 m)
SERVICE SPEED: 17 knots
PROPULSION: Geared turbines/single screw

These three Dutch vessels were among 413 "Victory" ships built in America, their original names being *Costa Rica Victory*, *Cranston Victory* and *La Grande Victory*. "Victory" ships were designed as enlarged and improved versions of the famous "Liberty" cargo ships, built during the war in America. Towards the end of the war, 97 "Victory" ships were completed as transports, able to carry up to 1597 troops. Bunks were installed in the 'tween decks; and galleys, washrooms, hospital facilities and a few public rooms were added. The entire accommodation area was fitted with a ventilation system and heating. To support these additions, the hull and decks had to be strengthened, but by the time most of these ships were completed, the war was over.

Cranston Victory was launched on 5 May 1944, and on completion was operated for the US Maritime Commission by the South Atlantic Steamship Corp., of Savannah. *Costa Rica Victory* was launched on 17 June 1944, completed three months later, and operated for the government by the American Hawaiian Steamship Corp., of New York. Last of this trio to be launched was *La Grande Victory*, on 16 January 1945, which was managed by the Shepard Steamship Co., of Boston. All three ships were laid up in 1946, and offered for sale the following year.

Purchased during 1947 by the Dutch Government,

ZUIDERKRUIS AND WATERMAN

BUILT: 1944/45 by Oregon Shipbuilding Corp., Portland
TONNAGE: 9178/9176 gross
DIMENSIONS: 455 × 62 ft (138.7 × 18.9 m)
SERVICE SPEED: 17 knots
PROPULSION: Geared turbines/single screw

they were renamed after the three major star formations, the Great Bear, the Southern Cross and Aquarius. *Groote Beer* was placed under the management of Nederland Line, while *Zuiderkruis* and *Waterman* were managed by Royal Rotterdam Lloyd. The trio were refitted to carry troops to the Dutch East Indies, with accommodation for 276 in cabins and 575 in dormitories. They remained in this service over the next four years, then in 1951 were refitted again, for the emigrant trade.

Each vessel was sent in turn to the Nederland Dock Co. shipyard in Rotterdam, where an extra deck was added, and the bridge moved forward atop an extension to the superstructure. Internally, the accommodation was rebuilt to carry 830 persons in cabins. *Zuiderkruis* was the first to be altered, returning to service in June 1951 with a voyage from Rotterdam to New York, then was placed on a service to Canada. In August she left Rotterdam with 800 migrants bound for New Zealand. *Waterman* was the second of the trio to be reconstructed, but during 1951, *Groote Beer* made three voyages to Australia before being rebuilt, the first departing Rotterdam on 28 February to reach Fremantle on 21 March, Melbourne on 27 March and Sydney three days later. She then called at Surabaya on her way back to Holland, leaving Amsterdam on her second voyage to

WATERMAN

GROOTE BEER

Australia on 26 May to follow the same route. Her third voyage also left from Amsterdam, this time bound for New Zealand with 450 migrants, then going to Australia.

On 2 November 1951 *Groote Beer* arrived at Nederland Dockyard, while on 14 November, *Waterman* left Rotterdam on her first voyage to Australia, berthing in Fremantle on 9 December, Melbourne on 14 December and Sydney on 17 December. *Groote Beer* returned to service in May 1952, and on 18 June left Rotterdam on a voyage to New York, followed by a trip to Quebec. She was now being managed for the government by Holland–America Line, with *Zuiderkruis* being transferred to the management of Nederland Line.

Over the next decade, the three ships made periodic voyages to both Australia and New Zealand, as well as being employed on various Atlantic trades. In January 1961, the Dutch Government formed their own shipping company, N. V. Scheepsvaart Maats. Trans– Oceaan, to which these vessels were transferred, though remaining under the same management as before. Their accommodation was upgraded to tourist class, as the demand for emigrant passages was declining.

During November 1962, *Groote Beer* and *Waterman* were berthed in Fremantle to provide accommodation for visitors to the Commonwealth Games. In January 1963, *Waterman* departed Amsterdam on what was to be the last voyage to Australia and New Zealand by these

vessels under the Dutch flag, as later that year all three were sold by the Dutch Government. *Zuiderkruis* went to the Dutch Navy as an accommodation ship, based at Den Helder, while in September 1963 the other pair was sold to the Greek shipowner, John S. Latsis.

Waterman was renamed *Margareta*, while *Groote Beer* became *Marianna IV*, and both were used for economy services in the Mediterranean and across the Atlantic. However, on 2 December 1964, *Marianna IV* left Piraeus for Australia, arriving in Melbourne on 28 December and Sydney two days later, leaving on 2 January 1965 to return to Piraeus. For this voyage, the ship's funnel was painted in Chandris cargo line colours.

Both Latsis ships were used for student travel across the Atlantic during the summer months. On 12 July 1966, *Marianna IV* was leaving Southampton when she collided with the sand dredger *Pen Avon* off the Isle of Wight. *Marianna IV* returned to Piraeus for repairs, but no work was done, and instead the vessel was laid up in Eleusis Roads on 17 March 1967. Also during 1967, *Margareta* was withdrawn from service, and sold to the Yugoslav shipbreaking firm, Brodospas, being towed out of Piraeus on 10 November 1967 bound for Split.

Zuiderkruis remained with the Dutch Navy until being sold to local shipbreakers in Rotterdam on 29 October 1969, who then resold the ship to Spanish breakers at Bilbao, where she arrived under tow on 27 November. *Marianna IV* remained laid up until June 1970, when she was sold to local shipbreakers.

LLOYD TRIESTINO TRIO

BUILT: *1951 by Cant. Riuniti dell'Adriatico, Trieste*
TONNAGE: *12 839 gross*
DIMENSIONS: *528 × 69 ft (161 × 21.1 m)*
SERVICE SPEED: *18 knots*
PROPULSION: *Sulzer diesels/twin screws*

Lloyd Triestino had re-established its Australian service with old and chartered tonnage, but began a rebuilding programme as soon as possible after the war, ordering seven liners. Two were for their Far East route, two for the African trade, and three for the Australian service. This trio were the first to be built, and all were launched during 1950. The first was named *Australia* when launched on 21 May, the second *Oceania* on 30 July, with *Neptunia* following on 1 October. Accommodation was provided for 280 first class, 120 second class and 392 third class passengers, with a crew numbering 236.

Australia departed Trieste on her maiden voyage to Australia on 19 April 1951, reaching Fremantle on 11 May, Adelaide on 15 May, and Melbourne on 17 May. Departing three days later, *Australia* arrived in Sydney on 22 May, and terminated the voyage at Brisbane on 24 May. The return voyage was made along the same route, and the ship returned to Genoa, from which port all her future sailings would depart.

Oceania departed Genoa on her maiden voyage on 18 August, and *Neptunia* on 14 September, reaching Brisbane on 18 October. With these three ships in service, Lloyd Triestino was once again able to offer a regular schedule of modern liners, and it enjoyed extremely good passenger loadings over the next decade. When the Suez Canal was closed in 1956, the vessels were routed around South Africa. *Oceania* was the first vessel bound for Australia to pass through the canal when it re-opened in April 1957.

During 1958, each of the liners was withdrawn from service in turn for a refit, during which the forward well deck was filled in, the accommodation altered to cater for 136 first class and 536 tourist class, the latter being subdivided into 304 tourist A and 232 tourist B. At the same time, the air-conditioning was extended to encompass the entire ship. On 15 June 1958, *Australia* made a call at Newcastle to load wool and board passengers, being the first large passenger vessel to visit the port since the war.

The changes effected in 1958 verified the gradual drift away from first class accommodation to the more popular tourist class, and reflected the decline in the emigrant trade from Italy with the removal of third class. From October 1960, *Neptunia* began operating as a one-class ship, but the other two were not altered in a similar way.

The three ships continued to carry good loads in both directions, so in 1960 Lloyd Triestino placed orders for two large liners more than twice the size of the *Australia* trio, for the Australian trade. They were due in service during 1963, at which time these three liners would be withdrawn, and transferred to Italia Line, to replace three cargo/passenger liners on the service from Italy to Central America and the west coast of South America.

Australia was the first to be withdrawn, departing Genoa for the last time on 18 January 1963, and after leaving Sydney on 21 February, made a call at Hobart on 23 February, before going back to Melbourne, Adelaide and Fremantle, from where she sailed on 4 March for Genoa. *Australia* was then handed over to Italia Line, and renamed *Donizetti*, departing Genoa on 4 June on her first voyage to Valparaiso. *Oceania* made her final departure from Genoa on 15 February 1963, leaving Sydney on 23 March, and on being handed over to Italia Line was renamed *Rossini*.

The first of the new liners, *Galileo Galilei* entered service in April 1963, but work on her sister was delayed, so *Neptunia* was retained on the route. She made her final departure from Genoa on 7 August 1963, departing Sydney on 11 September, and on being transferred to Italia Line was renamed *Verdi*. Little alteration was made to the vessels for their new service. On 16 April 1964, *Verdi* collided with the tanker *Pentelikon* in fog off Gibraltar, suffering bow damage, and had to return to Genoa for repairs.

The service to South America was heavily subsidised by the Italian Government, but the amount required to keep the ships operating increased greatly during the 1970s. Eventually the Italian Government could no longer support the shipping services, and they were all abandoned. The first to go was the South American service, and the three ships were withdrawn within a matter of months.

Donizetti arrived at La Spezia on 15 October 1976 to be laid up, being joined by *Rossini* on 19 November, and finally *Verdi* was laid up on 26 January 1977. All three were offered for sale, with *Donizetti* and *Verdi* being purchased by shipbreakers at La Spezia in June 1977. At the same time *Rossini* was transferred to another Italian company, Tirrenia, but they had no use for the ship, and in September 1977 she was also sold to shipbreakers at La Spezia.

These three liners all came from the same shipyard within months of each other, spent their entire careers operating together, and ended their lives at the same place within months of each other.

NEPTUNIA

OCEANIA

SKAUBRYN

BUILT: *1951 by Oresundsvarvet, Landskrona and Howaldtswerke, Kiel*

TONNAGE: *9786 gross*

DIMENSIONS: *458 × 57 ft (139.6 × 17.3 m)*

SERVICE SPEED: *16 knots*

PROPULSION: *Gotaverken diesel/single screw*

Of the many ships that carried new settlers to Australia in the post-war years, it is surprising that only one was lost whilst engaged in this service. Considering the age and size of some of the ships used, it is even more surprising that the sole casualty should be one of the more modern vessels of a reasonable size. It is a pity that *Skaubryn* is mainly remembered for her unfortunate end, as she was one of the best ships placed on the migrant service in the early 1950s.

Skaubryn was ordered just after the war ended by Norwegian shipowner Isak M. Skaugen as a shelter deck cargo ship for one of his companies, D/S A/S Eikland. Launched on 7 October 1950, she was being fitted out when Skaugen decided to rebuild her as an emigrant carrier. He had entered the trade in 1949 with *Skaugum*, and saw the possibility of placing a second ship on the route to Australia. Consequently, *Skaubryn* was taken from the Oresundsvarvet yard to the

Howaldtswerke yard at Kiel, where *Skaugum* had been refitted for passenger service.

An extensive superstructure was constructed, while in the hull accommodation was installed for 1221 passengers, with two-, six- and eight-berth cabins for half that number, and dormitories for the remainder. Facilities provided included several lounges, three dining rooms plus a separate dining room for children, two cinemas, a 78 bed hospital, and a large playroom for young children, as well as an open-air swimming pool. Compared to other migrant carriers of that time, *Skaubryn* was a fine vessel, and also looked very smart. *Skaubryn* ran trials, achieving 17 knots, on 22 February 1951, by which time a contract had been obtained from the IRO to transport displaced persons to Australia.

On 23 May 1951, *Skaubryn* departed Bremerhaven on her maiden voyage, reaching Fremantle on 20 June, and terminating in Melbourne on 25 June, leaving empty two days later for the return trip. On future voyages, *Skaubryn* departed from either Bremerhaven or Genoa, and most terminated in Sydney. However, on occasion the vessel was chartered out for other services, and on 11 June 1953 left Bremen on a migrant voyage to Montreal, then returned to the Australian trade again.

The French Government took *Skaubryn* on charter in

SKAUBRYN

SKAUBRYN AT MALTA

the mid–1950s to carry troops back to France from Vietnam, after the independence of former French colonies in the Far East. In September 1956, *Skaubryn* was chartered by the Dutch Government for one round trip from Rotterdam to Halifax and New York, then in November 1956, the vessel was chartered by the British Government to transport British troops from Singapore to Britain.

For three months in 1957, *Skaubryn* was chartered to the Greek Line, her first departure for them being on 18 June from Bremen to Le Havre and Southampton and then to Quebec, returning to Liverpool. She then made three round trips from Liverpool to Quebec, leaving the Canadian port for the last time on 8 September and returning to Bremen. *Skaubryn* then returned to the Australian emigrant trade once more.

On 14 March 1958, *Skaubryn* left Bremerhaven with 1288 passengers aboard, bound for Australia. Having passed through the Suez Canal and Red Sea, the vessel was crossing the Indian Ocean when, on 31 March, a fire broke out in the engine room. The crew attempted to extinguish the blaze, but were unsuccessful, and a call for help was answered by the Ellerman cargo ship *City of Sydney*. When she arrived on the scene, all the passengers on *Skaubryn* were put into lifeboats and transferred to the British ship, as fortunately the seas were smooth. One passenger suffered a heart attack while in a lifeboat, and subsequently died, but all the others reached safety. Next day the Lauro liner *Roma* arrived, and all the *Skaubryn* passengers were transferred again in lifeboats to her.

The fire destroyed the midships and forward part of *Skaubryn*, but left the stern almost untouched. On 2 April the frigate HMS *Loch Fada* arrived on the scene, putting a party aboard the abandoned vessel, and rigging a line, with the intention of towing the vessel to Aden. The following day the Dutch salvage tug *Cycloop* took over the tow, but *Skaubryn* was settling lower in the water each day, until on 6 April she sank.

RUAHINE

BUILT: *1951 by John Brown & Co., Clydebank*
TONNAGE: *17 851 gross*
DIMENSIONS: *584 × 75 ft (178.2 × 22.9 m)*
SERVICE SPEED: *17 knots*
PROPULSION: *Doxford diesels/twin screws*

Ruahine was the third new liner delivered to the New Zealand Shipping Co. after the war, enabling them to operate a regular four-weekly schedule of departures from London to New Zealand. Launched on 11 December 1950, she left London on 22 May 1951 on her maiden voyage to Wellington via the Panama Canal. Accommodation was provided for 267 passengers in one class, and there were six holds for cargo. Passengers were embarked at London, but on the return trip, disembarked at Southampton.

Ruahine led an uneventful life, giving excellent service to her owners. Over the years, additional ports were added to the itinerary, such as Madeira, Bermuda, Jamaica and Tahiti, to attract more passengers. During a refit at the end of 1965, the mainmast was removed, and the passenger accommodation increased to 310 in one class. At the same time, her funnel was repainted in the colours of the Federal Steam Navigation Co., a subsidiary of the New Zealand Shipping Co., while in

1967 ownership of *Ruahine* was officially transferred to the Federal Line.

Through these changes, the actual operation of the ship was not affected, but the decline in passenger numbers soon rendered the vessel uneconomic. In April 1968, *Ruahine* left London for New Zealand on her final voyage, departing Auckland for the last time on 19 June. On her return to London, the vessel was laid up briefly, then sold to International Export Lines Ltd, a member of the C. Y. Tung Group of companies, based in Hong Kong.

Renamed *Oriental Rio*, she was refitted at the Taikoo Dockyard in Hong Kong to carry 229 first class passengers, and also had her foremast removed. In January 1969 she was transferred to another Tung company, Chinese Maritime Trust Ltd, registered in Taiwan. *Oriental Rio* then went to San Diego, sailing on 26 February 1969 to inaugurate a new round-the-world service, operating under the banner of Orient Overseas Line.

The world oil crisis of the early 1970s brought the career of *Oriental Rio* to a premature end, as in 1973 she was laid up in Hong Kong. Eventually she was sold to shipbreakers in Taiwan, leaving Hong Kong on 26 December, and being delivered at Kaohsiung three days later.

RUAHINE

RUAHINE AFTER 1965

THE SAME SHIP AS *ORIENTAL RIO*

SAN GIORGIO

BUILT: *1923 by Cantiere Navale Franco Tosi, Taranto*
TONNAGE: *8955 gross*
DIMENSIONS: *460 × 59 ft (140.2 × 18 m)*
SERVICE SPEED: *14 knots*
PROPULSION: *Geared turbines/twin screws*

San Giorgio made three voyages to Australia for Lloyd Triestino in 1952, at the end of her career, but she had first voyaged to Australia at the start of her career. She was built for Lloyd Sabaudo, one of the major Italian shipping companies, as the single funnelled *Principessa Giovanna*, with a sister ship, *Principessa Maria*. They were designed as large cargo ships but had 'tween deck accommodation for 400 migrants. This was only used on voyages from Italy, as on the return passage a full cargo would be loaded.

In August 1923, *Principessa Giovanna* made her maiden voyage from Genoa to Australia, and with her sister maintained a regular service until 1925, when they were transferred to the South American trade. In 1932, Lloyd Sabaudo amalgamated with another large Italian company, Navigazione Generale Italiana to form Italia Line, to which all the vessels of both their fleets were transferred.

Shortly after the merger, *Principessa Giovanna* was rebuilt, emerging with two funnels, a more extensive superstructure, and accommodation for 640 third class passengers. She continued on the South American trade, though in 1935 she was used as a troopship for the Abyssinian campaign for a short period. In 1940 she became a troopship for the Italians again, but after the surrender in 1944 was taken over by the British. Under management of British India Line, *Principessa Giovanna* then served as a British hospital ship, and later as a troopship.

In 1947 the vessel was returned to the Italians, and refitted at Genoa. Renamed *San Giorgio*, she resumed her place on the Italia Line trade to South America until 1952, when she was transferred to Lloyd Triestino. Repainted in their colours, *San Giorgio* departed Trieste on 17 February 1952 for Australia, arriving in Fremantle on 25 March and Melbourne on 1 April, berthing in Sydney on 6 April. She remained in port for a week, then returned to Trieste. Her second voyage departed on 18 June, and her third on 10 October. Leaving Sydney on 28 November, *San Giorgio* was in Melbourne on 3 December, and Fremantle on 11 December, and then returned to Trieste.

A fourth voyage, scheduled to depart on 27 January 1953, was cancelled, and *San Giorgio* was instead laid up. She remained idle through the year, then in December was sold to shipbreakers, arriving on 30 December at their Savona yard.

SAN GIORGIO

ORONSAY

BUILT: *1951 by Vickers–Armstrong Ltd, Barrow*
TONNAGE: *27 632 gross*
DIMENSIONS: *708 × 93 ft (216 × 28.5 m)*
SERVICE SPEED: *22 knots*
PROPULSION: *Geared turbines/twin screws*

Oronsay was built to the same basic design as *Orcades*, but with a more rounded superstructure and thicker mast. Launched on 30 June 1950, she was being fitted out when a fire erupted in No. 1 hold on 28 October. Firemen pumped so much water into the ship, she began to list heavily against the wharf, and there were fears she would capsize, so a hole was cut in her side to let the water out. This incident caused only a minor delay to her completion, and on 23 April 1951, *Oronsay* ran trials, achieving 25.23 knots.

Delivered to Orient Line early in May, *Oronsay* went to Tilbury to prepare for her maiden voyage. Leaving on 16 May 1951, *Oronsay* reached Fremantle on 8 June, then visited Adelaide and Melbourne before arriving in Sydney on 18 June. Reflecting the gradual swing away from first class travel, *Oronsay* had accommodation for 668 first class and 833 tourist class passengers. For the early years of her career, *Oronsay* voyaged only between Britain and Australia. On 14 February 1953 she left Sydney on her first cruise, which became an occasional feature of her itineraries.

Oronsay was the first Orient Line vessel to make a voyage across the Pacific, departing Sydney on 1 January 1954 for Auckland, where she berthed on 4 January. She then went on to visit Suva, Honolulu and Vancouver before arriving in San Francisco on 21 January, then returned to Sydney. She made two further voyages across the Pacific in 1954, leaving Sydney on 21 May and 19 November. In future years, *Oronsay* would make frequent voyages in the Pacific, but it was 1956 before she transited the Panama Canal to complete her first voyage around the world. On 11 October 1960, *Oronsay* left Sydney on her first cruise to the Far East, visiting several Japanese ports, Hong Kong and Singapore.

During 1960, P & O absorbed the Orient Line, but *Oronsay* retained her corn coloured hull until early 1964. She was then the first of the Orient liners to be repainted white, departing Tilbury for the first time in her new colours on 18 April 1964. In future years, *Oronsay* would make an increasing number of cruises from Sydney, and also from Southampton.

On 14 January 1970, *Oronsay* arrived in Vancouver on a voyage to Australia, but was found to have typhoid on board. The vessel was quarantined, and anchored out in the harbour until 4 February, when she was able to leave. The cause of the outbreak was traced to sewerage pipes that had been wrongly connected during a recent refit.

From 1973 *Oronsay* spent most of each year cruising. She was never altered to a one–class ship, which did not help her cruising career. On 4 August 1975, *Oronsay* left Southampton for the last time, passing through the Panama Canal and calling at ports on the west coast of America. She arrived in Sydney on 15 September, and the next day left on a one-way cruise to Hong Kong. After calls at Brisbane and Manila, *Oronsay* arrived in Hong Kong on 28 September, where she was destored. On 7 October 1975, *Oronsay* arrived in Kaohsiung, to be broken up.

ORONSAY WITH A WHITE HULL

ROMA AND SYDNEY

ROMA

BUILT: *1943 by Seattle–Tacoma Shipbuilding Corp.,*
  Tacoma
TONNAGE: *14 687 gross*
DIMENSIONS: *492 × 69 ft (150 × 21.1 m)*
SERVICE SPEED: *17 knots*
PROPULSION: *Geared turbines/single screw*

This pair were typical examples of post-war
conversions from warships to passenger vessels.
Intended to be standard C3-type cargo ships, they were
ordered by the US Government, for allocation to
American shipping companies on completion. The keel
of *Sydney* was laid down on 5 September 1941, but
shortly after she was redesigned as an auxiliary aircraft
carrier, being launched on 4 April 1942 and named USS
Croatan, commissioning into the US Navy in August
1942. *Roma* was laid down on 9 June 1942, and launched
on 7 September 1942 as the USS *Glacier*, being
commissioned in June 1943.

    Both these ships were handed over to the British
under the lend-lease agreement, *Croatan* being
commissioned into the Royal Navy on 27 February
1943 as HMS *Fencer*, while *Glacier* became HMS
Atheling on 31 July 1943. They could carry 20 aircraft,
and had a pair of 5 inch guns for defence. *Fencer* was part
of the British Pacific Fleet that arrived in Sydney on 16
March 1945. When the war ended, both vessels were
returned to the Americans, *Fencer* on 11 December

SYDNEY

BUILT: *1942 by Western Pipe & Steel Co., San Francisco*
TONNAGE: *14 708 gross*
DIMENSIONS: *492 × 69 ft (150 × 21.1 m)*
SERVICE SPEED: *17 knots*
PROPULSION: *Geared turbines/single screw*

1946, *Atheling* two days later, and laid up at Hampton
Roads pending disposal.

    In mid-1949, both vessels were bought by Flotta
Lauro, and had their flight decks and other wartime
fittings removed by Gibbs Corporation at Jacksonville.
Atheling arrived there on 23 September 1949, followed
by *Fencer* on 28 October. *Atheling* left Jacksonville on 9
April 1950 for Trieste, followed soon after by *Fencer*,
bound for Genoa. Work began immediately converting
them into passenger liners, during which a full
superstructure was built atop the existing hull. Due to
extensive use of a new non-flammable lining called
marinite, they were called the "ships that cannot burn",
but fortunately this claim was never put to the test.
Roma had accommodation for 92 first and 680 tourist
class passengers, while *Sydney* could carry 94 first and
708 tourist class.

    The ships were scheduled to operate regular
monthly departures from Genoa to Australia. *Roma*
made the first sailing, in August 1951, arriving in
Fremantle on 1 October, Melbourne on 9 October, and

ROMA

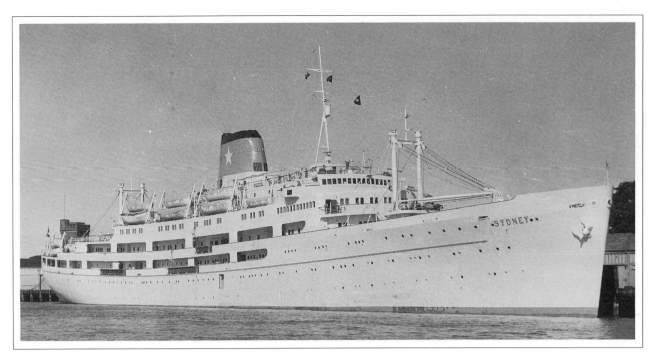

SYDNEY

Sydney on 14 October. She then called at Brisbane on 17 October en route to Jakarta and Singapore on her return trip. *Sydney* followed the same route in September 1951, reaching Fremantle on 17 October, then calling at Melbourne, Sydney and Brisbane.

When *Roma* returned to Genoa in April 1953, she was transferred to the North Atlantic trade, leaving Genoa on 3 May bound for New York. *Roma* remained on this trade for over three years, her place on the Australian route being taken by *Surriento*. From July to September 1953, *Sydney* operated four round trips between Liverpool and Quebec, then returned to the Australian service. On 24 January 1957, *Roma* departed Genoa bound for Australia again, and the two sisters remained on this route for the next nine years.

As demand for passages from Italy increased, both ships were refitted in 1960. *Sydney* could now carry 119 first class and 994 tourist class, while *Roma* had berths for 119 first and 1026 tourist class. An open-air swimming pool was now provided for each class, and air-conditioning extended throughout the vessels. Despite these changes, the ships still could not meet the demand, so in 1962 Flotta Lauro announced plans for the construction of two 30 000 ton liners with accommodation for 1700 passengers each for the Australian trade, to replace *Roma* and *Sydney*. Before construction began, Flotta Lauro was able to purchase two second-hand liners instead, *Willem Ruys* and *Oranje*, which were rebuilt in Italy, and due to enter service in 1965, as *Achille Lauro* and *Angelina Lauro*. In mid-1965, *Roma* was withdrawn from the Australian trade, and transferred to a service from Italy to Central America. However, serious fires on board both *Achille Lauro* and *Angelina Lauro* delayed their delivery dates, so *Roma* had

to return to the Australian service again. With the new ships finally ready for service in early 1966, *Roma* made her final departure from Genoa for Australia on 4 January 1966, departing Sydney on 3 February and Brisbane two days later on her return trip. *Sydney* left Genoa on 11 February 1966, departing Sydney for the last time on 14 March.

Both *Roma* and *Sydney* were then transferred to the service from Naples and Genoa to Barcelona, Funchal, Teneriffe and La Guaira. Unfortunately the route was no longer viable, so in 1967 *Roma* was withdrawn and sold to shipbreakers in Savona.

Flotta Lauro decided to join the booming Mediterranean cruise market, using *Sydney*, but just to confuse matters, she was renamed *Roma*. Her first season of Mediterranean cruising was not a success, so in 1968 she was offered for sale. Another Italian concern, Aretusa S.p.A. di Nav. bought the vessel in 1969, and operated her for a season of Mediterranean cruises, but in October 1970 she was laid up in La Spezia, again for sale. This time the vessel was bought by Sovereign Cruises, a new Cypriot flag firm formed by a British tour operator. Renamed *Galaxy Queen*, she was given a major refit, and on 20 March 1971 began cruising under her new name. Numerous mechanical and other failures dogged *Galaxy Queen*, so in 1972 she was sold again, to G. Kotzovilis, and renamed *Lady Dina*, but remained laid up. In 1973, she was chartered to the Siosa Line, who had recently lost their vessel, *Caribia*. Renamed *Caribia 2*, she made some cruises during 1973, but was in very poor condition. In 1974, the old vessel was disposed of to shipbreakers, Terrestre Marittima of La Spezia, who began demolition work on 1 September 1975.

CALEDONIEN AND TAHITIEN

BUILT: *Caledonien 1952 by At. et Ch. de France, Dunkirk*
  Tahitien 1953 by Naval Dockyard, Brest
TONNAGE: *12 712/12 614 gross*
DIMENSIONS: *548 × 67 ft (167.3 × 20.6 m)*
SERVICE SPEED: *17 knots*
PROPULSION: *B & W diesels/twin screws*

Messageries Maritimes had established a link between France and Australia in 1882, with a service through Suez. In the 1920s it established a second route through the Panama Canal to Tahiti and Noumea, and during the war this was extended to Australia, while the Suez route was abandoned. After the war, the company re-established its operation using old tonnage, but placed orders for a series of nine new liners for their various routes, two of which were designated for the Australian trade.

The first of these to be launched was *Caledonien*, on 26 April 1952, being completed five months later. She departed Marseilles on 1 October on her maiden voyage to Australia. *Tahitien* was launched on 4 October 1952, and entered service exactly seven months later, with a departure from Marseilles on 4 May 1953 for Australia. The two ships provided accommodation for 74 first class, 84 tourist class and 208 third class passengers, the latter being subdivided into two grades. *Caledonien* and *Tahitien* gave useful but unspectacular service on the route from France to Australia for the next twenty years.

These ships followed a route across the Atlantic and through the Panama Canal, then to Tahiti and on to Noumea, terminating in Sydney. Three ships were required to maintain a regular schedule, and initially this pair were partnered by *Changchow*, then by *Melanesien*, and finally *Oceanien*. In 1963 Messageries Maritimes ordered a new liner to be built for the route, which was to have been named *Australien*, but by the time she was launched in June 1966, her name had been changed to *Pasteur*, and she entered service in 1966 on the route to South America.

With the withdrawal of *Oceanien* in the middle of 1966, *Tahitien* and *Caledonien* were left to maintain the service on their own for the first time. The only major incident to mar their careers happened to *Tahitien*, which was disabled by an engine room fire on 12 May 1969, when bound from Panama to Tahiti. Fortunately

another Messageries Maritimes ship, the freighter *Marquisien*, was nearby, and towed *Tahitien* back to Balboa, where they arrived on 19 May. Inspection of the damage showed that extensive repairs were required, so *Marquisien* was delegated to tow the crippled liner across the Atlantic to Marseilles, arriving on 31 August. Repairs lasted three months, and to fill the gap in the sailing schedule, *Cambodge* was despatched to Australia for one trip.

Messageries Maritimes was in the process of withdrawing from the passenger business, and in 1971 decided to withdraw from the Australian trade. *Caledonien* left Sydney on 9 July 1971 on her final voyage back to Marseilles, leaving *Tahitien* to make the final departure for the company from Sydney on 14 September 1971. On their arrival back in Marseilles, both ships were offered for sale, and found new owners the following year.

Caledonien was sold to the Greek shipping company, Efthymiadis Line, and renamed *Nisos Kypros*. She was refitted as a car ferry, with doors cut in her side and holds converted into garage space. On 10 June 1972 she entered service between Piraeus and Cyprus, and shortly after her name was anglicised to *Island of Cyprus*. Within a matter of months, Efthymiadis Line was in financial ruin, and all their ships had to be laid up. In 1975 *Island of Cyprus* was sold to shipbreakers in Taiwan.

Tahitien has been more fortunate, having been sold in 1972 to another Greek concern, Med Sun Lines, though the ship was registered under the ownership of Aphrodite Cruises Ltd, of Limassol in Cyprus. Renamed *Atalante*, she too was refitted for the car ferry trade, and on 6 May 1972 entered service between Ancona and Patras. Several years later she was transferred to the longer route from Ancona to various Greek islands and Piraeus. This service operates only between May and October, and is advertised as a cruise. During the winter the ship is usually laid up.

In 1980 the Sydney based travel company, Port Royale Charters, announced it had chartered *Atalante* for a series of South Pacific cruises from Sydney, the first being scheduled to depart on 28 November 1980. This did not eventuate, as the company went out of business during the year. *Atalante* is still going strong in the Mediterranean, and has been highly successful for her present owner.

CALEDONIEN

TAHITIEN

155

CASTEL FELICE

BUILT: *1930 by A. Stephen & Sons, Glasgow*
TONNAGE: *12 150 gross*
DIMENSIONS: *493 × 64 ft (150.3 × 19.6 m)*
SERVICE SPEED: *16 knots*
PROPULSION: *Geared turbines/twin screws*

Castel Felice was the first vessel owned by Sitmar Line to have been built as a passenger carrier. Ordered by British India Line, she was launched on 27 August 1930 as *Kenya*, and completed four months later. She was designed to trade across the Indian Ocean from Bombay to East Africa and Durban, with her sister, *Karanja*. Accommodation was provided for 66 first class, 120 second class and 1700 third class passengers. First and second class consisted of cabins, but third class was very basic accommodation, consisting of open deck spaces allocated on the main and lower decks, which were well ventilated. This was restricted to Indian passengers, mostly emigrants to East Africa, and to feed them there were six galleys, with special cooks provided to prepare meals according to religious requirements. The crew was composed of British officers and engineers, lascars and firemen, and Goanese stewards.

Kenya remained on the Indian Ocean trade for ten years, then in June 1940 she was requisitioned by the British Government, as was her sister. Returning to Britain for the first time since being completed, she was converted into a landing ship, infantry, carrying ten landing craft, and 1500 troops. To avoid confusion with a Royal Navy cruiser, she was renamed HMS *Keren*. During an active war career, *Keren* took part in a number of Allied landings, including Madagascar in May 1942, and those in North Africa in November 1942, during which her sister was sunk. *Keren* later took part in the Sicily landings and was back in the Indian Ocean, preparing for operations against the Japanese, when the war ended.

British India Line did not want the ship back, so on 3 April 1946 she was purchased by the Ministry of Transport, only to be sent to Scotland and laid up in Holy Loch. For three years the vessel lay idle, then early in 1949 the Vlasov Group began negotiations to purchase the vessel. While these were in progress, on the night of 19 February 1949, *Keren* broke her moorings and was swept ashore during a severe storm. Quickly refloated, the vessel was drydocked in Glasgow for repairs.

It was at this time that a sale was finalised to the Vlasov Group, and *Keren* passed into the ownership of the Alva Steamship Co., of London. She was towed to Rothesay Bay and laid up again, and over the next two years underwent a number of name changes. Initially

THE BRITISH INDIA LINER *KENYA*

MAIDEN ARRIVAL IN SYDNEY OF *CASTEL FELICE*, 7 NOVEMBER 1952

she was renamed *Kenya*, but later reverted to *Keren*, then *Kenya* again. In 1950 she was transferred to Panamanian registry, renamed *Fairstone*, and towed back to Holy Loch again. In June 1950 she became *Kenya* once more, and in October 1950 was transferred to Sitmar Line, under the Italian flag. In March 1951 her name reverted to *Keren* again, and it was under this name that the vessel finally left the Holy Loch on 15 October 1950, being towed to Falmouth.

The initial work of rebuilding the vessel for passsenger service began in Falmouth, then on 10 March 1951, she was towed to Antwerp, where further work was done. In August the vessel was towed from Antwerp to Genoa, where the final work would be done. During this period a raked bow was fitted, the promenade deck extended to the stern, and a new funnel fitted, along with new masts and derrick posts. The interior was completely rebuilt, with cabins installed for 596 cabin class and 944 third class passengers. The work was completed in September 1952, at which time the vessel was renamed *Castel Felice*.

On 6 October 1952, *Castel Felice* left Genoa on her maiden voyage, arriving in Fremantle on 1 November, Melbourne four days later, and Sydney on 7 November. She then returned to Genoa, and was placed in regular service to Central and South America, making her first departure in January 1953. In July 1954 *Castel Felice* made the first of two voyages from Bremen to Quebec, followed by several voyages from Havre and Southampton to New York. On 7 October 1954, she left Bremen on her second voyage to Australia, going to Fremantle and Melbourne only, then returning to Genoa to resume the South American service.

Early in 1955 air-conditioning was installed, and the accommodation altered to 28 first class and 1173 tourist class. On 26 February *Castel Felice* left Trieste on her third voyage to Australia, then spent several months on the South American trade, ending the year with two more voyages to Australia. The first departed Cuxhaven on 21 September, the second being from Naples on 1 December, followed by another departure from Naples on 3 March 1956. *Castel Felice* spent the rest of 1956 and much of 1957 operating across the Atlantic, making her final departure from New York on 19 September. She was then given another refit, as Sitmar had obtained a government contract to carry assisted migrants from Britain to Australia.

On 6 April 1958, *Castel Felice* made her first departure from Southampton, and spent the rest of her career on the Australian trade. Occasional voyages were extended to New Zealand, some return trips passed through the Panama Canal, and she also made infrequent cruises from Sydney. In 1970 Sitmar lost the migrant contract, and it was decided to retire *Castel Felice* at the end of the year.

Preparing for her final departure from Southampton, *Castel Felice* suffered damage from a fire that broke out in the accommodation on 15 August. The damage was not repaired, and she carried a reduced number of passengers to Australia, passing through Fremantle on 16 September, then proceeding direct to Sydney. Arriving on 26 September, the ship was destored, her crockery and linen being sent to Italy for use on the recently purchased *Fairsea* and *Fairwind*. On 7 October 1970, *Castel Felice* left Sydney, and arrived on 21 October at the shipbreaker's yard in Taiwan.

ARCADIA

BUILT: *1954 by John Brown & Co., Clydebank*
TONNAGE: *29 734 gross*
DIMENSIONS: *721 × 90 ft (219.7 × 27.5 m)*
SERVICE SPEED: *22 knots*
PROPULSION: *Geared turbines/twin screws*

Arcadia was one of the most popular liners to voyage to Australia in the post-war era, and is also fondly remembered as a cruise liner in the last years of her career. She was destined to be the last of the traditional design P & O liners to operate out of Australia. *Arcadia* was launched on 14 May 1953, the same day as *Orsova* of the Orient Line. The two ships had virtually identical hulls, but very different superstructures, and fitting out of *Arcadia* was completed first, with accommodation for 675 first class and 735 tourist class passengers. She ran trials in January 1954, then was handed over to P & O, and on 22 February departed Tilbury on her maiden voyage to Australia.

Arcadia went first to Suez, Aden, Bombay and Colombo before arriving in Fremantle on 18 March, Melbourne on 22 March and Sydney two days later. On her return to Britain, *Arcadia* made a series of cruises from Southampton, the first being to the Mediterranean. When the liner returned to Tilbury on 26 September, to prepare for her second voyage to Australia, she collided with the tug *Cervia*, which sank with the loss of five lives.

It was not until October 1954 that *Arcadia* departed on her second voyage to Australia. By then her sister ship, *Iberia*, had also joined the service, and the two were easily distinguishable by their funnels, *Arcadia*'s having a black painted domed top. For the first five years of her career, *Arcadia* combined line voyages to Australia with cruises from Britain. On 1 April 1959, she arrived at the Harland & Wolff shipyard for an extensive refit. Air-conditioning was extended through the ship, and all cabins and public rooms were upgraded and refurbished. Leaving Belfast on 11 June, *Arcadia* made a series of cruises from Southampton before returning to the Australian trade.

On 22 November 1959, *Arcadia* departed Sydney on her first cruise from an Australian port. With P & O expanding their route network, *Arcadia* then left Sydney on 11 December on her first voyage across the Pacific, going to San Francisco and returning to Sydney on 19 January 1960, then returning to Britain through the Suez Canal. Throughout the 1960s, *Arcadia* combined line voyages with cruises from Britain and Australia, and also trans-Pacific voyages, some of which transited the Panama Canal rather than returning to Australia.

Early in 1970, *Arcadia* had her mainmast removed during a refit, while her accommodation was converted to carry 1372 passengers in one class. On 26 April she left Southampton for Sydney, then went to San Francisco. From there the liner made a series of cruises to Alaska until October, when she transferred to cruises from San Francisco to Mexican ports. These cruises were so successful that P & O left *Arcadia* on the west coast of America permanently. They also bought a cruise ship still under construction, which entered service as *Spirit of London* in 1973. For a year *Arcadia* remained on the west coast of America cruise trade to partner the new ship.

In October 1974, *Himalaya* was withdrawn from the Australian cruise trade, and *Arcadia* was brought to Sydney to replace her. In 1975 and 1976, she made one return trip to Britain, but she made her final departure from Southampton on 8 May 1976, voyaging by way of Cape Town to arrive in Sydney on 11 June. For the next two and a half years, *Arcadia* was based permanently in Sydney, cruising to the South Pacific and Asia. Her accommodation was reduced to 1240 in one class at this time.

As *Arcadia* approached her twenty-fifth anniversary, P & O began seeking a replacement, and purchased *Kungsholm* during 1978, which was renamed *Sea Princess*. On 29 January 1979, *Arcadia* left Sydney for the last time, being escorted to the Heads by a flotilla of small craft. Two days later she received a similar send-off from Brisbane, then headed for Manila, and on to Hong Kong. The cruise was to have terminated there, and the passengers were to transfer to *Sea Princess*, but the new ship had been delayed. *Arcadia* went on to Singapore, berthing on 21 February next to *Sea Princess*.

Once the passengers had transferred to *Sea Princess*, *Arcadia* steamed away from Singapore on her final voyage to Taiwan. Arriving in Kaohsiung on 28 February, *Arcadia* was handed over to a firm of shipbreakers.

ARCADIA

THE MAINMAST WAS REMOVED IN 1970

AROSA STAR

BUILT: *1931 by Bethlehem Shipbuilding Corp., Quincy*
TONNAGE: *7114 gross*
DIMENSIONS: *466 × 60 ft (142 × 18.3 m)*
SERVICE SPEED: *15 knots*
PROPULSION: *Geared turbines/single screw*

Arosa Star made three trips to Australia with migrants over a 15 month period. She had been launched on 24 September 1930 as *Borinquen* for the New York & Porto Rico Steam Ship Co., fitted out with accommodation for 261 first class and 96 second class passengers, and entered service in 1931 between New York and San Juan.

In January 1942, *Borinquen* was taken over by the US Engineers Corps, and refitted to carry 1289 troops. She made many trips across the Atlantic during the war, as well as to South Africa, and was involved in the landings in North Africa. Returned to her owner in February 1946, *Borinquen* resumed her pre-war service until 1948, when the N.Y. & P.R. Line ceased trading.

Transferred to the associated Bull Line, she was renamed *Puerto Rico*, and refitted to carry 186 first class only, then placed on the San Juan route again. In 1951 she was laid up, then chartered to American Export Line for a brief period before being sold to Cia. Internacional Transportadora, a Swiss-owned firm registered in Panama. Renamed *Arosa Star*, the vessel was rebuilt, with a lengthened superstructure, glassed-in promenade deck and new raked bow. Accommodation was increased to 38 first class and 768 tourist class, and on 18 May 1954, *Arosa Star* departed Bremerhaven on her first voyage, to Montreal.

Arosa Star came to Australia under an I.C.E.M.

contract, her first voyage departing Bremerhaven on 20 November 1954, arriving in Fremantle on 24 December and Melbourne five days later. She then returned to Piraeus, to make a second voyage to Australia, calling at Fremantle and Melbourne before arriving in Sydney on 4 March, leaving the next day for Malta. *Arosa Star* then returned to the Canadian trade for the summer, but on 22 January 1955 left Bremerhaven on her third Australian voyage. She visited Fremantle, Melbourne and Sydney, leaving on 5 March for Auckland, arriving on 9 March. *Arosa Star* then returned to Bremerhaven through the Panama Canal, and resumed the Canadian trade.

Arosa Star spent the next two northern winters cruising from New York, but Arosa Line were sliding into deep financial trouble. On 7 December 1958, *Arosa Star* was arrested in Bermuda, and during 1959, was sold at auction to McCormick Shipping, who operated as Eastern Steamship Line.

Renamed *Bahama Star*, she was refitted for cruising from Miami to the Bahamas all year, with 600 passengers. On 13 November 1965, she rescued survivors from another elderly cruise ship, *Yarmouth Castle*, when it burned and sank off Nassau. This disaster brought about new safety regulations for cruise ships operating from American ports, and as the cost of upgrading *Bahama Star* to the new standards was prohibitive, she was withdrawn from service in 1968.

In 1969 the vessel was sold to a California group, for conversion into a floating hotel. Renamed *La Janelle*, she was anchored off Port Hueneme, but on 13 April 1970 drove ashore during a severe storm. Declared a total loss, she was broken up where she lay.

AROSA STAR

ORSOVA

BUILT: *1954 by Vickers–Armstrong Ltd, Barrow*
TONNAGE: *28 790 gross*
DIMENSIONS: *723 × 90 ft (220.3 × 27.5 m)*
SERVICE SPEED: *22 knots*
PROPULSION: *Geared turbines/twin screws*

Orsova was the first large liner to be built without masts, though her general outline was similar to *Oronsay*. She was also the first liner to have an all welded hull, and was launched on 14 May 1953, the same day as *Arcadia*. Running trials in March 1954, *Orsova* reached 26 knots. On 17 March 1954, she departed Tilbury on her maiden voyage to Australia, arriving in Fremantle on 9 April, then visiting Adelaide and Melbourne before reaching Sydney on 19 April. Accommodation was provided for 681 first class and 813 tourist class, and the crew numbered 620.

After three return voyages from Britain to Australia, *Orsova* left Sydney on 28 January 1955 to cross the Pacific to San Francisco. Leaving there, she reached Honolulu in 89 hours, at an average speed of 23.39 knots, breaking a record that had stood since 1921. On 27 April 1955, *Orsova* left Tilbury on the first round-the-world voyage to be operated by the Orient Line. This took her out to Australia through the Suez Canal, then across the Pacific to the west coast of America, and through the Panama Canal, returning to Tilbury on 13 July.

Orsova had begun making occasional cruises, and in 1960 she went to the Vickers–Armstrong Ltd shipyard in Newcastle for a ten-week refit, during which air-conditioning was installed. It was also in 1960 that the Orient Line was absorbed into P & O. *Orsova* retained her corn coloured hull until 1964, when it was repainted white. She arrived in Fremantle on 23 May 1964 on her first voyage in the new colours. In 1965, *Orsova* was transferred to the ownership of P & O, and the Orient Line name disappeared.

In the early 1970s, *Orsova* was used more extensively for cruising, though retaining her two-class configuration. On 25 November 1972 she arrived at the Vosper–Thorneycroft shipyard at Southampton for an extensive refit to upgrade her accommodation for cruising, though still in two classes. On 9 January 1973 *Orsova* departed Southampton on what was destined to be her final voyage to Australia, as on her return to Britain she began a lengthy programme of cruises from Southampton. These proved to be highly successful, so she was scheduled for a world cruise departing in January 1974.

Also during 1973, *Canberra* was operating a less than successful series of cruises from New York, and returned to Britain in November 1973, while a decision was made as to her future. At one time it was considered that *Canberra* would be sold for scrap, but instead *Orsova* became a victim of her own success. The response to the proposed world cruise was more than *Orsova* could handle, so *Canberra* was substituted, and then programmed to replace *Orsova* on the rest of the 1974 cruise schedule.

Orsova berthed in Southampton on 25 November 1973 at the end of her final cruise, and then was sold to Taiwanese shipbreakers. The liner made the long voyage east under her own power, and on 14 February 1974 was handed over to the shipbreakers in Kaohsiung.

ORSOVA

IBERIA

BUILT: *1954 by Harland & Wolff Ltd, Belfast*
TONNAGE: *29 614 gross*
DIMENSIONS: *718 × 90 ft (219 × 27.5 m)*
SERVICE SPEED: *22 knots*
PROPULSION: *Geared turbines/twin screws*

Iberia was the final unit in the P & O post-war passenger ship rebuilding programme, yet her career was destined to be the shortest of all these liners. Her keel was laid down on 8 February 1952, and she was launched on 21 January 1954. After spending nine months fitting out, *Iberia* achieved a maximum of 24.9 knots on trials, then was handed over to P & O on 10 September 1954. Accommodation was provided for 673 first class and 733 tourist class, and she had a crew of 711 personnel.

Iberia could be distinguished from her sister, *Arcadia*, by her funnel, which was topped by a smoke deflector. On 28 September 1954, *Iberia* departed Tilbury on her maiden voyage to Australia, passing through Suez to reach Fremantle on 22 October, then calling at Adelaide and Melbourne before berthing in Sydney on 1 November.

On 14 March 1956, *Iberia* left Tilbury for Australia, but en route from Aden to Colombo, she collided with a tanker, *Stanvac Pretoria*, during the night of 27 March. *Iberia* suffered extensive damage to her port side, but was able to complete her voyage to Sydney, arriving on 16 April. Workmen from Cockatoo Dockyard spent 17 days repairing the damage while *Iberia* was berthed at Pyrmont, and she left two weeks behind schedule.

Iberia was used for occasional cruises from Southampton, and during 1958 made a cruise to New York. In the mid-1950s, *Iberia* began operating across the Pacific to the West Coast of America. On 15 December 1959, *Iberia* left Tilbury on her first voyage around the world, passing through the Panama Canal and visiting West Coast ports and Honolulu before arriving in Sydney, and returning to Britain through Suez. On 19 January 1960 *Iberia* left Sydney on her first cruise from an Australian port, 14 days around the South Pacific. In January 1961 *Iberia* was given an extensive refit, during which air-conditioning was extended throughout the accommodation, which was also upgraded and refurbished.

Throughout her career, *Iberia* was plagued by engine problems, which grew worse during the 1960s. During one voyage to Britain late in 1969, there was a fire in the funnel while *Iberia* was berthed at Pago Pago, followed a few days later by engine trouble that made her a day late into Honolulu. Shortly after leaving Acapulco the starboard engine failed, but was repaired by the engineers, then while taking on bunkers in Curacao, some oil escaped into the first class baggage room. *Iberia* eventually reached Southampton a week late, and was drydocked for an overhaul. On her next voyage, a power failure blacked out the ship only three days out from Southampton, but this was repaired and the voyage continued.

In the early 1970s, with the rising price of oil, P & O were forced to prune their fleet. *Iberia* became the first victim, despite being the youngest of the liners under consideration, as her engine problems told against her. At one time a plan to re-engine *Iberia* was considered, but not accepted. On 5 November 1971, *Iberia* departed Southampton on her final voyage to Australia, and made a short series of cruises from Sydney. Her final departure from Sydney was on 16 March 1972, returning to Southampton on 19 April 1972. She was then withdrawn from service, and soon after sold to Taiwanese shipbreakers. On 27 June 1972, *Iberia* left Southampton with a small crew aboard, and only two lifeboats. Voyaging around South Africa, she arrived in Kaohsiung on 5 September, and shortly after was scrapped.

IBERIA

IBERIA AFTER THE MAINMAST WAS REMOVED

SOUTHERN CROSS

BUILT: *1955 by Harland & Wolff Ltd, Belfast*
TONNAGE: *20 204 gross*
DIMENSIONS: *604 × 78 ft (184 × 23.9 m)*
SERVICE SPEED: *20 knots*
PROPULSION: *Geared turbines/twin screws*

In 1952, Shaw Savill & Albion decided to build a new passenger liner, which would carry no cargo at all, unlike all their previous vessels, to inaugurate a round-the-world service. The design of the new ship produced a number of other breaks with tradition, in particular locating the engines aft. On 17 August 1954 the vessel was launched by Queen Elizabeth and named *Southern Cross*, the first British merchant vessel to be launched by a reigning monarch. Work on fitting out the liner took six months, during which 405 cabins were installed for 1160 passengers, all tourist class. After running trials in late January 1955, *Southern Cross* was handed over to Shaw Savill on 23 February.

On 29 March 1955, *Southern Cross* left Southampton on her maiden voyage, going across the Atlantic and through the Panama Canal, then to Tahiti, and on to Wellington, where she arrived on 2 May. On 9 May, *Southern Cross* berthed in Sydney, then visited Melbourne two days later, and Fremantle on 16 May. The liner then crossed the Indian Ocean to Cape Town,

and back to Southampton. She then made three cruises from Southampton before departing on her second line voyage, in the reverse direction to her maiden voyage.

Southern Cross was scheduled to make four voyages around the world each year, taking 76 days for the trip at an average speed of 20 knots, having a reserve of two knots in case of delay. Within a short time it was clear that *Southern Cross* was a great success, as the engines–aft design gave passengers much more open deck space, and public rooms were not obstructed by funnel casings.

To make the round-the-world service fully efficient, it needed two ships. Consequently, a second ship of similar design was built, entering service as *Northern Star* in July 1962. From this time, *Southern Cross* operated only in a westward direction, with *Northern Star* proceeding eastward. However, by the end of the 1960s, demand for liner passages was declining, and *Southern Cross* began making more cruises.

In May 1970, *Southern Cross* was extensively overhauled and refurbished, to better suit her for cruising, then spent several months cruising from Southampton. A line voyage was made to Sydney, from where she operated another series of cruises, returning to Southampton again in May 1971, and completing another programme of cruises. In August

SOUTHERN CROSS

SOUTHERN CROSS

1971, *Southern Cross* left Southampton on her final voyage around the world, returning to Southampton in November, and being laid up there. In April 1972 she was moved to the River Fal.

Southern Cross was on the market for over a year before a sale was finalised for 500 000 pounds to Cia. de Vapores Cerulea, a Greek company, but registered in Panama. Renamed *Calypso*, the liner went to Piraeus for a major refit, which cost 10 million pounds. The interior of the ship was stripped out, and new cabins with private facilities installed, to accommodate 950 passengers in one class. The indoor pool on the lowest deck became a discotheque, while a new pool was built on the sun deck forward of the bridge, this area being fully enclosed, the only major external difference.

Calypso entered service as a full-time cruise ship in April 1975, being based again at Southampton, under charter to a British tour company, Thomson Tours. During 1976 she was based in Rotterdam, and also Leith in Scotland, while 1977 found her back at Southampton again. Throughout this period she made a variety of cruises to the Mediterranean, Altantic Islands and Scandinavia. At the end of 1977 the Thomson Tours charter ended, and *Calypso* was then operated by her owner under the banner of Ulysses Cruises.

Calypso spent most of 1978 cruising in the Mediterranean, then at the end of the year went to South Africa for a short season. Returning to the Mediterranean in February 1979, *Calypso* cruised there until the end of the year, then on 16 December 1979 left Piraeus, bound for Miami.

Under charter to Paquet Cruises, *Calypso* operated out of Miami to the Caribbean until May 1980, when she transferred to the west coast of America, cruising out of Los Angeles to Vancouver and Alaska. This series ended in September, and on 29 September 1980, *Calypso* was sold to Western Cruise Line, a subsidiary of Eastern Cruise Line, of Miami, and part of the Gotaas–Larsen Group of shipping companies. Renamed *Azure Seas*, the swimming pool forward on the sun deck was removed, and the open deck enclosed to form a large new public room, used as a casino, with an open observation deck above. In November 1980, *Azure Seas* began operating a regular cruise service from Los Angeles to Ensenada in Mexico, departing every Monday and Friday evening. Five years later, when she celebrated her five-hundredth departure, she had carried over 67 000 passengers on these highly successful short cruises.

In October 1987, the fleets of Eastern Cruise Line, Western Cruise Line and Sundance Cruises, were combined into a new company, Admiral Cruises, under which banner *Azure Seas* continues to operate.

AURELIA

BUILT: *1939 by Blohm & Voss A. G., Hamburg*
TONNAGE: *10 022 gross*
DIMENSIONS: *488 × 60 ft (148.7 × 18.4 m)*
SERVICE SPEED: *17 knots*
PROPULSION: *MAN diesel/single screw*

This vessel has had a long and varied career. Ordered by Hamburg–America Line, and launched on 15 December 1938, she was named *Huascaran*, entering service in April 1939. At 6951 gross tons, and primarily a cargo ship, she had accommodation for up to 58 passengers, and joined her sister, *Orsono* on the trade from Hamburg to the west coast of South America via Panama.

When war broke out, *Huascaran* was taken over by the German Navy and converted into a submarine depot ship, and later a repair ship, seeing considerable service in Norwegian waters. *Huascaran* survived the war, to be seized by the Allies as a prize, being allocated to Canada on 14 November 1945.

The Park Steamship Co. managed the ship on behalf of the Canadian Government until, on 2 September 1947, *Huascaran* was bought by Canadian Pacific, and refitted at a shipyard in Sorel to carry 773 passengers in one class. Renamed *Beaverbrae*, she was intended to carry migrants from Europe to Canada, and a full cargo on the return trip. Her first voyage departed from St Johns on 8 February 1948, for Bremerhaven, and over the next six years, *Beaverbrae* made 51 round trips between Canada and European ports.

As the demand for migrant passages declined, *Beaverbrae* was no longer needed, so on 1 November 1954 she was sold to Cia. Genovese di Armamento, better known as Cogedar Line. Renamed *Aurelia*, she went to Trieste for rebuilding as a passenger liner. The original small superstructure was greatly enlarged, air-conditioning installed, and berths for 1124 passengers. A few cabins had private facilities, and amenities included an outdoor swimming pool and a theatre.

On 13 May 1955, *Aurelia* left Trieste on her first voyage to Australia, but later that year her European terminal port became Genoa. Her first departure from there was on 15 November, with calls at Naples, Messina, Malta and Piraeus added to the itinerary. *Aurelia* made four round trips per year to Australia, and in 1958 was withdrawn for further alterations.

During this work, her original MAN diesels were replaced by a new pair of the same type, and the superstructure further enlarged both fore and aft, though her passenger numbers were not increased. *Aurelia* then entered a new service to Australia from Bremerhaven, her first departure being on 12 June 1959.

In June 1960, *Aurelia* made a round trip from Bremerhaven to New York under charter to the Council of Student Travel, and in each year up to 1969 she made between two and five return trips to New York under similar charter, during the northern summer months. On the Australian trade, *Aurelia* began calling at Southampton, her first visit being on 14 September 1961.

BEAVERBRAE OF CANADIAN PACIFIC

Aurelia operated through Suez, or round Africa when the canal was closed, until the end of 1964, when she began a new round-the-world service. On 9 December, *Aurelia* left Rotterdam, and after calling at Southampton crossed the Atlantic to pass through the Panama Canal, and cross the Pacific to Auckland and then Sydney, returning through Suez. After two more voyages on this route, *Aurelia* reverted to the Suez route again in both directions, with an extension to Auckland, the first of these voyages leaving Rotterdam on 8 December 1965.

The closure of the Suez Canal in 1967, combined with a decline in the migrant trade to Australia, eventually brought about the end of Cogedar Line service to Australia. On 23 September 1968, *Aurelia* left Rotterdam on her final voyage, going around South Africa in both directions, departing Sydney for the final time on 29 October. On her return to Europe, *Aurelia* was refitted for service as a cruise ship, with her accommodation reduced to 470 passengers. The work took longer than expected, and her first three sailings had to be cancelled, but finally she left Southampton on her first cruise on 5 February 1969.

This cruise programme finished in May 1969, and *Aurelia* then made six round trips to New York. She returned to cruising from Southampton again in September, but returns were poor, so the vessel was offered for sale, being purchased by Chandris Cruises in September 1970, and renamed *Romanza*. Chandris rebuilt the ship internally, installing 238 new cabins, most with private facilities, for 650 passengers in one class. On 1 April 1971, *Romanza* left Venice on her first cruise for Chandris, and spent most of her subsequent career cruising in the Mediterranean.

A charter to Crown Cruises late in 1976 came to an abrupt end when the company went bankrupt, and then *Romanza* spent most of 1977 cruising out of Brazil under another charter. She also cruised in the Indian Ocean from South African ports over several years between November to March, but usually spent April to October cruising in the Mediterranean.

On 17 October 1979, *Romanza* ran aground on Dhenousa Island in the Aegean Sea, and suffered considerable bow damage. Refloated two days later, she was towed to Syros, and later back to Piraeus, where she was repaired, and returned to her Mediterranean cruising circuit. During the 1980s *Romanza* has spent periods laid up, and in 1988 was reported to be under charter as a floating hotel in the Canary Islands.

AURELIA AS FIRST CONVERTED

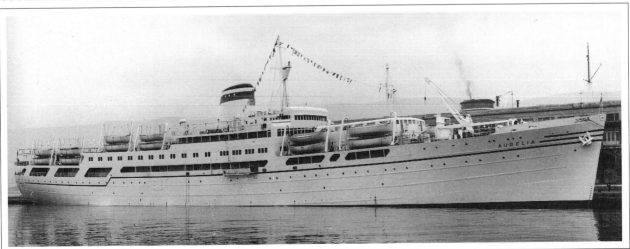

AFTER REBUILDING IN 1959

FLAMINIA

BUILT: *1922 by Merchant Shipbuilding Corp., Chester, Pennsylvania*
TONNAGE: *8779 gross*
DIMENSIONS: *462 × 60 ft (140.5 × 18.2 m)*
SERVICE SPEED: *14 knots*
PROPULSION: *Sulzer diesels/twin screws*

This vessel was launched on 14 December 1921 as the *Missourian*, and completed in June 1922. She was one of a pair of funnel-less freighters, her sister being named *Californian*, built for the American–Hawaiian Steamship Co., yet they commenced their careers operating from the west coast of America to Europe. After several years this was changed to a service from the west coast to New York.

In 1940 both these vessels were among a group of 90 ships transferred by the United States Government to Britain. *Missourian* was renamed *Empire Swan*, and managed by Runciman (London) Ltd. In 1942 *Empire Swan* was transferred to the Belgian Government, then in exile in London, and renamed *Belgian Freighter*. Managed by Cie. Maritime Belge, she was purchased outright by them in 1946, and renamed *Capitaine Potie*, being placed in service from Belgium to the Congo, and later to South America.

In May 1948 she was sold to Cia. Genovese d'Armamento, better known as Cogedar Line. Renamed *Genova*, she was sent to Trieste for an extensive rebuilding, during which the cargo holds were removed and accommodation installed for 800 third class passengers. An extensive superstructure was added, while for the first time a conventional funnel was fitted. During 1949, *Genova* entered service from Genoa to River Plate ports, maintaining this for five years, then returning to the Monfalcone shipyard in Trieste for further alterations.

Her original B & W diesels were removed, and replaced by Sulzer diesels, while the superstructure was further enlarged to allow for more public rooms and cabins, as well as an outdoor swimming pool. She could now carry 1024 passengers in 154 cabins, most of which contained eight berths. When the rebuilding was completed in March 1955, she was renamed *Flaminia*, and placed on a new service to Australia.

Her first voyage was from Trieste in April 1955, and took the vessel only to Cairns, where she berthed on 30 May, departing three days later for Italy. On 16 July, *Flaminia* left Trieste on her second voyage, arriving in Fremantle on 14 August, and terminating in Melbourne on 19 August. For the next three years, *Flaminia* operated from Italian ports to Australia.

On 15 December 1958, *Flaminia* left Rotterdam, and Bremerhaven the next day on a new service to Australia. She served on this new route a further three years, then on 4 August 1961 had a fire in the accommodation when between Trieste and Bari. *Flaminia* made one more trip to Australia, departing Fremantle on 22 November 1961 on her return trip.

The vessel was then chartered by Zim Line, of Israel, for a service between Haifa and Marseilles, and while still under this charter was sold in 1963 to another Italian firm, Covena S.p.A., of Genoa. When the Zim charter expired in October 1964, the vessel was sold again, to Saudi Lines, being given her seventh name, *King Abdelaziz* under her fifth flag, that of Saudi Arabia.

Placed in the pilgrim trade to Jedda, she had the misfortune to run aground on Algaham Reef, off Jedda, on 30 April 1965. Sent back to Italy for repairs, she then resumed the pilgrim trade in September 1965. Early in 1970 the old ship was withdrawn, and on 23 April 1970 arrived at Kaohsiung in Taiwan to be broken up.

FLAMINIA

GRUZIA

BUILT: *1939 by Swan, Hunter & Wigham Richardson Ltd,*
Newcastle
TONNAGE: *11 030 gross*
DIMENSIONS: *512 × 67 ft (156.1 × 20.4 m)*
SERVICE SPEED: *16 knots*
PROPULSION: *B & W diesels/twin screws*

Although, strictly speaking, this vessel does not come
within the confines of this book, it is well worth
recording the visit of *Gruzia* to Melbourne in
connection with the Olympic Games in 1956. The
decision to hold the Olympics in the southern
hemisphere for the first time in 1956, meant that athletes
from European countries had a considerable distance to
travel for the first time. The Russians overcame this
problem to some extent by despatching the bulk of their
team to Melbourne on the *Gruzia*.

This ship was launched on 25 August 1938, and
named *Sobieski*, having been built for the Polish
company, Gdynia–America Line. She had a sister,
Chrobry, which was built in Denmark at the same time,
and both were placed on a service from Gdynia to South
America. *Gruzia* had accommodation for 44 first class,
250 second class and 860 third class. She left Gdynia on
15 June 1939 on her maiden voyage, and was outbound
on her second voyage when Poland was invaded.
Sobieski headed for Dakar, where she was taken over by
the British, and converted into a troopship. *Chrobry*
was in Brazil on her maiden voyage at that time, and
was also taken over by the British as a troopship.

Both *Sobieski* and *Chrobry* were sent to Norway in

May 1940, but *Chrobry* was bombed by German aircraft
off Bodø, and sunk. *Sobieski* survived to take part in
further landings in Madagascar, North Africa, Sicily,
Salerno and finally Normandy. In 1947, the vessel was
handed back to Gdynia–America Line, and after a refit
in Genoa, made a voyage from there to New York,
returning to Gdynia. She now had accommodation for
70 first class, 270 cabin class and 450 tourist class
passengers.

In 1950, *Sobieski* was transferred to the flag of the
USSR, under the ownership of Sovtorgflot. Renamed
Gruzia, she was registered in Odessa, and operated in
the Black Sea, mainly on the route between Odessa and
Batumi. Having been selected to convey the Soviet
Union's Olympic team to Melbourne, *Gruzia* left
Odessa during October 1956, and arrived in Melbourne
on 7 November. For five weeks she lay alongside there,
being used as a floating hotel by many athletes and
officials. On 11 December, *Gruzia* departed, bound for
Vladivostok according to the local papers. She
eventually returned to the Black Sea, and resumed her
regular trade from Odessa.

Gruzia operated from Odessa to Eupatoria, Yalta,
Novorossiysk, Tuapse, Sochi, Sukhumi, Poti and
Batumi, a route known as the Black Sea Express. In
1964, the vessel began making voyages from Odessa to
Cuba, and also voyaged to Indonesia when that country
established close ties with the Soviet Union. *Gruzia*
finished her career back in the Black Sea, being
withdrawn early in 1975. On 14 April 1975, she arrived
at La Spezia, having been sold to shipbreakers there.

GRUZIA IN MELBOURNE

GUMHURYAT MISR

BUILT: *1928 by Cammell Laird & Co., Birkenhead*
TONNAGE: *7830 gross*
DIMENSIONS: *437 × 59 ft (134.5 × 18.1 m)*
SERVICE SPEED: *12.5 knots*
PROPULSION: *Geared turbines/twin screws*

Gumhuryat Misr was originally named *Lady Nelson*, the first of a group of five liners built for Canadian National Steamships. With accommodation for 130 first class and 32 second class passengers, these vessels carried general cargo to the West Indies, returning with sugar or fruit. *Lady Somers* was requisitioned late in 1940, only to be sunk in July 1941. In January 1942, *Lady Hawkins* was also sunk, as was *Lady Drake* four months later, when both were still in commercial service. On 9 March 1942, *Lady Nelson* was torpedoed whilst alongside at Castries in St Lucia, and settled on the shallow bottom. Refloated on 26 March, she was towed to Mobile, and converted into the first Canadian hospital ship, with 515 beds. The fifth ship, *Lady Rodney*, became a troopship, and in November 1946, the two survivors were handed back to Canadian National Steamships.

Lady Nelson and *Lady Rodney* resumed their pre-war service in August 1947, but in December 1952 were withdrawn, and sold in February 1953 to Khedivial Mail Line, of Egypt. *Lady Nelson* was renamed *Gumhuryat Misr*, her sister became *Mecca*, and they were refitted in Alexandria to carry 118 first class, 115 tourist class, and hundreds of pilgrims in the 'tween decks. During the pilgrim season they operated to Jedda, being laid up or chartered at other times.

On 15 August 1956, *Gumhuryat Misr* departed Piraeus with 914 Greek migrants on board. The ship was refused entry to Colombo until her owner forwarded payment for the harbour dues. Leaving Colombo, *Gumhuryat Misr* headed for Fremantle, where 47 migrants were to disembark. Arriving in Gage Roads on 16 September, with little fresh water left in her tanks, the local port authorities had not been advised of her arrival in advance, so no arrangements had been made for health, migration and customs clearances, nor had the owner appointed any agents in Australia.

For 30 hours, *Gumhuryat Misr* rode at anchor off Fremantle. An agent was hurriedly appointed, and money forwarded from Egypt to cover port costs, then on the evening of 17 September, the vessel finally berthed. An inspection of her lifesaving equipment resulted in seven of the 21 lifeboats being found unserviceable, some with holes in their hulls, others unable to be launched as the davits would not move. *Gumhuryat Misr* was held in port, awaiting further payments from Egypt to allow for repairs to be carried out, which did not commence until 21 September.

The repairs to the lifeboats were completed on 23 September, and at noon the next day, *Gumhuryat Misr* departed for Melbourne, where she berthed on 30 September. The bulk of her passengers disembarked there, then the vessel went on to Sydney, arriving on 3 October, and remaining in port for eight days. Some 4000 tons of flour were loaded, with more being taken on back in Melbourne during a 10 day stay at Victoria Dock. After passing through Fremantle again, *Gumhuryat Misr* went to Port Sudan to unload her cargo, then returned to Egypt. Not surprisingly, she never returned to Australia.

During 1960, all Egyptian shipping companies were nationalised as The United Arab Maritime Co., and *Gumhuryat Misr* was renamed *Al Wadi*. On 18 December 1965, she was badly damaged in a collision, and laid up in Alexandria, until sold to local shipbreakers during 1968.

GUMHURYAT MISR

POLYNESIE

BUILT: *1955 by S.A. des Anciens Chantiers Dubigeon, Nantes*
TONNAGE: *3709 gross*
DIMENSIONS: *344 × 49 ft (104.8 × 14.9 m)*
SERVICE SPEED: *14 knots*
PROPULSION: *B & W diesel/single screw*

Messageries Maritimes began operating a feeder service between Sydney and Noumea in 1882, using small vessels, usually near the end of their careers. In 1938 the *Polynesien*, of 1422 gross tons, was purchased for the route, but it was abandoned during the war. *Polynesien* returned to the feeder service in 1947, but she provided only a limited passenger capacity. When Messageries Maritimes commenced a post-war rebuilding programme, they left the construction of a new ship for the Sydney to Noumea route to last, so it was not until the middle of 1953 that a new ship was ordered.

Launched on 17 September 1954 as *Polynesie*, fitting out took nine months. *Polynesien* was sold to Hong Kong shipbreakers in April 1955, and on 11 June *Polynesie* left Marseilles on her delivery voyage. After calls at Colombo and Singapore, the vessel reached Noumea on 15 July, departing again five days later on her first voyage to Sydney, where she berthed on 25 July.

Polynesie was a very smart little ship, having 20 outside cabins with private facilities for 36 passengers.

Initially she had a black hull with a white line and a black funnel, but later her funnel was repainted white. In the 1960s her hull was also painted white, giving her the appearance of a luxury yacht. Her port of registry was changed several times, from Marseilles to Noumea then back to Marseilles again, while for a brief period in 1972 it was La Verdun, a small port on the Gironde River. Subsequently *Polynesie* was registered in Port Vila, as her route had been extended to include calls in the New Hebrides.

Polynesie was a regular visitor to Sydney for 20 years, but in the early 1970s, Messageries Maritimes began withdrawing from the passenger trades. *Polynesie* was the last of their vessels to be withdrawn from service, departing Sydney for the final time on 22 October 1975, and going to Port Vila and Noumea, where she was laid up for over a year, pending sale. The feeder service was then taken over by a chartered cargo ship, *La Bonita*.

Late in 1976, *Polynesie* was bought by Guan Guan Shipping (Pte.) Ltd, a well known Singapore company, which owned a large fleet of second-hand tonnage. Renamed *Golden Glory*, she went to Singapore, but it is doubtful if the new owner ever used her, as she seemed to be mostly laid up off the island port. Three years later she was sold to Taiwanese shipbreakers, Gi Yuen Steel Enterprises Co. Ltd, and arrived at their Kaohsiung yard on 14 June 1979, with demolition work commencing nine days later.

POLYNESIE

MELANESIEN

BUILT: *1926 by Kon. Maats. de Schelde, Flushing*
TONNAGE: *9905 gross*
DIMENSIONS: *508 × 60 ft (154.8 × 18.3 m)*
SERVICE SPEED: *17 knots*
PROPULSION: *Sulzer diesels/twin screws*

To maintain a regular service between France and Australia in the post-war years, Messageries Maritimes needed to charter a vessel to partner *Caledonien* and *Tahitien*, and initially operated *Changchow*. When she was returned to her owner in 1958, Messageries Maritimes chartered *Melanesien*.

This vessel had been built for Rotterdam Lloyd, being launched on 21 March 1925. Originally to have been called *Wajang*, she was instead named *Indrapoera*, and on 10 February 1926 left Rotterdam bound for the Dutch East Indies. She provided accommodation for 141 first class, 184 second class and 68 third class passengers. In 1928 she was joined by the slightly larger *Sibajak*, which also came to Australia after the war.

Indrapoera proved to be slower than her running mates, so in 1931 she went back to her builder's yard to have a more powerful set of Sulzer diesels installed. At the same time she was lengthened at the bow, these changes increasing her speed from 15 to 17 knots. *Indrapoera* had been back in service for only two years when, on 27 November 1933, her superstructure was almost destroyed by fire when she was berthed in Rotterdam. Following rebuilding, the liner returned to service during 1934.

When the Germans invaded Holland in May 1940, *Indrapoera* was on a voyage to the East Indies, and was taken over by the Allies. Retaining her Dutch crew, she served as a troopship until 1947, then was handed back to her owner, which was now known as Royal Rotterdam Lloyd. Instead of being restored to her pre-war state, *Indrapoera* was rebuilt as a cargo/passenger vessel, with her accommodation reduced to 96 passengers only, all first class. The central superstructure was retained, but the promenade deck extension to the stern was removed, and an extra pair of cargo derricks fitted aft, while the funnel was shortened to half its original height.

Indrapoera returned to her pre-war service to the East Indies, where demand for passages was greatly reduced due to civil unrest in the area. *Indrapoera* was withdrawn from service in 1956, and soon after sold to Providencia Shipping Co., Panama, being renamed *Assuncion*. However, later the same year the ship was resold to the Costa Line, and renamed *Bianca C*.

Costa offered the vessel for charter, and she was taken up by Messageries Maritimes. Her accommodation was altered to carry 100 first class and 80 third class passengers, and the ship renamed *Melanesien*. On 13 May 1958, the vessel left Marseilles on her first voyage, passing through the Panama Canal, then visiting Tahiti and Noumea before arriving in Sydney on 7 July.

Over the next three years, *Melanesien* made three round trips each year, then on 14 March 1963 she left Marseilles on her final voyage, being in Sydney for three days before departing on 10 May. With her charter expired, the vessel was handed back to Costa Line, who sold her to shipbreakers in Italy during October 1963.

MELANESIEN

EASTERN QUEEN

BUILT: *1950 by Wm Denny & Bros, Dumbarton*
TONNAGE: *8644 gross*
DIMENSIONS: *468 × 63 ft (142.6 × 19.2 m)*
SERVICE SPEED: *15 knots*
PROPULSION: *Geared turbines/single screw*

The Indo–China Steam Navigation Co. was formed in 1882 to operate a variety of services from Hong Kong along the China coast to Shanghai, later extending to Singapore and Calcutta.

Many of the company staff were interned in Hong Kong following the Japanese invasion in December 1942. To pass the time, some of the staff began designing a new ship for the service from Japan, China and Hong Kong to the Straits and Bay of Bengal, and after the war ended this ship was ordered. Launched on 5 April 1950 as *Eastern Queen*, she was the largest ship yet owned by the Indo–China Steam Navigation Co., and the fastest, reaching 18.7 knots on trials. Unlike the other ships of the line, *Eastern Queen* was also given some passenger accommodation, with 28 first class and 28 second class in cabins, 522 unberthed and 180 deck passengers. In common with other ships on the China coast, there were also extensive anti-pirate safeguards fitted.

Eastern Queen proved to be a very expensive ship to operate, so at the end of 1955 she was taken off the Bay of Bengal trade, and replaced the cargo ship *Eastern Saga* on the Australian trade. Departing Japan in December 1955, *Eastern Queen* left Hong Kong on 4 January 1956, arriving in Sydney on 17 January, and Melbourne a week later, then going on to Adelaide and Port Pirie. Northbound, the vessel also called at Brisbane, then went directly to Yokkaichi in Japan, setting a record for this voyage in 1958, 9 days 14 hours and 42 minutes.

In 1960, *Eastern Queen* was chartered by Messageries Maritimes to transport Tonkinese refugees from Noumea to North Vietnam. The ship arrived in Sydney on 1 September 1960 to begin the charter, but did not leave for Noumea until 23 December, then carried the refugees to Haiphong.

Her appearance was altered at various times. When she first appeared on the route she had a black hull and squat funnel, which was later heightened, while her hull was at one time repainted white. In 1966, Indo–China S. N. Co. went into partnership with the Dominion Line, forming Dominion Far East Line, and the hull of *Eastern Queen* was repainted grey-green. This joint service was not a success, as the day of the passenger–cargo liner was all but over, and in 1970 *Eastern Queen* was replaced by a container vessel.

On 30 June 1970, *Eastern Queen* left Sydney for the last time, having been sold to Wicklow Shipping Co., of Gibraltar. Renamed *Wicklow*, she operated as a cargo ship until 22 February 1974, when she arrived at Whampoa to be broken up.

EASTERN QUEEN

BERGENSFJORD

BUILT: *1956 by Swan, Hunter & Wigham Richardson,*
  Newcastle
TONNAGE: *18 739 gross*
DIMENSIONS: *578 × 72 ft (176.2 × 22 m)*
SERVICE SPEED: *20 knots*
PROPULSION: *Stork diesels/twin screws*

Between 1974 and 1978, thousands of Australians
cruised from Singapore around the Indonesian islands
on the *Rasa Sayang*. Though never a visitor to Australia
under this name, the vessel did make a number of
voyages here under her original name, *Bergensfjord*, in
the course of world cruises. Launched on 18 July 1955
by Princess Astrid of Norway, *Bergensfjord* was
completed in May 1956, and handed over to Norwegian
America Line. Designed as a dual-purpose liner, she
could accommodate 103 first class and 775 tourist class
passengers on regular voyages between Oslo and New
York, but for cruises this number was reduced to 500 in
one class.

On 10 January 1958, *Bergensfjord* left New York on
her first cruise to the South Pacific, calling at Tahiti on
her way to Auckland, Wellington and Hobart before
arriving in Melbourne on 18 February, and Sydney two

days later. She then went to Port Moresby, and back
across the Pacific to New York. Two years later,
Bergensfjord returned, leaving New York on 15 January
1960. This time she called at Sydney first, on 18
February, then Hobart on 22 February, before crossing
to Wellington and Auckland. Her final visit to Australia
and New Zealand was during February 1963, as in
future years the liner cruised to ports in the Far East.

In 1971 Norwegian America Line offered
Bergensfjord for sale, and the French Line made an
immediate offer, needing a ship to replace their *Antilles*,
recently lost by grounding and a subsequent fire. In
March 1971 the vessel changed hands, being renamed
De Grasse, and began a regular service from France to
the West Indies, with some cruises, but was not a
success.

In October 1973, *De Grasse* was sold to a new
company, Cruise East, a subsidiary of the Norwegian
Thoreson shipping concern. Renamed *Rasa Sayang*, she
was refitted in Singapore to carry 800 passengers in one
class, then on 8 July 1974, left on her first cruise around
the Indonesian islands. For a few years this operation
was very successful, but on 2 June 1977 a fire broke out
when the ship was off the Malaysian coast, and she had

BERGENSFJORD

RASA SAYANG

to be abandoned. Towed back to Singapore, repairs were effected, then *Rasa Sayang* returned to service again on 4 July, but she would never regain her popularity.

On 19 June 1978, *Rasa Sayang* completed her final cruise, and then was withdrawn. Soon after, she was sold to Sunlit Cruises, and renamed *Golden Moon*. Arriving in Piraeus in December 1978, the vessel was laid up while a charter was arranged with a new Dutch company, who intended to rename her *Prins Van Oranje*. This deal fell through, so the liner remained idle in Piraeus.

In May 1980, the Australian Government banned Soviet cruise ships in local ports, effectively putting an end to the operation of CTC Line. They sought alternative tonnage to charter, and selected *Golden Moon*. Under the arrangement, the vessel would be

again named *Rasa Sayang*, and marketed in Australia under the banner of Rasa Sayang Cruises. It was planned that the ship would be overhauled, then go to Southampton in November 1980 to board passengers and bring them to Sydney. On 23 December, she was scheduled to depart on the first of a long programme of South Pacific cruises.

Work on refitting the interior and overhauling the engines was done in Piraeus, and on 27 August 1980 an engine test was run. During this, a fire broke out, but was thought to have been extinguished. However, that night the fire erupted again, and soon engulfed the entire ship. Her aluminium superstructure melted in the heat, and after being towed into Peráma bay to burn out, the ship turned on her side and sank in shallow water. The wreck was later used to form part of a land-filling programme in Peráma bay.

KUNGSHOLM

BUILT: *1953 by Kon. Maats. de Schelde, Flushing*
TONNAGE: *21 141 gross*
DIMENSIONS: *600 × 77 ft (182.9 × 23.5 m)*
SERVICE SPEED: *19 knots*
PROPULSION: *B & W diesels/twin screws*

One of the most attractive liners to visit Australia in the course of long-distance cruises during the post-war years was *Kungsholm*. She was owned by Swedish–America Line, having been launched on 18 October 1952, and completed a year later. Designed as a dual-purpose liner, *Kungsholm* could carry 176 first class and 626 tourist class passengers when on the regular trade between Gothenburg and New York, but for cruises would carry about 500 passengers in one class.

On 24 November 1953, *Kungsholm* departed Gothenburg on her maiden voyage to New York, and was employed on this trade for most of the year. During the off-season, the liner would make cruises from New York to the Caribbean. In 1957 she was joined by the similar *Gripsholm*, and the following year Swedish–America Line began sending their ships on long-distance cruises from America during the winter months.

On 21 January 1958, *Kungsholm* departed New York on a cruise around the Pacific, calling at numerous islands and Auckland before berthing in Sydney on 21 February for a two-day stopover. From there she went to Port Moresby, then on to Hong Kong and Japanese ports before returning to New York. Such was the success of that voyage that, in December 1958, *Kungsholm* left New York on a 98 day Pacific cruise, visiting 22 ports. Once again she visited Auckland, then Wellington before arriving in Sydney on 14 January 1959 for another two-day stay, returning to New York via Asia.

For the next few years, *Kungsholm* went to other parts of the world on her long cruises, then in January 1962, left New York bound for the South Pacific once more, visiting Auckland, Wellington and Sydney again. Her final visit to these parts as *Kungsholm* was in 1965, having departed New York on 8 January with 375 passengers on board. Following visits to Auckland and Wellington, the liner arrived in Sydney on 9 February, then headed north to Green Island, off Cairns, and Darwin, thence Bali, Hong Kong and Japan, returning to New York on 8 April.

During 1964 a sale had been negotiated for

KUNGSHOLM ARRIVING IN SYDNEY COVE

COLUMBUS C

Kungsholm to North German Lloyd, who took delivery of the ship on 16 October 1965. Renamed *Europa*, and now with a black hull, she spent the next six years combining cruises with regular summer voyages between Bremerhaven and New York. In 1970, North German Lloyd and Hamburg–America Line merged to form Hapag–Lloyd, with *Europa* operating for them, from 1972 exclusively as a cruise ship, having a white hull once again. In 1981, a new *Europa* was built, and features elsewhere in this book, so the original *Europa* was sold in November 1981 to Costa Line, of Italy.

Renamed *Columbus C*, but otherwise unaltered apart from funnel colours, she began cruising on the European market, and early in 1983 made a world cruise. Departing from Genoa on 22 December 1982, the liner passed through the West Indies and Panama Canal, then on to the South Pacific islands before stopping at Auckland, Wellington and Lyttelton, then across to Hobart and Sydney, arriving on 15 February. Leaving the next day, *Columbus C* stopped at the Great Barrier Reef and Cairns, before continuing north to Hong Kong, Canton and then Singapore. The final stage of the cruise took her to India and then through the Suez Canal, returning to Genoa on 12 April.

During 1984 it was planned to rename the ship *Costa Columbus*, but on 29 July 1984, the vessel struck a breakwater while entering Cádiz, and after berthing settled on the bottom, though with most of her hull above the water. The damage proved so serious that the liner was sold to local shipbreakers as soon as she was refloated.

FAIRSKY

BUILT: *1942 by Western Pipe & Steel Co., San Francisco*
TONNAGE: *12 464 gross*
DIMENSIONS: *502 × 69 ft (153 × 21.2 m)*
SERVICE SPEED: *17.5 knots*
PROPULSION: *Geared turbines/single screw*

Fairsky was the second converted aircraft carrier that Sitmar Line placed in passenger service to Australia, though the vessel had originally been laid down on 7 April 1941 as a standard C3 type cargo ship. Intended to be handed over to the Isthmian Steam Ship Co., of New York, on completion, the vessel was named *Steel Artisan* when launched on 27 September 1941. Three months later, the incomplete vessel was taken over by the United States Government, for conversion into an auxiliary aircraft carrier.

Intended to join the US Navy as the USS *Barnes*, she was one of a number of such vessels transferred to the Royal Navy under the lend-lease agreement, being commissioned on 30 September 1942 as HMS *Attacker*. In her new role, the ship could carry 18 aircraft, and initially served as a convoy escort on the North Atlantic. Her aircraft were later used to provide cover during the landings at Salerno in September 1943, and in the South of France in August 1944. HMS *Attacker* finished the war in the Pacific, then on 6 January 1946 was handed back to the Americans.

Laid up and offered for sale, the vessel was purchased by National Bulk Carriers, of New York, and in February 1947 work commenced on conversion into a cargo ship. The flight deck and other military fittings were removed, but then the work stopped. In 1950 the vessel was bought by Navcot Corp., the American company established by Alexandr Vlasov, founder of Sitmar. Renamed *Castelforte*, she was left idle until 1952, then was transferred to the ownership of Sitmar Line.

The vessel was sent to the Newport News shipyard for conversion into a reefer ship, destined for the lucrative meat trade from South America. In the event, the conversion was not completed, and instead she was again laid up, though her name was amended to *Castel Forte*. It was February 1957 before the ship moved again, this time going to the Bethlehem Steel shipyard in New York to commence conversion into a passenger ship.

A new superstructure was constructed atop the hull in New York, then in December 1957, she crossed to Genoa where the internal fitting out was completed. Renamed *Fairsky* early in 1958, she was registered in Liberia under the nominal ownership of a Sitmar subsidiary, Fairline Shipping Corp. A four year contract had been obtained from the Australian Government to transport British migrants, so accommodation was installed for 1461 passengers in one class.

On 26 June 1958, *Fairsky* left Southampton on her first voyage, with 1430 passengers on board. Arriving in Fremantle on 21 July, Melbourne on 27 July and Sydney on 29 July, *Fairsky* left the next day for Brisbane, where she berthed on 1 August, then retraced her route back to Southampton. It was not until December 1961 that *Fairsky* made her first visit to a New Zealand port, Auckland, and in 1962 she made her first cruise.

Fairsky remained on the migrant trade until 1970, though in the 1960s some return voyages were made through the Panama Canal. After the closure of the Suez Canal, *Fairsky* voyaged out around South Africa, and in November 1969 suffered engine trouble between Southampton and Cape Town. She spent several days there being repaired, and eventually reached Fremantle 12 days late. When Sitmar lost the migrant contract to Chandris in 1970, *Fairsky* continued to operate regular voyages from Britain to Australia until February 1972, when she was laid up in Southampton.

On 8 November 1973 *Fairsky* returned to service, departing Southampton for Australia again. On 2 June 1974, she left Southampton for the last time, following which she began permanent cruises from Sydney. In this role *Fairsky* enjoyed a great deal of success, operating both from Sydney and Darwin.

On 12 June, *Fairsky* departed Darwin on a cruise, but while leaving Jakarta on 23 June she struck a sunken wreck. Badly holed forward, *Fairsky* was beached on a sandbar to prevent her sinking. A concrete patch was placed over the hole, and on 9 July *Fairsky* entered drydock in Singapore. The damage was so severe it was not worth repairing, so *Fairsky* was offered for sale, and purchased in December 1977 by Fuji Marden & Co., for breaking up in Hong Kong. Arriving there under her own power on 18 December, *Fairsky* was awaiting her fate in Junk Bay when, in March 1978, she was sold to Peninsular Shipping Corp., from the Philippines.

Towed to Mariveles, she was converted into a floating casino and hotel, being renamed *Philippine Tourist*, and berthed in Manila South Harbour. On the night of 3 November 1978, the ship was swept by fire, and completely gutted. The wreck was sold back to Fuji Marden & Co., being towed back to Hong Kong, arriving on 24 May, and soon after was scrapped.

THE AIRCRAFT CARRIER *HMS ATTACKER*

FAIRSKY

UNDERGOING CONVERSION INTO *PHILIPPINE TOURIST*

MONTEREY

BUILT: *1952 by Bethlehem Shipbuilding Corp., Sparrow's Point*
TONNAGE: *14 799 gross*
DIMENSIONS: *561 × 76 ft (171.1 × 23.2 m)*
SERVICE SPEED: *20 knots*
PROPULSION: *Geared turbines/single screw*

In 1885 the Oceanic Steam Ship Co. commenced a service between California and the east coast of Australia. In 1926 the firm was taken over by the Matson Line, and during the 1930s they operated two large liners on the route, *Mariposa* and *Monterey*. After the war, Matson hoped to return these ships to the trade, but this did not eventuate. It was not until 1955 that Matson decided to reactivate their trans-Pacific service, when a pair of "Mariner" class cargo ships were obtained for conversion into passenger liners. They revived the names of the pre-war vessels, with *Free State Mariner* being renamed *Monterey* while *Pine Tree Mariner* became *Mariposa*.

Free State Mariner had been launched on 29 May 1952, and *Pine Tree Mariner* on 7 November 1952, and both were operated for a brief period by the US Maritime Commission, then laid up. Following their sale to Matson in 1955, both ships were sent to the Williamette Iron & Steel Corp. shipyard in Portland, where conversion work commenced. This involved the construction of a superstructure, and cabins for 365 passengers. They were the first American ships to be fitted with Sperry Gyrofin stabilisers.

MARIPOSA

BUILT: *1953 by Bethlehem Steel Co., Quincy*
TONNAGE: *14 812 gross*
DIMENSIONS: *561 × 76 ft (171.1 × 23.2 m)*
SERVICE SPEED: *20 knots*
PROPULSION: *Geared turbines/single screw*

Mariposa was the first finished, reaching 24.6 knots on trials. On 27 October 1956, she left San Francisco on her maiden voyage, calling at Honolulu and Papeete before arriving in Wellington on 15 November, then Melbourne on 19 November and Sydney on 21 November. *Mariposa* called at Auckland on her return voyage, which ended in San Francisco on 11 December.

Monterey was scheduled to enter service in November 1956, but it was not until 8 January 1957 that she left San Francisco for Sydney, where she berthed on 29 January. After a few voyages, the calls at Wellington and Melbourne were abandoned, with Nuku'alofa and Opua being added.

For 10 years the two vessels voyaged to the South Pacific all year, during which time calls at Suva and Pago Pago were added. From 1968 both ships were also used for cruises. *Mariposa* cruised from San Francisco to Alaska during the summer months of 1968 and 1969, while *Monterey* made two cruises to South America in 1969. An extensive cruise programme was scheduled for 1970, and into 1971.

On 13 August 1970, Matson Line announced they were going to terminate their passenger operation, and to sell *Mariposa* and *Monterey* to Pacific Far East Line,

MONTEREY AS A MATSON LINER

effective on 20 January 1971. *Mariposa* was handed over in San Francisco the following day, and *Monterey* on 15 February, on her return from the last voyage Matson would operate to the South Pacific.

The only change made to the ships was their funnel colours, and they continued to operate to the South Pacific and also cruise. The ships lost money for their new owner, despite the government subsidy, and that was only available while the pair were less than 25 years old. This meant that from 1978 the government would no longer be subsidising the pair, and without that assistance, Pacific Far East Line could not afford to continue the passenger service.

Mariposa departed San Francisco on 1 November 1977 on her final voyage to the South Pacific, being in Auckland on 21 November, and Sydney from 26 to 28 November, returning to San Francisco on 14 December. The final voyage by an America flag liner to the South Pacific commenced on 7 December 1977, when *Monterey* left San Francisco, calling at Auckland on 27 December, and being in Sydney from 1 January 1978 for three days. Following visits to Suva, Pago Pago and Honolulu, *Monterey* arrived back in San Francisco on 19 January, and was then laid up.

Mariposa remained in service slightly longer, cruising from California to Hawaii, but on 7 April 1978 she berthed in San Francisco for the last time, and then joined her sister in lay-up.

Both vessels were offered for sale, but then Pacific Far East Line went bankrupt, so on 10 April 1979 both ships were sold at auction, for $2.7 million, to Edward Daly, the president of World Airways. Despite this, they remained idle in San Francisco, as the new owner tried to either resell or charter them. *Monterey* was reported sold to a new company, Royal Hawaiian Cruise Lines, but this fell through, then in November 1980 the liner was sold to the International Organisation of Masters, Mates and Pilots. However, the ship was destined to remain idle in San Francisco for a further seven years.

Mariposa was sold to American World Line in October 1980. On 7 November she left San Francisco under tow, bound for Mihara in Japan, where *Mariposa* was once more laid up. In 1983, *Mariposa* was sold again, to Guangzhou Ocean Shipping Co., of China. The vessel was given an extensive refit in Japan, during which she was converted to diesel propulsion, and then renamed *Jin Jiang*. Since 1984 she has operated a regular service between Shanghai and Hong Kong under the banner of the Shanghai Jin Jiang Shipping Co.

Monterey remained idle in San Francisco, then in 1984 was sold to American Maritime Holdings. The vessel remained laid up until July 1986, when she was towed to Portland, Oregon. After a delay of several months, work began on converting *Monterey* into a luxury cruise ship. Steelwork was done at Portland's Northwest Marine Works, then in June 1987 *Monterey* was towed to the Tacoma Boatbuilding Co. yard to have a bowthruster and sponsons fitted. Following this, the vessel was towed to Finland, where the Wartsila shipyard completed the conversion work, which included installation of diesel engines.

In September 1988, *Monterey* was handed over to her owner, and entered a new cruise service around the Hawaiian islands, but six months later the company went bankrupt and *Monterey* was laid up.

MARIPOSA IN PACIFIC FAR EAST LINE COLOURS

ANKING AND ANSHUN

BUILT: Anking *1950 by Scotts Shipbuilding &*
  Engineering Co., Greenock
Anshun *1951 by Taikoo Dockyard, Hong Kong*
TONNAGE: *6160 gross*
DIMENSIONS: *418 × 57 ft (127.4 × 17.3 m)*
SERVICE SPEED: *15 knots*
PROPULSION: *Doxford diesel/single screw*

The post-war rebuilding programme initiated by China Navigation Co. included orders for two ships which were designed for the service from Chinese ports to Singapore. One was built in Britain, the second being the largest of her type to be built in Hong Kong after the war. *Anking* was launched on 23 August 1949, and arrived in Hong Kong early the following year, while *Anshun* was launched on 12 September 1950. Both were fitted out with cabin accommodation for 50 first class and 116 steerage passengers, while a further 1000 steerage could be carried on short sectors.

By the time these ships were completed, China was under Communist control, and China Navigation was no longer operating along the Chinese coast. Instead, they joined the pilgrim trade to Jedda for half the year, and operated a variety of routes for the rest of the year. On 3 July 1955, *Anshun* was damaged by shells from an Egyptian battery at the entrance to the Gulf of Aqaba.

Having established a successful service to the east coast of Australia, China Navigation decided to open a new service to Fremantle. On 8 August 1958, *Anshun*

departed Fremantle to inaugurate the service, to Indonesia, Hong Kong and Japan. *Anking* made occasional appearances on this route as well over the next few years.

For the first 10 years of their careers, *Anking* and *Anshun* had white hulls, but these were repainted black in 1961. The same year, the pair transferred to a new service, from Hong Kong, Manila and Port Moresby to Brisbane, Sydney and Melbourne, with monthly sailings in conjunction with *Taiyuan* and *Changsha*. This phase of their careers lasted four years, following which *Anking* and *Anshun* were transferred to different trades.

Anshun went back to the pilgrim trade, while *Anking* opened a new service from Hong Kong to Keelung in Taiwan. On 11 August 1965, *Anking* struck the breakwater of Keelung Harbour, and was holed. At times *Anshun* joined her sister on the Taiwanese trade. *Anking* was sold in May 1970 to Straits Steam Ship Co., of Singapore. Renamed *Klias*, she operated from Singapore to Borneo. In 1971, *Anshun* was sold to Pan-Islamic Steamship Co., of Pakistan, renamed *Safina-E-Abid*, and used on the pilgrim trade from Pakistani ports to Jedda for most of each year.

On 7 September 1976, *Klias* was berthing in Singapore when her stern became impaled on the dock. The damage proved so severe, the vessel was sold to shipbreakers in Hong Kong shortly thereafter. During 1978, *Safina-E-Abid* passed into the ownership of the Pakistan Shipping Corp., and when not engaged on the pilgrim trade, operated between Karachi and Kuwait.

ANSHUN

ORANJE

BUILT: *1939 by Netherlands Shipbuilding Co., Amsterdam*
TONNAGE: *20 551 gross*
DIMENSIONS: *656 × 84 ft (199.9 × 25.5 m)*
SERVICE SPEED: *21 knots*
PROPULSION: *Sulzer diesels/triple screws*

Oranje was built for the Nederland Line, which maintained a regular service between Holland and the Dutch East Indies in competition with Rotterdam Lloyd. On 2 July 1937, the keel was laid for a liner destined to be the finest, largest and last to be built for the Nederland Line. Named in honour of the Dutch Royal Family, the ship was launched by Queen Wilhelmina on 8 September 1938. Completed on 27 June 1939, *Oranje* achieved 26.5 knots on trials, giving her a good reserve of speed, and at the time she was the highest powered motorship in the world.

Accommodation on *Oranje* was divided between 283 first class, 283 second class, 92 third class and 52 fourth class. A striking feature of the ship was the shape of her hull. Instead of the sides being vertical, they flared out, the beam at the waterline being 17 ft (5.17 m) wider than at the Promenade deck. This was intended to make her more stable, reduce tonnage and, along with a cut-away bow, improve speed.

On 3 September 1939, Britain and Germany declared war, but this did not have an immediate effect on Holland, so on 4 September, *Oranje* departed on schedule for her maiden voyage to the Dutch East Indies. However, instead of following the regular route through the Mediterranean, she went around Africa, with a call at Cape Town. On arrival in Batavia, the ship was detained while a decision was made concerning her returning to Europe. It was decided to lay her up at Surabaya, where she arrived in December 1939.

Following the German invasion of Holland in May 1940, *Oranje* was handed over to the British by the Dutch Government in exile. In February 1941, she was offered to the Australians as a hospital ship, to be equipped at the expense of the Dutch, and manned by her regular crew. On 31 March 1941, *Oranje* arrived in Sydney, and was converted at Cockatoo Island. On 1 July she entered service as the second hospital ship attached to the Royal Australian Navy.

On her first voyage, *Oranje* went to Suez and back, and in all she operated 41 voyages as a hospital ship, painted all white with a wide red band around her hull, and red crosses on the hull and funnel, which were lit up at night. On 31 May 1942, *Oranje* left Sydney in the afternoon, and that night several Japanese midget submarines penetrated the harbour, though only causing minor damage. The final visit by *Oranje* to Australia as a hospital ship was during November 1945, following which she finally returned to her home port of Amsterdam, and a great welcome.

Oranje was then refitted, and restored to her original condition. In July 1947, the liner returned to commercial service, and made her first return trip to Batavia, seven years after being completed. However, the Dutch East Indies were in ferment, as the clamour for independence from Holland grew into open rebellion. Both Nederland Line and Royal Rotterdam Lloyd were forced to find alternative employment for many of their ships. The two companies decided to pool their resources on the Dutch East Indies service, with *Oranje* and *Willem Ruys* operating a joint service.

Indonesia gained full independence in 1949, but still retained many commercial links with Holland, so *Oranje* and *Willem Ruys* remained on their regular trade. On 6 January 1953, the two liners were scheduled to pass in the Rea Sea. To give their passengers a special treat, the captains tried to make the pass as close as possible, but unfortunately the manoeuvre went wrong, and the ships sideswiped each other, causing enough damage to *Oranje* for her to miss one voyage while undergoing repairs.

In December 1957, the Indonesian Government seized all Dutch possessions in the islands, and terminated relations with the Dutch. This brought about an immediate cessation of the joint Nederland–Royal Rotterdam Lloyd service to Indonesia, and *Oranje* was laid up pending a decision on her future. With *Johan van Oldenbarnevelt* already operating to Australia, Nederland Line decided to have *Oranje* join her. During 1958, she was refitted at Amsterdam, her accommodation being altered to carry 323 first class and 626 tourist class passengers.

In November 1958, *Oranje* left Amsterdam on her first commercial voyage to Australia, passing through the Suez Canal and arriving in Fremantle on 30 November, Melbourne on 5 December, and Sydney two days later. On 9 December she departed Sydney, following the same route back to Holland. Her second voyage left Amsterdam on 4 February 1959, and followed the same route to Sydney, but on the return journey called at Jakarta, Singapore and Penang.

In March 1959, *Willem Ruys* joined the Australian trade, and in conjunction with *Oranje* began a new round-the-world service. *Oranje* made four voyages a year westabout, including calls at Port Everglades, Tahiti, Auckland and Wellington, Sydney and Melbourne, and on occasion Fremantle, Singapore, Penang, Colombo and Port Said, while *Willem Ruys* operated the route in reverse. This service was maintained for four years, then the two Dutch companies decided to withdraw, and dispose of their liners. On 4 May 1964, *Oranje* left Amsterdam on her final voyage, being in Melbourne on 3 June, and departing Sydney on 10 June, then being laid up in Amsterdam on her return, and offered for sale.

ORANJE

ANGELINA LAURO

184

ANGELINA LAURO

REBUILT: 1966 by Cant. del Tirreno, Genoa
TONNAGE: 24 377 gross
DIMENSIONS: 674 × 83 ft (205.5 × 25.5 m)
SERVICE SPEED: 21 knots
PROPULSION: Sulzer diesels/triple screws

On 4 September 1964, *Oranje* was sold to Flotta Lauro, renamed *Angelina Lauro*, and sent to the Cant. del Tirreno shipyard in Genoa for extensive rebuilding. It had been planned to install new machinery, but when the engines were opened up, and found to be in excellent condition, they were retained. Externally the ship was altered so completely she was no longer recognisable as *Oranje*.

A raked bow was fitted, to improve her sea-keeping qualities, the forward well deck plated in, and Denny–Brown stabilisers fitted. The superstructure was extended forward, and the lower decks enclosed. The mainmast was removed, and replaced by two cargo derricks, while a signal mast was fitted above the bridge. The most unusual, and controversial feature was the unique new funnel, with its angled top, known as an "angel's wing", and lattice work on the sides and back.

The original accommodation was stripped out, and rebuilt to carry 189 first class and 946 tourist class, with an additional 377 berths classified as interchangeable. Over 90 per cent of the cabins had private facilities, and all were tastefully decorated. Air-conditioning was extended throughout the accommodation, and a new swimming pool with a sliding glass cover added for first class passengers, the two existing pools being allocated to tourist class. Several new public rooms were added as well, those for first class being located at the forward end of the saloon deck, with tourist class having the after end of the deck. Some facilities were shared between the classes, including the chapel and the two deck high cinema, with tourist class seating on the main deck, and first class in the balcony on the saloon deck. The work was almost finished when, on 24 August 1965, a fire broke out on board, which burned for two days. Six shipyard workers lost their lives in the blaze, and the completion of the vessel was put back six months while repairs were effected.

Angelina Lauro was finally handed over to Flotta Lauro in February 1966, and prepared for entry into the Australian trade. On 6 March, the liner departed Bremerhaven, then called at Southampton before proceeding through the Mediterranean and Suez Canal, arriving in Fremantle on 29 March, Melbourne on 2 April, and Sydney on 5 April, terminating the voyage at Wellington on 8 April, returning by the reverse route. She was joined in this service in April 1966 by her old running mate, *Willem Ruys*, now renamed *Achille Lauro*.

After 1967, *Angelina Lauro* had to voyage around South Africa, and on 28 September 1968, she left Sydney on her first homeward voyage across the Pacific, and around Cape Horn, with calls at several South American ports. Late in 1969, *Angelina Lauro* made her first cruise from Australia, and in 1970 also made some cruises from Southampton. From 1971 the vessel began making regular voyages around the world, returning to Europe through the Panama Canal, and the number of cruises she operated was increased.

During 1972, Flotta Lauro decided to withdraw from the Australian trade, due to a reduction in the demand for passages combined with tighter government controls on immigration. In April 1972, *Angelina Lauro* departed Southampton on her final voyage to Australia, leaving Melbourne on 14 May, and Sydney on 17 May. The liner was then refitted for full-time cruising, her passenger capacity being reduced to 800. From November 1972, *Angelina Lauro* was based on San Juan for regular seven day cruises in the Caribbean, being managed for Lauro by another Italian company, Costa Line.

On 10 October 1977, Costa Line took *Angelina Lauro* on charter for three years, during which her funnel would be repainted in their colours, and she would be advertised as *Angelina*, though her name was never officially altered. The ship had returned to Genoa for a refit, and Costa took her over there. On 21 October she departed on a line voyage to La Guaira in Venezuela, and on 5 November 1977, she began cruising from San Juan again.

On 30 March 1979, *Angelina Lauro* was berthed in St Thomas during a cruise, when a fire broke out in the aft galley, and rapidly spread to engulf the whole ship. Attempts to tow her away from the wharf failed, and the weight of water poured into the ship left her sitting on the shallow bottom, with a 25 degree list to port, away from the dock. Fortunately, all her passengers were ashore at the time of the fire, so there was no loss of life. Declared a total loss, the wreck was refloated on 6 July, having already been sold to shipbreakers in Taiwan. Leaving St Thomas under tow on 30 July, the pair passed through the Panama Canal, and were in the middle of the Pacific when *Angelina Lauro* began taking water on 21 September. Gradually her list worsened, and on 24 September 1979, *Angelina Lauro* rolled on her side and sank.

WILLEM RUYS

BUILT: *1947 by Kon. Maats. de Schelde, Flushing*
TONNAGE: *21 119 gross*
DIMENSIONS: *631 × 82 ft (192.4 × 25.1 m)*
SERVICE SPEED: *22 knots*
PROPULSION: *Sulzer diesels/twin screws*

Rotterdam Lloyd had operated a service from Holland to the Dutch East Indies since 1875, and in August 1938, it placed an order for a new vessel, to be the biggest, fastest, and last passenger liner they would own. The keel was laid down on 25 January 1939, and the new ship was scheduled to enter service during 1941. She was to be the Rotterdam Lloyd answer to the new *Oranje* of their main competitors, Nederland Line.

Work continued on the vessel until Holland was invaded by the German Army in May 1940, at which time the hull was complete, and the engines had been installed. The Germans tried to have the ship completed, but the Dutch resistance managed to prevent much real progress being made, and eventually the Germans gave up, and prohibited work on the ship. Extensive protection was built around the hull, and sand spread over the top deck to protect against incendiary bombs. The Allied air forces made numerous bombing raids on the Flushing area during the German occupation, but no damage was inflicted on the incomplete hull that overshadowed the town. When the Germans retreated from Holland, they tried to destroy the incomplete vessel with dynamite, but Dutch resistance workers removed the charges before they could be detonated.

Flushing had been severely damaged during the war, and the engines of the new ship were utilised while she was still on the slipway to supply electricity to the town. Meanwhile, work proceeded apace on completing the vessel, which throughout this long period had been known only as yard number 214, and she was launched on 1 July 1946 as *Willem Ruys*. This honoured the memory of the man who founded Rotterdam Lloyd, but was more in memory of his son, who was executed by the Nazis in August 1942, while being held as a hostage. The christening was performed by his widow.

A shortage of steel slowed completion of *Willem Ruys*, but in November 1947 she ran trials, achieving a maximum of 24.62 knots. Her eight diesel engines produced 38 000 bhp, but she could maintain 21 knots on only six engines. On 21 November, *Willem Ruys* was handed over to her owner and on the same day the company name was granted the prefix ''Royal'' by Queen Wilhelmina, in recognition of the service rendered by its ships during the war.

On 2 December 1947, *Willem Ruys* departed Rotterdam on her maiden voyage, going through the Mediterranean and Suez Canal to Malaya, Singapore and Batavia. She provided accommodation for 344 first class, 301 second class, 109 third class and 86 fourth class, but only the first class public rooms were air-conditioned. The ship had an unconventional appearance, accentuated by two squat funnels, and a very bulky superstructure, with lifeboats set much lower than usual.

WILLEM RUYS AS ORIGINALLY BUILT

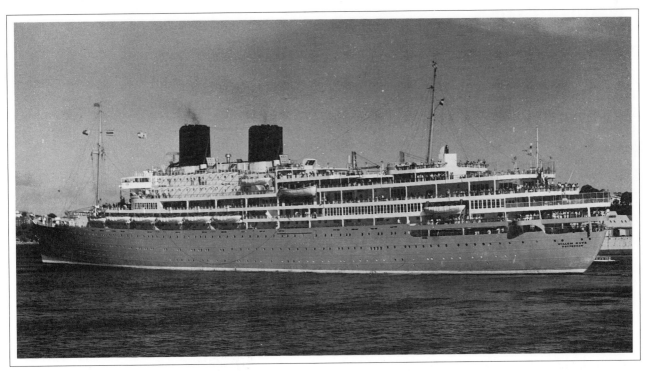

WILLEM RUYS AFTER 1958 ALTERATIONS

Unfortunately, the introduction of *Willem Ruys* coincided with an increase in political turmoil in the Dutch colony, clamouring for independence. This had a bad effect on the passenger trade, and many ships were withdrawn from the trade. Eventually, the two rivals, Royal Rotterdam Lloyd and Nederland Line, decided to operate a joint service, using *Willem Ruys* and *Oranje*. When the Dutch East Indies finally became the independent state of Indonesia, strong ties with Holland were retained, these two ships giving regular service together on the route for a number of years.

On 6 January 1953, *Willem Ruys* and *Oranje* were to pass in opposite directions off Port Sudan in the Red Sea. As the two ships approached at a combined speed of over 40 knots, they got too close, and the interaction of water forced them together. The two liners bumped and scraped along their entire lengths, causing so much damage to both that they had to miss a sailing to have repairs effected.

In December 1957, the Indonesian Government seized all Dutch possessions in the islands, which resulted in the immediate cessation of passenger services from Holland, and the laying up of *Willem Ruys*. In May 1958 she was chartered to Holland–America Line for two round trips to New York, then made two voyages to Montreal from Rotterdam for Europe–Canada Line. By this time, Royal Rotterdam Lloyd had decided to place the ship on a round-the-world service to Australia, so on 20 September 1958, she arrived at the Wilton–Fijenoord shipyard for a refit.

Internally, about 100 new cabins were installed, and air-conditioning extended throughout the entire accommodation, while the crew quarters were also upgraded. The ship could now carry 275 first class and 770 tourist class passengers, but some cabins were interchangeable and had extra berths if required, so the maximum capacity was 1167. Externally, fin stabilisers were fitted, several open sections of deck were plated in, and the forward funnel heightened, the work being completed in February 1959.

Once again, Royal Rotterdam Lloyd and Nederland Line linked to operate a new round-the-world service using *Willem Ruys* and *Oranje*. *Willem Ruys* was allocated the eastabout sailings, departing on her first voyage from Rotterdam on 7 March 1959. Her first call was at Southampton, then on to the Mediterranean and through the Suez Canal to Fremantle on 29 March, Melbourne on 3 April, and Sydney on 6 April, then to New Zealand and on to Tahiti, the Panama Canal and back to Rotterdam. She was scheduled to make four round trips per year, and maintained the service for five years.

In 1964, Royal Rotterdam Lloyd and Nederland Line decided to abandon their round-the-world service, and dispose of the two liners involved. *Oranje* was withdrawn first, then on 16 October 1964, *Willem Ruys* left Rotterdam on her twenty-sixth and last voyage. She left Melbourne on 14 November, and Sydney three days later, returning to Rotterdam in December. It had been announced during the year that *Willem Ruys* had been sold to Flotta Lauro, and in January 1965 they took delivery of the liner.

ACHILLE LAURO

REBUILT: *1966 by Cant. Nav. Riuniti, Palermo*
TONNAGE: *23 629 gross*
DIMENSIONS: *643 × 82 ft (196 × 25.1 m)*
SERVICE SPEED: *22 knots*
PROPULSION: *Sulzer diesels/twin screws*

In 1962, Flotta Lauro ordered two 30 000 ton, 1700 passenger liners to be built by the Ansaldo shipyard in Livorno. When *Willem Ruys* and *Oranje* came on the market in 1964, the company decided to purchase them, and cancelled the construction order. *Willem Ruys* was handed over to Flotta Lauro on 6 January 1965 in Rotterdam, and renamed *Achille Lauro*, after the founder of the company, who was born in 1887, and became a shipowner in 1922. This ship therefore had the rare distinction of bearing the names of two illustrious shipowners.

Achille Lauro was sent to Palermo for an extensive rebuilding, from which she would emerge bearing almost no similarity to the original *Willem Ruys*. A raked bow was added, the superstructure extended forward and modernised, both masts removed and a new signal mast fitted behind the bridge. The most notable alteration was the two new funnels, much taller and thinner than the originals, and topped by sloping double windvanes, to dispel smuts. Internally, the old accommodation was completely stripped out, and new cabins installed for 270 first class and 917 tourist class

passengers, plus 394 interchangeable berths, and 150 children's beds.

On 29 August 1965, when the conversion work was almost finished, *Achille Lauro* was swept by fire following an explosion aboard, which caused considerable damage. Her consort, *Angelina Lauro*, had been devastated by a similar outbreak just five days earlier, and both outbreaks were considered to be sabotage. Repairs set back the delivery date of *Achille Lauro* by six months, until March 1966.

Achille Lauro returned to her old home port of Rotterdam, from where she departed on 7 April 1966 on her first voyage, going to Southampton and then Genoa, from where she sailed on 13 April. The vessel arrived in Fremantle on 4 May, Melbourne on 8 May and Sydney two days later, then continued to Wellington, where the voyage ended on 14 May. She then retraced the route to Europe with an additional call at Singapore. When the Seuz Canal was closed in 1967, *Achille Lauro* was routed around Africa, and some return voyages went through the Panama Canal.

On 28 September 1968, *Achille Lauro* left Sydney, and after calling at Wellington, proceeded around Cape Horn, and called at Rio de Janeiro on her way back to Europe. She made one more voyage on this route, departing Sydney on 12 October 1969, but then the route was abandoned. *Achille Lauro* made five trips a year to Australia up to 1969, but during that year she

ACHILLE LAURO

ACHILLE LAURO

began making occasional cruises from Sydney and Rotterdam.

In May 1972, *Achille Lauro* went to Genoa for an overhaul, and while there the bridge structure and forward accommodation areas were swept by fire on 19 May, which put her out of service for five months while repairs were effected. During 1972, Flotta Lauro decided to withdraw from the Australian trade, so when *Achille Lauro* departed Rotterdam once more on 13 October 1972, it was to be her final voyage to Australia. Her final departure from Melbourne was on 13 November, but she made several short cruises from Sydney, then in February 1973 returned.

In April 1973, *Achille Lauro* began cruising in the Mediterranean from Genoa, and enjoyed considerable success. Her capacity was reduced to about 800 passengers in one class, and the vessel continued cruising from various European ports throughout the year. On 28 April 1975, *Achille Lauro* was proceeding through the Dardanelles when she collided with a small Lebanese cargo ship, which sank very quickly, though the liner was hardly damaged.

Achille Lauro was chartered by a German tourist company for several years, and also other tourist companies at various times. She was chartered by a South African company for cruises out of Durban between November 1979 and March 1980. This was repeated for the same period in 1980–81, and the charter was renewed for 1981–82. In November 1981 the liner was on her positioning cruise to South Africa when a fire broke out on board. Although it was quickly quelled, a panic-stricken passenger jumped overboard and drowned, while her husband, on hearing the news, died from a heart attack.

Towards the end of 1981, Flotta Lauro was encountering serious financial difficulties, and several of their cargo ships were impounded. *Achille Lauro* was returning to Genoa from her South African cruise season when she arrived in Teneriffe on 23 January 1982, and was arrested. She remained there for a year, but on 22 January 1983 was allowed to leave after the

Italian Government intervened. The liner proceeded to Genoa, where she was laid up on 28 January.

On 15 November 1983, the founder of the company, Achille Lauro, died at the age of 96, having seen the company he founded almost destroyed at the end of his life. Eventually *Achille Lauro* returned to service in July 1984, making five Mediterranean cruises from Genoa, then being laid up again. An arrangement was reached between Flotta Lauro and Chandris Line for *Achille Lauro* to operate a series of 20 cruises a year over three years from Genoa, commencing on 5 March 1985, and marketed by both companies.

On 7 October 1985, *Achille Lauro* was seized by terrorists shortly after leaving Alexandria, while bound for Port Said. The ship was held for two days, during which one of the American passengers was shot, then the terrorists surrendered to Egyptian authorities. This incident effectively destroyed the Mediterranean programmes of many shipping companies, as Americans refused to cruise in the region for several years. *Achille Lauro* was one of the few ships to remain in the Mediterranean, and on 6 April 1986, she ran aground off Alexandria, but was refloated without damage after six hours.

On 14 January 1987, *Achille Lauro* returned to Australian waters, when she arrived in Fremantle, having been chartered by Motive Travel for one month in connection with the America's Cup races. She had come direct from South Africa with 600 passengers on board, of whom 382 were migrants to Australia. During her stay in Fremantle, the liner made trips out to watch the yachts on race days, and on other days made a six-hour cruise to nowhere. On 16 February, *Achille Lauro* departed Fremantle, going first to South Africa, and then back to Europe to resume her Mediterranean cruising schedule. In January 1990, *Achille Lauro* returned to Australia on a voyage from South Africa. After calling at Fremantle and Melbourne, she arrived in Sydney on 28 January, then made a short cruise, leaving again on 8 February, on a voyage to Europe. The liner returned for more cruises in January 1991.

QUEEN FREDERICA

BUILT: *1927 by Wm Cramp Shipbuilding & Engineering Co., Philadelphia*
TONNAGE: *16 435 gross*
DIMENSIONS: *582 × 83 ft (177.3 × 25.4 m)*
SERVICE SPEED: *20 knots*
PROPULSION: *Geared turbines/twin screws*

Queen Frederica was one of four American built liners to be bought by Chandris in the 1960s, and all were designed by the same man, William Francis Gibbs. In fact, *Queen Frederica* was the first liner he designed, as *Malolo* for Matson Line.

Launched on 26 July 1926, *Malolo* was a very advanced liner for her time. The majority of her cabins were on the outside, and almost all first class had private facilities. Public rooms were spacious and finished in wood panelling, and a new feature was an indoor swimming pool, one of the first on a ship. Special attention was paid to safety, with a double bottom and twelve watertight bulkheads. The value of these were proved on trials, as on 25 May 1927, the Norwegian freighter *Jacob Christensen* collided with *Malolo*. Water flooded into the engine rooms, but with her intensive safety features, *Malolo* remained afloat, and was towed into New York, and put into drydock.

The collision delayed delivery of *Malolo* by five months, but in October 1927 she was handed over to Matson Line, and on 16 November she left San Francisco on her maiden voyage to Honolulu, which would be her regular route. Accommodation was provided for 457 first class and 163 cabin class passengers, and she was the outstanding ship on the Pacific. On 21 September 1929, *Malolo* left San Francisco on a cruise around the Pacific, going first to Japan, then Hong Kong, Manila, Singapore and Bangkok, and on to Australia, visiting Fremantle, Melbourne and Sydney. *Malolo* then crossed to Auckland, and on to Suva, Pago Pago and Hawaii en route back to San Francisco, arriving there on 20 December. This cruise was so successful, it was repeated at the same time in 1930 and 1931.

At this time, *Malolo* had a chocolate-brown hull, in common with other Matson ships, but in 1931 the company took delivery of the first of three new liners, *Mariposa, Monterey* and *Lurline*, all of which had white hulls, and *Malolo* had her hull repainted white to match them. In 1937, *Malolo* was withdrawn for an extensive rebuilding, which considerably altered her appearance. The lifeboats were raised two decks, and much of the open promenade space enclosed to provide more staterooms, including Lanai suites that were a feature on the new Matson liners. Accommodation was altered to 693 first class only, and the liner was renamed *Matsonia* prior to returning to service, with a departure from San Francisco on 14 January 1938.

Matsonia remained on the Hawaiian trade until 21 November 1941, when she was requisitioned by the US Navy as a transport. Quickly refitted to carry over 3000 troops, she was scheduled to leave San Francisco on 8 December for Manila, but the attack on Pearl Harbor changed this. The men and equipment destined for the Philippines were off-loaded, and instead ammunition and plane parts were taken aboard, along with 3277

MALOLO, AS BUILT

troops, and on 16 December *Matsonia*, in company with *Lurline* and *Monterey*, left San Francisco bound for Honolulu. *Matsonia* spent the next four years trooping in the Pacific, with several visits to Australian ports.

In April 1946, *Matsonia* was returned to Matson Line, having carried 176 319 persons during the war, and travelled 385 549 miles. Following a quick refit, *Matsonia* resumed the Hawaiian trade on 22 May 1946 from San Francisco, and maintained a lone-ship service until April 1948, when she was replaced by *Lurline*. *Matsonia* was then offered for sale, and bought by Mediterranean Lines, a Panamanian flag subsidiary of Home Lines.

At the Ansaldo shipyard in Genoa, the vessel was refitted to carry 349 first class, 203 cabin class and 626 tourist class passengers, though her external appearance was almost unaltered. Renamed *Atlantic*, she left Genoa on 14 May 1949 on her maiden voyage to New York. She remained on this route until February 1952, then was transferred to a new route from Southampton and Le Havre to Canada. During the winter months, *Atlantic* made cruises from New York to the Caribbean.

In 1954, Home Lines formed a Greek flag subsidiary, National Hellenic American Line, and on 23 December 1954 *Atlantic* was transferred to this company, and renamed *Queen Frederica*. Her accommodation was altered to 132 first class, 116 cabin class and 931 tourist class, and on 29 January 1955 she left Piraeus bound for New York. She remained on this route for several years, apart from seasonal cruises from New York.

On 15 December 1958, *Queen Frederica* departed Naples with migrants bound for Australia. Reaching Fremantle on 8 January 1959, the liner continued to Melbourne, where she berthed on 12 January, arriving in Sydney on 15 January. Next day she left on the return voyage, calling again at Melbourne and Fremantle to collect passengers, returning to Piraeus.

At the end of 1960, *Queen Frederica* was given an extensive refit, during which the after end of the superstructure was extended and the lower promenade deck plated in, while accommodation was increased to 174 first class and 1005 tourist class. The liner then began operating to Canada again, from Cuxhaven, and remained on this route until November 1965, when she was sold to Chandris Line.

Unaltered apart from new funnel colours, *Queen Frederica* left Piraeus on 10 December 1965 for Australia, arriving in Fremantle on 28 December, then proceeding directly to Sydney, berthing on 3 January 1966. She departed the next day for Piraeus, and a scheduled second trip to Australia was cancelled. Instead, Chandris placed the vessel on the North Atlantic trades again, from Piraeus to New York, with cruises in the winter months.

Queen Frederica did not return to Australia until November 1966, having departed Southampton on 22 October. Following this voyage she made a short series of cruises from Sydney. These were repeated in the summer of 1967–68, when the liner made her final appearance in Australian waters. From 1968, *Queen Frederica* began operating cruises in the Mediterranean under charter to Sovereign Cruises, until she was laid up in the River Dart on 22 September 1971.

In June 1972, *Queen Frederica* was moved to Piraeus, then given a refit prior to returning to service in April 1973 with weekly Mediterranean cruises from Palma de Mallorca, under charter to Blue Seas Cruises. When these ended in November 1973, the veteran liner was laid up again. In May 1977, *Queen Frederica* was sold to shipbreakers at Eleusis.

CHANDRIS LINER QUEEN FREDERICA ENTERING SYDNEY HEADS

PATRIS

BUILT: *1950 by Harland & Wolff Ltd, Belfast*
TONNAGE: *16 259 gross*
DIMENSIONS: *595 × 76 ft (181.3 × 23.3 m)*
SERVICE SPEED: *18 knots*
PROPULSION: *B & W diesels/twin screws*

Patris was the first liner to be operated by D. & A. Chandris, who bought her from Union–Castle Line. Launched on 25 August 1949, she was christened *Bloemfontein Castle*, and completed in March 1950. This liner had an identical hull and machinery to the *Durban Castle* and *Warwick Castle*, built in 1938, and very similar superstructure. However, *Bloemfontein Castle* had been built to meet an anticipated rush of migrants to South Africa, so was fitted out to carry 721 passengers in one class, unlike any other Union–Castle liner. She was also the only liner in the fleet to have only one mast, and had a large cargo capacity, much of it refrigerated. Placed on an independent schedule from London to Cape Town and Beira, *Bloemfontein Castle* departed for her maiden voyage on 6 April 1950.

Bloemfontein Castle was always the odd ship in an otherwise well-balanced fleet, being the only Union–Castle liner to operate without partners. The expected rush of migrants did not materialise, so the liner had to rely on regular passengers to a large extent. On 8 January 1953, *Bloemfontein Castle* answered a call for

help from the Dutch liner *Klipfontein*, which was sinking off the Mozambique coast, and rescued her 116 passengers and 118 crew. This was the only highlight in an otherwise unremarkable career under the British flag, as in 1959 *Bloemfontein Castle* was offered for sale. In October she was purchased by Chandris Line, and arrived in Southampton on 9 November at the end of her final voyage, then was delivered to Chandris later that month.

Renamed *Patris*, the vessel went to Smith's Dock at North Shields for a short refit. Externally she was not altered, apart from new hull and funnel colours, but internally the accommodation was enlarged to carry 36 first class and 1040 tourist class passengers, though after a short time this was changed to 1076 in one class. On 14 December 1959, *Patris* departed Piraeus on her maiden voyage to Australia, arriving in Fremantle on 2 January 1960, Melbourne on 7 January and Sydney on 9 January. Her return voyage departed Sydney on 12 January, following the same route back to Piraeus.

Patris remained on this route for several years. On the morning of 16 April 1960, she ran aground in the Suez Canal during a sandstorm, but was quickly refloated without damage the same evening. Her large refrigerated cargo spaces were utilised to transport meat to Greece, and on 9 January 1961, she made the first of several calls at Geelong to load mutton. It was also

BLOEMFONTEIN CASTLE

during 1961 that *Patris* made two return trips to Greece via Brisbane and Singapore, and in October paid her first visit to Wellington. She was also used for occasional cruises.

With the closure of the Suez Canal in 1967, *Patris* was forced to voyage around Africa to Australia, which she did for five years. On 18 June 1971, *Patris* was leaving Sydney Harbour when she collided with the collier *Rickie Miller* off Goat Island. The smaller ship was able to continue to her wharf, but *Patris* had to go to Banks Anchorage for repairs to her bow, eventually leaving Sydney on 20 June.

Early in 1972 *Patris* was placed on a new service, from Australia to Djibouti in the Red Sea. It was thought this would attract passengers to a faster service to Europe, with passengers flying to their destinations from Djibouti, but after several voyages the service was abandoned. On 6 October 1972, *Patris* inaugurated another route, from Sydney to Singapore via Melbourne and Fremantle, which was designed to compete with the booming "ship–jet" trade between Fremantle and Singapore. This route was maintained for almost two years, but on 6 July 1974, *Patris* was laid up in Singapore. At first it was announced that the ship would be sold, but then Chandris had her refurbished, and on 26 October 1974 she left Singapore on her old service again.

On Christmas Day 1974, Darwin was almost destroyed by Cyclone Tracy. With most of the population homeless, Chandris offered *Patris* to provide temporary accommodation, and on 15 February 1975 she arrived in the Northern Territory port. She remained there nine months, during which her condition deteriorated rapidly, and when she left on 13 November 1975, returned to Piraeus for an extensive

overhaul. Chandris had decided to convert her into a car ferry, for which purpose her lower decks were gutted to provide garage space for about 250 cars, and large doors cut in her sides. The accommodation was altered to carry 1403 passengers, and on 17 June 1976, *Patris* began operating betwen Patras and Ancona. This was a seasonal trade, and the vessel was laid up in October. Returning to service in 1977, she began a new service from Patras to Venice in June, again being laid up in October. This was repeated in 1978, then in 1979, *Patris* was sold to Karageorgis Line, and renamed *Mediterranean Island*.

Under her new name, the vessel remained in the ferry trade between Greece and Italy, then in 1981 her name was changed to *Mediterranean Star*. On 28 August 1982, on a voyage from Patras to Ancona, *Mediterranean Star* was disabled by a major engine room fire. All passengers and many crew abandoned the ship in lifeboats, while remaining crew eventually managed to extinguish the blaze. The vessel was sent to Perama for repairs, but due to her age, these were not effected immediately, and the ship was idle for several years.

In May 1986, *Mediterranean Star* was chartered to Star Navigation Co. Ltd, and began cruising from Piraeus to Rhodes, Limassol and Alexandria. Returns from this programme were very poor, and in October 1986, the liner was laid up again. During 1986, reports had appeared in the Australian press that *Mediterranean Star* had been chartered by newly formed Scandic Line, to cruise from Sydney during 1987 as *Scandic Star*, but that did not happen, as Scandic Line went out of business in 1986. Instead *Mediterranean Star* remained idle in Piraeus until August 1987. She was then sold to Pakistani shipbreakers, and under the name *Terra* was towed to Karachi to be scrapped.

PATRIS

ROYAL INTEROCEAN SISTERS

BUILT: *1950/51 by C. Van der Giessen, Krimpen*
TONNAGE: *8679 gross*
DIMENSIONS: *479 × 63 ft (146 × 19.2 m)*
SERVICE SPEED: *16 knots*
PROPULSION: *Werkspoor diesels/twin screws*

In June 1947, two Dutch companies, the Royal Packet Co. (KPM), and the Java–China–Japan Line, merged to form Royal Interocean Line. A number of ships were ordered for the new company, including a pair of passenger liners for the trade from the Dutch East Indies to Singapore, Hong Kong and Japan.

The first of these liners was launched on 29 April 1950 and named *Tjiwangi*, while *Tjiluwah* was launched on 9 May 1951. *Tjiwangi* was completed in December 1950, then voyaged to Hong Kong, where Royal Interocean Line had established their headquarters. *Tjiluwah* left Rotterdam on 10 November 1951 for her delivery voyage, arriving in Hong Kong on 21 December. Both ships provided cabin accommodation for 98 first class and 120 second class passengers, with space for a further 1700 deck passengers. These consisted mainly of Chinese travelling between Hong Kong and the Dutch East Indies.

For several years the ships traded very successfully, and during the 1954–55 financial year, the pair carried over 70 000 passengers. However, this figure dropped to 27 000 in 1957–58, as relations between the Indonesians and their former Dutch masters worsened culminating in the seizure of all Dutch property in the islands in December 1958. This resulted in the immediate suspension of all Royal Interocean Line services that included calls at Indonesian ports. For several months, *Tjiwangi* and *Tjiluwah* were idle in Hong Kong, then in May 1959 they began operating a shortened service between Singapore, Hong Kong and Japan, but passenger returns were very poor.

Since the war, Royal Interocean Line had been operating a service to Australia from Indonesia with *Nieuw Holland*, which was disposed of in February 1959. Royal Interocean decided to place *Tjiwangi* and *Tjiluwah* on the Australian trade, though on a different itinerary. On 9 July 1960, *Tjiwangi* departed Hong Kong for a direct voyage to Sydney, where she arrived on 21 July, then to Melbourne three days later. Leaving there on 29 July, she returned to Sydney, called at Brisbane, then made the 11 day passage to Yokkaichi in Japan, and on to Nagoya, Yokohama, Osaka and Kōbe before returning to Hong Kong.

Tjiluwah departed Hong Kong on 29 July, and called at Brisbane on 15 August before going to Sydney and Melbourne. She made her first northbound departure from Melbourne on 29 August. For this service, the deck accommodation was dispensed with, being replaced by a third class described as "deck with stretcher". This rather spartan grade was popular with Chinese students, and in the early days was also used by White Russian migrants from China, who were sponsored by the United Nations Refugee Organisation.

At the end of 1962 *Tjiwangi* was given a major refit, followed by *Tjiluwah* in early 1963. Air-conditioning was extended to include the entire accommodation areas, public rooms were improved, and a swimming pool installed for tourist class. The accommodation was altered to 104 first class, 118 tourist class and 202 third class. The peak demand for third class was reached in 1964, but from then it declined rapidly. The major external change was the repainting of their hulls white, which gave the ships a more graceful appearance, and

TJIWANGI

TJILUWAH

they became known as the 'White Sisters'.

The six-week round trip to Japan was advertised as a cruise, and on some voyages extra ports were visited, with Noumea featuring on at least one voyage each year from 1966. When *Tjiluwah* arrived in Yokohama in November 1966, the voyage was terminated and the ship drydocked there for her annual overhaul, the first time this had not been done in Hong Kong. When she came out of drydock, *Tjiluwah* made a 16 day cruise with over 300 Japanese passengers, leaving Yokohama on 26 December.

The day before *Tjiluwah* departed Yokohama, *Tjiwangi* had arrived for drydocking, her passengers transferring to *Tjiluwah*. *Tjiwangi* also made a cruise from Yokohama, leaving on 24 January, before returning to the regular schedule. These ventures were not repeated, as in subsequent years both ships returned to Hong Kong for their annual overhauls. During their 1969 overhauls, they were upgraded to meet the new standards for fire prevention, including the installation of double-closing fireproof doors in bulkheads. At the same time, third class was removed.

In November 1969, Royal Interocean Line tried another new cruise venture, with *Tjiwangi* departing Melbourne on a cruise to Dunedin, Lyttelton, Wellington and Auckland. This was so successful that

Tjiluwah made a similar cruise the following year, departing Melbourne on 11 November 1970 and visiting Hobart in addition to the four New Zealand ports.

During July 1971, Royal Interocean Line announced that *Tjiluwah* was to be withdrawn, and replaced by a larger vessel. *Tjiluwah* departed Melbourne for the last time on 15 December 1971, leaving Sydney on 20 December and Brisbane two days later on a regular voyage, which terminated on her arrival in Hong Kong on 16 January 1972, the next southbound voyage being taken by *Nieuw Holland*. *Tjiluwah* had been offered for sale prior to her final voyage, and been purchased by Pacific International Line, a major Singapore company. *Tjiluwah* was handed over in Hong Kong on 25 January 1972, and renamed *Kota Singapura*.

Tjiwangi remained in service a further two years, partnering *Nieuw Holland*, but the number of passengers carried was declining each year. On 17 December 1973, *Tjiwangi* departed Melbourne on her final voyage, leaving Sydney on 20 December and Brisbane two days later. She arrived in Hong Kong on 18 January 1974, where the 143 passengers disembarked, and *Tjiwangi* was withdrawn from service. She had also been sold to Pacific International Line, and was subsequently renamed *Kota Bali*.

KOTA SINGAPURA

KOTA BALI

196

Pacific International Line took delivery of *Tjiluwah* in Hong Kong on 25 January 1972, and renamed her *Kota Singapura*. It had arranged to charter the ship to a new Australian travel company, Travel House, for a service between Fremantle and Singapore. At first the ship was advertised in the Australian press as *Lion City*, but was never given this name. Following a brief refit in Hong Kong, in which the only change effected was in funnel colours, *Kota Singapura* went to Singapore, from where she departed on her first voyage to Fremantle on 10 March 1972, arriving on 16 March.

Travel House was one of a number of companies selling cheap "ship–jet" fares from Australia to Britain. This required passengers to travel from the eastern states by coach, train or plane to Fremantle, where they boarded a ship for the voyage to Singapore, there joining a charter aircraft for the flight to London. The first northbound voyage by *Kota Singapura* was marred by overbooking, which resulted in some passengers having to sleep in deckchairs during the five-night voyage. The new crew was also still finding its way about the ship, and the voyage caused a considerable amount of bad publicity for Travel House.

Over the next few months, *Kota Singapura* was arrested several times in Fremantle due to the non-payment of bills by Travel House. These incidents caused further bad publicity, and matters came to a climax in July 1972, when Travel House suddenly ceased trading. Thousands of intending travellers were left stranded and out of pocket, while *Kota Singapura* was immediately taken out of service, and laid up in Singapore.

Several months later, *Kota Singapura* returned to service between Singapore and Fremantle, this time on behalf of Pacific International Line, but this was not the end of her problems. On 8 December 1972, *Kota Singapura* berthed in Fremantle, and was due to depart two days later. However, Australian trade unions refused to let the ship go, because the wages and conditions of her crew, which were based on Singapore standards, were far below those enjoyed by Australian crews. The wrangle continued for several days, with no sign of resolution, as the crew of *Kota Singapura* was not in favour of the action being taken by the Australian unionists. On the night of 15 December, crew members on *Kota Singapura* dropped the lines to shore, and the ship left port without official clearance or a pilot on board. The irate Australian unionists declared that the ship would never be allowed to enter any Australian port again, so Pacific International Line placed *Kota Singapura* on a service from Singapore to China.

Pacific International Line must have been satisfied with *Kota Singapura*, as when her sister, *Tjiwangi*, became available, they purchased her too. Taking delivery in Hong Kong in January 1974, she was renamed *Kota Bali* and refitted to carry 220 passengers in one class, though again the only external change was to the funnel colours. *Kota Bali* was placed on a cruise service from Fremantle to Singapore, Bangkok, Jakarta and Bali, a service she was to maintain for several years, becoming quite popular with residents of Western Australia.

Meanwhile, the demand for 'ship–jet' passages to Britain continued, and more companies were formed to service the trade. One such firm was Palanga Line, which began by chartering a Russian ship, *Khabarovsk*, for the sector between Fremantle and Singapore. When she was handed back to her owner in December 1975, Palanga chartered *Kota Singapura* for the route. Apparently the problems of three years before were no longer an issue, as on 23 February 1976 *Kota Singapura* left Singapore on her first voyage back to Fremantle. The ship now provided accommodation for 302 passengers in one class, and enjoyed much better luck on the route.

Kota Singapura spent the next three years operating between Fremantle and Singapore, but when the Palanga charter ended, she left Fremantle for the last time on 16 May 1979. Pacific International Line had planned to utilise the ship on the pilgrim trade to Jedda from Indonesia, but instead she was laid up in Singapore, and then sold to shipbreakers in Taiwan. On 11 December 1979, *Kota Singapura* arrived in Kaohsiung, and on 5 January 1980 work began on scrapping the vessel.

Kota Bali continued to operate regular cruises out of Fremantle until early in 1981. On 9 February that year, *Kota Bali* arrived in Singapore, and was laid up. In March 1982, *Kota Bali* was chartered to Pelataran Nasional Indonesia, for inter-island service from Jakarta to Padang, Surabaya and Ujung Pandang. This charter lasted until early in 1984, and then the vessel was sold to shipbreakers in Shanghai, arriving at their yard on 23 April 1984.

ORIANA

BUILT: *1960 by Vickers–Armstrong Ltd, Barrow*
TONNAGE: *41 915 gross*
DIMENSIONS: *804 × 97 ft (245.1 × 29.6 m)*
SERVICE SPEED: *27.5 knots*
PROPULSION: *Geared turbines/twin screws*

The largest, and last, passenger liner to be built for the Orient Line, *Oriana* was launched by Princess Alexandra on 3 November 1959. A year later she managed 30.64 knots during trials in poor weather conditions. Accommodation was provided for 638 first class and 1496 tourist class passengers, and since *Oriana* was too large to berth at Tilbury, she became the first Orient Line vessel to be based on Southampton. Her maiden voyage departed on 3 December 1960, via the Suez Canal to Fremantle, Melbourne and Sydney, where she berthed on 30 December.

With her high speed and huge capacity, *Oriana* was able to reduce passage time to Sydney by a week, and thus replace two older vessels on the route. On 5 January 1961 she left Sydney on a cruise to Hobart, Wellington and Auckland, then made a circle-Pacific voyage with calls at Vancouver, San Francisco and Los Angeles. Returning to Sydney, *Oriana* then voyaged back to Britain through the Suez Canal, having been away 111 days when she arrived back in Southampton.

Oriana spent the early years of her career engaged mostly on the mail service between Britain and

Australia via Suez, with occasional cruises and circle-Pacific voyages. On 3 December 1962 she collided with the aircraft carrier USS *Kearsage* off Los Angeles, but suffered only minimal damage. In March 1964, she eclipsed the record established in 1936 by *Awatea* for the journey between Auckland and Sydney, with a 45 hour 24 minute passage at an average speed of 27.76 knots. *Oriana* made her first cruise from Southampton in July 1964, and on 2 October the same year, left Sydney on a cruise to Japan to coincide with the Tokyo Olympic Games.

Since entering service, *Oriana* had been operating under the banner of P & O–Orient Line, though the vessel remained under the nominal ownership of the Orient Line. When completed, she was given the regular Orient Line corn-coloured hull, but during 1964 *Oriana* was repainted with a white hull. On 31 March 1965, *Oriana* was transferred to the ownership of P & O Line, and in October 1966 the P & O–Orient Line name was discontinued in favour of P & O Line. These changes did not affect the actual operation of *Oriana* in any way.

While transiting the Panama Canal in September 1969, *Oriana* struck the side suffering damage to one propeller, but a more serious incident occurred on 11 August 1970. While departing Southampton a fire broke out in the electrical switchboard, which fortunately was quickly extinguished, but *Oriana* had to return to her

MAIDEN ARRIVAL OF *ORIANA* IN SYDNEY, 30 DECEMBER 1960

ORIANA WITH A WHITE HULL

berth where repairs took two weeks to complete.

With the demand for passages by sea between Britain and Australia declining, *Oriana* was used increasingly for cruises from both Southampton and Sydney. In 1973, her accommodation was modified to carry 1500 passengers in one class as a cruise ship. For most of the year she was based on Southampton, then in November voyaged to Sydney for a three month season of cruises in the South Pacific before returning to Southampton again. This schedule was followed for eight years, until 1981. Following her arrival in Sydney on 22 December that year, *Oriana* remained permanently on the Australian cruise trade, replacing *Sea Princess*.

In August 1985, P & O had announced that *Oriana* was to be withdrawn from service in March 1986. On 14 March 1986, *Oriana* sailed on her final cruise, returning to Sydney on 27 March, and then being laid up. Over the next two months a number of rumours spread about the ultimate future of the liner, ranging from a return to service under new ownership, to service as a floating hotel in Sydney Harbour, to sales to scrap yards. Eventually, on 21 May P & O announced that the vessel had been sold to the Japanese company, Daiwa House Sales. To be operated by a subsidiary, Royal Ocean Tourist Enterprises, *Oriana* would be used in a static role as a cultural and tourist centre at Beppu, on Kyushu island.

The oil rig service vessel *Lady Lorraine*, owned by P & O subsidiary Australian Offshore Services, was delegated to tow *Oriana* to Japan, with departure set for 23 May, but union problems delayed the last voyage of *Oriana*. Finally, on the afternoon of 28 May, *Oriana* slowly proceeded down Sydney Harbour, accompanied by a flotilla of small boats, and many thousands watching from the shore.

On reaching Japan, *Oriana* was handed over to her new owner, and sent to the Hitachi Zosen shipyard at Sakai for conversion to her new role. This involved the removal of all the original accommodation, and the installation of a variety of facilities, including conference rooms, exhibition hall, cinema, lounges and bars and restaurants. The work was delayed while negotiations were conducted with authorities over berthing rights in Beppu Bay, and the necessary fire prevention equipment required to meet local laws.

Eventually all the problems were resolved, and on 26 June 1987, *Oriana* arrived under tow at Beppu Port, in the Oita Prefecture. Amongst the huge crowd that gathered to watch the giant liner enter her new home was the mayor of Beppu, who described *Oriana* as being full of the culture and tradition of Europe. City officials expressed the hope that the vessel would attract many people from all over Japan, as well as overseas, and bring a welcome boost to the local economy.

On 1 August, the new look *Oriana* was opened to the public for the first time, and immediately began drawing large crowds. The owner needed to attract at least 1.5 million visitors a year to the ship, charging the quite high entrance fee of ¥2500 per adult, which would recoup the costs involved in purchasing and refitting *Oriana*.

MONTE UDALA

BUILT: *1948 by Cia. Euskalduna, Bilbao*
TONNAGE: *10 170 gross*
DIMENSIONS: *487 × 62 ft (148.5 × 19 m)*
SERVICE SPEED: *16 knots*
PROPULSION: *Sulzer diesels/single screw*

New settlers have come to Australia from every European country in the post-war years, and *Monte Udala* made two voyages to Australia with Spanish migrants. She was the second of a series of six cargo ships ordered by Empressa Nacional "Elcano", known as the "Monasterio" class. All were eventually redesigned while building into passenger–cargo liners, and sold to two other Spanish companies, Cia. Transatlantica Espanola, and Naviera Aznar, who purchased the first four vessels to be completed. The Aznar ships were subsequently named *Monte Urbasa*, *Monte Udala*, *Monte Urquiola*, and *Monte Ulia*, while the others became *Covadonga* and *Guadalupe*.

Launched on 1 May 1946, work on fitting out *Monte Udala* proceeded very slowly, due to the time taken to redesign the ship, and a shortage of materials. It was not until July 1948 that she was finally handed over to Aznar Line. Placed in service from Spanish ports to Buenos Aires and other cities in the River Plate estuary, *Monte Udala* was fitted out with accommodation for 62 first class, 40 second class and 290 third class passengers. The first class quarters were of a very high standard, while second class consisted only of ten four-berth cabins, and third class was reserved for migrants from Spain.

Aznar Line had never had any connection with the Australian trade, so it was a surprising move when they programmed *Monte Udala* for a voyage to Australia at the end of 1959. Departing Bilbao in December, *Monte Udala* brought 400 migrants to Melbourne, where she berthed on 20 January 1960. All the migrants disembarked there, then on 27 January *Monte Udala* moved across the bay to Geelong, where a cargo of wheat was loaded. On 2 February she left, returning to Spain and resuming her regular trade to South America.

In December 1960, *Monte Udala* departed Santander on her second voyage to Australia, arriving in Melbourne on 19 January 1961. She remained in port loading cargo until 7 February, then returned to Spain. This was the final visit to Australia made by *Monte Udala*, which then spent the rest of her career on the South American trade.

During the late 1960s, *Monte Udala* ceased carrying passengers, but continued to operate to South America as a cargo ship. The vessel was on a voyage from Buenos Aires to Spain when, on 8 September 1971, water was found to be leaking into the engine room. The crew were unable to stop the inrush of water, but as the ship was close to the Brazilian coast, rescue ships were soon on the scene. The crew abandoned ship, and were picked up by a passing freighter. *Monte Udala* finally rolled on her side and sank.

MONTE UDALA

CONTE GRANDE

BUILT: *1928 by Stablimento Technico, Trieste*
TONNAGE: *23 842 gross*
DIMENSIONS: *667 × 76 ft (203.3 × 23.8 m)*
SERVICE SPEED: *20 knots*
PROPULSION: *Geared turbines/twin screws*

Conte Grande made a single voyage to Australia on behalf of Lloyd Triestino, at the end of her career. *Conte Grande* was launched on 29 June 1927, and was completed in February 1928, having accommodation for 1720 passengers in three classes. She departed for her maiden voyage on 3 April 1928, from Genoa to New York, joining her sister, the British-built *Conte Biancamano*. This pair had been built for Lloyd Sabaudo, who operated a wide network of services, including one to Australia from 1921 until 1932, which eventually was taken over by Lloyd Triestino. In January 1932 the Italian Government reorganised the numerous Italian shipping companies into a few large concerns. Lloyd Sabaudo joined with Navigazione Generale Italiana and the Cosulich Line to form a new company, Italia Line. *Conte Grande* and her sister remained on the New York trade until 1933, when they were transferred to the South American route.

When Italy entered the war in 1940, *Conte Grande* was in Brazilian waters, so was laid up at Santos. Seized by the Brazilian Government on 22 August 1941, she was then sold to the United States on 16 April 1942. Refitted as a troopship, and renamed *Monticello*, she served as such until March 1946, then was laid up. In July 1947, the liner was handed back to Italy, and given an extensive refit, during which a raked bow and new funnels were fitted. With accommodation for 215 first class, 333 cabin class and 950 tourist class, she returned to service in July 1949 as *Conte Grande* once again, from Genoa to South America, once again partnered by *Conte Biancamano*. In the summer of 1956, *Conte Grande* and *Conte Biancamano* were returned to the New York trade for several months, following the sinking of *Andrea Doria*, and over the next few years both liners operated to New York during the peak summer season.

At the end of 1960, *Conte Grande* was chartered by Lloyd Triestino for one voyage, with her funnels repainted in their colours. On 15 December, *Conte Grande* departed Genoa with 1600 passengers on board, all in one class, comprising emigrants and fare-paying passengers. After calling at Fremantle on 7 January 1961, and Melbourne on 11 January, the liner arrived in Sydney on 13 January, remaining in port for two days. On her return voyage, she called again at Melbourne, then went to Adelaide, being there on 19 January, before passing through Fremantle on 22 January, to arrive back in Genoa on 14 February.

Conte Grande then returned to the South American trade, once again in Italia Line colours. *Conte Biancamano* had been withdrawn from service in April 1960, and subsequently sold to shipbreakers, so it was obvious her sister was also nearing the end of her career. In August 1961, *Conte Grande* arrived in Genoa at the end of her final voyage, and on 7 September she anchored off La Spezia, where she was broken up.

CONTE GRANDE IN SYDNEY HARBOUR

CANBERRA

BUILT: *1961 by Harland & Wolff Ltd, Belfast*
TONNAGE: *45 270 gross*
DIMENSIONS: *820 × 102 ft (249.9 × 31.1 m)*
SERVICE SPEED: *27 knots*
PROPULSION: *Turbo-electric/twin screws*

Canberra was destined to be the last, and largest, liner that P & O would build for the Australian trade. Designed to partner *Oriana* on the route, the two ships were totally dissimilar in appearance, with *Canberra* reflecting the latest ideas in liner design. Laid down on 27 September 1957 and launched on 16 March 1960, fitting out took a further 14 months, so it was 18 May 1961 before the vessel ran trials, averaging 29.27 knots. Unable to use the usual P & O berth at Tilbury because of her size, *Canberra* was based on Southampton, from where she sailed on 2 June 1961 on her maiden voyage to Australia via the Suez Canal.

Crossing the Indian Ocean from Colombo to Fremantle she was subjected to engine trouble, and arrived 31 hours late on 23 June. A crowed of 20 000 turned out to watch her depart for Melbourne and Sydney, where she berthed on 29 June. *Canberra* then continued across the Pacific to Auckland on 4 July and on to Suva, Honolulu, Vancouver, San Francisco and Los Angeles, and back to Sydney via Honolulu again, returning to Britain by way of the Suez Canal. During her first year of operation, *Canberra* suffered continual mechanical problems, so on 2 June 1962 she entered the King George V drydock in Southampton for an overhaul, which lasted six weeks. In addition to fixing the engines, additional ballast was added forward to keep the bow deeper in the water, making for a smoother passage. Returning to service, *Canberra* made a short cruise from Southampton, followed by two cruises from Southampton to New York.

Despite her early problems, *Canberra* was a popular ship with passengers. She provided berths for 548 first class and 1650 tourist class passengers, and spent most of her first 10 years on the Australian trade, apart from occasional cruises. Her mechanical problems continued, as on 4 January 1963 she was completely disabled off Malta by an engine room fire, which destroyed the main starboard switchgear. *Canberra* limped to Valetta, where her passengers were disembarked, and she returned to her builder's yard for repairs that lasted four months, returning to service again on 24 May.

During 1964, *Canberra* made four cruises from Southampton to New York, and early in 1966 made her first appearance in Asian waters. Passing through Yokohama on 15 March, she called at Kōbe and Nagasaki, then on 22 March became the first vessel to berth at the new Ocean Terminal in Hong Kong. In July 1967, *Canberra* was on a voyage from Britain when rumours that Egypt and Israel were about to start

fighting again prompted P & O to order the captain to turn his ship around out of Port Said, and divert around Africa. On the day *Canberra* was scheduled to transit the Suez Canal, Israel and Egypt went to war, and all ships in the canal were trapped there for seven years.

At the end of 1972, *Canberra* was withdrawn from the Australian trade, due to a steady decline in demand for passages. Instead, she was refitted to carry 1500 passengers in a single class as a cruise ship. P & O decided to base the ship on New York offering regular cruises to the West Indies, the first of which departed on 31 January 1973. Response from the Americans was so poor that, after just two cruises, *Canberra* was laid up at Wilmington in Delaware on 24 February. At the end of March, the vessel resumed her cruise schedule, but was not a success, and in November 1973 returned to Southampton and an uncertain future.

P & O were in the process of reducing their fleet, and committing those ships they retained to full time cruising. For a while it appeared that *Canberra* might join the sad procession of liners to the shipbreaker's yards of Taiwan and Hong Kong. However, the company had scheduled a world cruise, departing Southampton in January 1974 utilising *Orsova*, which had brought an excellent response in Britain. Eventually it was decided to send *Canberra* on this voyage, as she could accommodate all those wishing to travel, and the unfortunate *Orsova* went to the breaker's yard instead.

It was a fortunate move by P & O, as following her return from the world cruise, *Canberra* took over the cruises originally scheduled for *Orsova* out of Southampton, and was very successful. Each January, *Canberra* departed Southampton on a three-month cruise around the world, which included calls at Auckland and Sydney during mid–February. The itineraries for these cruises varied, with some including Japan and the Far East, while others took the vessel around Africa.

On 2 April 1982, *Canberra* arrived in Naples nearing the end of another world cruise, while half a world away, an Argentine force was invading the Falkland Islands. At first these two events seemed unconnected, and *Canberra* raised her anchor and sailed on to her next port of call. Meanwhile, in London plans were already afoot to use *Canberra* as a troopship for the expedition being mounted to free the Falklands. On 5 April the vessel was officially requisitioned by the British Government, but she did not reach Southampton for another two days. As soon as the passengers were disembarked, workmen swarmed aboard, erecting two helipads and converting the liner for a combat role within 48 hours. Some 2500 troops streamed aboard, and on the evening of 9 April, *Canberra* left Southampton, initial destination Ascension Island. After all the rush, *Canberra* spent over two weeks waiting at Ascension, then headed south in a convoy. On 21 May, *Canberra* anchored in San Carlos Bay, and within hours was under attack by Argentine aircraft, but miraculously avoided damage, although one of her escorting warships was sunk. The same night, *Canberra* slipped out to sea again, steaming in boxes until being sent to South Georgia to take on board troops from *Queen Elizabeth 2*. On 2 June, *Canberra* returned to San Carlos Bay to disembark these troops and their stores, which took two days, but air attacks were fewer during this period. Returning to sea again, *Canberra* awaited further orders, which came 10 days later, when the Argentine forces finally surrendered, and *Canberra* was directed to enter San Carlos Bay once again. This time the liner took on board 1121 Argentine prisoners-of-war, then she sailed to Port Stanley to take on more, until she had a total of 4167 Argentinians aboard. *Canberra* then departed for the Argentine port of Purto Madryn, where the troops were disembarked. Returning to the Falklands, *Canberra* entered San Carlos Bay for the fourth time, this trip being to embark British troops returning home, and on 25 June, the liner

left Falkland waters for the last time. Returning to Southampton on 11 July, *Canberra* received a rapturous reception, including a visit from Prince Charles. She had been away 94 days, and covered some 25 245 nautical miles without any mechanical malfunction of any kind.

Badly in need of a refit, *Canberra* spent the next two months in dock, then on 11 September, left Southampton on a cruise. In November, *Canberra* left Southampton on her scheduled voyage to Australia, receiving a fine welcome on reaching Sydney on 21 December. For the first time in many years, *Canberra* was scheduled to make five cruises from Sydney to the South Pacific, then in March 1983, she returned once more to Southampton and her British cruise programme. Since then, *Canberra* has reverted to making her annual round-the-world cruise, departing each January, and spending two days in Sydney in mid-February, and it is highly unlikely she will cruise again from Australian ports. In 1988, *Canberra* underwent a major refit, to enable her to continue in service for a further 10 to 15 years.

CANBERRA

KUALA LUMPUR

BUILT: *1936 by Barclay, Curle & Co., Glasgow*
TONNAGE: *12 598 gross*
DIMENSIONS: *517 × 63 ft (157.5 × 19.3 m)*
SERVICE SPEED: *15 knots*
PROPULSION: *Doxford diesels/twin screws*

Kuala Lumpur was originally built as a troopship. Launched on 17 October 1935, she was named *Dilwara*, having been built for British India Line as the first of a class of four vessels to operate under charter to the British Government. She was followed by *Dunera*, also owned by British India Line, then by *Ettrick* of P & O and *Devonshire* of Bibby Line. Completed in January 1936, *Dilwara* could carry 1150 troops, and also had cabin accommodation for 104 first class and 100 second class passengers. When not trooping, *Dilwara* would operate special cruises for schoolchildren from Britain.

Dilwara had a very hectic war career, which included participation in the landings at Madagascar, Sicily, Crete and the south of France. She finished the war in the Pacific theatre, then was used to repatriate British troops from the Far East and Middle East. In November 1949, *Dilwara* arrived in Southampton at the end of her final such voyage, then went to the Clyde to be refitted.

Dilwara was altered to carry 125 first class, 96 second class, 104 third class and 705 troops, with better facilities being provided. The forward well deck was closed in to provide more recreation space for the troops, and the funnel was heightened. On 4 October 1950, *Dilwara* left Southampton for Hong Kong on her first trooping voyage since the refit, and served in this role for a further ten years. When her trooping contract expired in 1960, it was not renewed by the British Government, so British India Line put *Dilwara* up for sale.

Purchased by China Navigation Co., the vessel was renamed *Kuala Lumpur*, and on 7 October 1960, left Southampton for Hong Kong, where she entered the Taikoo shipyard for refitting. China Navigation wanted to utilise *Kuala Lumpur* in the pilgrim trade to Jedda for part of each year, with cruising in the remaining months. She was given cabin accommodation for 242 first class passengers, while quarters for 1669 pilgrims were also installed, though these were very basic. Air-conditioning was also installed throughout the ship, and a swimming pool for the cabin passengers, while a mosque was added for the pilgrims. Apart from new funnel colours, the external appearance of the ship was not changed.

At the end of her first pilgrim season, *Kuala Lumpur* went to Fremantle, departing there on 8 September 1961 on the first of two 46 day cruises to the Orient. The second cruise departed on 30 October, returning on 3 December, following which *Kuala Lumpur* went on to Melbourne, arriving on 10 December, and then Sydney three days later, from where she made a voyage to Hong Kong. In 1962, *Kuala Lumpur* came to Sydney for cruises, the first departing on 28 October. These were marketed under the banner of Kuala Cruises, and over the next nine years the vessel came to Sydney for several months of cruising each year, carrying about 200 passengers, mostly in cabins with private facilities.

On 20 September 1971, *Kuala Lumpur* left Sydney for the last time, going first to Singapore, then Hong Kong. She was laid up for a short time, then sold to shipbreakers in Taiwan.

KUALA LUMPUR

The Second Chandris Liner

BUILT: *1952 by Ch. de Penhoet, St Nazaire*
TONNAGE: *16 335 gross*
DIMENSIONS: *581 × 73 ft (177 × 22.3 m)*
SERVICE SPEED: *18 knots*
PROPULSION: *Geared turbines/twin screws*

Bretagne was one of a pair built for Soc. Generale de Transports Maritimes. Launched on 20 July 1951, *Bretagne* was completed in January 1952, and departed Marseilles on 14 February 1952 for her maiden voyage to South America, joining her sister ship, the British built *Provence*. Accommodation was provided for 149 first class, 167 tourist class and 974 third class passengers.

On 18 November 1960, Chandris Line signed a charter agreement for *Bretagne*, with an option to purchase. The liner was sent to Genoa for refitting, during which an additional 242 cabins were installed, so that the ship could carry 150 first class and 1050 tourist class passengers.

Bretagne was used first for cruising, initially in the Mediterranean, then from New York. During this period, Chandris was negotiating to purchase the liner, and on 20 September 1961 the deal was finalised. At that time the vessel was in Southampton, preparing for her first voyage to Australia, which departed on 22 September.

Bretagne arrived in Fremantle on 19 October, then went to Melbourne, where she berthed on 24 October, reaching Sydney two days later. She then went north to Brisbane, where she docked on 29 October, continuing around the north of Australia to Singapore and back to Southampton through the Suez Canal. Her second voyage, departed Southampton on 30 November.

On her third voyage, *Bretagne* made a special call at Geelong on 5 March 1962 to load cargo, being one of the largest passenger vessels ever to visit that port. On returning from her third voyage, *Bretagne* was renamed *Brittany* in early April 1962, and under that name left Southampton on 10 April. At the end of that voyage, *Brittany* crossed to New York for another series of cruises, then on 12 September left Southampton again bound for Australia. This was followed by a departure on 22 November, then on 28 January 1963, *Brittany* left Southampton on her final voyage.

Leaving Sydney on 2 March, she called at Melbourne and Fremantle, then passed through Suez and called at Piraeus. Passing through the Mediterranean, *Brittany* suffered serious engine trouble, and returned to Piraeus on 28 March 1963. Her passengers were flown to their destinations, and the ship sent to the Hellenic Shipyard at Scaramanga for repairs.

The work was nearly complete when, on 8 April, a fire broke out in the engine room while the vessel was in drydock, and quickly spread to the accommodation. Before firemen could properly attack the blaze, *Brittany* had to be floated out of the drydock, but by then the fire had a firm hold, and the ship was beached in Vasilika Bay to burn out. Early in 1964, the wreck was sold to shipbreakers at La Spezia. She arrived there on 31 March 1964, under tow.

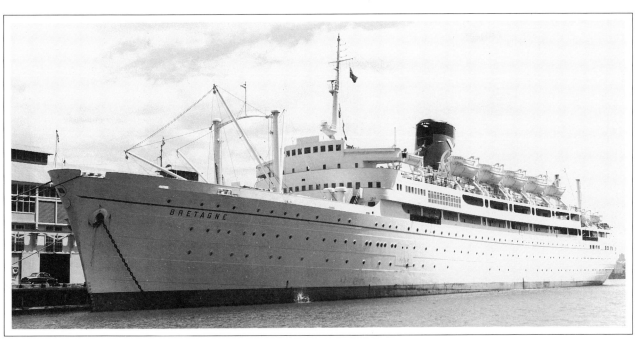

BRETAGNE

NORTHERN STAR

BUILT: *1962 by Vickers–Armstrong Ltd, Newcastle*
TONNAGE: *24 733 gross*
DIMENSIONS: *650 × 83 ft (198.1 × 25.5 m)*
SERVICE SPEED: *20 knots*
PROPULSION: *Geared turbines/twin screws*

Southern Cross was such a successful ship for Shaw Savill, it ordered a second vessel of the same type for its round-the-world service. Launched on 27 June 1961 as *Northern Star*, the liner was completed a year later, having tourist class accommodation for 1412 passengers. Although of the same basic design as *Southern Cross*, the new liner was longer and wider, and could carry an extra 250 passengers. *Southern Cross* had alternated the directions of her voyages, but when *Northern Star* entered service, she operated the eastward voyages, while *Southern Cross* travelled westabout.

On 10 July 1962, *Northern Star* departed Southampton on her maiden voyage, but on 16 July, in mid-Atlantic, the starboard engine had to be stopped, due to a fault in the high pressure turbine. This was disconnected and the engine re-started, only for the port engine to suffer identical problems on 20 July, and also

have the high pressure turbine disconnected. After making calls at Cape Town and Durban, *Northern Star* reached Fremantle two days late, on 11 August. She then went on to Melbourne and Sydney, where she remained for six days undergoing repairs and having the high pressure engines reconnected.

Departing Sydney on 24 August, *Northern Star* arrived in Wellington on 28 August, and after a call at Auckland, visited Suva and Papeete. Four days out from Tahiti, first the starboard engine and then the port engine had to be stopped again, and the high pressure turbines disconnected. *Northern Star* continued through Panama, and limped into Southampton on her two half-engines nine days late. Repairs were effected before she sailed on schedule for her second voyage, on 18 October. However, engine problems were to plague this ship throughout its lifetime, and bring about her early demise.

Northern Star settled into a pattern of four round-the-world trips a year, with some cruises as well. In December 1965, her funnel was repainted a deep green with a thin black top, and a four-pointed gold star attached to each side. In 1966 the funnel was returned to the regular Shaw Savill colours, but the star remained.

NORTHERN STAR

NORTHERN STAR

While the ship was in Durban on 13 November 1967, a fire caused considerable damage to the control equipment, resulting in a 10 day delay while repairs were effected.

As demand for line voyage passages declined, *Northern Star* began making more cruises, and by 1971 was scheduled for only two round-the-world voyages during the year. These were broken up by cruises out of Sydney, and she also cruised from Southampton. The mechanical problems she suffered became more frequent, and by 1973 there were also boiler problems. On 12 June 1973, a minor boiler explosion off Venice sent the ship limping back to Southampton, where the affected boiler tubes were replaced.

From November 1973 to March 1974, *Northern Star* cruised out of Sydney, then returned to Southampton for another programme of cruises, returning to Sydney

again at the end of the year. By now there were problems with the low pressure turbines, resulting in the ship missing a cruise departure on 28 January 1975 to be repaired in Sydney, resuming service again on 7 February. With the withdrawal of *Ocean Monarch* in May 1975, *Northern Star* was the last Shaw Savill passenger liner in service. She went back to Britain for a final season of 11 cruises, the last returning to Southampton on 1 November 1975. Having been sold to shipbreakers in Taiwan, *Northern Star* left Southampton for the last time on 7 November, with only a skeleton crew aboard, and made her way to Kaohsiung, arriving on 11 December 1975. Hers had been a very brief career of just over 13 years, plagued throughout by faulty engines.

REMUERA

ARAMAC

ARAMAC

BUILT: *1948 by Harland & Wolff, Belfast*
TONNAGE: *13 619 gross*
DIMENSIONS: *532 × 70 ft (162.1 × 21.3 m)*
SERVICE SPEED: *18 knots*
PROPULSION: *Geared turbines/twin screws*

Comparing the pictures of this ship with *Flavia* on the next page, it is difficult to believe that they were once identical sister ships, but such was the case. They were built for the Cunard Line, this vessel being named *Parthia*, and the first Cunard ship to be built by Harland & Wolff. Launched on 25 February 1947, *Parthia* was fitted out with comfortable accommodation for 250 passengers in one class. She was also fitted with fin stabilisers, but only the public rooms were air-conditioned. The liner also had a very large cargo capacity, carried in six holds.

These two ships were intended to operate a secondary service from Liverpool to New York, on which route *Parthia* made her maiden departure on 10 April 1948. Unlike the express liners, these voyages included calls at numerous ports enroute, but by the late 1950s, it was becoming increasingly uneconomic to operate passenger–cargo liners on the North Atlantic. During 1961, both ships were scheduled to be withdrawn, and offered for sale. *Parthia* made her final departure from Liverpool on 23 September 1961, and on her return was laid up.

Amongst those who showed an interest in buying the ship were H. C. Sleigh & Co., of Melbourne, who considered using her on a service to Japan, but the Australian Government refused to grant a currency licence. Also interested in *Parthia* was the New Zealand Shipping Co., which was about to retire two of their older liners, *Rangitata* and *Rangitiki*. They were seeking to replace them with a single ship, to maintain a regular schedule alongside *Rangitane*, *Rangitoto* and *Ruahine*. On 1 November 1961, the New Zealand Shipping Co. finalised the purchase of *Parthia*, and the ship was sent to the Glasgow shipyard of A. Stephen & Sons for refitting. The main deck was extended aft, and a mainmast installed, while internally her capacity was increased to carry 350 passengers in one class, and air-conditioning was extended throughout the accommodation.

Renamed *Remuera*, she departed London on 1 June 1962 on her first voyage to New Zealand, through the Panama Canal, reaching Auckland on 27 July, then going on to Wellington, Port Chalmers and Timaru. Unfortunately, *Remuera* was to prove to be a less than successful purchase by the company, becoming a misfit in the NZSC fleet as the only steamship in a fleet of motorships, and being much smaller than her running mates, though capable of carrying a similar number of passengers. However, the passenger trade between Britain and New Zealand was steadily declining each year, so on 19 November 1964, *Remuera* left London on her last voyage to New Zealand, having been a member of the NZSC fleet for little more than two years.

After discharging her passengers and cargo in New Zealand ports, *Remuera* crossed the Tasman to Sydney, arriving on 12 January 1965, and being transferred within the P & O Group of companies to the E & A Line. Renamed *Aramac*, the only visible change was a black painted funnel, to which a dome top was added. The liner went to Melbourne to load, sailing on 8 February for Sydney, Brisbane, Port Moresby and on to Hong Kong and ports in Japan.

Aramac was the first passenger ship to be operated by the E & A Line since the war, and quickly became popular on this route, the round trip being advertised as a cruise. However, once again she was to have only a few years of service, partly due to her own success. In October 1969, *Aramac* was withdrawn from service, and replaced by the larger *Cathay*, transferred from the parent P & O Line. On 15 October 1969, *Aramac* left Sydney on her final voyage to Hong Kong, from where she crossed to Kaohsiung, arriving on 20 November, having been sold to a firm of shipbreakers there.

FLAVIA

BUILT: 1947 by John Brown & Co., Clydebank
TONNAGE: 15 465 gross
DIMENSIONS: 556 × 70 ft (169.8 × 21.3 m)
SERVICE SPEED: 18 knots
PROPULSION: Geared turbines/twin screws

The second former Cunard Line passenger–cargo liner to enter service from Britain and Europe to Australia and New Zealand was *Flavia*, following one of the most comprehensive rebuildings given any vessel in the post-war years. *Flavia* was originally named *Media*, having been launched on 12 December 1946, and entering service on 20 August 1947 with a departure from Liverpool for New York. Providing accommodation for 250 first class passengers only, *Media* and her sister, *Parthia*, remained under Cunard Line ownership until 1961, when both were sold.

Media was bought by Cia. Genovese d'Armamento, better known as Cogedar Line, in July 1961, but did not complete her final Cunard voyage until 30 September, at Liverpool. On being handed over to her new owners, the vessel was renamed *Flavia*, and sent to Genoa to be rebuilt by Officine A & R Navi. The work took a year, during which the original superstructure was removed and a new one built, a raked bow was added, all cargo areas removed, and 378 cabins for 1224 passengers installed, comprising 152 two-berth, 221 four-berth and 5 eight-berth, the majority having private facilities. New amenities included two outdoor swimming pools, plus a third for children, two dining rooms, and a cinema.

On 2 October 1962, *Flavia* departed Genoa on her first voyage, arriving in Fremantle on 30 October, and being in Melbourne from 5 to 7 November before reaching Sydney on 9 November. Departing next day, *Flavia* retraced her course, but went on to Bremerhaven, which would be her European terminal,

her first sailing from there being on 22 December 1962. *Flavia* also made occasional cruises from Australia, the first being from Sydney on 8 April 1963 to Japan and the Far East, returning on 10 May. Later in 1963, *Flavia* began operating a round-the-world service, from Bremerhaven, Rotterdam and London through the Panama Canal to Tahiti, Auckland, Australian ports, and back through Suez.

With the closure of the Suez Canal in 1967, *Flavia* had to divert around South Africa, but the following year Cogedar Line withdrew from the trade. On 23 July 1968, *Flavia* left Rotterdam on her final voyage to Australia, and after a cruise from Sydney, left there on 18 October, and Melbourne two days later. On her return to Europe, *Flavia* was chartered to Atlantic Cruise Line, and after a quick refit, she began cruising from Miami on 20 December 1968, to the West Indies.

In 1969, *Flavia* was sold to the major Italian shipping company, Costa Line, but not renamed. With her accommodation upgraded and reduced to 850 in one class, she began operating three and four day cruises from Miami to the Bahamas throughout the year. *Flavia* was very popular and successful on this trade, and remained there until July 1977, when she went to South America for a series of cruises, then in April 1978 began cruising in the Mediterranean. However, in September 1978, *Flavia* returned to the short cruise circuit from Miami once again.

In 1982, *Flavia* was withdrawn, and sold to the C. Y. Tung Group of Hong Kong. With her name altered to *Flavian*, the vessel arrived in Hong Kong, for a new cruise service under the banner of Flavian Cruises, but instead was laid up. In 1986 she was sold to Virtue Shipping of Hong Kong, and her name amended to *Lavia*, but she remained idle at anchor off Lantau Island. On 7 January 1989, *Flavia* caught fire, and was completely gutted. The wreck was sold to Taiwanese shipbreakers.

CUNARD LINER *MEDIA*

FLAVIA

CHUSAN

BUILT: *1950 by Vickers–Armstrong Ltd, Barrow*
TONNAGE: *24 161 gross*
DIMENSIONS: *673 × 84 ft (205.1 × 25.6 m)*
SERVICE SPEED: *22 knots*
PROPULSION: *Geared turbines/twin screws*

Chusan did not appear in South Pacific waters until 1963, having been built for the P & O service to the Far East and Japan. She was the second liner built for P & O after the war, the first being *Himalaya*, and in many ways *Chusan* was a smaller version of that liner. Launched on 28 June 1949, and completed one year later, *Chusan* was fitted out with accommodation for 475 first class and 551 tourist class passengers. On 15 September 1950, *Chusan* left Tilbury on a return voyage to Bombay and on 7 November she made her first departure for Japan.

Chusan combined line voyages with cruises from Britain, but one problem to afflict her was smuts from the funnel falling on the afterdeck. To rectify this, a Thorneycroft smoke deflector was added in 1952. On 12 June 1953, as *Chusan* was heading down the English Channel at the start of a cruise, she collided with a cargo ship in fog near the South Goodwin lightship. Though not seriously damaged, *Chusan* returned to Tilbury for repairs, sailing again three days later.

As P & O expanded its network of services across the Pacific in the late 1950s, *Chusan* made the first P & O voyage around the world, in 1960. She had been given a refit in 1959, during which the accommodation was slightly reduced, to 464 first class and 541 tourist class. Returning to service early in 1960, she followed her normal route to Japan, then crossed to the west coast of America, and through the Panama Canal, the entire trip lasting 12 weeks.

With demand for passages to the Far East declining, on 6 June 1963, *Chusan* left Tilbury on her first voyage to Australia, arriving in Sydney on 10 July. Next day she left on a three-week cruise to Tahiti, then returned to Britain. Subsequently, she came to Australia several times a year, and also operated some more cruises.

Chusan continued making occasional voyages to the Far East until 1970, when the route was abandoned by P & O. During the summer of 1970, and again in 1971, *Chusan* made four cruises from Amsterdam, for the European market. *Chusan* seemed to be quite successful, and very popular whenever she made cruises, so it was a great surprise when P & O decided to withdraw her in 1973. Her final departure from Southampton was on 12 May 1973, on a voyage to Australia. She then made a cruise to Hong Kong, and after destoring, crossed to Taiwan, arriving in Kaohsiung on 30 June 1973, and was handed over to shipbreakers.

CHUSAN

OCEANIEN

BUILT: *1938 by P. Smit Jr, Rotterdam*
TONNAGE: *10 276 gross*
DIMENSIONS: *502 × 64 ft (152.9 × 19.5 m)*
SERVICE SPEED: *17 knots*
PROPULSION: *B & W diesels/twin screws*

Messageries Maritimes built two new liners after the war for the service from France to Australia, *Caledonien* and *Tahitien*, but the service required three vessels to maintain a regular schedule. The third vessel was always chartered for the trade, from 1958 to 1963 being *Melanesien*. In 1963, Messageries Maritimes did place an order for a new liner to join the Australian service, which would have been named *Australien*, but until she was completed in 1966, it would be necessary to charter another vessel. It was under these circumstances that *Oceanien* operated to Australia until 1966.

Oceanien was launched on 9 April 1938 as *Noordam*, the first of a group of four cargo–passenger liners built for Holland–America Line. On 28 September 1938 *Noordam* left Rotterdam on her maiden voyage to New York, having accommodation for 125 tourist class passengers. She was joined shortly after by her sister ship, *Zaandam*. The other two ships of the class, *Westerdam* and *Zuiderdam*, were not completed when war broke out, and only the former ship survived.

As the war in Europe intensified, *Noordam* was transferred to a safer route from New York to the Dutch East Indies in March 1941, but in April 1942 she was taken over by the US War Shipping Administration. Her sister, *Zaandam*, was also taken over, but sunk in November 1942, with three survivors being found in a lifeboat 82 days after the sinking. *Noordam* was handed back to Holland–America Line in 1945, and after refitting, during which her accommodation was reduced to 148 first class, returned to the New York trade in July 1946.

Noordam operated on the secondary service to New York with *Westerdam* until early in 1963, when she was withdrawn. On 27 April 1963, the vessel was sold to Cielomar S.A. of Panama, a subsidiary of the Costa Line, for the purpose of being chartered to Messageries Maritimes to replace their *Melanesien*. At first *Noordam* was to be renamed *Wallisien*, but this was changed to *Oceanien*. She was altered to carry 106 first class and 96 tourist class passengers, then on 2 August 1963 left Marseilles on her maiden voyage, to Papeete, Port Vila and Noumea, via the Panama Canal. Her second departure from Marseilles was on 19 November, and brought *Oceanien* to Sydney for the first time, arriving on 9 January 1964 and leaving on 12 January.

The vessel being built as *Australien* was allocated to the South American trade as *Pasteur* on completion, so *Oceanien* remained on the Australian trade. On 23 March 1966, she left Marseilles on her final voyage for Messageries Maritimes, leaving Sydney after a three day stay on 24 May. Her charter expired when she returned to Marseilles, and the vessel was handed back to her owner. Unable to obtain another charter for her, she was sold to Brodospas, the Yugoslav shipbreakers, arriving at their Split yard on 14 February 1967.

OCEANIEN

DOMINION LINERS

BUILT: *1947/48 by Vickers–Armstrong Ltd, Newcastle*
TONNAGE: *7743 gross*
DIMENSIONS: *440 × 61 ft (134.1 × 18.5 m)*
SERVICE SPEED: *15 knots*
PROPULSION: *Geared turbines/single screw*

H. C. Sleigh Ltd is a well-known Melbourne shipping company, which operated the vessels of the Dominion Navigation Co. Ltd, including *Francis Drake* and *George Anson*. This pair had been built as *Nova Scotia* and *Newfoundland* for the Johnston Warren Line, a member of the Furness Withy Group, to replace ships of the same names lost during the war.

Nova Scotia was launched on 8 November 1946, and made her maiden departure from Liverpool on 2 September 1947 to St John's, Halifax and Boston. *Newfoundland* was launched on 22 May 1947, making her first sailing from Liverpool on 14 February 1948. The ships provided accommodation for 62 first class and 92 tourist class passengers, and had a large cargo capacity in four holds. The hulls of these vessels were strengthened for ice, which was often encountered in the winter months at most of the ports they visited.

Nova Scotia and *Newfoundland* were among the last passenger–cargo liners operating a regular schedule across the North Atlantic, and for some years enjoyed considerable success. However, at the end of 1961 their capacity was reduced to 12 passengers only. In 1962 they were offered for sale, and purchased in November that year by H. C. Sleigh Ltd, of Melbourne, though

the registered owners were listed as Dominion Navigation Co. Ltd, Nassau.

Nova Scotia was renamed *Francis Drake*, while her sister became *George Anson*, and both went to the Glasgow shipyard of Barclay, Curle & Co., for a refit. The main deck was extended forward of the bridge, the Promenade deck opened up and an outdoor swimming pool installed. The accommodation was remodelled to cater for 130 passengers in one class, and air-conditioning installed. The ships were repainted with light grey green hulls and a plain yellow funnel.

In March 1963, *Francis Drake* entered service from Melbourne, Sydney and Brisbane to Manila, Taiwan and Japan. *George Anson* came into service in April 1963, and the pair maintained a schedule of monthly departures from Melbourne, with each round trip lasting 63 days. In 1965, the Indo–China Steam Navigation Co. and Dominion Navigation combined to form Dominion Far East Line, to which both these ships were transferred. The only change was to their funnels, which were repainted red with a black top.

The careers of *Francis Drake* and *George Anson* came to rather a sudden end early in 1971, when they were withdrawn from service and sold to shipbreakers in Taiwan. First to go was *George Anson*, which left Sydney on 14 January 1971 on a voyage to Hong Kong, from where she proceeded to the breaker's yard at Kaohsiung. *Francis Drake* followed a month later, leaving Sydney on 18 February for the final time, also bound for Hong Kong, and then Kaohsiung, where she arrived on 16 March 1971.

FRANCIS DRAKE

LLOYD TRIESTINO TWINS

BUILT: *1963 by Cant. Riuniti dell'Adriatico, Monfalcone*
TONNAGE: *27 905 gross*
DIMENSIONS: *702 × 94 ft (213.9 × 28.6 m)*
SERVICE SPEED: *24 knots*
PROPULSION: *Geared turbines/twin screws*

Lloyd Triestino had been operating their Australian service with three liners for ten years when they placed orders for two larger vessels, as replacements. The pair were constructed together on adjoining slips at Trieste, with the first being launched on 2 July 1961 as *Galileo Galilei*. The second was named *Gugielmo Marconi* when launched on 24 September 1961. Throughout their careers, these ships would be best known under their abbreviated names of *Galileo* and *Marconi*.

Fitting out of both ships was due to take 18 months, but in both cases took longer. *Galileo* was scheduled to make her maiden departure on 16 February 1963, but it was not until 22 April that the liner left Genoa on her maiden voyage. She arrived in Fremantle on 9 May, Melbourne on 13 May and Sydney two days later, leaving on 19 May to follow the reverse route home. *Marconi* was scheduled to enter service on 10 June 1963, but her fitting out lasted two years. Three round trips had to be cancelled before she eventually made her maiden departure from Genoa on 18 November. *Marconi* passed through Fremantle on 5 December, Melbourne on 9 December, and berthed in Sydney on 11 December.

With their higher speed, these ships reduced the passage time from Genoa to Sydney from 31 days to 23 days, and between them they could carry more passengers than the trio they replaced. Where the previous ships had offered three grades of accommodation, *Galileo* and *Marconi* were only divided into two, first and tourist. Depending on demand, first class berths could vary between 156 and 289, while tourist class could carry from 1358 to 1594 passengers. The only amenity shared by both classes was the cinema. The first class dining room could seat 149 persons, while that in tourist class had a 774 person capacity.

Up to 1967, both ships voyaged in each direction through the Suez Canal, but when it was closed, they had to make the longer passage around South Africa. On 7 October 1968, *Galileo* left Sydney on the first voyage by these ships across the Pacific, passing through the Panama Canal and back to Genoa. Over the next six years both ships made several round-the-world voyages each year, visiting more ports to attract passengers. In the early 1970s, one of pair would make an annual Christmas cruise from Sydney, but neither ship was ever engaged in cruising for any extended period.

The world oil crisis of the 1970s had an impact on the careers of these liners. *Marconi* had been programmed to depart Sydney on a cruise on 18 December 1973, but this was cancelled, and the ship lay in port until 3 January 1974, when she left on schedule for Italy. A year later, *Galileo* was on a voyage to Australia around South Africa when, on 13 January

GALILEO GALILEI

1975, she struck a reef off the coast of West Africa, and had to divert to Monrovia. Inspection showed extensive hull plate damage, so *Galileo* returned to Genoa on 24 January, and was drydocked for repairs, returning to service in March.

The service was heavily subsidised by the Italian Government, as were the ships operated by Italia Line on the Atlantic, but costs were rising so fast that the charge to the public purse was becoming excessive. The government decided to change the subsidy system, and this resulted in the abandonment of the Australian passenger service by Lloyd Triestino. On 20 October 1975, *Marconi* departed Genoa on her final voyage to Australia, passing through Cape Town to arrive in Fremantle on 16 November, Melbourne on 20 November and Sydney two days later. Departing on 23 November, *Galileo* arrived in Auckland on 26 November, then went across the Pacific and through the Panama Canal to reach Genoa on 30 December. *Marconi* was then transferred to Italia Line, and joined their service to South America, departing Naples for the first time on 20 January 1976.

This left *Galileo* to carry on the Australian trade alone, and she had been programmed to remain in service through 1977. However, at very short notice, her departure from Genoa on 26 May 1977 was cancelled, stranding over 1000 passengers. This meant that her final voyage to Australia had been from Genoa on 12 March, departing Sydney on 13 April and Auckland on 16 April for her return trip through the Panama Canal, arriving back in Genoa on 19 May.

Also during May 1977, the Italia Line service to South America was terminated at short notice, with *Marconi* returning to Naples on 7 June. The Italian Government had decided that both ships were to be transferred to the lucrative American cruise market, to be marketed jointly by Costa and Lauro Lines. This soon changed, as Lauro Line dropped out of the arrangement, so Costa Line and the Italian Government decided to form a new company, Italian Cruises International, to operate *Galileo* and *Marconi*, as well as two other Italian liners, *Leonardo da Vinci* and *Ausonia*.

In order to better suit *Galileo* and *Marconi* for the American cruise trade, they were refitted at the Cantiere Navale Riuniti shipyard in Palermo, with passenger capacity reduced to 900 in one class. It was programmed that one of the ships would be based all year in North America, while the other would cruise in the Mediterranean from April to October, then switch to the Caribbean for the rest of the year.

Marconi was chosen for the American market, commencing early in 1978, but her refit was protracted due to the failure of the Italian Government to pay the shipyard bills promptly. Eventually Costa Line decided to withdraw from their arrangement with the government, forcing the Italian Government to

undertake the operational duties themselves. *Marconi* eventually arrived in New York, and commenced a series of short cruises to the Caribbean on 27 December 1978. In spite of her US$6 million refit, the vessel could not pass the inspections conducted by the US Health Service. In July 1979 she failed for the seventh time, scoring 38 points out of 100, and Italian Cruises International were ordered to cease selling berths on the ship.

Galileo had entered Mediterranean cruise service in April 1979, and was due to cross to Port Everglades in October. However, *Marconi* was sent to the Florida port for modifications, then took over the programme scheduled for *Galileo*, which was laid up in Genoa. *Marconi* made her first departure on 20 October, but three days later in San Juan, again failed to pass the Health Service tests, this time scoring only 36 points. After further improvements, *Marconi* resumed on 22 December 1979, but on 12 January 1980 she was taken out of service, and returned to Genoa to join *Galileo* for the rest of the year.

In June 1981, *Galileo* returned to service under charter to Chandris Line, cruising in the Mediterranean until October, then was laid up again. Late in 1983, both ships were sold, *Galileo* going to Chandris, while *Marconi* was bought by Costa Line. *Galileo* was in the best condition, and needed only a brief refit, during which the forward part of the superstructure was extended, then returned to service. Her name was officially changed to just *Galileo*, and in June 1984 she began cruising from American east coast ports. The vessel is still active on this schedule, and looks very smart in the blue Chandris colours.

Marconi was in poor condition, especially mechanically, so she was given an extensive rebuilding by Costa Line, as well as having her engines and boilers overhauled. The work was done by the T. Mariotti shipyard in Genoa, and lasted over a year. The interior of the ship was almost gutted, and new accommodation for 984 passengers installed, along with new public rooms. Externally, the superstructure was totally changed, being extended fore and aft, while the original funnel was encased in a most unusual looking cage.

Renamed *Costa Riviera*, the vessel was delivered to Costa Line in November 1985, and placed on the American cruise market. Based at Port Everglades, *Costa Riviera* made her first cruise on 14 December 1985, and operates regular weekly departures throughout the year. With *Galileo* operating out of Miami for several months each year, the two sisters were occasionally seen in a Caribbean port together.

Late in 1989, *Galileo* was given an extensive refit at the Lloyd Werft shipyard in Bremerhaven, and was then renamed *Meridian*. Following this rebuild, the two ships are similar in appearance again.

GUGLIELMO MARCONI

MERIDIAN

HOLLAND-AMERICA LINERS

BUILT: *1951/52 by Wilton–Fijenoord N.V., Schiedam*
TONNAGE: *15 024 gross*
DIMENSIONS: *502 × 69 ft (153.2 × 21.1 m)*
SERVICE SPEED: *16.5 knots*
PROPULSION: *Geared turbines/single screw*

The liners of Holland–America Line are usually associated with the North Atlantic. In the immediate post-war years their veteran liner *Volendam* made several trips to Australia with migrants, and in the mid-1960s they sent two of their ships, *Ryndam* and *Maasdam*, to Australia on several voyages.

In 1949, Holland–America Line ordered two passenger–cargo ships, and the first was laid down on 17 December 1949 as *Dintledyk*, while the second was to be named *Diemerdyk*. Shortly after construction began, it was decided to redesign this pair as passenger liners, and the first was launched on 19 December 1950 as *Ryndam*. The same day the keel of the second ship was laid down on the same slipway, and she was launched on 5 April 1952 as *Maasdam*. Both ships were powered by the machinery intended for them as passenger–cargo ships, but were fitted out with accommodation for 39 first class and 854 tourist class passengers.

Ryndam entered service with a 16 July 1951 departure from Rotterdam for New York, while *Maasdam* made her maiden sailing on 11 August 1952. These ships were aimed at the economy market, and operated independently of the main Holland–America liners, often calling at extra ports as demand required. The introduction of *Rotterdam* in 1959 resulted in *Ryndam* being transferred in March 1960 to a new route from Rotterdam, Southampton and Le Havre to Quebec and Montreal. In the winter, both ships began operating cruises from New York to the West Indies.

On 15 February 1963, *Maasdam* was entering the mouth of the Weser River bound for Bremerhaven on her first visit, when she struck the wrecks of two ships that had recently been sunk in the main channel. *Maasdam* suffered serious underwater damage, and was abandoned by her 500 passengers, but the ship stayed afloat. She was repaired at the North German Lloyd shipyard, and returned to service on 16 April, with a voyage to New York.

In 1964, Nederland Line and Royal Rotterdam Lloyd withdrew from the Australian trade, so Holland–America decided to maintain a Dutch presence by taking their place, operating one voyage a year, working in conjunction with Cogedar Line. On 6 November 1964, *Ryndam* departed Rotterdam, and Southampton the next day, on her first voyage to the area, passing through Suez and calling at Fremantle and

Melbourne before arriving in Sydney on 14 December. The voyage then continued to Wellington, and on across the Pacific, through the Panama Canal, and back to Rotterdam.

The 1965 voyage was taken by *Maasdam*, which left Southampton on 20 October, and proceeded through Suez to Fremantle, Melbourne, Sydney and Wellington. *Maasdam* then made a cruise to the South Pacific islands, before resuming her voyage around the world, passing through the Panama Canal and back to Southampton and Rotterdam. For these voyages, both ships reverted to a one-class configuration for about 860 passengers, mostly emigrants on the outward passage.

On 8 February 1966, *Ryndam* departed Southampton on her second voyage to Australia, following the same route as on her first trip. In September 1966, *Ryndam* was transferred to Europe–Canada Line, in which Holland–America held an interest, and began operating between Bremerhaven and New York all year. *Maasdam* was then transferred to the trade from Rotterdam to Montreal, and her voyage to Australia scheduled to depart Rotterdam on 6 November 1966 was cancelled.

On 30 September 1967, *Maasdam* did depart Rotterdam bound for Australia once more, following the usual route to berth in Sydney on 7 November, the same day that fleetmate *Statendam* was also in port, the only time two Holland–America liners would be together in an Australian port. When *Maasdam* returned to Europe, Holland–America ended their interest in the Australian emigrant trade. In 1968, *Maasdam* was sold to Polish Ocean Line, and renamed *Stefan Batory*, being used for the next 20 years on the regular trade from Gdynia to Montreal as well as cruises.

From May to October 1968, *Ryndam* was chartered to Trans–Ocean Steamship Co. and renamed *Waterman*. She then reverted to her original name, and continued to operate for Europe–Canada Line until June 1971, when she was laid up in Schiedam. In August 1972, *Ryndam* was sold to Epirotiki Line, and extensively rebuilt in Greece for luxury cruising. Renamed *Atlas*, she entered service on 5 May 1973, cruising in the Mediterranean. In 1981 she was reported sold to Mexican interests, to be renamed *Royal Prince*, but this deal fell through, and the ship remained in the Epirotiki fleet as *Atlas*, though in recent years she spent some time laid up.

In April 1988, *Stefan Batory* completed her final voyage from Montreal to Copenhagen and Gdynia, and then was laid up until sold to Panamanian owners. To date, she has not returned to active service. In January 1989, *Atlas* was sold to Pride Cruises, and renamed *Pride of Mississippi*. The vessel is now cruising out of ports in the Gulf of Mexico.

MAASDAM

RYNDAM

CENTAUR

BUILT: *1964 by John Brown & Co., Clydebank*
TONNAGE: *8262 gross*
DIMENSIONS: *481 × 66 ft (146.6 × 20.1 m)*
SERVICE SPEED: *20 knots*
PROPULSION: *B & W diesels/twin screws*

Centaur was built to replace *Gorgon* and *Charon* on the Blue Funnel Line service between Fremantle and Singapore. Launched on 20 June 1963, she was completed in January 1964. *Centaur* was designed as a multi-purpose ship, to carry 196 first class passengers in air-conditioned comfort, and also a wide variety of cargoes. She could also carry livestock in the 'tween decks, up to 700 head of cattle or 4500 sheep, loaded at either Broome or Derby, ports with a vast tidal range, so *Centaur* had to be strengthened to sit on the bottom on an even keel at low tide.

On completion, *Centaur* went to Liverpool to load cargo for Australia, departing on 20 January. She passed through the Suez Canal en route to Singapore, but then went around the north of Australia to arrive in Sydney on 23 February. The vessel had been chartered by the Australian Chamber of Commerce as a floating trade mission to the Far East and Japan, and she returned from this trip to Sydney at the end of April. When the display material had been removed, *Centaur* went round to Fremantle, and on 27 May departed on her first voyage to Singapore, Port Klang and Georgetown.

Originally registered under the ownership of Ocean Steamship Co. Ltd, she was transferred within the Alfred Holt Group to China Mutual Steam Navigation Co., then in 1973 this changed again. Registered under the ownership of Eastern Fleets Ltd, her port of registry was changed from Liverpool to Singapore. In 1978 she came under yet another Alfred Holt subsidiary, Blue Funnel (S.E.A.) Pte. Ltd, but through all these alterations the ship retained her Blue Funnel colours.

The route of *Centaur* was changed in 1979, when she began making 25 day round trips from Fremantle to Singapore, Hong Kong and Manila, returning to Singapore and then back to Fremantle. This service was maintained for three years, but the trade in both passengers and cargo was declining. On 15 September 1982, *Centaur* left Fremantle on her final voyage to Singapore for Blue Funnel Line, who then abandoned the trade.

A one year charter of *Centaur* to the St Helena Shipping Co. had been arranged. With her funnel repainted in their colours, *Centaur* voyaged to Cape Town, from where she departed on 5 November 1982 bound for St Helena, Ascension Island, Cape Verde Island and Teneriffe en route to Bristol. A two-monthly schedule was maintained, passage time from Bristol to Cape Town being 24 days.

Blue Funnel had hoped St Helena Shipping would exercise a purchase option on *Centaur*, but when the charter ended in November 1983, she was handed back. Returning to Singapore from Cape Town, the vessel called once again at Fremantle arriving on 3 December for a three-day stay. She left on 6 December on a special voyage to Singapore, arriving on 12 December, then was laid up there, having been offered for sale. For over a year *Centaur* remained idle, then in 1985 she was purchased by the Shanghai Hai Xing Shipping Co., of China. Renamed *Hai Long*, she was sent first to Hong Kong, then entered service from there to Shanghai. In 1986 her name was changed to *Hai Da*, and she can often be seen in Hong Kong.

CENTAUR

ELLINIS

BUILT: *1932 by Bethlehem Shipbuilding Corp., Quincy*
TONNAGE: *24 351 gross*
DIMENSIONS: *632 × 79 ft (192.6 × 24.2 m)*
SERVICE SPEED: *20 knots*
PROPULSION: *Geared turbines/twin screws*

When Chandris Line realised that *Brittany* was a total loss, they immediately sought a replacement, and selected the Matson liner *Lurline*, which was renamed *Ellinis*. During 1932, Matson Line took delivery of three sister ships, the first pair being built for the trans-Pacific trade to Australia as *Mariposa* and *Monterey*. The third vessel was launched as *Lurline* on 18 July 1932, and completed in December the same year. With superb accommodation for 475 first class and 240 cabin class passengers, she was designed to operate on the lucrative service between California and Hawaii.

Prior to entering this trade, *Lurline* made a cruise around the Pacific, which departed San Francisco on 27 January 1933, and included calls at Auckland and Sydney, returning to San Francisco on 24 April. The liner then began her regular service to Hawaii. In 1934,

Lurline again visited Australia and New Zealand during a South Pacific cruise, but spent the rest of her time on the service from Los Angeles and San Francisco to Honolulu.

Lurline was two days out of Honolulu bound for San Francisco when the Japanese attacked Pearl Harbor on 7 December 1941. Blacked out, and travelling at top speed, she reached her destination safely two days later, and was immediately taken over by the US War Shipping Administration. Her luxury fittings were stripped out, and quarters for 3292 troops installed in just four days. *Lurline* then joined a convoy bound for Honolulu which included her sisters, *Mariposa* and *Monterey*. After several similar trips, *Lurline* was despatched to Pago Pago and Australia, travelling alone and relying on her 22 knot maximum speed to outrun any lurking Japanese submarines.

Lurline spent the war years on active duty in the South Pacific region. In 1943 she began carrying American troops from San Francisco to Brisbane, and in April 1944 took Australian Prime Minister John Curtin and his party to America to meet President Roosevelt.

LURLINE IN SYDNEY HARBOUR, FEBRUARY 1933

Between September 1944 and June 1945, *Lurline* made five return trips to Australia, then was sent to France to redeploy troops to the South Pacific, but before they arrived the Japanese surrendered.

On 11 September 1945, *Lurline* left Brisbane for San Francisco carrying 3560 passengers, including 500 war brides of American servicemen and 200 children. The liner continued to voyage to Australia, repatriating troops and taking American war brides to San Francisco, until 29 May 1946, when she was handed back to the Matson Line. She then went to the United Engineering Co. shipyard at Alameda for a refit.

Restoring *Lurline* to her former glory took two years, during which the cost soared from an estimated US$9.5 million to US$20 million. With accommodation for 484 first class and 238 cabin class, *Lurline* returned to service on 15 April 1948, when she left San Francisco for Honolulu.

Lurline quickly regained her pre-war popularity on the Hawaiian trade, and by 1955 she was enjoying a 97 per cent occupancy rate annually. As a result, Matson refitted *Monterey* to join her, under the name *Matsonia*, and carrying 761 first class passengers only. When she entered service, in June 1957, the accommodation on *Lurline* was altered to 722 first class. In December 1957, *Lurline* began making cruises, and on 7 January 1958, she left San Francisco with 575 passengers on a 73 day, 15 port cruise to the South Pacific and Orient, which included calls at Auckland and Wellington before arriving in Sydney on 31 January. Departing on 2 February, *Lurline* returned to San Francisco on 19 March. Subsequently *Lurline* made numerous short cruises each year, a scheduled cruise to the South Pacific in 1959 being cancelled, but in January 1960 she went as far as Tahiti.

By 1962, the Matson service to Hawaii was starting to lose money, so *Matsonia* was laid up in September. On 3 February 1963, *Lurline* arrived in Los Angeles from Honolulu with serious problems in the port turbine. She continued to San Francisco on one engine, and then was laid up, as repairs were considered too expensive. Subsequently, the liner was offered for sale, being purchased by Chandris Line on 3 September 1963, and renamed *Ellinis*.

After engine repairs, *Ellinis* left San Francisco, and went to Smith's Dock in North Shields for refitting. The superstructure was streamlined, the foremast removed and replaced by twin derricks, and a signal mast added above the bridge. Two new funnels were fitted, and a new raked bow, increasing her length to 642 ft (195.7 m). Internally, new cabins and extra berths in existing cabins increased capacity to 1668 passengers in one class. *Ellinis* left North Shields on 21 December

1963, bound for Piraeus, from where she departed on 30 December for her first voyage to Australia.

Passing through Fremantle on 16 January 1964, *Ellinis* arrived in Melbourne on 20 January, and Sydney two days later, then returned by the same route to Southampton. This was to be her European terminal port for future voyages to Australia, her first departure being in March 1964, though in later years some voyages would be extended to Rotterdam. For the next 10 years, *Ellinis* made regular line voyages to Australia, with occasional cruises, and for several years was employed on an eastward round-the-world route.

In April 1974, *Ellinis* was on a cruise to Japan when major problems developed in one engine, which was found to be out of alignment when the liner returned to Europe. At that time, her former sister *Mariposa*, which had been operating as *Homeric*, was being broken up in Taiwan, so Chandris Line bought one of her engines. It was transported to Rotterdam and installed in *Ellinis*, which then returned to service in March 1975. During the summer of 1975, *Ellinis* made Mediterranean cruises from Cannes, then in November 1975, voyaged to South Africa for three cruises from Cape Town to South America. She cruised in the Mediterranean for much of 1976, so it was not until March 1977 that *Ellinis* appeared again in Australian waters. She made a cruise to Japan from Sydney, then returned to the Mediterranean once more.

Chandris Line were gradually changing their operation from the Australian service to cruising. On 30 August 1977, *Ellinis* left Southampton on her final voyage to Australia. She spent six months cruising out of Sydney, the last being to Japan in April 1978. On 18 May, *Ellinis* departed Sydney for the last time, calling at Auckland three days later, on her way back to Britain. For the summer months of 1978 and 1979, *Ellinis* cruised in the Mediterranean, and was laid up in Piraeus during the winter.

In 1980, *Ellinis* again cruised during the summer, but when her season ended, she was laid up at Perama on 14 October 1980. For over six years, *Ellinis* would remain idle. Some of her mechanical parts were removed and installed in *Britanis*, and various plans for her further use were occasionally put forward. One such plan involved her returning to San Francisco as a floating hotel, but all came to nought. On 3 December 1986, *Ellinis* was towed away from Perama, bound for the scrap yard in Taiwan. She began taking water off Singapore on 11 March, and developed a 15 degree list to starboard. After this was rectified, she eventually arrived in Kaohsiung on 15 April 1987, where work on scrapping her commenced two months later.

LURLINE IN SYDNEY, 31 JANUARY 1958

ELLINIS

MALAYSIA

BUILT: *1955 by Cammell Laird & Co., Birkenhead*
TONNAGE: *8062 gross*
DIMENSIONS: *439 × 60 ft (133.8 × 18.3 m)*
SERVICE SPEED: *15 knots*
PROPULSION: *Geared turbines/single screw*

Austasia Line is part of the Vestey Group, which also owns Blue Star Line and Booth Line, and this vessel saw service with two of these companies. Launched on 31 August 1955, she was named *Hubert*, having been built for the Booth Line service to Manaus on the Amazon River from Liverpool, her maiden voyage commencing on 11 February 1955. Accommodation was provided for 74 first class and 96 tourist class passengers. *Hubert* joined her sister *Hilderband*, but she was wrecked on the Portuguese coast in September 1957.

Hubert operated to the Amazon for 10 years, the last three being partnered by *Anselm*, which would later join her in Australian waters. In November 1964, *Hubert* was withdrawn from Booth Line service, and transferred to Austasia Line, being renamed *Malaysia*. Austasia Line had operated a fleet of cargo ships from Australia to the Malayan peninsular, but this was their first entry into the passenger trade. The only change made to the ship was the new funnel colours.

On 3 December 1964, *Malaysia* left London with a full cargo, going around South Africa to Lourenco Marques, then crossing to Albany, where she arrived on 21 January 1965. *Malaysia* arrived in Sydney on 28 January, then went to Melbourne, departing there on 6 February on her first Austasia voyage. This took her to Sydney, Brisbane, Port Moresby, Singapore, Malacca, Penang and Port Swettenham, then back to Singapore.

Later a call at Jakarta was added, and in May 1970 she ran aground off that port, not being refloated for five days.

For some time, *Malaysia* was partnered by *Australasia*, the former *Anselm*, but in 1970 she was transferred to a new service from Fremantle to Singapore. At the end of 1972, *Australasia* was disposed of, and *Malaysia* abandoned her east coast service, and began operating out of Fremantle in December 1972. *Malaysia* spent just over three years on this trade, but on 5 May 1976, she left Fremantle on her final voyage for Austasia Line.

Malaysia was sold to Atlas Shipping Agency, of Singapore, who took delivery on 14 May 1976. Renamed *United Challenger*, she was extensively rebuilt to carry livestock, with pens for sheep being installed in the former cargo and passenger areas. The rebuilding was completed in October 1976, at which time the ship was renamed *Khalij Express*. She was to operate out of Australian ports again, where live sheep were loaded and transported to the Middle East. Her first voyage on this trade was from Fremantle, and over the next seven years the ship visited numerous ports where livestock were handled.

In 1977, *Khalij Express* was sold to Halena Shipping, also of Singapore, but not renamed. In 1981 she changed hands again, passing into Saudi Arabian ownership when purchased by Arabian Maritime Transport Co. Ltd, again without change of name. *Khalij Express* remained a regular visitor to Australia until the end of 1983, when she was withdrawn. The vessel was then sold to shipbreakers at Karachi, where she arrived in April 1984.

MALAYSIA

AUSTRALASIA

BUILT: *1950 by John Cockerill S.A., Hoboken*
TONNAGE: *10 868 gross*
DIMENSIONS: *504 × 64 ft (153.7 × 19.6 m)*
SERVICE SPEED: *16 knots*
PROPULSION: *B & W diesels/single screw*

Australasia was the fifth name to be carried by this vessel. She was the fourth of a class of five liners built in Belgium for the Compagnie Maritime Belge, being launched on 4 March 1950 as *Baudouinville*. On 19 September 1950, she left Antwerp on her maiden voyage to Matadi, in the Belgian Congo. Accommodation was provided for 248 first class passengers, with a large cargo capacity. These ships were rather underpowered, and in 1957 were fitted with turbo-chargers, increasing their speed by one knot.

In 1957, Cie. Maritime Belge built two larger vessels for the Congo service, and decided to name one of these ships *Baudouinville*, in honour of the king. On 1 June, the older vessel was renamed *Thysville*, and fitted with her turbo-charger in August. She remained on the Congo trade a further three years, then was withdrawn and offered for sale. On 13 March 1961 she was purchased by the Vestey Group, and allocated to Booth Line as *Anselm*.

During a refit at the Mercantile Marine Engineering & Graving Dock Co., in Antwerp, the accommodation was altered to 135 first class and 101 tourist class. This involved changes to the lounges and dining room, a new galley and hospital, while refrigeration machinery was installed in the cargo holds. On 16 June 1961, *Anselm* departed Liverpool on her first voyage to South America, going up the Amazon River as far as Manaus. She was partnered by *Hubert*, which later became *Malaysia*.

Unfortunately, *Anselm* was not a success, and on 19 April 1963 she was transferred within the Vestey Group to Blue Star Line, being renamed *Iberia Star*. Refitted at the Bremer Vulkan shipyard, her accommodation was reduced to only 76 first class, while air-conditioning was extended throughout the ship, having previously only been piped to the public rooms. *Iberia Star* began operating from London to the River Plate, but again was not a success, so remained under the Blue Star flag a mere eighteen months.

On 22 August 1965, *Iberia Star* was transferred again within the Vestey Group, to Austasia Line, and renamed *Australasia*. She voyaged from London via Beira to Sydney, arriving on 15 December 1965, and then went to Melbourne, berthing on 19 December. On 9 January 1966, she began her first voyage on her new route, calling at Sydney and Brisbane en route to Singapore, where she docked on 30 January. The ship then went on to Port Swettenham, Penang and Malacca before returning to Singapore, and back to Australia. For three years, *Australasia* maintained this route with *Malaysia*, then on 30 January 1969 she left Sydney for the last time.

On reaching Singapore, *Australasia* was transferred to a new route, from there to Fremantle. On 28 July 1970, *Australasia* was transferred from British to Singapore registry, but by then the ship was suffering considerable engine problems. They became worse over the next two years, and on 10 December 1972, the vessel was sold to Euroasia Carriers Ltd, of Singapore, who resold her the same day to Nissho-Iwai Co. Ltd, of Osaka. *Australasia* was in Fremantle that day, and left there on 11 December for the last time. Arriving in Singapore on 16 December, she was handed over to her new owners, but they had already negotiated her sale to Taiwanese shipbreakers. *Australasia* arrived at their Hualien yard on 27 December 1972, having been towed from Singapore.

AUSTRALASIA

FAIRSTAR

BUILT: *1957 by Fairfield Shipbuilding & Engineering Co.,
Glasgow*
TONNAGE: *21 619 gross*
DIMENSIONS: *613 × 78 ft (186.9 × 23.8 m)*
SERVICE SPEED: *18 knots*
PROPULSION: *Geared turbines/twin screws*

The most popular and successful cruise ship to have
operated from Australian ports must be *Fairstar*. She is
always kept in immaculate condition, and has a modern
appearance despite her thirty years. This liner was
ordered by the Bibby Line, a British company that had
been involved in trooping for the government for many
years. Launched on 15 December 1955, she was named
Oxfordshire, and was destined to be the last vessel built
to transport troops.

Oxfordshire was handed over to Bibby Line on
13 February 1957, and began a 20 year contract as a
troopship, which would take her to many parts of the
world. As built, *Oxfordshire* could carry 1000 troops,
plus 500 dependents in cabins. The cabins could also be
divided up into 220 first class, 100 second class and 180
third class when fare-paying passengers were carried. In
this service, she was partnered by her sister, *Nevasa*,
owned by British India Line.

In 1962, after a mere five years duty, the trooping
career of *Oxfordshire* came to a sudden end. The British
Government decided that all future troop movements
would be by plane, so on 19 December 1962,
Oxfordshire arrived in Southampton at the end of her
final voyage. She then went to Falmouth to be laid up,
and was offered for charter. In May 1963, Sitmar Line
took the vessel on a six-year charter, with an option to
purchase. She was despatched to the Wilton–Fijenoord
shipyard in Holland, to be refitted for the Australian
emigrant trade. This involved a major enlargement of
the superstructure, and the installation of extra cabins in
the original troop and cargo spaces.

A dispute arose between Sitmar and Bibby Line
regarding some of the alterations being made to the
vessel, so in March 1964, Sitmar decided to exercise its
option, and purchased *Oxfordshire*. She was then
renamed *Fairstar*, and the conversion work continued.
Sitmar then had a dispute with the Dutch shipyard, so in
April 1964, *Fairstar* was moved to Southampton, where
the conversion was completed by Harland & Wolff.
Fairstar provided accommodation for 1870 passengers in

one class, and on 19 May 1964, she left Southampton on
her first voyage to Australia. Fremantle was reached on
12 June, followed by Adelaide on 17 June and
Melbourne the next day, with *Fairstar* arriving in
Sydney for the first time on 21 June.

On her outbound voyages, the bulk of passengers on
Fairstar were migrants on assisted passages, while the
return trip was made with fare-paying passengers.
Voyages were regularly made out and back through the
Suez Canal, with four return trips each year. In January
1965, *Fairstar* made a three-day cruise from Sydney on
charter to Massey Ferguson, this being the first
Australian business convention held on a ship. On 22
December 1965, *Fairstar* left Sydney on her first
commercial cruise, which lasted 22 days. In subsequent
years, *Fairstar* made an annual Christmas cruise from
Sydney.

The closure of the Suez Canal in 1967 resulted in
Fairstar being diverted around South Africa, and
eventually she began making round-the-world voyages,
returning to Britain through the Panama Canal. In 1970,
Sitmar lost the British migrant charter to Chandris Line,
but *Fairstar* remained on her regular trade to Australia
for a while, relying on fare-paying passengers in both
directions. Eventually the demand for such passages
was insufficient to keep the vessel in service all year. In
July 1973, *Fairstar* made a voyage to Australia and New
Zealand, then returned to Sydney to commence a
programme of cruises, which lasted until April 1974.
She then voyaged to Southampton, and cruised from
there for several months, but with only limited success.
On 13 November 1974, *Fairstar* departed Southampton
for the last time, travelling via Cape Town to Sydney
and Auckland, then returning to Sydney to enter
permanent cruise work on 23 December 1974, carrying
a maximum of 1280 passengers.

Since that time, *Fairstar* has cruised from Sydney
throughout the year. Most of her trips are around the
South Pacific islands, but most years she has also made
one or two longer cruises to the Far East and Japan.
These finished temporarily in 1982, but from 1986 she
has again made one cruise each year to Singapore, where
she is drydocked and overhauled. During her 1988 refit,
Fairstar had her funnel repainted in new colours adopted
by Sitmar that year. Following the takeover by
Princess Cruises of Sitmar Cruises, *Fairstar* is the only
Sitmar ship not to have been renamed. Her 1990 cruise
schedule did not include any trips to the Orient.

THE TROOPSHIP *OXFORDSHIRE*

FAIRSTAR

Statendam

BUILT: *1957 by Wilton–Fijenoord N.V., Schiedam*
TONNAGE: *24 294 gross*
DIMENSIONS: *642 × 81 ft (195.8 × 24.7 m)*
SERVICE SPEED: *19 knots*
PROPULSION: *Geared turbines/twin screws*

This attractive liner was built in a graving dock, being floated out on 12 June 1956, but not christened. Over the next six months she was fitted out with accommodation for 84 first class and 867 tourist class passengers, then began her sea trials. On 15 December, the liner suffered an embarrassing total breakdown of her engines, and had to be towed back to the shipyard. Following repairs, a further series of trials were conducted, and on 23 January 1957 she was officially named *Statendam* at sea during her delivery voyage from Schiedam to Rotterdam. On 6 February, *Statendam* left Rotterdam on her maiden voyage to New York, and also made short cruises from New York during the off-peak periods.

Statendam was used increasingly for cruising, and by 1965 she was spending most of the year in this trade, with only an occasional Atlantic voyage in the summer season. In October 1965 she left New York on her first cruise around the world. She visited numerous islands in the South Pacific, and also called at Auckland and Sydney.

In October 1966, *Statendam* made another visit to the South Pacific, including visits to Australian and New Zealand ports, returning for a third time in 1967. On this occasion, *Statendam* was in Sydney on 7 November, the same day as *Maasdam*, the only time that two Holland–America ships would be in the port together. It would be a further five years before *Statendam* again visited the South Pacific, when she arrived in Sydney on 19 November 1972, and sailed the next day. This was her final visit to the region.

Upon completion of this cruise, *Statendam* was given an extensive refit. The accommodation was altered to carry 740 passengers in one class, and she was repainted in the new Holland–America Line colours, deep blue hull and orange funnel carrying their new logo. Subsequently, *Statendam* cruised out of American east coast ports until 1981, when she switched to the west coast to operate from Vancouver during the summer season.

At the end of 1981, *Statendam* was offered for sale, and soon purchased by Paquet Cruises, a French company. They had to wait until November 1982 to take delivery of the ship, which was then renamed *Rhapsody*, and painted all white. She continued to operate from Vancouver in summer, and Port Everglades in winter. On 1 April 1984, *Rhapsody* ran aground on a reef off Grand Cayman Island, and for some time was thought to be a total loss. After several weeks of frantic work, she was refloated and found to be only slightly damaged, so after repairs she returned to service.

Early in 1986, the liner was again offered for sale, and bought by a Greek firm, Regency Cruises. *Rhapsody* arrived in Port Everglades on 4 May 1986, at the end of her final cruise under the French flag, then was laid up there for several months after being handed over to her new owners. Eventually the liner crossed to Piraeus, where she spent a considerable time being refitted, having been renamed *Regent Star*. A major alteration was the removal of the original engines, which were replaced by diesels removed from a large container ship also purchased by Regency Cruises, and originally to have been rebuilt as a cruise liner. When the conversion work was completed, *Regent Star* entered service during May 1987 as a full-time cruise liner, still operating on the American market, but based on Montego Bay, in Jamaica, in winter and Vancouver in the summer.

STATENDAM

AUSTRALIS

BUILT: *1940 by Newport News Shipbuilding & Drydock Co., Newport News*
TONNAGE: *26 485 gross*
DIMENSIONS: *723 × 93 ft (220.4 × 28.4 m)*
SERVICE SPEED: *22 knots*
PROPULSION: *Geared turbines/twin screws*

Australis was the most notable of all the ships Chandris Line purchased for their service from Europe to Australia, having been built as *America* for the United States Line. Designed by William Francis Gibbs, who was also responsible for the *United States*, the fastest liner ever built, *America* was built for the North Atlantic trade. The keel was laid on 22 August 1938, and the liner launched by Mrs Franklin Roosevelt on 31 August 1939. When *America* was completed in July 1940, she had accommodation for 543 cabin class, 418 tourist class and 241 third class passengers, but could not operate to Europe because of the war. Instead the vessel was sent cruising, departing New York for the first time on 10 August for the Caribbean.

One problem to arise early in her career was smuts falling on the afterdeck. To counter the problem, both funnels were raised some 15 ft (5 m), to retain a balanced appearance. *America* continued to operate cruises until 15 July 1941, when she was taken over by the US Navy and converted into a troopship.

Fitted out with quarters for 8175 men, the vessel was renamed USS *West Point*, and allocated pennant number AP23. Entering service in November 1941, *West Point* joined a convoy from Halifax, bound for Egypt, but then was rerouted to Singapore via Cape Town. By the time Singapore was reached, the Japanese were closing in, and *West Point* was frequently attacked by aircraft while anchored off the island. Eventually, she went to Bombay to disembark her troops, then to Suez to collect Australian troops and rush them to Singapore,

returning to Bombay with civilian evacuees. *West Point* then proceeded to Fremantle, Adelaide, Melbourne and Auckland, where American troops were embarked and carried to Noumea. *West Point* visited many ports in Europe, Africa and South America, and returned to the Pacific at the end of the war.

Having steamed over 500 000 miles during her war career, and carried 505 020 persons, *West Point* was released by the government on 22 July 1946, and handed back to United States Line. Returning to her builders' yard, the liner was refitted for commercial service, with accommodation for 516 first class, 371 cabin class and 159 tourist class passengers. Given back her original name, *America* left New York on 14 November 1946, with 972 passengers aboard, for her first commercial voyage across the Atlantic, calling at Cobh, Southampton and Le Havre. After three voyages, her French terminal port was changed to Cherbourg, but in May 1948 she again began calling at Le Havre.

From October 1951, *America* extended her voyages to Bremen, a route she would maintain for the remainder of her career on the North Atlantic. In July 1952, *America* lost her position as the premier American flag liner, when *United States* entered service, and immediately broke all the Atlantic speed records. These two ships operated the United States Line service together for the next 12 years.

During 1961, the cabin and tourist classes were combined into a single tourist class for 530 passengers, and incentive fares offered. *America* managed to remain competitive for a while longer, but just before her scheduled departure from New York on 14 September 1963, an inter-union dispute resulted in the engineers going on strike. The 900 passengers were left stranded, and *America* was towed to Hoboken and laid up. It was 7 February 1964 before she returned to service, being programmed to operate 13 Atlantic voyages and three

AMERICA OF UNITED STATES LINE

short summer cruises during the year. Sadly, it soon became evident that the vessel was totally uneconomic to operate, and on 9 October 1964 *America* left New York on her final voyage, departing Bremen on 19 October to return to New York on 27 October. During her 18 years on the Atlantic, *America* had carried 476 462 passengers while making 288 voyages.

On 5 November came the announcement that *America* had been sold to Chandris Line, with the Greek flag being raised on 17 November, at which time she was renamed *Australis*. The same day her funnels were repainted light blue with a thin black top, and on 18 November, *Australis* left Newport News for Piraeus. There, Chandris' own shipyard set about converting the liner for the Australian trade. The accommodation was more than doubled, to 2258 passengers in one class, and air-conditioning installed. External changes were minor, though the superstructure was extended aft, and the hull painted white.

On 21 August 1965, *Australis* departed Piraeus on her maiden voyage to Australia, reaching Fremantle on 6 September, Melbourne on 13 September, and Sydney two days later. She then crossed the Tasman to Auckland, and on to Tahiti and through the Panama Canal, calling at Port Everglades on 3 October before terminating the voyage at Southampton. On 16 October, *Australis* left Southampton on her second voyage to Australia and New Zealand, but went to Wellington, then returned to Melbourne and on to Britain via the Suez Canal.

Australis remained on the regular trade between Britain and Australia through Suez until the canal was closed in 1967, when she was diverted around South Africa, with calls at Cape Town and Durban. Occasionally, *Australis* made cruises from Australia during the summer. During a refit in 1968, the mainmast was removed, as well as a pair of kingposts aft, while a short signal mast was added on the after funnel, and the hull was repainted light grey. In 1969, *Australis* was transferred from Greek to Panamanian registry.

On 22 October 1970, a fire broke out in the galley when *Australis* was between Auckland and Suva. The crew managed to control the blaze, but not before the galley was badly affected, and water damaged forty cabins and the ballroom. Temporary repairs were effected in Suva, and *Australis* was able to continue her voyage on 30 October.

In 1970, Chandris Line secured the government contract to transport British migrants to Australia, but over the next few years the number being carried decreased, as more were choosing to travel by airplane. By 1976, *Australis* was the only liner offering regular sailings between Britain and Australia, her former consorts having been transferred to cruising. It was during 1976 that *Australis* was returned to Greek registry, but the following year was to be her last. On 18 November 1977, *Australis* departed Southampton for the final time, carrying among her passengers 650 assisted migrants, the last to be transported to Australia by sea. The voyage terminated in Sydney on 17 December, as *Australis* had been chartered to operate a "rock and roll cruise", but this was cancelled due to lack of patronage. Instead the vessel left Sydney for Auckland, arriving on 20 December, and then went to the small port of Timaru to be laid up.

At one time it was announced that *Australis* had been sold to Taiwanese shipbreakers, but early in 1978 the liner was bought by a newly formed company, America Cruise Line for US$5 million. On 23 April 1978, she left Timaru for New York, arriving on 19 May and going into drydock. The ship was completely refurbished internally, while the hull was repainted dark blue and the funnels the same blue with a red band. Once again she was named *America*, though her new owner was forced to change its name to Venture Cruise Line, to avoid confusion with another company.

On 30 June 1978, *America* left New York on a three-day cruise to nowhere, with 950 passengers aboard, but workmen were still swarming over the ship and many cabins and public rooms were out of use. Six hours out, *America* turned back, and anchored off Staten Island to disembark 250 disgruntled passengers in lifeboats. *America* made a second cruise from New York, with 641 passengers, but the next two cruises had to be cancelled while faulty plumbing was repaired. On 18 July, *America* was arrested by the District Court, then two days later Venture Cruise Line ceased operations, and *America* was laid up in Brooklyn.

On 28 August, *America* was put up for auction, and the surprise successful bidder was Chandris Line, who bought back the liner for US$1 million. She left New York for the last time on 6 September bound for Piraeus, where she arrived on 12 September. Chandris refitted the ship for their cruise service, during which the dummy forward funnel was removed, and replaced by a mast, and she was then renamed *Italis*. On 28 July 1979, she left Genoa on the first of three Mediterranean cruises, then was laid up again on 12 September 1979, at Peráma. Her planned cruise programme for 1980 was transferred to *Ellinis*, and *Italis* remained idle, being offered for sale.

Italis was sold to Inter Commerce Corp., a subsidiary of Hilton Hotels, for conversion into a floating hotel to be based at Lagos. Renamed *Noga*, the liner remained idle at Peráma. In subsequent years, there have been a number of schemes promoted for the liner, and her ownership has changed. She is presently owned by a Panamanian concern, Silver Moon Ferries, under the name *Alferdoss*, but after so many years idle, it is unlikely the vessel will ever return to active service again.

The long period of idleness had a most destructive effect on the hull of the liner, and in December 1988 she had to be run aground near Piraeus to stop her sinking.

AUSTRALIS INITIALLY HAD A WHITE HULL

AUSTRALIS AFTER ALTERATIONS AND REPAINTING IN 1968

KUNGSHOLM

BUILT: *1966 by John Brown & Co., Clydebank*
TONNAGE: *26 678 gross*
DIMENSIONS: *660 × 86 ft (201.2 × 26.3 m)*
SERVICE SPEED: *21 knots*
PROPULSION: *Gotaverken diesels/twin screws*

The last liner to be built for Swedish America Line, and also the last vessel to be built by the famous John Brown shipyard, *Kungsholm* was launched on 14 April 1965. On 19 November, the liner made her first sea trials, but problems were discovered so it was not until 17 March 1966 that *Kungsholm* was delivered to her owner, and left Gothenburg on 22 April 1966 for her maiden voyage to New York.

Kungsholm had been designed as a dual-purpose liner, mainly intended for cruising, but also capable of making occasional trans-Atlantic voyages. In the latter role, accommodation was provided for 108 first class and 605 tourist class passengers, but on cruises this was reduced to 450 in one class.

Kungsholm made her first excursion into the South Pacific in 1967, calling at Auckland and Wellington before arriving in Sydney on 6 February and departing the next day. She returned in February 1968, and was back in Sydney on 23 February 1969 for a one-day stopover. It was a further three years before *Kungsholm* returned, arriving in Sydney on 19 February 1972. Due to depart the next day, she was delayed by problems with the air-conditioning and generator, and had to be moved from Circular Quay to Woolloomooloo for

repairs. Eventually leaving on 22 February, a scheduled call at Brisbane was dropped, the ship going direct to Vila.

On 19 September 1975, *Kungsholm* arrived in Gothenburg and was laid up, to bring to an end the Swedish America Line participation in the passenger trade, which had commenced in December 1915.

Within days, *Kungsholm* had been sold to Flagship Cruises, of Norway, which had recently sold their only ship, *Sea Venture*, to Princess Cruises, to be renamed *Pacific Princess*. Flagship retained the name *Kungsholm*, but her cruising capacity was increased to a more economic 600 in one class. The liner had been programmed by Swedish America Line for a cruise to the South Pacific early in 1976, and Flagship retained this in their schedule. *Kungsholm* visiting Auckland and then Sydney, where she berthed on 25 February 1976. This was to be her final voyage to the area as *Kungsholm*, as subsequently she cruised from New York to the West Indies.

As 1978 progressed, Flagship Cruises were in financial difficulties. Eventually these problems became so serious that Flagship decided to withdraw from the trade, and *Kungsholm* was offered for sale. At this time, P & O Line was seeking a replacement for *Arcadia* on the Australian cruise trade, and decided to purchase *Kungsholm*. The vessel left New York on 10 August 1978 for her final cruise on behalf of Flagship Cruises, following which she was handed over to P & O, and renamed *Sea Princess*.

KUNGSHOLM

SEA PRINCESS

REBUILT: *1979 by Bremer Vulkan, Bremen*
TONNAGE: *27 670 gross*
DIMENSIONS: *660 × 86 ft (201.2 × 26.3 m)*
SERVICE SPEED: *21 knots*
PROPULSION: *Gotaverken diesels/twin screws*

Having purchased *Kungsholm* from Flagship Cruises, P & O Line took delivery of the vessel in New York on 21 August 1978, and renamed her *Sea Princess*. P & O sent the ship to the Bremen shipyard of Bremer Vulkan for an extensive rebuilding and refurbishment.

The forward funnel, which was a dummy, was reduced to a stump, while a conical top was fitted to the remaining funnel. The mainmast was removed, while the after end of the superstructure was extended, and the after end of the promenade deck rebuilt, incorporating 80 new cabins and more open deck space with a new outdoor swimming pool. These alterations increased the passenger capacity to 840 in one class. The work was delayed by the severe winter weather, the worst experienced in Europe for many years.

Sea Princess left the Bremer Vulkan shipyard on 20 January 1979, bound for Southampton. There she boarded her first passengers, and departed for Australia. Meanwhile, the ship she was replacing, *Arcadia*, had left Sydney on her final cruise to Singapore, where the two ships met up, and passengers were transferred from the old to the new ship.

Sea Princess then continued her voyage, visiting Bali before arriving in Fremantle on 28 February, and after a visit to Melbourne, arrived in Sydney on 6 March. For the next three years, she was based on Sydney for cruises around the South Pacific, with an occasional longer trip to Asian ports.

In 1982, P & O decided to transfer *Sea Princess* to the British cruise market, replacing her in Australia by *Oriana*. On 4 February 1982, *Sea Princess* left Sydney on a cruise to Asia, returning on 10 March, then departed the next day on a voyage to Southampton. *Sea Princess* was then based on Southampton, but in January 1983 left on a world cruise, arriving in Sydney on 21 February for a two–day stopover. This voyage was repeated in 1984 and 1985, but then *Sea Princess* was transferred to the West Indies, to operate fly/cruises for British passengers throughout the year.

In November 1986, *Sea Princess* was transferred to Princess Cruises. She was given an extensive refit, her accommodation was upgraded, and her funnel repainted white, with the Princess Cruises logo on the sides. During early 1987, she was based on Port Everglades for Caribbean cruises, then spent the rest of the year in the Pacific. For several months she operated to Alaska from San Francisco, then was cruising between Asian ports until December, when she returned to Australia.

On 26 January 1988, *Sea Princess* anchored in Sydney Harbour for the Bicentennial Day celebrations, then went back to sea for the final two days of that cruise. Her final cruise from Sydney was 28 days to Tahiti, returning on 25 February, and the same day *Sea Princess* left for Singapore, to resume her Asian cruise schedule. In December 1988, the liner returned to Sydney for another programme of four cruises, extending into February 1989, and she was back again in December 1989 for another season of cruises.

SEA PRINCESS

SHAW SAVILL TRIO

BUILT: *1960 by Harland & Wolff Ltd, Belfast*
TONNAGE: *18 575 gross*
DIMENSIONS: *583 × 78 ft (177.7 × 23.8 m)*
SERVICE SPEED: *17.5 knots*
PROPULSION: *B & W diesels/twin screws*

The appearance of *Akaroa, Arawa* and *Aranda* on the Shaw Savill service from Britain to Australia and New Zealand was so brief, they are almost forgotten today. They were built too late to be successful on their initial trade, and spent only two years under Shaw Savill ownership before being sold.

This trio was ordered by Royal Mail Line to replace its "Highland" class liners on the trade between London and Buenos Aires. The first was launched on 7 July 1959 as *Amazon*, being completed in December that year, and departing on her maiden voyage on 22 January 1960. The second was named *Aragon* when launched on 20 October 1959, entering service on 29 April 1960. The last to be built was *Arlanza*, launched on 13 April 1960, and making her maiden departure from London on 7 October. These ships provided accommodation for 107 first class, 82 cabin class and 275 third class passengers, the latter being used primarily by Spanish migrants.

There was also 480 000 cu ft (13 592 m³) of cargo space, of which 435 000 cu ft (12 318 m³) was refrigerated, for carrying meat to Britain. This meant that much of the cargo space was empty on the outward voyages, which was to have an adverse effect on the economic viability of these three ships. They were fully air-conditioned and fitted with stabilisers, and also were the first British ships to use alternating current for their electrical systems.

Sadly, from the beginning these three ships were not a paying proposition for Royal Mail Line. Many potential passengers were lost to the airlines, and increasingly meat was consigned on new types of fast cargo ships that operated to quicker timetables. After eight years operation, Royal Mail Line decided to cut their losses, and withdraw these three ships from service, and they were subsequently transferred within the Furness Group to Shaw Savill.

In March 1968, *Amazon* was transferred to Shaw Savill, and renamed *Akaroa*. The original three class layout was modified to carry 516 passengers in a single class, the only external change being the funnel colours. On 28 May 1968, *Akaroa* departed Southampton on her first voyage, arriving in Sydney on 4 July, then crossing to New Zealand. Once passengers had been disembarked, *Akaroa* spent some time loading meat at various ports, then returned to Britain through the Panama Canal.

In January 1969, *Arlanza* was transferred to Shaw Savill and renamed *Arawa*. After being altered in a similar fashion to her sister, *Arawa* departed Southampton on 28 February 1969, arriving in Sydney on 6 April, then going on to New Zealand and back to Britain. *Aragon* made the final Royal Mail Line passenger voyage to South America, which returned to London on 21 February 1969. She was then handed over to Shaw Savill, renamed *Aranda*, and on 28 March left Southampton. Passing through Sydney on 3 May, *Aranda* went on to New Zealand to load meat, then

AKAROA

THE SAME SHIP AS THE CAR CARRIER *AKARITA*

came back to Sydney on 30 May, on her return voyage to Britain.

These ships never achieved a high acceptance rate with travellers, as the length of time required to load frozen cargo in New Zealand was a major drawback, and timetables were frequently disrupted by strikes. Shaw Savill tried using these ships for occasional cruises out of Australia, but they were totally unsuited to this trade. They then purchased *Ocean Monarch*, and for a brief time, Shaw Savill were operating six passenger liners to Australia and New Zealand.

On 15 April 1970, *Akaroa* suffered extensive damage to her boilers when a fire broke out as she was passing the Azores, though the ship was able to limp into port safely. This was the only major mishap to befall these ships during their brief period under Shaw Savill ownership. They proved to be such enormous economic burdens, that during 1971 all three were sold.

On 15 April 1971, *Akaroa* was sold to Uglands Rederi, of Norway. Renamed *Akarita*, she was sent to the Nymo Shipyard at Grimstad to be converted into a car carrier. *Arawa* and *Aranda* were both purchased by Leif Hoegh & Co., also of Norway, and sent to Yugoslavia for conversion into car carriers at the Viktor Lenac shipyard in Rijeka. In April 1972, *Akarita* also

arrived at the same shipyard to have her conversion completed.

Arawa was renamed *Hoegh Transit*, while her sister became *Hoegh Traveller*, and on completion the three vessels operated on a joint service known as Hoegh–Ugland Auto Liners. In their new guise their appearance had been totally changed, with a new, box-like superstructure. They were used to transport cars around the world, and returned to Australian and New Zealand ports on several occasions.

In June 1972, *Hoegh Transit* was renamed *Hoegh Trotter*. In 1977 all three ships were sold to Ace Navigation Co. Ltd, and renamed *Hual Trotter, Hual Traveller* and *Hual Akarita* under the Liberian flag. During 1980 the "Hual" was dropped from their names, so they were known simply as *Trotter, Traveller* and *Akarita*. By then their careers were nearing an end, as all three were sold to shipbreakers in Taiwan during 1981.

Trotter arrived in Kagoshima on 4 October 1981, and was laid up until being sold, arriving in Kaohsiung on 9 December. *Traveller* left New Orleans on 29 October on her final voyage, arriving in Kaohsiung on 6 November. *Akarita* ended her final voyage at Sasebo on 22 November 1981, and subsequently arrived in Kaohsiung in early January 1982.

FRENCH STOPGAPS

BUILT: *Pacifique 1952 by Ch. Navals de la Ciotat, La Ciotat*
Cambodge *1953 by At. et Ch. de France, Dunkirk*
TONNAGE: *13 520 gross*
DIMENSIONS: *532 × 72 ft (162.1 × 22 m)*
SERVICE SPEED: *21 knots*
PROPULSION: *Geared turbines/twin screws*

Following the withdrawal of *Oceanien* from the Pacific service in 1967, Messageries Maritimes still required a third vessel to partner *Caledonien* and *Tahitien* on the route from France to French Pacific possessions, if not all the way to Australia. Messageries Maritimes also operated a service from France to the Far East, using three ships, *Viet-nam, Cambodge* and *Laos*. This service was in decline, so one of those ships, *Viet-nam*, was withdrawn and transferred to the Pacific trade, being renamed *Pacifique* in 1967.

Viet-nam launched on 14 October 1951, entering service in July 1952 with a voyage from Marseilles to Yokohama. *Cambodge* was launched on 8 July 1952, and entered service a year later, while *Laos* joined the route in July 1954. Each had accommodation for 117 first class, 110 tourist class and 312 third class passengers.

Pacifique began operating from Marseilles to Tahiti, Vila and Noumea. In September 1967, she left Marseilles on a voyage that extended to Australia, arriving in Sydney on 6 November 1967. Instead of returning to France across the Pacific, *Pacifique* continued on to Melbourne, where she berthed on 10 November, then went around South Africa to return to Marseilles. This was to be her only visit to Australia, and in 1970 *Pacifique* was sold to Cia. de Nav. Abeto, of Hong Kong.

Renamed *Princess Abeto*, she was initially announced as returning to Australia to commence a cruise service from Townsville, but this did not eventuate. Instead, she was refitted for the pilgrim trade, to carry 1612 persons. In 1971 her name was changed to *Malaysia Baru*, then *Malaysia Kita* in 1972, but on 12 May 1974 the vessel was gutted by fire off Singapore, and sank in shallow water. In 1975 the wreck was raised, and scrapped in Taiwan.

In May 1969, *Tahitien* was badly damaged by a fire, and had to miss a voyage to Australia for repairs. *Cambodge* was on her final voyage from the Far East at the same time, so was called on to make a single voyage to Australia. Departing Marseilles in August 1969, she arrived in Sydney the following month for a two-day stopover, then returned to France. In December 1969, *Cambodge* was sold to Sun Line, a Greek cruise firm, and given the temporary name, *Stella V*.

The vessel was then totally rebuilt, emerging as the luxury cruise liner *Stella Solaris*, bearing no resemblance at all to her original appearance. She entered service in her new role in June 1973, cruising in the Mediterranean in summer, and the Caribbean or South American waters in winter. In the summer of 1986 and 1987, *Stella Solaris* stayed on the east coast of America, cruising to Bermuda and the West Indies from New York, but in 1988 she returned again to the Mediterranean.

PACIFIQUE

THE RUSSIAN 'WRITERS'

BUILT: *1964–1972 by Mathias–Thesen Werft, Wismar*
TONNAGE: *19 872–20 502 gross*
DIMENSIONS: *578 × 77 ft (176.1 × 23.6 m)*
SERVICE SPEED: *20 knots*
PROPULSION: *Sulzer diesels/twin screws*

This group of five, comprising *Ivan Franko, Alexandr Pushkin, Taras Shevchenko, Shota Rustaveli* and *Mikhail Lermontov*, are named after famous Russian writers. The first was launched on 15 June 1963, and named *Ivan Franko*, being completed in November 1964. Allocated to the Black Sea Steamship Co., she initially operated between Leningrad and Montreal. *Alexandr Pushkin* was the second launched, on 26 March 1964, and on completion in June 1965 joined the fleet of the Baltic Steamship Co. On 16 January 1965, *Taras Shevchenko* was launched, being delivered on 26 April 1967 to the Black Sea Shipping Co. The fourth, *Shota Rustaveli* was also allocated to the Black Sea Shipping Co. when completed in May 1968.

Each of these ships could carry 750 passengers in one class, with a crew numbering 220. They soon proved themselves to be highly successful both on line voyages and for cruises, being available for charter by travel companies in western countries. During the mid-1960s, Charter Travel Club was formed in London, to provide cheap cruises to club members on chartered ships. Within a couple of years, a branch had also been formed in Australia, hoping to introduce low cost travel to and from Britain. In 1968, it sought the charter of one of the new Russian liners, and were allocated *Ivan Franko*, but then *Shota Rustaveli* was substituted. On 14 October 1968, she left Southampton bound for Australia, arriving in Sydney on 15 November, and departing the next day to return to Britain.

The success of this voyage resulted in the expansion of Charter Travel Club into CTC Lines. It chartered *Shota Rustaveli* again, which left Southampton on 24 November 1969 for Australia, and made two cruises from Sydney, the first departing on 26 December. *Shota Rustaveli* returned to Britain, and in March 1970 left Southampton on another return voyage to Australia, following which she cruised out of Southampton for CTC Line. *Shota Rustaveli* voyaged again to Australia in November 1970, 1971 and 1972, and made several cruises from Sydney before returning to Britain each year.

The success of the four liners resulted in an order for a fifth member of the class, launched on 31 December 1970 as *Mikhail Lermontov*. Externally she was identical to the earlier vessels, but designed mainly for cruising, so her accommodation was reduced to 700 in one class. Completed in February 1972, *Mikhail Lermontov* was allocated to the Baltic Steamship Co., and entered service as a cruise ship, though she was also used on the route between Bremerhaven and Montreal in summer. On 28 May 1973, *Mikhail Lermontov* departed Leningrad on a voyage to New York, where she arrived on 11 June, the first Russian liner to berth there in 25 years.

Late in 1973, *Shota Rustaveli* was taken out of service for a lengthy overhaul. In her place, CTC chartered *Taras Shevchenko*, which left Southampton in November 1973, operated several cruises out of Sydney, and returned to Britain in March 1974. *Shota Rustaveli* returned for the 1974–75 summer season in Australia. The popularity of the CTC operation was

SHOTA RUSTAVELI

such that, in 1975 both *Shota Rustaveli* and *Taras Shevchenko* were chartered for the summer season.

Up to 1975, all voyages to and from Australia had been through the Panama Canal, the same route *Taras Shevchenko* followed in November 1975. When *Shota Rustaveli* left Southampton on 5 November 1975, she went around South America, calling at Rio de Janeiro and Buenos Aires, then proceeding directly to Auckland, with 15 days at sea between ports. *Taras Shevchenko* made a return trip to Australia from Britain in March 1976, interrupted by a cruise from Sydney.

For the 1976–77 season, *Shota Rustaveli* was available, but *Taras Shevchenko* was being overhauled, so in her place *Mikhail Lermontov* was chartered. *Shota Rustaveli* made her regular voyage to Australia in November 1976, but *Mikhail Lermontov* did not leave Southampton until January 1977, arriving in Sydney on 6 February. The next day, she left on a Pacific circle cruise that did not return to Sydney until 4 April. The same day, *Mikhail Lermontov* departed for Britain, calling at Melbourne and Fremantle, and passing through the Suez Canal to reach Southampton on 10 May.

In March 1977, *Shota Rustaveli* left Southampton on a voyage around the world, coming out to Australia through the Suez Canal, and returning through the Panama Canal. *Shota Rustaveli* was the only CTC ship to visit Australia in the 1977–78 season, and in April 1978, she left Southampton on another voyage around the world. This was to be the final visit to the region by *Shota Rustaveli*, which departed Sydney on 20 May, and Auckland four days later. Since that time, *Shota Rustaveli* has been used primarily for cruising from European ports. In the early 1980s she was extensively refitted, during which the stern was built up, and she is now painted completely white.

On 14 November 1978, *Taras Shevchenko* took the Australian voyage for CTC Line, cruising from Sydney until early February 1979, then returning to Britain around South America. On 4 January 1979, *Mikhail Lermontov* departed Southampton on a voygae to Australia through the Panama Canal, arriving in Sydney on 6 February. The next day, she left on a cruise around the Pacific, becoming the first Soviet passenger vessel to visit Honolulu on her way to the west coast of America, returning via Tahiti and Auckland to Sydney on 3 April. The next day she left for Britain via the Suez Canal. *Taras Shevchenko* took the 1979 round-the-world sailing, departing Southampton on 30 March, but broke the voyage in Sydney for a 14-day cruise, leaving on 19 May to return to Britain through the Panama Canal.

The November 1979 voyage to Australia was made by *Ivan Franko*, the first of the class to be built, but previously employed on a regular service between Leningrad and Montreal. Arriving in Sydney on 7 December, *Ivan Franko* made two South Pacific cruises, then on 26 January 1980, she left Sydney on a 66 day cruise around South America, returning through the Panama Canal to Sydney. She then made a further two South Pacific cruises before returning to Britain again.

Early in 1980, the Commonwealth Government announced that from May that year, Russian passenger ships would be banned from Australian waters, a move caused by the Soviet invasion and occupation of Afghanistan. When not engaged on voyages to Australia, these vessels were chartered out for cruising in the northern hemisphere, or operated regular voyages across the Atlantic, so the Australian ban did not affect them in any major way. In the early 1980s, *Mikhail Lermontov* and *Taras Shevchenko* were given extensive refits, and repainted white, in similar fashion to *Shota Rustaveli*. The New Zealand Government did not follow the Australian example, so both *Mikhail Lermontov* and *Taras Shevchenko* visited the country on world cruises. With a change of government in Australia in 1983, the ban on Soviet passenger ships was lifted early in 1984, and at the end of the year two of these vessels were cruising from Sydney again.

Mikhail Lermontov arrived back in Sydney on 19 December 1984, and commenced an extended season of

IVAN FRANKO

cruises until March 1985, when she returned to Britain. On 21 December 1984, *Alexandr Pushkin* arrived in Sydney for the first time. This vessel had spent her career to date operating out of European ports, and was the last of the class the make a voyage to Australia. She, too, commenced a series of South Pacific cruises, which lasted until the end of May, when she left the region. It was during 1985 that *Alexandr Pushkin* was transferred from the Black Sea Shipping Co. to the Far East Shipping Co., her home port becoming Vladivostok.

For the 1985–86 summer season, both *Mikhail Lermontov* and *Alexandr Pushkin* returned to Australia for cruises from Sydney commencing in mid-December. On 7 February 1986, the two sisters were berthed together at the Pyrmont docks in Sydney, and departed several hours apart on cruises. *Mikhail Lermontov* went to New Zealand, calling at Auckland and Wellington, then Picton on the northern tip of South Island. Leaving Picton on the afternoon of 16 February, *Mikhail Lermontov* headed for Milford Sound but through faulty navigation, at about 6 pm, passed inside the lighthouse off Cape Jackson.

Two impacts with the bottom were felt, and water began pouring in. The captain tried to run his ship aground in Port Gore, but the power failed, and the prevailing wind blew the crippled liner away from the shore. By now the ship was down by the bow and listing heavily to starboard, but it was only then that passengers and crew were evacuated, though the lifeboats on the port side could not be lowered due to

the list. At around 11 pm, *Mikhail Lermontov* sank, settling on her starboard side in about 100 ft (33 m) of water. One crew member lost his life in the disaster, but everyone else was rescued. Attempts to salvage the wreck were abandoned.

Two days after the sinking, *Taras Shevchenko* arrived in Sydney on a world cruise, and *Alexandr Pushkin* continued her cruises as programmed, eventually remaining in the region until September. She then went back to Vladivostok for a refit, and on 18 December 1986, resumed her cruising out of Sydney. For the 1986–87 season she operated alone, as no replacement could be obtained for *Mikhail Lermontov*. The same day that *Alexandr Pushkin* returned, her sister ship, *Ivan Franko*, also arrived back in Sydney on a world cruise. Still with a black hull, this vessel had left Genoa on 1 November on a 100 day odyssey under charter to a West German tour company. She arrived in Auckland on 13 December, Sydney on 18 December and Brisbane on 21 December, having come through the Panama Canal, returning via the Far East and Suez Canal.

Alexandr Pushkin spends most of each year cruising from Sydney, and is only away for a couple of months being refitted. She spent the majority of 1988 cruising out of Sydney as well, being joined for some of the year by the newer *Belorussiya*. In February 1988, *Taras Schevchenko* passed through Australia on a world cruise.

In May 1989, *Alexandr Pushkin* left Sydney for Vladivostok, but has not returned. It is presently laid up with her future uncertain.

ALEXANDR PUSHKIN

CATHAY

BUILT: *1957 by Cockerill S.A., Hoboken*
TONNAGE: *13 809 gross*
DIMENSIONS: *559 × 70 ft (170.5 × 21.4 m)*
SERVICE SPEED: *16.5 knots*
PROPULSION: *Geared turbines/single screw*

This pair were regular visitors to Australia for just six years, but they are fondly remembered by all who travelled on them. They were very attractive ships, having been built for the Belgian firm, Cie. Maritime Belge, to operate a regular service from Antwerp to the Belgian Congo. The first was launched on 30 November 1955, and named *Jadotville*, entering service in July 1956. Her sister was launched on 10 January 1957 as *Baudouinville*, and made her maiden departure from Antwerp on 2 November the same year. They provided comfortable accommodation for 300 passengers in one class, and also had a large cargo capacity.

At the time these ships entered service, the Congo was torn by civil war, aimed at achieving independence from Belgium. This happened in 1960, forcing Cie. Maritime Belge to withdraw most of their ships from the Congo trade. At the same time, P & O was withdrawing the veterans *Corfu* and *Carthage* from its Far East trade, and in January 1961 it purchased the two Belgian ships to replace them. *Jadotville* was renamed *Chitral*, while *Baudouinville* became *Cathay* and their accommodation was reduced to 226 in one class. On 2 March 1961, *Chitral* left Tilbury on her first voyage to Hong Kong and Japan, followed by *Cathay* on 14 April, the pair being partnered by *Chusan*, and for a short while *Canton* as well.

The closure of the Suez Canal in 1967, causing a long detour around Africa, made these ships uneconomic for the Far East trade, so in the middle of 1969, *Cathay* was withdrawn, and transferred within the P & O Group to the E & A Line, as a replacement for *Aramac*. On 13 December 1969, *Cathay* left Melbourne for Sydney and Brisbane, then north to ports in Japan and Hong Kong.

Chitral was also withdrawn from the Far East trade in 1969, but then laid up and offered for sale. When no buyer was forthcoming, P & O used her for a series of Mediterranean cruises from Genoa, commencing in

CHITRAL

BUILT: *1956 by Ch. de Penhoet, St Nazaire*
TONNAGE: *13 821 gross*
DIMENSIONS: *557 × 70 ft (169.8 × 21.4 m)*
SERVICE SPEED: *16.5 knots*
PROPULSION: *Geared turbines/single screw*

March 1970, but she was totally unsuitable for this type of work. Noting the success of *Cathay* on the E & A service, P & O decided to transfer *Chitral* as well, so in October 1970 she joined her sister in Australia. The six-week round trip was advertised as a cruise, but large amounts of cargo were also carried.

The increasing price of fuel in the early 1970s, plus the introduction of container ships on the Far East cargo trade, gradually rendered *Cathay* and *Chitral* uneconomic once more. Variations to the route were tried, with *Chitral* leaving Melbourne on 14 January 1974 for Fremantle, then Singapore, Hong Kong and Keelung, the usual Japanese ports, then back via Manila, Bangkok, Singapore, Bali, Fremantle and Adelaide. She made several similar voyages, but results were poor, as were returns from the regular route. In 1975, calls at Auckland were introduced, with *Chitral* calling there on 16 June and 1 August.

Chitral used for more fuel than her sister, and in September 1975, she was offered for sale. Purchased by shipbreakers in Taiwan, she left Australia for the last time in November, and arrived on 3 December 1975 at Hualien, where she was scrapped. *Cathay* was scheduled to remain in service, but at very short notice she too was withdrawn. On 1 December 1975, *Cathay* left Melbourne on her final voyage, terminating in Hong Kong on 17 December. The vessel was then sold to the People's Republic of China, and renamed *Kenghshin*, reportedly to be used as a training ship. Soon after her name was changed to *Shanghai*, and in January 1980 she returned to commercial service again, operating for China Merchants Steam Navigation Co. Ltd on the short route between Shanghai and Hong Kong. As with several other vessels once familiar in Australian waters, *Shanghai* can often be seen in Hong Kong, and still looks very smart.

CATHAY

CHITRAL

AMERICAN PRESIDENT LINERS

BUILT: *1947/48 by Bethlehem Alameda Shipyard, Alameda*
TONNAGE: *15 456 gross*
DIMENSIONS: *609 × 75 ft (185.6 × 23 m)*
SERVICE SPEED: *19 knots*
PROPULSION: *Turbo-electric/twin screws*

American President Line was formed in 1938 to take over the financially troubled Dollar Line. The company operated regular services around the world and across the North Pacific, but usually did not venture into the South Pacific. As the demand for passenger services across the North Pacific declined, American President Line sent their remaining passenger ships cruising, which included visits to the South Pacific.

The two ships to come to Australia were *President Cleveland* and *President Wilson*. During the war, the United States Government built several series of troopships, and this pair were ordered as the last of 10 standard P2–SE2–R1 type troopships. Whilst they were under construction, the war ended, so these ships were redesigned for commercial service. *President Cleveland* was launched on 23 June 1946, and departed San Francisco on 15 December 1947 for her maiden voyage to Asian ports. *President Wilson* was launched on 24 November 1946, making her maiden departure from San Francisco on 27 April 1948.

These ships were the first post-war American liners, and the largest to be built on the Pacific coast of America, introducing new standards of comfort to the Pacific trade. Each ship could carry 324 first class and 454 tourist class passengers. For 20 years *President Cleveland* and *President Wilson* operated all year from San Francisco and Los Angeles to Honolulu, Japan, Hong Kong and Manila. In 1960, both ships were refitted to carry 304 first class and 380 "economy tourist" class passengers, with further improvements in 1963.

As the regular passenger trade declined, American President Line turned to cruising to keep its ships active. Early in 1969, *President Cleveland* made the first cruise by the company to the South Pacific, including a three day visit to Sydney from 4 February. On 29 January 1970, *President Wilson* arrived in Sydney on her first visit, returning again on 19 February 1972. *President Cleveland* made her second visit to Sydney at the end of 1972, being in port from 30 November to 2 December. The final cruise to the region by one of these ships was taken by *President Wilson*, which berthed in Sydney on 30 January, departing on 1 February. For these voyages, passenger numbers were reduced to about 500 in one class.

When these ships passed 25 years in service, their government subsidy ceased, and American President Line could not operate them without this assistance, so during 1972 they were offered for sale. Negotiations with Chandris Cruises for *President Cleveland* collapsed, but then the ship was sold to the C. Y. Tung Group, of Hong Kong. Handed over in San Francisco on 9 February 1973, she was renamed *Oriental President*. The same firm also bought *President Wilson*, which finished her last cruise in San Francisco on 26 April 1973, and was then renamed *Oriental Empress*. Both ships were refitted in Kaohsiung for further service, but the sudden increase in the price of oil brought their careers to a premature end. *Oriental President* was laid up in Hong Kong in 1973, then sold to Taiwan shipbreakers in June 1974. *Oriental Empress* did see some service, but was laid up in Hong Kong on 11 September 1975, and sold in June 1984 to local shipbreakers.

PRESIDENT CLEVELAND

ITALIA

BUILT: *1967 by Cant. Nav. Felszegi, Trieste*
TONNAGE: *12 219 gross*
DIMENSIONS: *492 × 68 ft (150 × 20.7 m)*
SERVICE SPEED: *19 knots*
PROPULSION: *Sulzer diesels/twin screws*

The giant P & O liner *Canberra* was considered to be of a unique appearance, but *Italia*, though much smaller, was very similar, apart from the funnel. *Italia* was ordered as a speculative venture by Sunsarda SpA, a subsidiary of an Italian bank. Launched on 28 April 1965, fitting out proceeded very slowly, as the bank sought a buyer or long term charter deal for the ship. In August 1967 the vessel was delivered, and almost immediately sold to Crociere d'Oltremare, of Cagliari.

The new owner was able to arrange a long term charter with Princess Cruises, to operate on the west coast of America. Her funnel was repainted in the Princess Cruises colours, and the ship was advertised as "Princess Italia", but her name was never officially changed, nor did she carry any name other than *Italia* on her bows and stern. The vessel provided very comfortable accommodation for 420 passengers in one class, with a crew numbering 252, and was particularly noted for the size and elegance of her public rooms. A major feature was the large open deck area between the bridge and the funnel, containing an extensive lido area surrounded by attractive mosaic work.

In 1969, Princess Cruises was looking to expand its sphere of operation, and developed plans to build two further ships for cruising to and within the South Pacific, based on Suva. As an experiment, *Italia* was despatched from Los Angeles on a cruise to the South Pacific in October 1969. After calling at Auckland, *Italia* arrived in Sydney on 19 November for a two-day stopover, berthing at the Circular Quay Passenger Terminal. Unfortunately, only 250 passengers were carried on this cruise, which caused Princess Cruises to abandon their plans to expand into the area.

Italia resumed her place on the west coast of America cruise trade, but when her charter ended in October 1973, it was not renewed. On 1 February 1974, *Italia* was chartered by Costa Line, and began cruising in the Mediterranean and Caribbean, depending on the season. The only external alteration was a change in funnel logo. Costa Line was so pleased with the ship that, in October 1974, it purchased her outright, but did not give her a new name.

In 1979, *Italia* was chartered by a major West German travel firm, Neckermann und Reisen, and began making long-distance cruises. In January 1980, she left Genoa on a world cruise, calling at Fremantle and Melbourne before arriving at Sydney on 3 February. Once again the ship berthed at Circular Quay, and created a great deal of interest, before departing on 4 February for the South Pacific, and then back to Genoa.

Italia remained in the Costa Line fleet until 1983, when she was sold to a recently formed company, Ocean Cruise Line. Following an extensive refit at Peráma in Greece, she was renamed *Ocean Princess*. In 1984 she began cruising in the Mediterranean and also from northern European ports in the peak summer season. In 1986, *Ocean Princess* began cruising out of ports on the east coast of America, then in 1988 returned to the Mediterranean for the summer season. Ocean Cruise Lines does not operate long-distance cruises, so it is probable this interesting little ship will not be seen in Australian waters again.

ITALIA ALONGSIDE THE SYDNEY PASSENGER TERMINAL

ENNA G

BUILT: *1961 by De Merwede, Hardinxveld*
TONNAGE: *9336 gross*
DIMENSIONS: *456 × 61 ft (139 × 18.5 m)*
SERVICE SPEED: *17 knots*
PROPULSION: *MAN diesels/single screw*

The tiny island republic of Nauru embarked on an ambitious venture in the 1960s, establishing their own shipping line. One new passenger–cargo ship was built, and three second-hand vessels were purchased, the largest of which was *Enna G*. This vessel had been operated by three different Dutch shipping companies before she was purchased. Laid down on 1 March 1960, and launched on 10 December that year as *Prinses Margriet*, she was handed over to the Oranje Line on 4 July 1961, to operate from Rotterdam, Antwerp and Hamburg to the Great Lakes ports of Toronto and Chicago. Accommodation was provided for 111 passengers, all first class.

Unfortunately, this service was on its last legs, and a mere two years after entering service, *Prinses Margriet* left Rotterdam on 3 April 1963 for her final voyage to the Great Lakes. On returning to Holland, the ship was chartered by Holland America Line, to replace *Noordam* on their secondary service to New York. Her first departure on this route was from Rotterdam on 8 June 1963. In November 1964, Holland America Line purchased the vessel outright, and she remained on the service to New York a further three years. On 2 December 1967, *Prinses Margriet* left Rotterdam on her final voyage for Holland America, and after unloading at New York, commenced a charter to the Royal Netherlands Steamship Co. Departing New York on 15 December, the vessel went to various Dutch outposts in the West Indies, remaining on this route until 1969, when she was offered for sale.

Purchased by Nauru Pacific Line, and renamed *Enna G*, she came to the Pacific, to operate from the tiny republic to neighbouring islands and Australia. At first the only Australian port she visited was Melbourne, making her first arrival there on 24 October 1970. She ran a regular service to New Guinea, Nauru and Guam, then in 1971 Sydney was added to the itinerary. Early in 1972 *Enna G* went to Japan for a refit, during which a swimming pool was installed on the starboard side, aft of the superstructure. The ship was then placed on a cruise service from Sydney, making her first departure on 5 May 1972. This was not a success, as on 10 January 1973 she left on her final cruise, returning to Sydney on 23 January. She then went to New Zealand, to start a new service from there to Pacific islands, but this also came to a premature end. Late in 1973, *Enna G* returned to Australia to commence a direct service between Melbourne and Nauru. In 1975, calls at Tarawa and Ocean island were added, but late in 1976 the service was abandoned, and *Enna G* left Australian waters for good.

Early in 1977, *Enna G* began yet another new service, from San Francisco to Honolulu, Majuro and Nauru, returning via Ponape, Truk and Saipan, but surprisingly, the call at Nauru was soon deleted. The round trip was sold as a cruise. In 1979, the vessel was refitted, during which the original masts were removed, and replaced by two large cranes, which rather spoiled her appearance. About 1982, *Enna G* was laid up in San Francisco, and as far as I am aware, she is still idle there.

ENNA G

MARCO POLO

BUILT: *1962 by Soc. Española de Const. Naval, Bilbao*
TONNAGE: *9232 gross*
DIMENSIONS: *478 × 61 ft (145.7 × 18.5 m)*
SERVICE SPEED: *17 knots*
PROPULSION: *B & W diesels/twin screws*

Marco Polo enjoyed several years of great popularity as a cruise ship from Australian ports, mostly to the Far East. She was operated by Dominion Far East Line, and jointly owned by Dominion Navigation Co. Ltd and the Indo-China Steam Navigation Co.

Before coming to Australia, this vessel had an interesting history, having been built in Spain for a Brazilian company, Costeira Line, as *Princesa Isabel*. With her sister, *Princesa Leopoldina*, she traded along the Brazilian Coast, providing accommodation for 200 first class and 280 tourist class passengers. At times the vessel was used for cruises, but their operation was not a financial success, so in 1966 both *Princesa Isabel* and her sister were taken over by the Brazilian Government owned Cia. de Nav. Lloyd Brasiliero. For a short time they continued on the coastal trades, but in 1967 both ships were laid up in Rio de Janeiro, and offered for sale.

Princesa Leopoldina was bought by China Navigation, and features elsewhere in this book as *Coral Princess*. *Princesa Isabel* remained idle until 1969, when she was bought by Dominion Far East Line. On 6 September 1969, she was towed out of Rio de Janeiro, bound for the Barclay, Curle shipyard in Glasgow. Arriving there on 5 October, the next six months were spent refitting the ship for the Australian cruise market, with accommodation for 363 passengers in one class. Renamed *Marco Polo*, she departed Melbourne on 30 June 1970 for her first cruise, but was usually based on

Sydney, operating lengthy cruises to Singapore, Hong Kong and Japan. For the summer of 1973–74 she was chartered by the New Zealand tour operator, Trans Tours, for a series of cruises from Australia to New Zealand and the Pacific Islands.

Marco Polo seemed to be enjoying great success, so it was a considerable surprise when she was withdrawn from service in 1978. Her last cruise terminated in Sydney on 23 August 1978, and then the vessel went to Singapore to be laid up. Within a short time, she had been sold to Arkley Navigation Co., connected with the well-known Greek shipping company, Kavounides Line.

During a refit in Greece, an extra deck was added to the superstructure forward of the bridge, following which the vessel was renamed *Aquamarine*. She then returned to the Far East, being based on Hong Kong for a series of cruises to mainland China and Japan, the first departing on 16 April 1979, but early in 1980, *Aquamarine* was laid up in Hong Kong. On 27 April 1980, she was arrested, and on 7 July was sold at auction to a major creditor, the Commercial Bank of Greece.

The bank tried to arrange a charter of *Aquamarine*, and in October 1980 came to an agreement with Rasa Sayang Cruises, to charter the ship for four years cruising out of Sydney, but this arrangement was soon cancelled. In January 1981, a sale to American Global Cruises failed to be completed, so the vessel returned to Greece, and was laid up near Piraeus.

Early in 1988, *Aquamarine* was finally sold, after eight years of idleness, to a major Greek operator, Epirotiki Line. They immediately began refitting the ship in Piraeus, to suit her for Mediterranean cruising, for which she was renamed *Odysseus*.

MARCO POLO

Ocean Monarch

BUILT: *1957 by Vickers–Armstrong Ltd, Newcastle*
TONNAGE: *25 971 gross*
DIMENSIONS: *640 × 85 ft (195 × 26 m)*
SERVICE SPEED: *20 knots*
PROPULSION: *Geared turbines/twin screws*

Ocean Monarch could well be described as the vessel that destroyed Shaw Savill Line. They spent a great deal of money purchasing and refitting the vessel, but she was never popular with travellers, suffered endless engine problems, and just five years after her purchase was sold to shipbreakers. Built for Canadian Pacific as *Empress of England*, she was launched on 9 May 1956, and entered service in April 1957 between Liverpool and Montreal, joining her sister *Empress of Britain*. Accommodation was provided for 160 first class and 898 tourist class passengers.

By the early 1960s, the passenger trade to Canada had declined so much that both *Empress of England* and *Empress of Britain* were spending much of each year cruising. In November 1964, *Empress of England* was chartered by the Travel Savings Association for cruises from British ports, and also South Africa. During the summer of 1967, the liner returned to the Atlantic service for the duration of Expo '67, held in Montreal, then resumed her cruising charter.

In February 1970, *Empress of England* was sold to Shaw Savill Line. The liner arrived in Liverpool on 31 March at the end of a cruise, and the next day was handed over to her new owner. Renamed *Ocean Monarch*, her funnel was repainted in Shaw Savill colours, and the ship prepared for an early entry into service. On 14 April, she left Southampton on a line voyage to Australia, which terminated in Sydney on 15 May. With an Expo being held in Japan in 1970, *Ocean Monarch* then made two cruises there from Sydney, the first departing on 22 May and the second on 27 June. The vessel then made a line voyage back to Britain, and was sent to the Cammell Laird shipyard for an extensive refit.

Several major structural alterations were made, with all cargo handling gear being removed, and the extension of the superstructure aft, where several public rooms were added, along with a new swimming pool and extensive open deck areas. New cabins were built into the former cargo holds, and existing cabins refurbished, so that the liner could carry 1372 passengers in one class. The work was continually delayed by industrial and other problems, so instead of the ship being ready for service again in June 1971, it was October before she was handed back to Shaw

Savill. A programme of cruises from Southampton had been scheduled from June, but *Ocean Monarch* only operated the last one, departing on 16 October, following which the ship left for Australia again on 5 November.

For several months, *Ocean Monarch* cruised out of Sydney, then returned to Britain in May 1972 for another season from Southampton. In October 1972, she returned to Australia again, having been scheduled to make just two long cruises from Sydney during the 1972–73 summer season. This was revised to a longer programme of short cruises, which was not appreciated by some of the crew. Just as the ship was about to depart on 22 January 1973, 191 stewards, seamen and pantrymen walked off the ship. For three days the vessel remained in dock at Sydney, then sailed without the striking crew, the passengers helping out with shipboard chores where possible. The dissatisfied crew were flown back to Britain, and new staff brought out to replace them.

Ocean Monarch eventually spent the rest of 1973 cruising from Sydney, and into 1974, then departed in May to return to Britain once again. By this time she was suffering from frequent engine problems, and her programme from Southampton was often disrupted. In November 1974, the liner returned to Sydney for another season of cruises, but her mechanical defects were now a major concern. Early in 1975, a cruise was cancelled so that *Ocean Monarch* could be drydocked in Sydney, but all efforts to rectify the faults failed. A line voyage to Britain was scheduled for April 1975, and Shaw Savill announced that the vessel would then be withdrawn from service.

On 26 April 1975, *Ocean Monarch* was due to leave Sydney for the last time, but shortly before sailing time, crew started hurling bottles, cans and other missiles from the ship, hitting people on the balcony of the Overseas Passenger Terminal who had come to farewell passengers. Police had to be called to restore order, and the ship was detained in Sydney overnight. Next day she finally got away, a humiliating end to an unfortunate career in Australian waters.

Returning to Southampton in May, *Ocean Monarch* was immediately offered for sale, and soon purchased by Taiwanese shipbreakers. On 13 June the liner slipped quietly out of Southampton, arriving in Kaohsiung on 17 July, where she was handed over to Chi Shun Hwa Steel Co. Ltd, who commenced demolition of the ship on 12 October 1975. By contrast, the former sister ship, *Empress of Britain*, is still in service, making short cruises from Florida to the Bahamas as *Carnivale* of Carnival Cruise Lines.

OCEAN MONARCH ARRIVING IN SYDNEY FOR THE FIRST TIME, 15 MAY 1970

EXTENSIVE ALTERATIONS WERE MADE TO THE STERN AREA IN 1971

BRITANIS

BUILT: *1932 by Bethlehem Shipbuilding Corp., Quincy*
TONNAGE: *18 254 gross*
DIMENSIONS: *632 × 79 ft (192.6 × 24.2 m)*
SERVICE SPEED: *20 knots*
PROPULSION: *Geared turbines/twin screws*

When the "new" *Britanis* first arrived in Sydney in March 1971, it was in fact the return of a vessel that first visited the city almost forty years earlier. At that time she was *Monterey*, of Matson Line, the second of three liners built during 1931–32. *Monterey* joined *Mariposa* on the trade from California to Sydney, while *Lurline* voyaged only to Honolulu.

Monterey was launched on 10 October 1931, and handed over to Matson on 20 April 1932. She left New York on 12 May on her delivery voyage to San Francisco, from where she made her maiden voyage across the Pacific. *Monterey* provided accommodation for 472 first class and 229 cabin class passengers, and made six round trips each year.

Monterey remained on the South Pacific route until the end of 1941. Arriving in San Francisco from Sydney on 1 December, the vessel was taken over by the US Maritime Commission on 3 December, and converted to carry 2950 troops. It was planned that she would depart on 8 December for Manila, but the attack on Pearl Harbor changed this. Instead, she was loaded with plane parts and other war material, and 3349 troops were crammed aboard. In company with *Matsonia* and *Lurline*, she left San Francisco on 16 December for Honolulu, returning with casualties, wives and children, some 240 passengers being under 12 years old.

Monterey was then further converted to carry 3841 troops, and she took on board 3674 men to be carried to

Australia. The vessel called at Brisbane, Fremantle, Adelaide and Melbourne on a 62 day voyage. *Monterey* then made a voyage from San Francisco to Adelaide, returning through the Panama Canal into the Atlantic, to spend a year ferrying troops to Europe. On most of these trips she carried over 6000 men, many of whom had to sleep on the deck.

In November 1942, *Monterey* took part in the Allied landings on North Africa, making four trips in all to Casablanca, and in June 1943 she finally returned to San Francisco again. Following another voyage to Brisbane, *Monterey* went back to the Atlantic, and on one trip from New York to Oran, carried 6855 soldiers, and then transported 6747 men to Naples.

Monterey returned to the Pacific for the final stages of the war, making several visits to Brisbane during this time. After the war, *Monterey* was used for some time to return American troops home, then on 15 June 1946 she left San Francisco on a voyage to Sydney, arriving on 2 July and departing four days later. Upon her return to San Francisco, *Monterey* was returned to her owners on 26 September 1946.

Monterey was sent to the United Engineering shipyard at Alameda to be refitted for commercial service again, but the cost of the conversion began to rise due to inflation. On 11 July 1947, work stopped, and *Monterey* was laid up. On 6 August 1952, the vessel was sold to the US Maritime Commission, then towed to Suisun Bay and laid up again.

The only Matson liner to return to full service after the war was *Lurline*, which resumed the Honolulu route in April 1948. By 1955, passenger loads were so good, Matson were seeking a second ship for the service. On 3 February 1956, the company bought back *Monterey* from the US Government, and she went to the

MATSON LINER *MONTEREY*, A REGULAR PRE-WAR VISITOR TO SYDNEY

Newport News shipyard for conversion. A raked bow was added and the funnels modernised, while accommodation was installed for 761 first class passengers. Renamed *Matsonia*, the vessel returned to service on 22 May 1957, making a delivery cruise from New York to California. She then joined *Lurline* on the Hawaiian trade, departing Los Angeles on 11 June.

By 1962, the two Matson ships were losing passengers, and money, so on 5 September *Monterey* was laid up in San Francisco. *Lurline* continued to operate, but in February 1963 she suffered engine trouble. As a result, *Lurline* was laid up, while *Monterey* was reactivated, and resumed her place on the service to Hawaii. In September 1963, *Lurline* was sold to Chandris Line, and renamed *Ellinis*. In a confusing move, *Matsonia* was renamed *Lurline* by Matson.

Under her third name, *Lurline* remained on the Hawaiian trade for a further seven years. From 1966, the liner was also used for cruises to other islands of Hawaii, and in March 1969 went further afield to the Caribbean, followed by a cruise to South America early in 1970. By 1970, *Lurline* was losing money to such an extent that she was offered for sale, and purchased on 27 May by Chandris Line. *Lurline* arrived in San Francisco for the last time on 25 June 1970, then five days later was handed over to her new owner, and renamed *Britanis*. She immediately was sent to Piraeus, to be converted by Chandris' own shipyard for the Australian trade.

The foremast was removed and replaced by sampson posts, and a new signal mast installed on top of the bridge, while the funnels were given raked backs and dome tops. The upper deck was extended forward to allow for extra cabins, and a number of other cosmetic changes made. New cabins were installed on most decks, while some existing cabins were given extra berths, requiring new staircases and a further lift. Accommodation was increased to 1655 passengers in one class, but surprisingly the Hawaiian decor and names were retained for many of the public rooms.

On 21 February 1971, *Britanis* departed Southampton on her first voyage to Australia, being scheduled to make four round-the-world trips each year, in conjunction with her former sister, *Ellinis* and *Australis*. However, *Britanis* was destined to spend only three years on this trade, during which she became a very popular ship with travellers.

The enormous increase in the price of oil in the early 1970s caused many shipping companies to rationalise their operations, and Chandris was no exception. On 19 May 1974, *Britanis* left Southampton on her final voyage to Australia, passing through Fremantle on 12 June and Adelaide on 15 June before reaching Melbourne on 17 June. She arrived in Sydney on 19 June, leaving the next day for Wellington, where she berthed on 23 June, then returned to Southampton through the Panama Canal.

Britanis then began her cruising career, first from Southampton, later moving to the Caribbean. For several years, *Britanis* spent the summer months cruising out of European ports, and the winter in the Caribbean, based on San Juan. Going into the 1980s, she continued to operate, passing her fiftieth anniversary in 1982, and being the oldest active cruise ship in the world. In 1986 I was fortunate enough to see *Britanis* in Miami, and she was still in excellent condition. In an age when most shipowners are seeking to lure passengers with large, modern vessels, *Britanis* continues to operate with great success, and could well pass her sixtieth year of service before being withdrawn.

BRITANIS

KHABAROVSK

BUILT: *1961 by Mathias–Thesen Werft, Wismar*
TONNAGE: *4722 gross*
DIMENSIONS: *401 × 52 ft (122.2 × 15.8 m)*
SERVICE SPEED: *17 knots*
PROPULSION: *DMR diesels/twin screws*

The Russians have built several groups of passenger ships, the largest of which is known as the "Mikhail Kalinin" class after the first ship to be completed, in 1958. Over a six-year period, a total of 19 ships of this type were built, of which *Khabarovsk* was the thirteenth. They were used on a diversity of services, from voyages between Leningrad and London to supplying Russian bases in the Arctic and Antarctic. Each ship could accommodate 333 passengers in either one or two classes, depending on the service they were operating.

Khabarovsk was assigned to the Far Eastern Shipping Co., and placed in service between Vladivostok and Providenie. A few years later, she began operating the international route from Nakhodka to Yokohama, some voyages extending to Hong Kong. In the Russian manner, there was no discrimination in the cabin arrangements, with males and females being berthed together regardless of relationship.

In the early 1970s a number of companies were formed in Australia to offer cheap travel to Europe, by taking advantage of the very low air fares available out of Singapore. This required the use of a ship between Australia and Singapore, and Fremantle became the main departure point for these "ship–jet" operators. One of the pioneers in this field was the Far East Travel Centre, who also formed Singapore–Australia Shipping Co. to charter and operate a passenger vessel between Fremantle and Singapore.

They were able to secure *Khabarovsk* on a one-year charter, and on 7 November 1971 she departed Singapore on her first voyage to Fremantle, where she arrived five days later. For these voyages her capacity was reduced to 250, due to restrictions on the amount of water that could be carried. *Khabarovsk* departed Fremantle every two weeks, but proved to be too small to meet the growing demand for "ship–jet" passages. In May 1972, the charter of *Khabarovsk* was terminated, and she was replaced by the larger *Eastern Queen*. *Khabarovsk* returned to her former trade from Nakhodka.

Singapore–Australia Line suffered three years of unending problems with *Eastern Queen*, and then her successor, *Eastern Princess*. The latter ship was eventually arrested in Singapore in March 1975 on a writ issued against the owner by Singapore–Australia Line, but it also left them without a ship. Once again they were able to charter *Khabarovsk*, which began running between Singapore and Fremantle in May 1975.

In August 1975 Far East Travel Centre folded, which also meant the end of Singapore–Australia Shipping Co. The operation, including the charter of *Khabarovsk*, was taken over by Palanga Line. They rapidly built up the "ship–jet" business again, so that within a short time *Khabarovsk* had to be replaced by the larger *Kota Singapura*.

On 14 December 1975, *Khabarovsk* left Fremantle for the last time, and has not returned to Australia. The vessel resumed her place on the service between Nakhodka and Yokohama. At a later date, two of her sisters, *Turkmenia* and *Felix Dzerjinsky* were chartered for cruises from Australia, and are described elsewhere.

KHABAROVSK ALONGSIDE THE FREMANTLE PASSENGER TERMINAL

EASTERN QUEEN

BUILT: *1953 by Ch. de Penhoet, St Nazaire*
TONNAGE: *11 684 gross*
DIMENSIONS: *531 × 65 ft (161.8 × 19.8 m)*
SERVICE SPEED: *16 knots*
PROPULSION: *B & W diesels/twin screws*

In the early 1970s, "ship–jet" services from Australia to Europe proliferated. One of the early firms in this market was Far East Travel Centre, who in 1972 had planned to charter *Fairsky*, but when this fell through, selected *Malaysia Raya*, owned by Cia. de Nav. Abeto, of Hong Kong, otherwise known as the Fir Line, but then that company purchased another liner from Philippine interests, which they named *Eastern Queen*. This vessel was offered to FETC and was taken on charter by them.

This vessel had been built for Cie. de Nav. Fraissinet et Cyprien, a French company, being launched on 9 July 1952 as *General Mangin*. Completed in March 1953, she was placed in service between Marseilles and French West Africa, having accommodation for 132 first class, 125 second class and 101 third class passengers, and also 500 troops. She was joined in 1957 by a sister, *Jean Mermoz*, which later came to Australia as the cruise liner *Mermoz*. In 1965, both these ships were transferred to Nouvelle Cie. de Paquebots, but remained on their original trade. When the French Government stopped providing subsidies for these liners in 1968, *General Mangin* was offered for sale, and bought by Chandris Line, for conversion into a cruise ship.

Chandris soon decided *General Mangin* was not suitable for conversion, and in 1969 sold her to Philippine President Line. Renamed *President*, she commenced a passenger service from Manila to Hong Kong and Japan, but after only two years in this trade, she was again offered for sale. Purchased by Cia. de Nav. Abeto, she became *Eastern Queen* early in 1972, and in April made one return trip from Singapore to Fremantle. She was then withdrawn for renovations, and resumed the trade from Singapore on 4 June.

Eastern Queen provided accommodation for 580 passengers in cabins and 156 in large dormitories, but unfortunately suffered a string of misfortunes. Her 29 August departure from Singapore had to be cancelled due to generator trouble, and she missed one round trip, her passengers having to be flown from and to Singapore. Early in 1973, she was taken out of service for another overhaul, during which her accommodation was upgraded and capacity reduced. She left Singapore again on 19 April, but suffered further engine problems, not reaching Fremantle until 27 April.

In May 1974, the charter of *Eastern Queen* was terminated at very short notice, the ship leaving Fremantle for the last time on 12 July 1974. She then joined the pilgrim trade, and at other times of the year operated a regular service from Singapore to Madras.

In September 1977, *Eastern Queen* was sold to Bangladesh Shipping Corp., and renamed *Hizbul Bahr*. She began a new service between Dacca and Singapore, carrying 930 passengers in three classes. On 16 February 1980, the vessel left Chittagong to inaugurate a service to Dubai via Colombo and Bombay, but on 11 December 1980, she arrived at Chittagong for the last time, and was then transferred to the Bangladesh Navy, being renamed *Shaheed Salahuddin*.

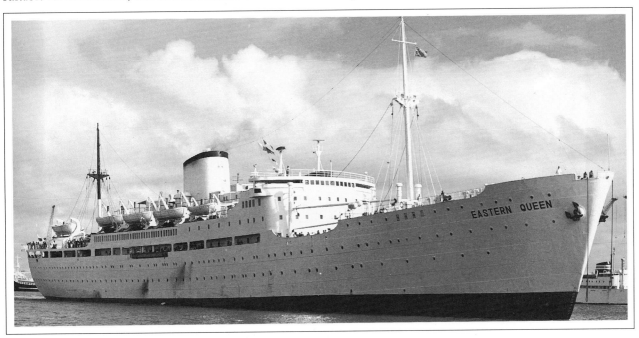

EASTERN QUEEN

SOVIET EX-CUNARDERS

BUILT: *1954/55 by John Brown & Co., Clydebank*
TONNAGE: *21 406 gross*
DIMENSIONS: *608 × 80 ft (185.3 × 25.4 m)*
SERVICE SPEED: *20 knots*
PROPULSION: *Geared turbines/twin screws*

This pair of Soviet liners came to the South Pacific under their third names, having been built for the Cunard Line, the first pair of four sister ships designed for the Canadian trade. On 17 February 1954, the first of these ships was launched as *Saxonia*, and completed six months later, departing Liverpool on 2 September for her maiden voyage to Montreal. The second ship was launched on 14 December 1954 as *Ivernia*, making her maiden departure for Canada on 1 July. Each ship provided accommodation for 110 first class and 820 tourist class passengers.

In June 1956 they were joined by the third ship of the class, *Carinthia*, followed by *Sylvania* exactly one year later. These four liners maintained the Cunard Line service from Liverpool to Canada in the summer months, and operated to New York in winter. However, in 1957 *Saxonia* and *Ivernia* were transferred to a new service from Southampton to Montreal.

At the end of the 1962 season, both ships went back to the John Brown shipyard for extensive refitting. The superstructure was extended aft to provide new lido areas, while internally the accommodation was upgraded to cater for 119 first class and 728 tourist class passengers. At the same time, they were repainted in the famous Cunard cruising green colours. To further promote the changes to these ships, *Saxonia* was renamed *Carmania*, while her sister became *Franconia*, reviving memories of two famous Cunard cruising liners of the 1930s.

Carmania resumed service in April 1963, followed by *Franconia* in July. Both ships operated on the Canadian trade during the summer months, but in winter began making cruises from New York. This pattern continued up to 1966, but in November that year, *Franconia* made her final voyage to Canada, and after a refit, during which she was repainted white, began a year-round service between New York and Bermuda. *Carmania* was withdrawn from the Canadian trade in November 1967, then was also repainted white, and began cruising year round from New York to the West Indies. On 12 January 1969, *Carmania* ran aground on a reef off the Bahamas, being refloated after five days with serious bottom damage, and had to go to the Newport News shipyard for repairs.

Franconia and *Carmania*, which were withdrawn in October 1971, and offered for sale two months later. In

LEONID SOBINOV

FEDOR SHALYAPIN

January 1972 they were nearly sold to a Japanese firm, Toyo Yusen Kaisha, but that deal fell through. The two ships were moved from Southampton to Falmouth in May 1972, and laid up there. It was not until August 1973 that they were sold to Nikreis Maritime Corp., a Panamanian concern acting on behalf of Morflot, the Soviet state-owned shipping organisation. Transferred to Soviet registry under the ownership of the Far East Shipping Co., *Franconia* was renamed *Fedor Shalyapin*, while *Carmania* became *Leonid Sobinov*.

Both ships went to the Swan Hunter shipyard on the Tyne for refitting, during which no structural alterations were made, but the accommodation was altered to carry 700 passengers in one class. A charter was arranged with CTC Lines to operate both ships for two years. On 21 November 1973, *Fedor Shalyapin* departed Southampton on her first voyage under the flag of the Soviet Union, to Australia through the Panama Canal, and on arrival in Sydney she made a series of cruises. *Leonid Sobinov* left Southampton on 26 February 1974 for her first voyage to Australia, going around South Africa to Mauritius, then Colombo and Singapore before arriving in Fremantle on 4 April, Melbourne on 9 April and Sydney two days later. The following day she departed on a cruise to Singapore.

Up to the middle of 1975, both these ships were frequent visitors to Australia on behalf of CTC Lines, but when the charter of *Fedor Shalyapin* expired, it was not renewed. Instead, the ship was chartered to Shaw Savill Line, and from October 1975 she began cruising permanently from Sydney. The CTC charter of *Leonid Sobinov* was renewed, and that ship continued to combine line voyages with cruises from Sydney, and also British ports. Shaw Savill Line did not enjoy much success with *Fedor Shalyapin*, and terminated the charter one year early. On 5 October 1976, the vessel arrived in Sydney at the end of her final Shaw Savill cruise, and was immediately taken on charter again by CTC Lines.

Leonid Sobinov was used mainly for line voyages between Europe and Australia, with only occasional cruises, but *Fedor Shalyapin* spent most of her time cruising from Sydney. She also made numerous voyages to Hong Kong under a ship–jet arrangement, her passengers then flying to Europe from Hong Kong. On 8 December 1979, *Leonid Sobinov* arrived in Sydney for the last time, then made a one-way cruise to Hong Kong, and was returned to her owners. *Fedor Shalyapin* had her 1980 programme suddenly cancelled, and following her arrival in Sydney on 8 February 1980, she too was handed back to Far East Shipping Co.

The Soviet Union used both ships as troop transports for a while, but in 1982 they were transferred to the Black Sea Shipping Co., and returned to cruising, this time in the Black Sea and Mediterranean, carrying Soviet passengers. Recently, the Soviet Union announced that most of their older passenger ships would be withdrawn, so it seems the careers of these two ships could soon be over.

NIPPON MARU

BUILT: *1958 by Mitsubishi Heavy Industries Ltd, Kōbe*
TONNAGE: *10 770 gross*
DIMENSIONS: *514 × 67 ft (156.6 × 20.4 m)*
SERVICE SPEED: *16 knots*
PROPULSION: *Geared turbines/single screw*

During November 1972, the Japanese cruise ship *Nippon Maru* visited ports in the South Pacific in the course of a Japanese Youth Goodwill Cruise, the first such trip to include Australia and New Zealand. These Youth Goodwill voyages were designed to give young Japanese a chance to improve their understanding of other countries and cultures.

Nippon Maru was originally named *Argentina Maru*, having been built for Osaka Shosen KK for its service from Japan to the east coast of South America. Launched on 8 February 1958, the vessel entered service four months later, providing accommodation for 12 first class, 82 second class and 960 third class passengers, and also having a large cargo capacity. In the early 1960s the demand for migrant passages from Japan to South America fell away, and on 1 April 1964, the two major firms on the route, Osaka Shosen and Mitsui amalgamated to form Mitsui–OSK Line. The accommodation on *Argentina Maru* was reduced to 23 cabin class and 352 tourist class, and in August 1965 the vessel entered a new service from Japan to the west coast of America and then through the Panama Canal to South American ports.

Meanwhile, in 1968 the Japanese Government instituted the Youth Goodwill Cruise programme, utilising *Sakura Maru*, managed by Mitsui–OSK Line.

This vessel had been built in 1962 to be a floating exhibition of Japanese goods, but when not engaged in this area, was used on the South American trade. *Sakura Maru* only visited Australia once, in June 1970, in her capacity as a floating fair. In 1971, *Sakura Maru* was replaced by a new ship, and sold to other Japanese owners. In February 1972 *Argentina Maru* was converted for use as a cruise ship.

During this conversion the ship was painted white, retaining her deep-red funnel, and then renamed *Nippon Maru*. In this guise, she embarked on her new career as a cruise ship, carrying groups selected by government departments rather than fare-paying passengers. In October 1972, *Nippon Maru* left Japan bound for the South Pacific, having on board 256 youths, 30 group leaders and 30 interpreters, as well as 27 guest lecturers. Ranging in age from 20 to 25, the members were selected from youth groups in the various prefectures of Japan, and all costs covered by the Prime Minister's Office of the Japanese Government.

Nippon Maru spent several days in Sydney, where she arrived on 15 November, and Melbourne, where the passengers had ample opportunity to meet and mix with local people of their own age. The visits were a great success, but in later years the Youth Goodwill Cruises operated by *Nippon Maru* did not return to Australia. In many ways, the vessel was not ideally suited to the task, still having her extensive cargo facilities, which were not used in her cruising capacity. *Nippon Maru* remained in service only four years, before being disposed of to shipbreakers in Taiwan in December 1976.

NIPPON MARU MADE ONLY ONE VISIT TO AUSTRALIA

UNIVERSE CAMPUS

BUILT: *1953 by Sun Shipbuilding & Dry Dock Co.,*
Chester, Pennsylvaniu
TONNAGE: *13 950 gross*
DIMENSIONS: *564 × 76 ft (171.9 × 23.2 m)*
SERVICE SPEED: *20 knots*
PROPULSION: *Geared turbines/single screw*

This vessel was originally built as a standard "Mariner" class freighter, *Badger Mariner*, having been launched on 1 July 1953 and delivered to the US Maritime Commission four months later. In 1957, the vessel was sold to the newly formed American Banner Line, and rebuilt as a passenger liner by the Ingalls Shipyard at Pascagoula, with accommodation for 40 first class and 860 tourist class passengers. Renamed *Atlantic*, she was placed in service in June 1958 between New York and Amsterdam, but in October 1959 American Banner Line ceased trading. *Atlantic* was sold to American Export Line, and without any name change entered their service from New York to the eastern Mediterranean in May 1960. In 1965 her accommodation was altered to 840 in one class, but in October 1967 *Atlantic* was withdrawn from service.

Eventually *Atlantic* was offered for sale, and on 25 July 1971 was purchased by the Hong Kong based C. Y. Tung Group, to be converted into a floating university for worldwide service, under the name *Universe Campus*.

Minimal conversion work was done on the ship following its purchase. Some existing public rooms were transformed into six classrooms, while the sundeck could also be used for classes in good weather. The dining room was altered to serve meals cafeteria style, and doubled as two further class rooms or a study hall at other times, and the theatre on the lower deck was used for lectures.

When rebuilt in 1958, the vessel was fitted with the largest swimming pool afloat, aft on the promenade deck, and this feature was retained. A wide variety of courses were offered during each cruise, while fares charged were very reasonable. The first cruise operated by *Universe Campus* departed Los Angeles on 4 September 1971. This voyage took the vessel around the world in about 16 weeks, and included a visit to Darwin in December.

Universe Campus was scheduled to make two cruises per year around the world, and shorter cruises within the Pacific for the rest of the year. It was in the course of one shorter cruise that *Universe Campus* came to Sydney on 29 September for a three-day stay, being berthed in Pyrmont for this time. This was destined to also be her last visit to Australia, although the ship continued to operate as a floating university for three more years.

In January 1976 the vessel completed a world cruise in Miami. She was then renamed *Universe*, and entered service as a cruise ship from Los Angeles to Mexican ports in February 1976. Since then, *Universe* has operated cruises to many parts of the world, and each summer spends several months operating in Alaskan waters.

UNIVERSE CAMPUS IN SYDNEY, 29 SEPTEMBER 1972

NIEUW HOLLAND

BUILT: *1958 by Wilton–Fijenoord N.V., Schiedam*
TONNAGE: *13 568 gross*
DIMENSIONS: *585 × 70 ft (178.3 × 21.4 m)*
SERVICE SPEED: *18 knots*
PROPULSION: *MAN diesels/twin screws*

This vessel was built for the Holland Africa Line service from Dutch and German ports to South Africa and Mozambique. Built in a graving dock, she was floated out on 28 June 1958, and named *Randfontein* on 24 November, when she was handed over to her owner. Accommodation was divided between 123 first class and 166 tourist class, combined with a large cargo capacity. Entering service in January 1959, *Randfontein* operated in conjunction with a number of smaller vessels, which were gradually withdrawn during the 1960s, until by 1969 *Randfontein* was the only ship left on the route.

In mid-1971, *Randfontein* was withdrawn from the African service, and then sold to Royal Interocean Line in July. Renamed *Nieuw Holland*, she was despatched to Hong Kong for an extensive refit. One pair of derrick posts forward was removed and replaced by a large crane, while internal alterations resulted in accommodation for 122 first class and 142 tourist class passengers. On 21 January 1972, *Nieuw Holland* left Hong Kong on her first voyage to Australia, arriving in Brisbane on 30 January and Sydney on 2 February, terminating in Melbourne on 7 February. She remained in port a week, then returned through the same ports on her first voyage to Japan, and then back to Hong Kong, which was to be her regular route. *Nieuw Holland* replaced *Tjiluwah*, and was partnered by *Tjiwangi*.

Nieuw Holland was involved in one unfortunate incident during her career. On 9 August 1972, as she was approaching her berth in Melbourne, the tug *Melbourne*, which had the bow line, was capsized by the bow wash, and sank quickly, drowning five crewmen. The tug was later raised and returned to service. In October 1973, *Nieuw Holland* made a 14 day cruise to New Zealand, carrying only 250 passengers, and visiting Dunedin, Wellington and Auckland, the only such voyage she would make.

In January 1974 her running mate, *Tjiwangi*, was withdrawn, and at the same time *Nieuw Holland* was transferred to a new route. On 12 February 1974, she left Adelaide, going first to Melbourne, then Risdon in Tasmania. Following a visit to Sydney, the vessel went directly to Port Moresby, then Bali, Surabaya, Jakarta, and Singapore, arriving on 10 March. Two days later *Nieuw Holland* went on to Penang, then Belawan, returning to Singapore and so back to Adelaide, but calling at Brisbane instead of Risdon. Unfortunately, this new service was a failure, and after only four round trips it was abandoned, and Royal Interocean Line pulled out of the Australian passenger trade. Leaving Adelaide on 9 October 1974, Melbourne on 15 October, and Sydney on 22 October, *Nieuw Holland* voyaged to Singapore, arriving on 6 November. She then went empty to Hong Kong, to be laid up.

When offered for sale, the ship was purchased by the People's Republic of China, being placed under the ownership of China Ocean Shipping. Renamed *Yu Hua*, she was placed in service from China to several ports in East Africa, carrying Chinese "technicians" and their families to assist in countries friendly with China. More recently *Yu Hua* has been used on coastal services, and is frequently seen in Hong Kong harbour.

NIEUW HOLLAND

GRIPSHOLM

BUILT: *1957 by Ansaldo, S.A., Sestri-Ponente.*
TONNAGE: *23 191 gross*
DIMENSIONS: *631 × 82 ft (192.3 × 24.9 m)*
SERVICE SPEED: *19 knots.*
PROPULSION: *Gotaverken diesels/twin screws*

The third Swedish–America Line vessel to visit the South Pacific in the course of cruises was *Gripsholm*, an enlarged version of the first *Kungsholm. Gripsholm* was launched on 8 April 1956, and departed Gothenburg on 14 May 1957 on her maiden voyage to New York. Accommodation was provided for 150 first class and 692 tourist class passengers.

Gripsholm was used on the North Atlantic trade in the summer months, and cruised from New York in the winter. By 1972, *Gripsholm* was being used for cruising most of the year, with only a few Atlantic voyages in the height of the summer season. On 14 October 1972, *Gripsholm* departed New York on her first cruise to include the South Pacific. After passing through the Panama Canal, *Gripsholm* headed north to the Far East, then came south to arrive in Sydney on 15 November. Leaving that night, *Gripsholm* called at Brisbane on 17 November, then headed back to New York through the South Pacific islands.

A year later, *Gripsholm* repeated this cruise, departing New York on 11 October 1973, to arrive in Sydney on 11 November, for a two day stay, After calling at Brisbane on 14 November, *Gripsholm* cruised back to New York. Three months later, *Gripsholm* was back again, arriving in Sydney on 26 February 1974, and departing the next day, this being her final appearance in local waters.

In November 1975, *Gripsholm* was sold to M.A. Karageorgis, of Greece. Renamed *Navarino*, the liner was refitted, then began a new career as a permanent cruise liner, based mainly in the Mediterranean. *Navarino* also cruised from South Africa in the winter of 1979 and the following two years. In August 1981, *Navarino* ran aground, and entered a drydock in Piraeus, but she toppled over and partially sank in the dock. Refloated with great difficulty, she was laid up, then sold in 1983 to Multiship Italia, and renamed *Samantha*. However, the ship remained laid up, having been moved to Spezia, but in October 1984 she was sold to Regency Cruises, another Greek company.

Renamed *Regent Sea*, she was towed back to Piraeus for extensive refitting. The interior was completely rebuilt, and minor external alternations made, mainly to the funnels. *Regent Sea* commenced a new cruise operation in November 1985, based in Montego Bay, Jamaica. In the summer months, *Regent Sea* moved north for the lucrative Alaskan summer season, returning to the Caribbean again for the winter months, and is still active.

GRIPSHOLM

THE 'ROYAL VIKINGS'

BUILT: *1972/73/73 by Wartsila A/B O/Y, Helsinki*
TONNAGE: *21 848 gross*
DIMENSIONS: *583 × 83 ft (177.7 × 25.2 m)*
SERVICE SPEED: *21.5 knots*
PROPULSION: *Sulzer diesels/twin screws*

Royal Viking Line was formed in 1970 as a consortium of three Norwegian shipping companies, Bergen Line, Det Nordenfjeldske D/S and A. F. Klaveness & Co. The first two had experience of passenger ship operation, Bergen Line having owned several cruise ships, and both companies having vessels on the famous route from Bergen to North Cape along the coast of Norway. The Klaveness company had only operated cargo ships since being founded in 1898. It was agreed that each company would order one ship for the consortium.

The Bergen Line vessel was the first to be built, being floated out of the Wartsila building dock on 12 May 1971. Named *Royal Viking Star*, she was delivered in June 1972, and commenced her first cruise from Copenhagen on 21 July. On 25 May 1972, the Det Nordenfjeldske ship was floated out and named *Royal Viking Sky*, being delivered in June 1973. The Klaveness vessel was named *Royal Viking Sea* when floated out on 19 January 1973, and was handed over to her owner on

16 November that year. There were minor internal differences between the vessels, but each carried some 536 passengers in luxurious accommodation, with a crew numbering 324 men and women.

Royal Viking Line was formed to provide worldwide cruising throughout the year, a new concept in the cruise trade. However, on completion *Royal Viking Sea* was chartered by Bergen Line for their ferry service between Bergen and Newcastle while the regular ship was out of service temporarily, making five return trips on the route. On 17 December 1973, *Royal Viking Sea* departed on her first cruise.

On 2 January 1973, *Royal Viking Star* left Los Angeles on her first cruise to the South Pacific, including visits to Auckland and Sydney as well as Cairns. On 24 September 1973, *Royal Viking Sky* departed New York on a 67 day cruise that included visits to Auckland, Wellington, Lyttelton and Sydney and terminated in San Francisco. This was typical of the cruises being operated by the company, which could either be taken in total or sectors by passengers. On 14 December, *Royal Viking Star* left Fort Lauderdale on a 66 day cruise following the same itinerary as her sister. *Royal Viking Sea* followed the same route as well on her maiden South Pacific cruise, which left from Fort Lauderdale on 16 January 1974.

The Royal Viking Line concept of luxury world

ROYAL VIKING SKY PASSING THE SYDNEY OPERA HOUSE

cruising was a great success, and the ships were always fully booked, with more demand for berths than they could provide. At one stage there was a problem, when Det Nordenfjeldske decided to opt out of the consortium in 1977 and sell their ship, *Royal Viking Sky*, but she was jointly purchased by Bergen Line and Klaveness to maintain the fleet. Instead of building a fourth ship, the two consortium partners decided to have all three existing vessels stretched, to jointly provide an extra 600 berths.

On 30 August 1981, *Royal Viking Star* arrived at the A. G. Weser shipyard in Bremerhaven, where she was cut in two, and a prefabricated section 91 ft (27.7 m) in length inserted. The three sections were then joined together, producing a vessel 674 ft (205.5 m) long with accommodation for 750 passengers, and a 28 221 gross tonnage. The lengthening also improved the overall appearance of the vessel. Late in 1982, *Royal Viking Sky* was given an identical lengthening, as was *Royal Viking Sea* at the end of 1983. Each ship was out of service for only four months while being rebuilt, and the whole operation was much cheaper and quicker than building a new vessel.

The first appearance in Australian waters by the new-look ships was made by *Royal Viking Star*, which departed Sydney on 6 February 1983 on a 44 day cruise around the Pacific, returning to Sydney on 22 March. This was the first time a Royal Viking Line cruise was scheduled from Australia. *Royal Viking Star* was to become a familiar sight in Sydney, while her sisters only appeared infrequently in future years. In 1984, *Royal*

Viking Star made a series of three cruises between Sydney and Tahiti in January and February, and two more early in 1985. Her 1986 programme included two further cruises to Tahiti. For 1987, *Royal Viking Star* made two cruises to New Zealand, the first calling at Melbourne, Hobart, Lyttelton and Wellington, the second also calling at Adelaide. In between the vessel made a cruise to the South Pacific islands and New Zealand, then at the end of March left for Tokyo.

Royal Viking Line provided Sydney with the nautical highlight of 1987 on 29 January, when *Royal Viking Star* and *Royal Viking Sky* made a spectacular entry into the harbour together, passing between the Sydney Heads side by side, and then in procession past the Opera House and under the Sydney Harbour Bridge.

Royal Viking Star returned to Sydney in December 1987 for another series of cruises, but this was to be her final season of operating in the South Pacific. On 15 March 1988, *Royal Viking Star* left Sydney for the last time, to spend the next year cruising to many parts of the world for Royal Viking Line. In April 1989, *Royal Viking Star* began cruising from New York to Bermuda, and in the winter months joined the Caribbean trade from Miami.

To replace *Royal Viking Star* in the South Pacific, *Royal Viking Sea* arrived in Sydney on 30 January 1989, making two long cruises to Tahiti and return. On 19 March, *Royal Viking Sea* left for other regions of the world, but returned in December 1989 and December 1990 for further cruises.

ROYAL VIKING STAR AFTER LENGTHENING IN 1981

SAGAFJORD

BUILT: *1965 by Forges et Chantiers de la Mediterranee, La Seyne*
TONNAGE: *24 002 gross*
DIMENSIONS: *620 × 82 ft (189 × 24.9 m)*
SERVICE SPEED: *20 knots*
PROPULSION: *Sulzer diesels/twin screws*

With the growth in cruising, Norwegian America Line ordered a new liner designed as much for cruising as trans-Atlantic voyages, which was launched as *Sagafjord* on 13 June 1964. Completed in September 1965, she departed Oslo on 2 October on her maiden voyage to New York, but then commenced her cruising career. Accommodation was provided for 85 first class and 704 tourist class passengers, but for cruising this was reduced to 462 in one class.

Sagafjord took over the long-range cruises previously operated by *Bergensfjord*, and in January 1967 left New York on her first voyage to the South Pacific, which included being in Sydney from 3 March for two days. The vessel was to make irregular appearances in the South Pacific, her second visit to Sydney being from 8 February 1969 for three days. *Sagafjord* did not return to the area again until February 1972, then spent two days in Sydney in February 1976, and a further two days in port in February 1980.

In 1980 Norwegian America Line decided to add an extra deck atop the existing superstructure, containing luxury staterooms. The work was done by the Blohm & Voss shipyard in Hamburg over a six-week period, which increased the cruising capacity to 505 passengers, while her tonnage rose to 24 108 gross.

The Norwegian shipowner, Leif Hoegh & Co., bought a 50 per cent interest in the company, which resulted in the formation of Norwegian America Cruises on 1 May 1980. However, by the end of 1980, Leif Hoegh had acquired the other 50 per cent shareholding in the company, though the operation of *Sagafjord* was not affected.

The first visit to Sydney by *Sagafjord* since her rebuilding occurred in February 1982, on a cruise that also included visits to Auckland and Brisbane. However, being under Norwegian registration, her crew expenses were enormous, and over the next couple of years the company found it increasingly difficult to break even. To overcome these problems, Leif Hoegh decided to sell Norwegian America Cruises, and in May 1983 the company was purchased by Cunard Line, with delivery of *Sagafjord* and *Vistafjord* in October that year. To be known as Cunard–NAC Cruises, the ships would be registered in the Bahamas.

In December 1983, *Sagafjord* was drydocked in San Francisco for extensive refurbishing, which included the addition of a further 25 luxury suites, enlarging the dining room, casino and nightclub, and general upgrading of other areas. The only external alteration was the repainting of the funnel in Cunard colours. *Sagafjord* then resumed her cruising programme, but was not scheduled to visit the South Pacific again until February 1985, when she again spent two days in Sydney. However, on the same day she arrived, *Queen Elizabeth 2* also entered port, on 14 February. This was the first occasion that two Cunard vessels had been in Sydney together.

Sagafjord returned to Sydney in February 1986 for another two-day stopover, but her 1987 world cruise took the ship to two other Australian ports, Cairns on 4 February and Darwin three days later. For her 1988 world cruise, *Sagafjord* again returned to the South Pacific, being in Sydney on 22 and 23 February.

In 1990, *Sagafjord* visited Cairns and Darwin in February, on her world cruise. She then returned to Sydney on 7 October, operated a cruise around New Zealand, then, on 21 October, left for Brisbane and the South Pacific islands.

SAGAFJORD

FRANCE

BUILT: *1961 by Ch. de Penhoet, St Nazaire*
TONNAGE: *66 348 gross*
DIMENSIONS: *1035 × 110 ft (315.5 × 33.7 m)*
SERVICE SPEED: *30 knots*
PROPULSION: *Geared turbines/quadruple screws*

During 1969, it was announced that the fastest passenger liner ever built, *United States*, would be making her first visit to the South Pacific early in 1970, in the course of a world cruise. Sadly, this did not eventuate, as in November 1969 *United States* was laid up, and has remained idle since then. Four years later, it was announced that the longest liner ever built, *France*, would be including Australia in the course of an 88 day world cruise in 1974, and this voyage did eventuate.

Launched on 11 May 1960, *France* was 18 months being fitted out, and ran trials in November 1961. The following month the liner was handed over to her owner, Cie. Generale Transatlantique, better known as the French Line. Her first voyage was a short cruise from Le Havre on 19 January 1962 to the Canary Islands, then on 3 February she departed the French port on her maiden crossing of the Atlantic to New York. Accommodation was provided for 407 first class and 1637 tourist class passengers. *France* was a beautiful liner, but unfortunately her completion coincided with the advent of jet commercial aircraft.

France waged a mighty battle against her faster competition, and from 1969 operated a joint service with *Queen Elizabeth 2*, a far cry from the days when the French Line and Cunard were deadly rivals on the North Atlantic. Due to her great length, *France* could

not enter many ports around the world, which made it very difficult to arrange cruises for her during the winter off-peak season. Early in 1972, *France* was despatched on a world cruise, which was quite successful, so a second such trip, with a different itinerary, was scheduled for 1974.

Departing New York on 9 January 1974, *France* went around South America, being too long for the Panama Canal, and after visiting Tahiti, called at Auckland and Wellington prior to arriving in Sydney on 16 February. A planned visit to Hobart, the only other Australian port she could enter, was cancelled, and instead *France* turned north for Port Moresby. Returning around Africa, *France* arrived back in New York on 11 April.

In July 1974, French Line announced that *France* was to be withdrawn from service in three months. Her final voyage ended outside Le Havre on 11 September, when her crew took over, and anchored the liner in the main channel, to protest her pending withdrawal. A month later, *France* finally entered port, and was laid up. In 1977 she was sold to a Saudi Arabian financed Swiss group, but remained idle until being sold again, to Norwegian Caribbean Lines, in June 1979.

Renamed *Norway*, she was extensively refitted for service as a permanent cruise liner. Among the changes made were the removal of some machinery and two propellers, while the after end of the superstructure was extended. With a passenger capacity of 2200 in one class, she began making weekly cruises from Miami to the Caribbean, and until the start of 1988 was the largest operational passenger vessel in the world.

FRANCE, THE LONGEST LINER EVER BUILT

THE 'LOVE BOATS'

BUILT: *1971/72 by Rheinstahl Nordseewerke, Emden*
TONNAGE: *19 907 gross*
DIMENSIONS: *554 × 81 ft (168.8 × 24.6 m)*
SERVICE SPEED: *20 knots*
PROPULSION: *Fiat diesels/twin screws*

In August 1974, P & O expanded their interest in the North American cruise market by purchasing Princess Cruises, and subsequently two sister ships to join that fleet. They were renamed *Pacific Princess* and *Island Princess*, and both have spent one summer season cruising from Sydney, and also paid a number of other visits to Australia in the course of South Pacific cruises from Los Angeles. However, their main claim to fame is from their use in the popular American television series, "The Love Boat".

This pair were built for Norwegian Cruiseships, jointly owned by two Oslo-based shipping companies, O. Lorentzen, and Fernley & Eger. They were designed for the lucrative summer short cruise trade between New York and Bermuda, with cruises to the West Indies at other times, to be operated under charter by Flagship Cruises. The first of the pair was launched on 9 May 1970, and named *Sea Venture*, entering service from New York in June 1971. Her sister was launched on 6 March 1971 as *Island Venture*, leaving New York for the first time on 4 January 1972. Accommodation was provided for 767 passengers in one class, but within six months it was apparent that the Bermuda trade could not support both ships.

The joint ownership arrangement was terminated in September 1972, with *Sea Venture* going to O. Lorentzen, and *Island Venture* to Fernley & Eger. *Sea Venture* remained on the Bermuda and West Indies trade, but *Island Venture* was chartered to Princess Cruises, and renamed *Island Princess*. She then commenced cruises on the west coast of America, mostly from Los Angeles to Mexico.

When P & O bought Princess Cruises, they also bought *Island Princess* from Fernley & Eger, then approached O. Lorentzen about acquiring *Sea Venture*. This they succeeded in doing in October 1974, though the ship would not be handed over until April 1975. Renamed *Pacific Princess*, she joined her sister once again, cruising the west coast of America to Mexico and Alaska.

Pacific Princess left San Francisco on 22 November 1975, and Los Angeles the following day, on a cruise to Australia, passing through Auckland on 13 December

and Wellington two days later before arriving in Sydney on 18 December. The next day *Pacific Princess* left on a 15 day South Pacific cruise, the first of 10 to be operated from Sydney over a five-month period, becoming the first true luxury cruise ship to regularly operate from Australia. Her longest cruise was of 25 days duration, going to Tahiti. The ship enjoyed some popularity during her stay, but had trouble with the South Pacific swell, and was often late into ports as a result. On 22 May 1976, *Pacific Princess* left Sydney to return to Los Angeles, and resumed her west coast schedule.

P & O in Australia decided not to repeat the *Pacific Princess* cruise programme in the summer of 1976–77. For a while Princess Cruises scheduled one cruise a year to Australia, the first of these being taken by *Island Princess*, which departed Los Angeles on 1 October 1976, arriving in Sydney on 22 October, and departing the next day. The October 1977 cruise was taken by *Pacific Princess*, while *Island Princess* came again in October 1978 on her second visit, this pattern continuing until 1982. In 1979, P & O expressed an interest in having both these ships lengthened. This process had been successful on several other cruise ships of similar age, but eventually the idea was abandoned. *Pacific Princess* made the October 1982 cruise, then returned four months later, arriving in Sydney on 21 February 1983, and departing the next day to return to Los Angeles. This was the last such cruise either of these ships has operated to Australia.

When *Royal Princess* joined the fleet in 1984, some operational changes were made. In June 1985, *Pacific Princess* was transferred to the Mediterranean for several months, and was to have returned in 1986. However, the *Achille Lauro* hijacking had made Americans wary of the Mediterranean, so *Pacific Princess* remained on the west coast of America.

When *Oriana* was withdrawn from the Australian cruise market in March 1986, P & O had no ship with which to replace her. Instead there was a gap of six months, but then *Island Princess* made a voyage from Los Angeles to Sydney, arriving on 30 October 1986. The next day she departed on a cruise to Hobart and Melbourne, then made a series of South Pacific cruises. These were aimed at the American market as much as the Australian trade, and were not a great success in either. Her final cruise terminated in Sydney on 29 April 1987, and the next day *Island Princess* left for Los Angeles, and her regular place on the Alaskan summer cruise trade. *Pacific Princess* returned to Australian cruise in February 1991 for a short season.

PACIFIC PRINCESS

ISLAND PRINCESS

LINDBLAD EXPLORER

BUILT: *1969 by Nystads Varv A/B, Nystad*
TONNAGE: *2346 gross*
DIMENSIONS: *250 × 46 ft (76.2 × 14 m)*
SERVICE SPEED: *15 knots*
PROPULSION: *Sulzer diesels/single screw*

Lindblad Explorer was ordered by Lindblad Travel, and designed to operate cruises to unusual places far from the usual tourist areas, in particular Antarctica, for which purpose her hull was strengthened for operations in ice. The keel was laid on 9 January 1969, and she was launched on 18 June. Accommodation was provided for a maximum of 118 passengers, for whom there was a main lounge, dining room, auditorium, and cinema, observation lounge, and small outdoor swimming pool.

Handed over to Lindblad Travel on 10 December, the vessel went to Southampton, and on 17 December departed on a voyage to Buenos Aires. From there she made three voyages into the Antarctic, then repositioned to Mombasa for a series of expeditions in the Indian Ocean. She then returned to South America for further voyages to Antarctica. During 1970 and 1971 *Lindblad Explorer* also paid her first visits to local waters, calling at several New Zealand ports as well as Hobart and Fremantle.

In November 1981, *Lindblad Explorer* passed through the Whitsunday Passage, visiting several islands, en route from New Guinea to Bluff, in New Zealand. She then cruised to Antarctica before returning to New Guinea, with a call at Norfolk Island. The vessel very seldom visited a major port, but on 2 March 1983 she arrived in Sydney for a two-day stopover.

A visit to *Lindblad Explorer* was most interesting, with a great deal crammed into the small ship. Testimony of the rough waters in which she sometimes operates was a network of ropes across the roof of the main lounge, for passengers to hang on to in bad weather. Several zodiac boats were carried to ferry passengers ashore on otherwise inaccessible shores. The cabins, though small, were well appointed, each having a porthole and private facilities. The strengthened hull of *Lindblad Explorer* twice saved her from disaster when she ran aground in the Antarctic. These voyages were as much scientific expeditions as cruises, with expert lecturers carried to give talks to passengers.

Early in 1984, *Lindblad Explorer* was sold to Society Expeditions, with delivery in October. In the meantime, Society Expeditions chartered the ship, and in September 1984 she made the first voyage by a passenger vessel through the notorious North West Passage. She then went to the Sembawang shipyard in Singapore in July 1985 for an extensive refit. The accommodation was upgraded, and a wide white band painted around the red hull. Prior to returning to service, the ship was renamed *Society Explorer*. Under this name she continues to operate expedition-type cruises to Antarctica and other areas.

LINDBLAD EXPLORER ALONGSIDE THE FREMANTLE PASSENGER TERMINAL

WORLD DISCOVERER

BUILT: *1974 by Unterweser AG, Hamburg*
TONNAGE: *3153 gross*
DIMENSIONS: *280 × 50 ft (85.3 × 15.2 m)*
SERVICE SPEED: *17 knots*
PROPULSION: *Atlas diesels/twin screws*

In 1972 a new company was formed in Denmark, Bewa Cruises, who planned to build two small cruise ships. They were designed for the exclusive American long-range cruise market to areas not visited by regular cruise liners, such as Indian Ocean islands and Antarctica, the ships would carry only 150 passengers. The first ship was launched on 8 December 1973 as *Bewa Discoverer*.

During fitting out, a fire destroyed the sauna on 17 May 1974, delaying completion. Unfortunately, Bewa Cruises was suffering financial difficulties, and in mid-1974 the company collapsed. The builders decided to complete the ship, which was then laid up in Hamburg under the name *Discoverer*. With a strengthened hull for operating in ice conditions, she was fully air-conditioned, had 75 cabins with private facilities, a small outdoor swimming pool, and a lounge above the bridge offering 360 degree panoramic views.

Attempts the find a buyer were unsuccessful, and eventually the builders managed to charter the ship out for several months during 1975, for cruises between Chicago and Montreal. Late in 1975, the vessel was purchased by De Vries & Co., who established a new company, Discoverer Cruises. Renamed *World Discoverer*, she began a wide-ranging programme of cruises to many parts of the world. During the northern summer, the ship would operate from European ports into far northern waters, while in the southern summer, she would be found on the Amazon River, in the Indian Ocean or the waters of Antarctica.

In the 1980s, *World Discoverer* was chartered by Society Expeditions, and it was then that she began including the South Pacific in her itinerary. On 19 February 1983, *World Discoverer* departed Invercargill on a cruise to New Guinea, which included calls at various ports and islands en route, such as Lord Howe Island, the Whitsunday Passage islands, Cairns on 1 March, Lizard Island and Port Moresby. In February 1984, she made a similar cruise from Invercargill to Port Moresby. In mid-1984, the Society Expeditions charter ended, and a new charter began with Heritage Cruises, a more up-market company.

During a four-month refit in Singapore, the ship was upgraded considerably, and as a luxury cruise ship, *World Discoverer* was to be based in the Pacific, mainly cruising from Suva to nearby islands, but also from Hong Kong to Japan and China. After a mere two months operation, Heritage Cruises cancelled the charter, and from May 1985, *World Discoverer* was once again chartered to Society Expeditions.

In December 1990, *World Discoverer* returned to Australian waters, visiting Queensland ports and islands, Sydney and Hobart.

WORLD DISCOVERER

SOVIET MINI-LINERS

BUILT: *1961/1958 by Mathias – Thesen Werft, Wismar*
TONNAGE: *4781 gross*
DIMENSIONS: *401 × 52 ft (122.2 × 15.8 m)*
SERVICE SPEED: *17 knots*
PROPULSION: *DMR diesels/twin screws*

The first of the "Mikhail Kalinin" class of Soviet passenger ships to appear in Australian waters was *Khabarovsk*, in 1971, and eight months after her final departure, a second ship of this group arrived, *Turkmenia*. The twelfth of this class of 19 to be completed, *Turkmenia* had joined the Black Sea Shipping Co. fleet, operating a service between Odessa and Batum. In 1975, *Turkmenia* was refitted, and upgraded for cruise work. This included improvements to cabins and public rooms, with the original capacity of 333 passengers being reduced to 250. The superstructure was also extended to the stern, to allow for an outdoor swimming pool with lido area, and an extra lounge.

Turkmenia was then offered for charter, and taken up by CTC Line, to operate between Fremantle and Singapore, as had *Khabarovsk*. CTC Line had established their own "ship–jet" service, using the Soviet airline Aeroflot from Singapore to Europe. On 2

August 1976, *Turkmenia* departed Singapore on her first voyage to Fremantle, arriving on 9 August. CTC were very happy with the ship, which provided much better accommodation than *Khabarovsk*, and they decided to commence a regular cruise operation from Fremantle as well, for which they chartered *Felix Dzerjinsky*.

The second of the "Mikhail Kalinin" class ships to be completed, *Felix Dzerjinsky* had also been operated by Black Sea Shipping Co., from Odessa to Batum. Then she was transferred to the Far East Shipping Co., for service from Nakhodka to Yokohama, partnering *Khabarovsk*. In 1975, *Felix Dzerjinsky* was upgraded in an identical manner to *Turkmenia*, and then chartered by the West German tour company, Neckermann und Reisen. She made a series of 13 day cruises between Manila and Singapore, from November 1975 to April 1976, her passengers being flown out to join the ship. *Felix Dzerjinsky* then returned to her regular service from Nakhodka again, until being chartered by CTC Line.

In February 1977, *Felix Dzerjinsky* began cruising out of Fremantle, being engaged in this for just over a year. Then her cruise programme was taken over by *Turkmenia*, and *Felix Dzerjinsky* voyaged into the South Pacific. From 28 May 1978 until 13 August, the vessel

FELIX DZERJINSKY

TURKMENIA

was based on Lautoka for weekly cruises around the Fijian islands, her passengers flying from Australia to Nadi to join the ship. She then came to Sydney, and began a series of cruises from there to the South Pacific islands.

During 1979, *Turkmenia* cruised from Fremantle, while *Felix Dzerjinsky* was based in Sydney, but late in the year her charter ended, and she returned to the Nakhodka service. *Turkmenia* then left Fremantle and came to Sydney, taking over the cruise programme of *Fedor Shalyapin*, which had also been withdrawn. *Turkmenia* made her first departure from Sydney on 8 February 1980, but then the Australian Government banned Soviet cruise ships from local waters. In May 1980, *Turkmenia* left Australian waters, and cruised for CTC Line from Singapore.

When the ban on Soviet ships was lifted late in 1983, *Turkmenia* returned to Australian waters. She arrived in Fremantle on 26 February 1984 from Singapore, then visited Adelaide and Melbourne before reaching Sydney on 5 March, to commence a programme of cruises. Late in 1984, *Turkmenia* went back to Fremantle, from where she cruised until 28 August 1985, when she left on a voyage to Singapore, having ended her charter to CTC Line.

By this time, *Turkmenia* had been transferred to the Far East Shipping Co., and she joined *Khabarovsk* and *Felix Dzerjinsky* on the service from Nakhodka to Yokohama and Hong Kong. *Turkmenia* was also used for occasional cruises, and on 11 November 1986, suffered major damage to her engine room when a fire broke out when she was about 60 miles from Nakhodka. At the time she had 300 children on board for an educational cruise, all of whom were safely evacuated. *Turkmenia* was towed into Nakhodka, and after repairs returned to service.

QUEEN ELIZABETH 2

BUILT: *1968 by John Brown & Co, Glasgow*
TONNAGE: *67 107 gross*
DIMENSIONS: *963 × 105 ft (293.5 × 32 m)*
SERVICE SPEED: *28.5 knots*
PROPULSION: *Geared turbines/twin screws*

Liners of the Cunard Line had been infrequent visitors to Australia for many years, as they were usually engaged on the trans-Atlantic trade, but they did make an occasional cruise around the world. During World War Two, the giant *Queen Elizabeth* and *Queen Mary* made a number of trips to and from Australia in their trooping capacities, and in the 1950s and 1960s, *Caronia* made a number of visits during cruises. By far the largest and most famous of present day ships to have visited Australia is *Queen Elizabeth 2*, flagship of the Cunard Line.

Launched by her namesake on 20 September 1967, *Queen Elizabeth 2* began sea trials late in November 1968, but suffered a series of problems, resulting in Cunard refusing to take delivery on the planned date, 1 January 1969. Instead *Queen Elizabeth 2* spent a further four months in her builder's hands, finally being handed over to Cunard on 18 April 1969. On 2 May the vessel left Southampton on her maiden voyage to New York. As a North Atlantic liner, *Queen Elizabeth 2* could accommodate 564 first class and 1441 tourist class

passengers, but this was reduced to 1400 in a single class when the liner went cruising. For the summer months the vessel makes a number of trans-Atlantic crossings, but most of the year is devoted to cruises, mostly from New York.

During 2 refit in 1972, the accommodation was altered to allow for 640 first class and 1223 tourist class in liner service, or 1740 in one class for cruises. Unfortunately, mechanical problems were to plague the liner, including a total breakdown in mid-Atlantic which resulted in all 1654 passengers having to be transferred to another vessel by lifeboats while large tugs were despatched to tow the crippled liner into Bermuda for repairs. Despite these problems, *Queen Elizabeth 2* was popular with Americans, but did not provide sufficient luxury suites. During a refit at the end of 1977, a new block containing 14 suites was added between the bridge and funnel, while other cabins were upgraded.

In January 1978, *Queen Elizabeth 2* left New York on a 90-day world cruise that took in the South Pacific for the first time, including a number of ports in New Zealand and Australia. On 13 February she anchored in the Bay of Islands, then berthed in Auckland the following day. From there the vessel went on to Wellington, Milford Sound, Hobart and Melbourne before arriving in Sydney on 24 February for a two-day

QUEEN ELIZABETH 2 BEFORE RE-ENGINING IN 1986

stay, then proceeding to Port Moresby. Also in port on 24 February was *Oriana*, with *Canberra* arriving two days later, so Sydney was host to the three largest British passenger ships in as many days.

It would be a further three years before *Queen Elizabeth 2* came to the South Pacific again, on her 1981 world cruise, calling at much the same ports as before and berthing in Sydney on 16 February for a two-day stay. Once again, she was followed in port by *Canberra* and *Oriana* on successive days.

Queen Elizabeth 2 was not scheduled to visit the South Pacific in 1982, but her routine was disrupted during May that year when she was requisitioned by the British Government to transport troops to the Falklands conflict. Leaving Southampton on 12 May, *Queen Elizabeth 2* proceeded to South Georgia, being considered too vulnerable to actually enter the war zone, and there transferred her troops to *Canberra* and *Norland*, who carried them the final 700 miles to the Falkland Islands. *Queen Elizabeth 2* then returned to Southampton, and was given a refit prior to returning to service on 14 August. A number of internal changes were effected, but the most notable alterations were external, as the liner was repainted with a pebble-grey hull, while her funnel carried the Cunard Line colours for the first time.

It was in this guise that *Queen Elizabeth 2* returned to the South Pacific again early in 1983, visiting Auckland and Wellington before arriving in Sydney on 21 February, and departing the next day for Brisbane, and also a day at anchor close to the Great Barrier Reef. The pebble grey hull proved very difficult to maintain, so later in 1983 the hull was repainted black.

The 1985 visit of *Queen Elizabeth 2* to the South Pacific was to produce a memorable morning for Sydney shipwatchers, and for Cunard in Australia. Having recently purchased Norwegian America Cruises, Cunard scheduled *Queen Elizabeth 2* and *Sagafjord* to arrive in Sydney on the morning of 14 February, though a plan for the ships to proceed down the harbour together had to be abandoned. An application to the Maritime Services Board for *Sagafjord* to actually berth alongside *Queen Elizabeth 2* for a short time to transfer passengers was refused, but as the sun rose on the appointed day, thousands crowded every vantage point ashore and afloat to witness *Sagafjord* come down the harbour, pass under the bridge and berth at Pyrmont, to be followed by *Queen Elizabeth 2*, going to her regular berth at Circular Quay, the only wharf able to accommodate the liner.

In October 1986, *Queen Elizabeth 2* was taken out of service for six months to have new engines installed amongst other major changes intended to extend her life by 20 years, and cut running costs by 50 per cent. The contract was awarded to the German shipyard, Lloyd Werft, who installed diesel-electric machinery, renovated all the cabins, revamped each of the public rooms, and added a further eight suites to the existing block atop the superstructure. One of the most notable external changes was the removal of the old funnel and its being replaced by one of a different design.

Returning to service in late April 1987, the rejuvenated vessel suffered an embarrassing series of problems on her first voyage across the Atlantic, but these were rectified as the liner settled back into service. For 1987 she was scheduled to make 25 trans-Atlantic crossings, seven cruises from Southampton and eight from New York, but all these were of relatively short duration. However, in January 1988, *Queen Elizabeth 2* departed New York on another global cruise which took her back to the South Pacific for the fifth time, and with her appearance altered for the fourth time.

Although publicised as a world cruise, this three-month voyage to 27 ports and five continents was a circuit of the Pacific and Indian Oceans. Departing New York on 13 January, *Queen Elizabeth 2* transited the Panama Canal and visited Los Angeles before turning south to Tahiti and on to Auckland, Wellington and Milford Sound, thence to Sydney, arriving on 15 February for her regular two-day stopover. As usual, a number of passengers left the ship here, and others joined for the second half of the cruise, which included calls at Melbourne, Adelaide and Fremantle, then across the Indian Ocean to Mauritius and Mombasa. Turning east, *Queen Elizabeth 2* called at ports in India, South East Asia and Japan before returning to Los Angeles, and back through the Panama Canal to New York.

At the time of her 1988 visit to Australia, Cunard announced that they had arranged a 72-day charter for *Queen Elizabeth 2* with the Japanese port of Yokohama, where she would be berthed from 30 March to 9 June 1989. Prior to starting this charter, the liner made a 37-day cruise from New York to South America.

En route to Japan, *Queen Elizabeth 2* made another excursion into the South Pacific, being in Sydney on 10 March, and Brisbane two days later, then going on to Yokohama. The fascination of the Japanese people for this giant liner resulted in a further charter being arranged for 1990, this time lasting 180 days. In the early months of 1990, the liner would be a major attraction at the World Exposition in Osaka, and would then be used for fly/cruises from Japanese ports. *Queen Elizabeth 2* would then return to the North Atlantic for the peak summer season sailings.

EASTERN PRINCESS

BUILT: *1953 by Chantiers de la Gironde, Bordeaux*
TONNAGE: *10 909 gross*
DIMENSIONS: *492 × 64 ft (150 × 19.6 m)*
SERVICE SPEED: *17 knots*
PROPULSION: *B & W diesels/twin screws*

This vessel replaced *Eastern Queen* under charter to Far East Travel Centre for the "ship–jet" service between Fremantle and Singapore in 1974. She was built for Messageries Maritimes as the last of a class of four passenger–cargo liners for their service from Marseilles to Mauritius. Launched on 12 July 1952 as *Jean Laborde*, she made her maiden departure on 31 July 1953, and provided accommodation for 88 first class, 112 tourist class and 299 third class passengers. With her sister ships, *La Bourdonnais, Ferdinand de Lesseps* and *Pierre Loti, Jean Laborde* remained on the Mauritius service for 17 years. In 1968, Messageries Maritimes sold two of these ships to the Greek Efthymiadis Line, and in 1970 *Jean Laborde* and *Pierre Loti* were also sold to them.

Jean Laborde and two others were refitted for service as ferries. Initially renamed *Mykinai*, this was changed to *Ancona* before she entered her new service in 1971, operating between Patras and Ancona. On 5 October 1973, *Ancona* suffered an engine-room fire, which was extinguished by the crew, but not before all 253 passengers had been evacuated. The ship was towed to Piraeus for repairs.

The opportunity was taken to refit her as a car ferry, with accommodation for 300 passengers, while the former cargo holds were converted to garage space. She returned to the service between Patras and Ancona for the summer of 1974, then was chartered by Far East Travel Centre, to be operated for them by Singapore Australia Shipping Co.

With her accommodation increased to 506 passengers in one class, the vessel was renamed *Eastern Princess*, and arrived in Singapore for a scheduled departure on 18 October 1974. However, a fault in the air-conditioning caused this to be postponed, and it was 16 November before she finally got away. The voyage was plagued by engine trouble, and she did not reach Fremantle until 24 November. *Eastern Princess* suffered continual engine problems, and was constantly anything from two days to a week behind schedule.

When she was put out of action again by an engine-room fire in March 1975, FETC obtained a writ against Efthymiadis Line, which resulted in *Eastern Princess* being arrested in Singapore on 19 March. *Eastern Princess* remained idle in Singapore for over a year, during which Efthymiadis went bankrupt. The vessel was then offered for sale by creditors, and bought by another Greek company, Epirotiki Line.

Eastern Queen left Singapore after repairs to her engines on 7 July 1976, arriving back in Piraeus on 29 July. There she was rebuilt as a luxury cruise liner, with accommodation for 540 passengers in 235 cabins. Renamed *Oceanos*, she began operating as a cruise liner from Piraeus on 5 May 1978. In October 1978, the vessel returned to the shipyard for further alterations, during which an extra deck was built forward of the bridge. Since then *Oceanos* has operated regular summer cruises in the Mediterranean.

EASTERN PRINCESS

NIPPON MARU

BUILT: *1962 by Brodogradiliste, Split*
TONNAGE: *10 451 gross*
DIMENSIONS: *492 × 62 ft (150 × 19 m)*
SERVICE SPEED: *17 knots*
PROPULSION: *B & W diesels/twin screws*

The second passenger vessel of this name to be operated by Mitsui–OSK Line and visit Australia, *Nippon Maru* was originally built in Yugoslavia for the Brazilian company, Cia. Nacional de Nav. Costeira. Launched on 29 December 1961, she was named *Rosa de Fonseca*, being completed in October 1962 and placed in service on the Brazilian internal route between Manaus, Belem, Rio de Janeiro and Santos, and on to Montevideo and Buenos Aires. Accommodation was provided for 208 first class and 274 tourist class passengers. This vessel and her sister, *Anny Nery*, were the first new vessels built for service along the Brazilian coast in 30 years.

In 1968 the Costiera Line went out of business, and all their ships were purchased by Lloyd Brasileiro. Apart from new funnel colours, the operation and appearance of the ships were not affected by this change, but the Brazilian coastal services were suffering from a decline in patronage. *Rosa de Fonseca* was often laid up, or used for cruising over a period of several years. Finally she was offered for sale. In 1975 the vessel was purchased by Cosmos Passenger Service, a Panamanian registered concern. Renamed *P/S Seven Seas*, she was then chartered to Mitsui–OSK Line for four years, as a cruise ship.

Apart from new funnel colours once more, the appearance of the ship was not altered externally, but internally she was refitted to better suit her for the Japanese cruise market. On 6 August 1975, *P/S Seven Seas* departed Yokohama on her first cruise, to Hawaii,

but most of her cruises would be of shorter duration to places close to Japan. Passengers were drawn from mutual interest groups who chartered the whole ship, a system peculiar to the Japanese cruise market at that time.

In December 1976, Mitsui–OSK disposed of its old liner *Nippon Maru*, and in 1977 they bought *P/S Seven Seas* outright, and renamed her *Nippon Maru*. She continued to operate cruises from Japan, but now her passengers were selected by government departments. In addition, each year the ship was used for a Japanese Youth Goodwill Cruise, when a group of students selected from throughout Japan would make a lengthy cruise to a variety of ports around the Pacific.

Nippon Maru can presently accommodate a maximum of 530 passengers. Each cabin has a porthole, and the majority have private facilities. The ship is fully air-conditioned and fitted with stabilisers. On her student cruises, the total cost is covered by the Japanese Government, while on her charter cruises the passengers are sponsored by a government department, or a group.

In the course of making these Youth Goodwill Cruises, *Nippon Maru* has visited Australian ports on four occasions. The first visit occurred in early 1979, during which the vessel was in Sydney for several days from 11 February. Three years later, *Nippon Maru* made her second visit, this time staying in Sydney four days from 13 February 1982. It was a further four years before the ship made her third visit, being in Sydney for five days from 11 February 1986. In 1988 *Nippon Maru* returned for the fourth time, being in Sydney for several days before departing on 29 January. It is highly likely that this vessel will continue to make visits to Australian ports at irregular intervals.

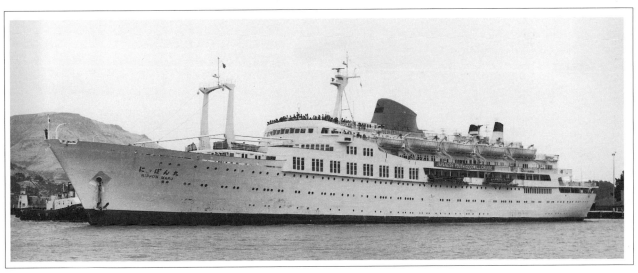

NIPPON MARU

MINGHUA

BUILT: *1962 by Ch. de Penhoet, St Nazaire*
TONNAGE: *14 225 gross*
DIMENSIONS: *549 × 71 ft (167.5 × 21.8 m)*
SERVICE SPEED: *22 knots*
PROPULSION: *B & W diesels/twin screws*

Minghua became the first Chinese vessel to cruise in the western world when she began operating from Sydney in January 1980. She had been built as *Ancerville* for the French company, Cie. de Nav. Paquet. Launched on 5 April 1962, *Ancerville* entered service on 5 September that year with a cruise from Marseilles to the Canary Islands, then was placed on a regular service from Marseilles to ports in French West Africa as far as Dakar. Accommodation was provided for 171 first class, 346 tourist class and 253 third class passengers, but when cruising, a maximum of 500 in one class were carried.

The West African shipping services died in the late 1960s, and from 1970 *Ancerville* was transferred to permanent cruising, operating out of both European and American ports. Early in 1973 *Ancerville* was offered for sale, being bought immediately by the Peoples Republic of China. It wanted early delivery, so

on 24 March *Ancerville* was withdrawn at very short notice, and handed over to her new owner a few days later.

Renamed *Minghua*, which translates as Spirit of China, she joined the China Ocean Shipping fleet, operating to East Africa, particularly Tanzania, where the Chinese were building a railway. At one time *Minghua* was anchored off Dar es Salaam as a floating hotel for Chinese diplomats attached to the local mission, but in 1977 she was laid up in the Whampoa River, near Canton.

In 1979, Asian Pacific Cruises was formed in Sydney, arranging a charter of *Minghua* for South Pacific cruises. The liner was given a refit in Hong Kong, her accommodation being altered to 580 in one class. In December 1979, *Minghua* boarded 300 Australian passengers in Hong Kong, for a positioning cruise to Sydney, which included a call at Cairns. Arriving in Sydney on 31 December, many of the passengers complained about numerous aspects of the voyage, including problems with the Chinese crew, and lack of facilities on board. Despite this, *Minghua* sailed on 1 January 1980 as scheduled for her first South Pacific cruise, which included a call at Auckland.

Meanwhile, back in Sydney, Asian Pacific Cruises

MINGHUA INITIALLY HAD A LIGHT GREEN HULL

THE LINER LOOKED BETTER WHEN PAINTED ALL WHITE

and the representatives of China Ocean Shipping were in dispute, which was suddenly resolved when the Chinese terminated the charter agreement. Instead, they organised the managers of the ship, Burns Philp, to operate the ship, as Minghua Cruises. The liner followed her scheduled programme, but as complaints about the operation grew, *Minghua* returned to Hong Kong in June 1980 for a major refit. The interior was upgraded and refurbished, while externally the light green hull was repainted white. Returning to Australia at the end of 1980, *Minghua* was a much improved ship, and gradually her popularity grew.

During another refit in 1981, the accommodation was reduced to 450 in one class, by the elimination of many small cabins, and at the end of that year, *Minghua* made a series of cruises from Darwin. Now nicknamed the "Friendship", *Minghua* had finally found a niche for

herself in the Australian market, by offering longer cruises to the Orient, and also to Hawaii. In February 1982, the vessel called at Adelaide and Fremantle at the start of a cruise to Japan, and the future success of the vessel in the Australian cruise market seemed assured.

It was quite a shock when, on 2 February 1983, the announcement was made that *Minghua* would be withdrawn in three months. On 20 May, the liner left Sydney for the last time, with a full complement of passengers, on a one-way cruise to Hong Kong. *Minghua* then made two cruises from Hong Kong under charter to a Japanese company, following which she was laid up. In June 1984 the vessel was sold to a joint Hong Kong–Chinese concern, Sea World Ltd, and converted into a floating hotel. Renamed *Sea World*, she is now anchored in Shek Kou Bay, servicing a popular Pearl River holiday resort.

DALMACIJA

BUILT: *1965 by Brodogadiliste Iljanik, Pula*
TONNAGE: *5651 gross*
DIMENSIONS: *383 × 50 ft (116.5 × 15.3 m)*
SERVICE SPEED: *19 knots*
PROPULSION: *Sulzer diesels/twin screws*

A shortlived cruising venture in Western Australia was Australian Ocean Line, formed in 1981 in Perth, which chartered a Yugoslav vessel, *Dalmacija,* for cruises out of Fremantle. *Dalmacija* and her sister, *Istra,* were ordered by the government-owned shipping company, Jadrolinija, for regular service in the Mediterranean. *Dalmacija* was the first of the pair to be built, being launched in March 1964.

On 27 August 1964, there was an explosion on board the incomplete ship, followed by a fire, which blazed out of control for some time. Firemen poured so much water into the ship that eventually she sank alongside her fitting-out berth. Raised and repaired, *Dalmacija* finally entered service at the end of 1965, having accommodation for 165 first class and 52 tourist class passengers, while several hundred deck passengers could also be carried on short sectors. Her route took the ship from Venice, Trieste and Rijeka to Piraeus, Alexandria, Beirut and Limassol.

Dalmacija and *Istra* were very advanced for this type of service, being fitted with stabilisers, fully air-conditioned, and having an outdoor swimming pool, with a sliding glass top. In 1969, both vessels were refitted to operate as cruise ships, with the accommodation being enlarged to carry 310 passengers in one class. From April to October each year, *Dalmacija* would cruise in the Mediterranean under charter to a West German tour company, while in winter she would either be laid up, or cruise under charter in the Caribbean. Australian Ocean Line took her on charter for two seasons in Australian waters.

Handed over in Venice, *Dalmacija* left on 12 November 1981 on her positioning cruise, calling at Djibouti, Colombo and Singapore before arriving in Fremantle on 8 December. Her first cruise departed on 11 December, and should have been three days to nowhere, but the seas were so rough the vessel had to seek shelter in Geograph Bay, anchoring there for two days. A varied programme had been arranged for *Dalmacija*, combining short cruises with 25 day ventures to the Far East, and around Australia.

On 14 December, *Dalmacija* left Fremantle on her first long cruise to Hong Kong, taking six days to reach Singapore. As her tanks held only five days supply of fresh water, it had to be rationed. Heavy seas were also encountered, and some passengers left the ship in Singapore and flew home. The resultant publicity affected bookings very badly, and the remaining two scheduled cruises to the Far East were not selling at all well. As a result one was cancelled, and the ship made a series of short cruises from Fremantle.

Dalmacija did make two cruises around Australia, visiting Adelaide, Melbourne, Sydney, Brisbane, Cairns, and Darwin twice, and Port Headland and Wyndham once each. The venture lost money through the season, and on 25 April 1982, *Dalmacija* left Fremantle for the last time, returning to Venice. Shortly afterwards, Australian Ocean Line ceased trading. Since 1982, *Dalmacija* has continued to cruise in the Mediterranean.

DALMACIJA

PRINCESS MAHSURI

BUILT: *1980 by Howaldtswerke–Deutschewerft, Kiel*
TONNAGE: *7813 gross*
DIMENSIONS: *402 × 57 ft (122.5 × 17.5 m)*
SERVICE SPEED: *17.5 knots*
PROPULSION: *Main K diesels/twin screws*

Blue Funnel Line had a long association with Australia, mostly operating passenger–cargo ships. Early in 1982, they formed Blue Funnel Cruises, and arranged the charter of a small cruise liner, *Berlin,* to be based on Sydney for part of each year. This vessel had been launched on 12 January 1980, and completed 10 months later. She was owned in West Germany by Schiffahrtsgesellschaft MS Berlin Beteilgungs GmbH & Co., and managed for them by Rederie Peter Deilmann.

Berlin provided accommodation for a maximum of 330 passengers in 150 cabins, and on completion was chartered by a West German tourist operator, Neckermann und Reisen. She spent several months in the Mediterranean, then went to the Caribbean, but unfortunately was not a great success. During 1982 Neckermann und Reisen sought to terminate their charter agreement. Blue Funnel Line were looking for a cruise ship with which to enter the Australian and Indonesian markets. They selected *Berlin,* and she was handed over to them in October 1982 at Genoa.

The vessel was renamed *Princess Mahsuri,* after a Malayan folklore figure, and on 2 November 1982 left Genoa bound for Singapore, calling at Djibouti, the Maldive Islands and Phuket on the way. From Singapore, the vessel cruised to Australia, visiting Townsville, Hayman Island and Brisbane before arriving in Sydney on 18 December. Next day, she departed on her first South Pacific cruise, and over the next five months made a series of cruises, varying in duration from 9 to 16 days.

In May 1983, *Princess Mahsuri* returned to Singapore, from where she made fourteen-day cruises around the Indonesian islands over a five-month period, returning to Sydney again in November 1983. She repeated her cruise programme of the previous year, but was not enjoying much success. This was mainly due to the high fares, as well as a lack of imagination in the itineraries being operated. On 14 June 1984, *Princess Mahsuri* left Sydney for the last time, going to Hong Kong for a brief refit, then to Singapore. A second season of Indonesian island cruises was then operated.

An extensive new programme of cruises for 1985 was announced by Blue Funnel Cruises, comprising lengthy voyages to the Orient from both Singapore and Sydney, and also longer South Pacific cruises, for which she was best suited. Unfortunately, in September 1984 it announced that the ship would be returned to her owner two months later. The vessel resumed her original name, *Berlin,* and began cruising in the Mediterranean.

Berlin was sent to the Werft Nobiskrug shipyard at the end of 1986, to be lengthened. The ship was cut in two, and a new midships section inserted, increasing her length to 458 ft (139.6 m), and her tonnage to over 10 000 gross. More importantly, passenger capacity rose to 470, making her a more economic ship to operate. Since the rebuilding, *Berlin* has cruised in the Mediterranean and northern European waters.

In December 1988, *Berlin* left Europe on her first cruise around the world, which included visits to Australian ports. The liner arrived in Sydney on 27 January 1989, and departed two days later.

PRINCESS MAHSURI

ODESSA

BUILT: *1974 by Vickers Ltd, Barrow*
TONNAGE: *13 758 gross*
DIMENSIONS: *446 × 70 ft (136.3 × 21.5 m)*
SERVICE SPEED: *19 knots*
PROPULSION: *Pielstik diesels/twin screws*

This vessel had been ordered by A/S Nordline in 1968, for student and economy cruising from New York and in the Pacific. Construction began in 1969, but before it had progressed very far, the shipyard advised of a huge increase in the construction cost. A/S Nordline sought a buyer for the incomplete vessel, and work came to a halt, but then owner and builder reached an agreement which enabled construction to recommence in September 1971. At that time it was intended to name the ship *Prins Henrik af Denmark*.

On 20 December 1972, the vessel was launched without ceremony or a name, as A/S Nordline were still suffering serious financial problems, and would be unable to take delivery of the completed ship. Attempts to arrange a charter were unsuccessful, so for three months the vessel lay idle. On 27 March 1973, she was towed from Barrow to Newcastle, where Swan, Hunter & Wigham Richardson took over completion of the ship. This work took a year, during which time the ship was named *Copenhagen*, and then in March 1974 she ran trials. The following month, *Copenhagen* was laid up, and offered for sale by the shipyard.

After a year idle, *Copenhagen* was finally sold to the Soviet Union in May 1975, and allocated to the Black Sea Steam Ship Co., being renamed *Odessa*, and registered at that port. She was handed over to her new owner at Liverpool on 18 July 1975, making a voyage to Leningrad, and then entering a general cruise service. Since then, *Odessa* has cruised out of American and European ports, including several years based on Vancouver for cruises to Alaska.

Odessa provides very comfortable accommodation for 600 passengers, all cabins being outside and having private facilities. Public rooms are located on the upper decks, and include a two deck high cinema. The vessel has often been chartered by American, German and British organisations, and has cruised around the world several times under charter to the London office of CTC Cruises.

Odessa made her first visit to Australia in February 1984, and returned at the same time in 1985. Her world cruise in 1986 did not include Australia, but in 1987 *Odessa* made her third visit. This time the ship was under charter to Transocean Tours, a West German organisation, and was on a 98 day cruise from Genoa. The trip included a visit to Auckland, then *Odessa* arrived in Sydney on 4 February, sailing the next day for Brisbane, then on to New Guinea and Asian ports, returning to Genoa through the Suez Canal. *Odessa* again missed out on Australian ports in 1988, but it is highly likely that she will return to the area on future long cruises.

ODESSA

EUROPA

BUILT: *1981 by Bremer Vulkan, Bremen*
TONNAGE: *33 819 gross*
DIMENSIONS: *653 × 92 ft (199.9 × 28.5 m)*
SERVICE SPEED: *21 knots*
PROPULSION: *MAN diesels/twin screws*

The name *Europa* has been associated with major German passenger liners since 1879, and the present vessel is the fifth to bear the name. The four previous ships were owned by North German Lloyd, but in 1972 they amalgamated with their main rivals, Hamburg America Line, to form Hapag–Lloyd, under whose banner the present vessel operates. She replaced a vessel of the same name, which is described elsewhere in this book under her original name, *Kungsholm*.

Launched on 22 December 1980, *Europa* was delivered to Hapag–Lloyd on 5 December 1981, and entered service with a departure from Genoa on 8 January 1982 on a lengthy cruise around Africa. Accommodation is provided for 758 passengers in 316 cabins. The layout of the liner follows the latest trends in ship design, with all cabins being located in the forward section of the vessel, and public rooms spread over several decks aft. These include several lounges, a nightclub, theatre and 500 seat restaurant. There is also an observation lounge above the bridge. The 280 crew have a separate swimming pool, and high standard accommodation.

Europa cruises out of various European ports, mainly catering to the West German market. Each year the vessel makes a world cruise, and it is the course of

some of these voyages that she has visited ports in Australia and New Zealand. In January 1984, *Europa* made her first excursion into the South Pacific, calling at Auckland on 11 March and Wellington on 13 March before arriving in Sydney on 16 March.

The success of the 1984 cruise resulted in a more extensive itinerary being arranged for 1985. This time, *Europa* stopped in Sydney four days, arriving on 26 February. While in Sydney, there was some transferring of passengers, either leaving or joining the liner from Europe. For the next two years, *Europa* did not visit the South Pacific, but in 1988 she returned. This time the liner followed a different route, and visited Fremantle for the first time, arriving there from Bali on 2 February for a one day stay. She then went on to make her maiden visit to Adelaide, and after calling at Melbourne, arrived in Sydney on 12 February. This was another four-day stopover, and the liner berthed at the Passenger Terminal at Circular Quay. She had to vacate the berth on 15 February to make way for *Queen Elizabeth 2*. In an unusual move, *Europa* was taken to a buoy off Neutral Bay. There she remained until leaving the same evening, her passengers being transported to and from the city by small ferries. This is one of the very few occasions that a visiting liner has anchored out in Sydney Harbour.

Europa returned to Australia again in 1989, once again being in Sydney four days, and having to change berths as usual. She is certainly one of the most attractive of the new generation of liners to visit Australia.

EUROPA

MERMOZ

BUILT: *1957 by Chantiers de l'Atlantique, St Nazaire*
TONNAGE: *13 804 gross*
DIMENSIONS: *527 × 65 ft (160.6 × 19.8 m)*
SERVICE SPEED: *17 knots*
PROPULSION: *B & W diesels/twin screws*

From 1973 to 1977, a vessel named *Eastern Queen* operated between Fremantle and Singapore, and in 1985 her former sister, *Mermoz*, made an appearance in Australian waters. Both these ships were built for Cie. de Nav. Fraissinet et Cyprien Fabre, a French company engaged in the trade to French West Africa.

Eastern Queen had been built in 1953 as *General Mangin*, but it was not until 17 November 1956 that her sister was launched, as *Jean Mermoz*. Completed in May 1957, *Jean Mermoz* had accommodation for 142 first class, 140 second class and 110 third class passengers, plus quarters for 470 troops, with 160 crew. The vessel departed Marseilles on her maiden voyage to Point Noire in French Equitorial Africa, including calls at Dakar, Conakry, Abidjan, Takoradi, Lome, Lagos and Duala.

During 1969 the Fabre fleet was absorbed into Nouvelle Cie. de Paquebots, but *Jean Mermoz* and her sister remained on their original route until 1969. Then *General Mangin* was sold, while *Jean Mermoz* was despatched to the Mariotti shipyard in Genoa, to be rebuilt as a full-time cruise liner. The work lasted eight months, during which the appearance of the ship was totally altered by an enlargement of the superstructure and heightening of the funnel. The interior of the ship was completely stripped out, and a completely new accommodation block constructed, with cabins for 757 passengers in one class. For her new role, the number of crew was increased to 264, and the ship was painted all white, including the funnel.

Prior to entering her new role, the name of the vessel was amended to *Mermoz*, and her owner changed their name to Paquet Cruises. In September 1970, *Mermoz* entered service, and for many years cruised in the Mediterranean from May to October, then spent the remainder of the year in the West Indies, based on Port Everglades.

In the 1980s, *Mermoz* began making long-distance cruises, and in 1985 came to the South Pacific for the first time. She called at Brisbane on 17 November, then proceeded to Sydney. Her arrival on 19 November was delayed eight hours by very rough seas, and no sooner was she tied up at Circular Quay than a tugboat union declared her black, in protest against French nuclear testing in the South Pacific. Another union then refused to allow *Mermoz* to sail until a dispute over payments to crew members was resolved. The liner had to be moved to Pyrmont on 20 November instead of sailing on schedule, and did not get away until late on 21 November, bound for Noumea.

At the time of this ill-fated visit, Paquet Line had established an office in Sydney, and were planning to bring another of their ships, *Azur*, for a series of seven-day cruises from Sydney to Noumea, commencing in November 1986. Wary of further union action against their ships, the company cancelled this programme of cruises, and then closed their Sydney office.

MERMOZ

MAXIM GORKI

BUILT: *1969 by Howaldswerke–Deutsche Werft, Hamburg*
TONNAGE: *25 022 gross*
DIMENSIONS: *638 × 87 ft (194.7 × 26.6 m)*
SERVICE SPEED: *20 knots*
PROPULSION: *Geared turbines/twin screws*

This vessel was ordered by German Atlantic Line, and launched as *Hamburg* on 21 February 1968. Completed with accommodation for 652 passengers, and 403 crew, she ran trials in February 1969, and was delivered to her owner the following month. *Hamburg* departed Cuxhaven on 28 March on a 36 day cruise to Africa and South America, arriving in New York for the first time on 26 June. For most of her career under the West German flag, *Hamburg* would be based on New York for cruises throughout the year. Early in her career she was widely advertised as the "space ship", referring to the small number of passengers carried for her size, allowing more space per person.

Early in 1973, *Hamburg* was transferred to the west coast of America, but this was not a successful move. German Atlantic Line were suffering financial problems, which eventually caused them to sell their other cruise ship, *Hanseatic*, which subsequently visited Australia as *Royal Odyssey*. On 25 September 1973, *Hamburg* was renamed *Hanseatic*, and returned to the east coast cruise trade, but within three months German Atlantic Line had to cease trading. On 1 December, *Hanseatic* was laid up in Hamburg, and offered for sale.

A sale to a Japanese firm, Ryutsu Kaiun KK, fell

through, but then the vessel was sold to the Soviet Union. On 25 January 1974, she was handed over to the Black Sea Steam Ship Co., registered in Odessa, and renamed *Maxim Gorki*. Before commencing her new career, though, the vessel was chartered to the makers of the film "Juggernaut", for which she was renamed *Britannic*. When this charter ended, *Maxim Gorki* began cruising under the Soviet flag, operating out of New York from May to September 1974. *Maxim Gorki* is presently the largest and fastest passenger ship owned by the Soviet Union.

In subsequent years, *Maxim Gorki* has cruised to most parts of the world, often under charter to West German tourist companies. She began making an annual cruise around the world, and it was in the course of such voyages that *Maxim Gorki* visited Australian ports. Between 1980 and 1983, when Russian cruise ships were banned from Australian ports, *Maxim Gorki* made several visits to New Zealand ports. On 28 February 1986, the vessel arrived in Fremantle, then went on to visit Melbourne before arriving in Sydney on 7 March 1986 for a three-day stopover. She returned to Australian ports in 1987, being in Sydney for three days from 22 February 1987, but on her 1988 world cruise, was in Sydney for one day only, 15 January.

On 20 June 1989, *Maxim Gorki* struck an iceberg while cruising off the Norwegian coast. She was able to reach port and later be repaired. In 1990, the vessel made another world cruise, including visits to Australian and New Zealand ports, during February.

MAXIM GORKI

SHIN SAKURA MARU

BUILT: *1972 by Mitsubishi Heavy Industries Ltd, Kōbe*
TONNAGE: *16 431 gross*
DIMENSIONS: *577 × 81 ft (175.8 × 24.6 m)*
SERVICE SPEED: *20 knots*
PROPULSION: *Mitsubishi diesel/single screw*

To promote their products overseas, the Japanese have frequently utilised large vessels to voyage to various ports as a floating fair, displaying a wide variety of goods. In 1962, a ship was built specifically for this purpose, being named *Sakura Maru*. In November 1970, *Sakura Maru* visited Australian ports in the course of her ninth voyage on behalf of the Japanese Industry Floating Fair Association. The following year, this vessel was sold.

On 18 December 1971, a replacement for *Sakura Maru* was launched as *Shin Sakura Maru*. In design the two ships were totally different, whereas *Sakura Maru* resembled a passenger liner, *Shin Sakura Maru* gave the appearance of a cargo ship, with a large superstructure aft. On being delivered to the Japanese Industry Floating Fair Association in July 1972, *Shin Sakura Maru* provided accommodation for 92 passengers only. She was painted in the colours of Mitsui–OSK Line, who managed the vessel, and was used on their service to South America when not engaged as a floating fair.

The maiden voyage of *Shin Sakura Maru* took her to European ports to promote Japanese industrial goods. In 1973, it was decided to dispense with carrying passengers, and when not in service as a floating fair, the vessel subsequently traded as a freighter. It was in this role that she first visited Australian ports, during 1978. In 1981, *Shin Sakura Maru* was purchased outright by Mitsui–OSK, and returned to her builder's yard for conversion into a modern cruise ship.

The work involved the removal of all cargo handling gear, converting the former holds into accommodation areas, extending the superstructure forward and relocating the bridge. A total of 142 cabins were installed, varying in capacity from two-berth to six-berth, for a maximum of 552 passengers. A variety of spacious public rooms were also built, including a large main lounge, and a large main hall two decks high, which when used as a cinema could seat 75 in the gallery and 295 in the stalls. There were also lecture rooms and meeting rooms for students. For recreation, a large sports deck was provided, with a swimming pool.

Shin Sakura Maru returned to service in December 1981, and immediately took over the charter cruises formerly operated by *Nippon Maru*. Unlike most western countries, Japan does not sell cruises on an individual basis, but parties from a religious group, company or region will charter the complete ship, and select members to partake of a cruise. Most are of about 10 days' duration, and visit nearby ports in Korea and China as well as Hong Kong.

Usually every second year, *Shin Sakura Maru* makes a long cruise, carrying students selected from all over Japan. It was in the course of such a cruise that *Shin Sakura Maru* came to Australia early in 1986, her longest stopover being five days in Sydney from 8 March. The vessel returned to Australia again in March 1989, remaining in Sydney for several days.

SHIN SAKURA MARU

ROYAL ODYSSEY

BUILT: *1964 by Chantiers de l'Atlantique, St Nazaire*
TONNAGE: *17 884 gross*
DIMENSIONS: *629 × 81 ft (191.7 × 24.8 m)*
SERVICE SPEED: *20 knots*
PROPULSION: *Geared turbines/twin screws*

Royal Odyssey spent two summer seasons cruising out of Sydney to the South Pacific. She was a liner with an interesting and varied history, and was operating under her fourth name and owner as *Royal Odyssey*. She was launched on 10 November 1962 as *Shalom*, the last and largest passenger vessel to be owned by the Zim Line, of Israel. Fitted out with accommodation for 72 first class and 1018 tourist class passengers, *Shalom* departed Haifa on 17 April 1964 on her maiden voyage to New York. She was an attractive liner, with twin exhausts similar to *Canberra*.

In October 1964, the accommodation was altered to carry 148 first class and 864 tourist class, to make her more suitable for cruising. Departing New York on a cruise on 26 November 1964, *Shalom* collided with a tanker, which was cut in two, while *Shalom* limped back to port with serious bow damage. *Shalom* continued to operate Atlantic voyages and cruises until May 1967, when she was sold to German Atlantic Line.

Renamed *Hanseatic*, she continued to operate Atlantic voyages, from Hamburg to New York, and cruises, until 1969, when she became a full-time cruise ship. In 1973, German Atlantic Line went out of business, and *Hanseatic* was sold to Home Lines, being renamed *Doric*. During a refit, the superstructure was extended aft, and the accommodation reduced to 725 in one class. *Doric* cruised out of New York to Bermuda from April to October, and the rest of the year was based on Port Everglades for West Indies cruising.

Having ordered a new cruise liner, Home Line offered *Doric* for sale in 1980, with forward delivery. The ship was purchased by Royal Cruise Line, but it had to wait until February 1982 to take over the ship, which was then renamed *Royal Odyssey*. During a four-month refit in Greece, the twin uptakes were replaced by a conventional funnel, and accommodation increased to 814 in one class. *Royal Odyssey* cruised in the Mediterranean and northern European waters from May to October, then spent the rest of the year based on Port Everglades.

In October 1986, she left Los Angeles bound for the South Pacific, passing through Auckland on 12 November. After visits to Wellington and Milford Sound, *Royal Odyssey* arrived in Sydney for the first time on 25 November. She made four cruises from Sydney, the last departing on 13 February 1987, then returned to Los Angeles.

Royal Odyssey returned to Australia for a second season, arriving in Sydney on 24 December 1987, and making two cruises. By then Royal Cruise Line was preparing to take delivery of a new liner, and *Royal Odyssey* was up for sale. By the time she left Sydney for the last time on 10 February 1988, *Royal Odyssey* had been sold to Regency Cruises, with delivery later in the year. On being handed over to her fifth owner, the liner was renamed *Regent Sun*, and in December 1988 began cruising from Montego Bay.

ROYAL ODYSSEY

Danae

BUILT: 1955 by Harland & Wolff Ltd, Belfast
TONNAGE: 12 123 gross
DIMENSIONS: 533 × 70 ft (162.3 × 21.4 m)
SERVICE SPEED: 17 knots
PROPULSION: B & W diesels/twin screws

The first arrival of *Danae* in Sydney in February 1986 was in fact the return of a former frequent visitor to the port, though in a very different guise. She was launched on 10 March 1955 as *Port Melbourne*, the second of a pair of large cargo liners built for the Port Line, her sister being *Port Sydney*. When completed in July 1955, *Port Melbourne* provided accommodation for 12 passengers, but was primarily a cargo ship.

For over 15 years, *Port Melbourne* and *Port Sydney* plied between Britain, Australia and New Zealand, until superseded by container ships. In 1972, both ships were sold to J. C. Carras of Greece, for conversion into passenger vessels. At this time, *Port Melbourne* was given the temporary name *Therisos Express*, and went to the Carras shipyard at Chalkis for rebuilding alongside her sister, which was renamed *Akrotiri Express*. The original superstructure was removed, and a much larger new one built. Internally, apart from the engines, everything was removed, and totally new accommodation installed. By the time the conversion was complete, the ships had been altered beyond recognition.

Akrotiri Express was the first to be completed, being renamed *Daphne* prior to entering service in July 1975. *Therisos Express* was renamed *Danae* in 1975, and entered service the following year, as a full-time cruise ship, with luxury accommodation for 512 passengers. Although not the most attractive of cruise ships in appearance, *Danae* and *Daphne* offer superb facilities, with large and bright public rooms and ample open deck space.

For three years *Danae* and *Daphne* cruised in the Mediterranean and Caribbean for Carras Cruises, then in 1979 both were taken on long-term charter by Costa Cruises, and adopted their funnel colours. Their general spheres of operation remained unchanged for some years, but in December 1985, *Danae* departed Genoa on a world cruise that included ports in the South Pacific.

After passing through the Panama Canal, *Danae* arrived in Auckland on 7 February 1986, then crossed to Sydney, berthing on 11 February. Departing the next day, *Danae* continued on to Melbourne and then Fremantle, and via African ports back to Genoa. For her 1986–87 world cruise, *Danae* did not visit Australia, but on 18 December 1987 she departed Genoa on her second cruise to this area. After passing through the Panama Canal and calling at several islands, *Danae* called at Auckland on 4 February and Wellington on 6 February for a two-day stay. She then crossed to Sydney, arriving on 11 February. Departing two days later, after exchanging passengers, *Danae* went to Brisbane, spent a day anchored in the Whitsunday Passage and visited Cairns before heading off to Asian and Indian ports, and passing through the Suez Canal to return to Genoa.

So far *Daphne* has not been seen in Australian waters, but it is hoped that one of these ships will continue to make regular visits to the area in the course of world cruises. The extent of their conversion is equal to that of *Flavia*, described earlier in this book.

THE PORT LINE CARGO SHIP *PORT MELBOURNE*

THE SAME SHIP AFTER REBUILDING INTO THE *DANAE*

Sea Goddess I

BUILT: *1984 by Wartsila A/B O/Y, Helsinki*
TONNAGE: *4253 gross*
DIMENSIONS: *340 × 47 ft (104.8 × 14.6 m)*
SERVICE SPEED: *17.5 knots*
PROPULSION: *Wartsila Vasa diesels/twin screws*

Undoubtedly the most luxurious cruise vessel attracted to Australia by the America's Cup races was *Sea Goddess I*. Built in a drydock, and floated out on 12 July 1983, she was the first of a pair of "ultra-luxury cruisers" ordered by Norske Cruises of Norway, being delivered in April 1984. Operated by a crew of 71, her accommodation consisted of 60 luxurious staterooms for a maximum of 120 passengers, though they were always referred to as "guests". They had virtually a free run of the ship, with no set meal times, nor any cruise directors and programmed activities.

Entering service in April 1984, *Sea Goddess I* began operating in the Mediterranean, then transferred to the Caribbean in October 1984. In April 1985 her sister, *Sea Goddess II*, entered service, and took over the Mediterranean cruise schedule. Norske Cruises aimed their ships at the very top end of the cruise market, but this did not ensure a viable financial future. By August 1986, Norske Cruises were in deep financial difficulty, and the Wartsila shipyard was threatening to repossess both ships. In a surprise move, the Cunard Line stepped in at the last moment, and took both ships on a 12-year charter. During that period, they will operate under the banner of Cunard Sea Goddess Cruises, but will not carry the Cunard colours on their funnels.

Westpac Travel chartered *Sea Goddess I* for a season of cruises in Australian waters, which brought one of these ships into the South Pacific for the first time. Following a cruise through numerous Pacific islands, *Sea Goddess I* arrived in Sydney on 23 December 1986, after a very stormy passage from Noumea. For the duration of the Westpac charter, a large red "W" was attached to the rear section of the funnel. Over a 10-day period, *Sea Goddess I* spent some time at anchor near the Opera House, made a one-day excursion to follow the start of the yacht race to Hobart on 26 December, and also a one-night excursion up to Broken Bay, anchoring off Cottage Point.

On 1 January 1987, *Sea Goddess I* left Sydney bound for Melbourne, and then went to anchor off Portsea. Her cruise continued across the Great Australian Bight to Albany, and then to Fremantle, arriving on 15 January. She was the first of a flotilla of cruise ships to descend on Fremantle for the America's Cup racing. On race days, the vessel followed the yachts, but on other days she made excursions to nearby locations, such as Rottnest Island. With the unexpected early finish to the racing, *Sea Goddess I* also made several two-night excursions, going south to Geograph Bay twice and once north to Geraldton.

Sea Goddess I was the last of the visiting cruise ships to leave Fremantle, on the evening of 16 February, when she headed for Bali and Singapore, and a series of cruises in Far Eastern waters. Unfortunately, the charter proved to be a financial disaster, as few Australians could afford the high cost of cruising on *Sea Goddess I*, and it is highly unlikely she shall visit Australia again.

SEA GODDESS I

VISTAFJORD

BUILT: *1973 by Swan Hunter Shipbuilders, Newcastle*
TONNAGE: *24 116 gross*
DIMENSIONS: *628 × 82 ft (191.4 × 24.9 m)*
SERVICE SPEED: *20 knots*
PROPULSION: *Sulzer diesels/twin screws*

The last passenger vessel to be built for Norwegian America Line, *Vistafjord* was designed specifically for year-round cruising. Launched on 15 May 1972, she was delivered exactly a year later, having run trials during April 1973. Luxurious accommodation had been installed for up to 620 passengers, but on long cruises a maximum of 550 would be carried, with a crew numbering 390 to look after them. On 22 May 1973, *Vistafjord* left Oslo on a voyage to New York, and then began her cruising career.

Since entering service, *Vistafjord* has usually cruised from European ports between May and October, either to Scandinavia or in the Mediterranean. For the remainder of the year, she has operated out of ports on the east coast of America, mainly Port Everglades, to the West Indies and South America. There was also an annual cruise around the world, which usually went to the North Pacific.

Norwegian America Line had an excellent reputation for the high standard of their ships, but they were having difficulty in remaining financially viable due to the increasing costs involved in keeping the ships on the Norwegian registry, and employing a

Norwegian crew. Eventually the cost factor became too much for them, and in May 1983 the company and its ships were sold to Cunard Line, the actual transfer of ownership taking place in October 1983. *Vistafjord* was transferred to Bahamas registry, and her crew became cosmopolitan, but the high standard was retained. In December 1983, *Vistafjord* entered the Malta Drydocks shipyard for a refit, during which an extra 25 luxury suites were installed, and several public rooms enlarged. Returning to service in January 1984, she now carried the famous Cunard colours on her funnel.

Cunard Line have been sending their premier cruise liners to Australia for over 30 years, but it was not until 1987 that *Vistafjord* was scheduled for her first visit to the region. On 5 January the liner departed Los Angeles, on an 80-day "America's Cup Odyssey", calling at several Pacific islands before arriving in Sydney early in the afternoon of 25 January. *Vistafjord* departed the following night for Melbourne, and also visited Adelaide on 30 January.

On 2 February *Vistafjord* arrived off Fremantle, as the third race of the final series was in progress. She made a day trip for the fourth and final race of the America's Cup, then remained in port three days. On 7 February, *Vistafjord* left Fremantle for Bali, then on to Singapore, Hong Kong, and the remainder of her cruise around the Pacific.

Vistafjord returned to Australia during her 1990 world cruise, arriving in Sydney on 13 February and departing the next day for Brisbane.

VISTAFJORD IN CUNARD COLOURS

CORAL PRINCESS

BUILT: *1962 by Cia. Euskalduna, Bilbao*
TONNAGE: *9639 gross*
DIMENSIONS: *478 × 61 ft (145.7 × 18.5 m)*
SERVICE SPEED: *17 knots*
PROPULSION: *B & W diesels/twin screws*

The cruise ship *Marco Polo* operated from Australian ports between 1970 and 1978, but it was not until 1985 that her former sister made her first appearance in local waters, as *Coral Princess*. This vessel was launched on 17 March 1961 as *Princesa Leopoldina*, having been built for Costeira Line to operate a network of services along the coast of Brazil. Accommodation was provided for 200 first class and 280 tourist class passengers.

During 1968, the Costeira Line fleet was absorbed into the state-owned Lloyd Brasiliero, but *Princesa Leopoldina* and her sister remained on the coastal trades, with occasional cruises. In 1970, both ships were withdrawn from service, and offered for sale. *Princesa Leopoldina* was purchased by China Navigation Co. Ltd, a Hong Kong based subsidiary of the Swire Group. China Navigation had a long association with Australia, and a number of their vessels feature in this book. In the 1960s they enjoyed considerable success in the region with *Kuala Lumpur*, but their best remembered vessels would be *Taiyuan* and *Changsha*.

Renamed *Coral Princess*, she was adapted for cruising, carrying 480 passengers in one class. The vessel made cruises from Hong Kong for her owners, and was also frequently chartered to Japanese groups. During 1982, *Coral Princess* was chartered by the New

South Wales based NRMA Travel, for a series of fly/cruises from Singapore. This programme was repeated over the next few years. In 1985, *Coral Princess* made her first visit to Australia, arriving at Fremantle on 13 March. The next day she departed on a cruise to Asia, returning on 1 April, and leaving the following day to return to Hong Kong. This was repeated in 1986, *Coral Princess* being in Fremantle on 16 March and 6 April.

In connection with the America's Cup races, *Coral Princess* spent longer in Australian waters in 1987. She visited the east coast for the first time, arriving in Brisbane on 20 January and Sydney two days later. She then called at Melbourne before proceeding to Fremantle, where she berthed on 30 January. Over the next two weeks, *Coral Princess* made day trips to watch the final cup races, and then had an extended stay in port, broken by a two-night cruise to Geograph Bay.

On 14 February, *Coral Princess* left Fremantle on a cruise, returning on 17 March, and again on 6 April, then returned to Hong Kong. In January 1988, *Coral Princess* returned to east coast ports again, departing Sydney on 22 January for a two-week cruise to New Zealand, followed by a cruise to Fremantle around the northern coastline of Australia. Arriving in Fremantle on 20 February, she left the same day to return to Hong Kong.

Coral Princess has been extensively altered in recent years, the most notable changes being a box-like extension to the aft superstructure, and a higher funnel. She returned for a short cruise programme in early 1989. In 1990, the vessel was sold, and renamed *Cora Princess*.

CORAL PRINCESS

ROYAL PRINCESS

BUILT: *1984 by Wartsila A/B O/Y, Helsinki*
TONNAGE: *44 348 gross*
DIMENSIONS: *751 × 95 ft (231 × 29.2 m)*
SERVICE SPEED: *22 knots*
PROPULSION: *Pielstick diesels/twin screws*

When the overseas passenger terminal at Circular Quay in Sydney was opened in December 1960, the first vessel to berth there was *Oriana*, at the end of her maiden voyage. Twenty-five years later, she became the last vessel to use the terminal before it was closed for an extensive rebuilding and modernisation. It was fitting that, when the new terminal was opened, another vessel making its maiden arrival in Sydney should be the first to berth there, being *Royal Princess*, which arrived on 12 March 1987.

Royal Princess was the first ship to be built for Princess Cruises, a subsidiary of P & O Line since 1974. The previous three ships operated by the company had all been operated by other companies prior to joining the Princess Cruises fleet, and were of medium size. *Royal Princess* was of a similar tonnage to *Oriana*, though shorter, but with a much bulkier superstructure.

Royal Princess was built in a covered drydock, and floated out on 17 February 1984. The vessel was completed on the date indicated in the contract, and voyaged to Southampton. On 15 November, she was officially named by the Princess of Wales, and four days later departed on her maiden voyage, going first to Miami, and then to Los Angeles.

Royal Princess can accommodate a maximum of 1260 passengers in 600 staterooms, which include a number of luxury suites. All have a window or porthole, and in a break from tradition, the public rooms are located in the hull, with the staterooms in a five deck high block above. This enables 160 of the suites and deluxe cabins to have a private balcony. Every stateroom is also fitted with a colour television, radio and music channels, air-conditioning, and private bathroom facilities. Amenities include four swimming pools, two spa pools, a gymnasium and jogging track, as well as the usual lounges, nightclub, cinema, and a discotheque wrapped around the funnel, with a magnificent 360 degree view.

For the first two years of her career, *Royal Princess* operated two types of cruises. In winter she voyaged through the Panama Canal between Acapulco and San Juan, and in summer from San Francisco to Vancouver and Alaska. Princess Cruises decided to transfer *Royal Princess* to Asian waters for part of her 1986–87 winter season. For her positioning cruise, the liner travelled through the islands of the South Pacific, calling at Auckland on 9 March, then crossing the Tasman to visit Sydney for two days. On departing Sydney, *Royal Princess* headed north to the Whitsunday Passage, where the photograph below was taken. The cruise ended in Hong Kong, from where she operated a series of cruises to China and Japan.

It had been planned that *Royal Princess* would return to the South Pacific in December 1987, but this cruise was cancelled, and *Royal Princess* returned to the west coast of America.

ROYAL PRINCESS ANCHORED IN THE WHITSUNDAY PASSAGE

ILLIRIA

BUILT: *1962 by Cant. Nav. Pellegrino, Naples*
TONNAGE: *3851 gross*
DIMENSIONS: *333 × 48 ft (101.5 × 14.6 m)*
SERVICE SPEED: *17 knots*
PROPULSION: *Fiat diesels/twin screws*

Just two weeks after the giant *Royal Princess* docked at the overseas passenger terminal in Sydney, the berth was host to one of the smallest passenger vessels to visit Australia in recent years. The Greek flag *Illiria* was under charter to Salens, and returning from a voyage to Antarctica, a far distance from the trade for which she was originally designed and built.

Launched on 28 September 1962, *Illiria* was built for the tourist trade between Italy and Greece. Owned by Adriatica Line, of Italy, she made regular 13-day voyages from Trieste and Venice to ports in Yugoslavia and on to the Greek islands and Piraeus between March and October each year. For the remainder of the year, the vessel would be laid up, although on occasion she was chartered for cruising. Fully air-conditioned and fitted with stablilisers, *Illiria* provided very comfortable accommodation for 181 passengers, mostly in cabins with private facilities.

Early in 1976, *Illiria* was sold to Blue Aegean Sea Line, and passed to the Greek flag without change of name. Her passenger capacity was slightly reduced, to 160, and she began making seasonal three- and four-day cruises out of Piraeus to the Greek islands. As before, *Illiria* was laid up for the winter months. This operation was disrupted in 1986, when as an aftermath of the *Achille Lauro* hijacking off Egypt, the Mediterranean cruise trade came to a virtual halt.

Illiria was despatched to Singapore, to operate a variety of cruises in Far Eastern waters, but also spent some periods laid up. Eventually the ship was chartered by the Salen organisation, to operate lengthy cruises to off-beat places. From Singapore, *Illiria* went south to the Antarctic islands, then came to Sydney.

Despite her size, *Illiria* offers most of the amenities found on large cruise liners. Public rooms include a large lounge, two bars, and a dining room large enough to seat all passengers together. A glass screen aft protects the outdoor swimming pool and surrounding lido areas.

Illiria has recently been operating out of Argentine ports on seasonal cruises to the Antarctic, and on other expedition-type cruises for the remainder of the year. It is highly likely that she will not return to Australian waters again.

ILLIRIA TAKES ON A PILOT OFF SYDNEY HEADS

SEA CLOUD

BUILT: *1931 by Fried. Krupp, Kiel*
TONNAGE: *2323 gross*
DIMENSIONS: *316 × 49 ft (97.2 × 15.1 m)*
SERVICE SPEED: *15 knots*
PROPULSION: *Enterprise diesels/twin screws*

Not normally a visitor to the Pacific, *Sea Cloud* came to the area in 1987, when under charter to Special Expeditions. During a series of cruises to many islands off the beaten track to the north-east of Australia, the vessel departed Bali on a voyage that terminated in Cairns on 11 August, having called at Lizard Island the previous day. On leaving Cairns, *Sea Cloud* followed the Great Barrier Reef south, and also stopped at Lord Howe Island and Norfolk Island en route to Nadi.

Built as a private yacht for E. F. Hutton and his wife, the former Marjory Merriweather Post, she was named *Hussar V*, and cost over US$1 million dollars. Fitted out in the most luxurious manner, she provided 13 staterooms for her owners and their guests.

In 1935 the Huttons divorced, with Mrs Hutton receiving title to *Hussar V*, which she promptly renamed *Sea Cloud*. In December 1935, she remarried, her new husband, Joseph E. Davies, later becoming an ambassador. When war broke out, Mrs Davies sold *Sea Cloud* to the US Government for the amount of one dollar, and at Baltimore the vessel had her masts taken out, was repainted grey, and was fitted out with extensive radar, sonar and radio equipment.

When peace returned, *Sea Cloud* was handed back to Mrs Davies, had her masts refitted, and once again became a luxury private yacht. However, in 1955 Mrs Davies sold *Sea Cloud* to the dictator of the Dominican Republic, Rafael Trujillo. Renamed *Angelita*, she remained a private yacht, and was later renamed *Patria*.

In 1967, *Patria* was purchased by a Miami businessman, but registered in Panama under the name *Antara*, being chartered by Oceanics Inc., of New York to cruise as a floating high school, with 60 students aboard at a time. This lasted until the mid-1970s, when the vessel was laid up in Cristobal. Then in 1978, a consortium of 10 West German businessmen bought the ship, and had her extensively rebuilt for service as a cruise ship at a cost of US$6.5 million.

The original public rooms and staterooms were retained intact, complete with original oil paintings, antique furniture, fireplaces and wood panelling. In addition, 28 new staterooms were added in an enlarged superstructure, designed in keeping with her original appearance, and overall style. In her new guise, the vessel could accommodate a maximum of 75 passengers, always referred to on board as guests. Being a genuine sailing ship, a crew of 60 is required at all times, as the sails all have to be set and furled by hand.

Prior to returning to active service, the vessel was renamed *Sea Cloud*. Taken on charter by an American tour firm, Heritage Cruises, *Sea Cloud* usually divides her year between the Caribbean and European waters.

SEA CLOUD

THE BELORUSSIYA CLASS

BUILT: *1975–76 by Wartsila A/B O/Y, Turku*
TONNAGE: *16 631 gross*
DIMENSIONS: *515 × 71 ft (157 × 21.8 m)*
SERVICE SPEED: *22 knots*
PROPULSION: *Pielstick diesels/twin screws*

These ships were named after regions of the Soviet Union, with the first being named *Belorussiya* when launched on 6 March 1974. She was followed by *Gruziya* on 18 October 1974, *Azerbaidzhan* on 14 April 1975 and *Kazakhstan* on 17 October 1975. The last of the series was launched on 14 April 1976 and named *Kareliya*.

In their original form, each of these ships was fitted out to accommodate 504 passengers in cabins, 114 in reclining seats, and 390 unberthed on short coastal sectors, with garage space for up to 256 cars and 23 trucks. When cruising, they would carry 350 passengers only.

Belorussiya was delivered to the Black Sea Steam Ship Co. on 15 January 1975, while the subsequent four ships were delivered at six-month intervals to the same company. All were based on Odessa, but almost immediately they were being used as much for cruising as in their car ferry role.

In June 1981, *Kareliya* was sent to the Tyne ship repairing yard at Newcastle to have the garage space converted into cabins, which increased her capacity to

650 passengers for cruises. *Kareliya* returned to service in January 1982, and was renamed *Leonid Brezhnev* the following year. In 1984, *Kazakhstan* went to the Lloyd Werft shipyard in Hamburg for a major refit, and in 1986 the same yard also refitted *Azerbaidzhan* and *Belorussiya*.

The first of these vessels to appear in the South Pacific was *Kazakhstan*, which made a world cruise early in 1986. After calling at Auckland on 13 February, she arrived in Sydney on 16 February. In 1987, *Azerbaidzhan* was selected to make the world cruise, being in Sydney on 17 and 18 February. The 1988 world cruise was taken by *Leonid Brezhnev*, departing Tilbury on 6 January, voyaging through the Panama Canal, arriving in Auckland on 14 February and Sydney on 17 February. Leaving the next day, the vessel called at Brisbane on 20 February, then continued via the Far East, Indian Ocean and Suez Canal back to Tilbury.

The loss of *Mikhail Lermontov* had left CTC Cruises in Australia short of an extra cruise ship for the 1986–87 season, but they were able to secure *Belorussiya* for the following season. *Belorussiya* arrived in Sydney on 23 December 1987, and began making regular cruises around the South Pacific during the summer season.

Belorussiya returned to Australia for the summers of 1988/89 and 1989/90, spending the rest of each year in European waters. The 1989 and 1990 world cruises were both operated by *Azerbaidzhan*, and included calls at New Zealand and Australian ports.

BELORUSSIYA

FAIR PRINCESS

BUILT: *1956 by John Brown & Co., Clydebank*
TONNAGE: *16 627 gross*
DIMENSIONS: *608 × 80 ft (185.3 × 24.5 m)*
SERVICE SPEED: *20 knots*
PROPULSION: *Geared turbines/twin screws*

During 1971, Sitmar Cruises announced that two new ships would be entering the South Pacific cruise trade within a year. To be named *Fairsea* and *Fairwind*, they would combine island cruises with trans-Pacific voyages between Sydney and Los Angeles. This plan was abandoned and both ships went into the American cruise trade. It was not until November 1988 that one of them made a voyage to Australia, but when *Fairsea* arrived she was under her new name, *Fair Princess*.

Fair Princess was launched on 14 December 1955 as *Carinthia*, for the Cunard Line. The third of four sister ships built for the Canadian trade, *Carinthia* left Liverpool on 27 June 1956 on her maiden voyage to Montreal. She joined *Saxonia* and *Ivernia*, and a year later *Sylvania* was completed. The first pair were refurbished for cruising in the 1960s, being renamed *Carmania* and *Franconia*, while *Carinthia* and *Sylvania* were offered for sale.

Purchased by Sitmar Line in January 1968, *Carinthia* was handed over at Southampton on 4 May 1968, and *Sylvania* two months later. They were renamed *Fairland* and *Fairwind*, but were to lie idle in Southampton for the next two years. When Sitmar bought this pair, they intended to convert them for the Australian migrant trade, replacing the veterans *Fairsea* and *Castel Felice*.

However, in 1969 the next five-year migrant contract, to commence in 1970, was awarded to Chandris Line, so *Fairland* and *Fairwind* remained idle while plans were drawn up for their conversion into cruise liners.

In January 1970, *Fairland* and *Fairwind* both arrived at the Arsenale Triestino shipyard for extensive rebuilding, during which *Fairland* was renamed *Fairsea*. She was the first to enter service, in December 1971, cruising on the west coast of North America, to Mexico and Alaska, where *Fairwind* joined her in June 1972.

In mid-1988, Sitmar Cruises announced a merger with rivals Princess Cruises, to form one of the largest cruise liner fleets in the world. As part of the agreement, the Sitmar ships would be given Princess names, and repainted in their colours. *Fairsea* completed her scheduled series of cruises to Alaska in September 1988, then went into drydock for a refit. At this time, the vessel was repainted in Princess colours, and her name changed to *Fair Princess*. She then departed Los Angeles on a cruise to Tahiti, from where she continued to New Zealand and Australia, arriving in Sydney on 10 November. She then made a series of cruises to South Pacific islands and around New Zealand. In April 1989, *Fair Princess* left Sydney to return to the west coast of America.

In 1973, the former sister ships of this pair, *Carmania* and *Franconia*, were sold to the Soviet Union. Renamed *Fedor Shalyapin* and *Leonid Sobinov*, they began operating to Australia, being described elsewhere in this book. A comparison of photographs of this pair will illustrate how extensively *Fair Princess* was rebuilt.

FAIR PRINCESS

ROYAL VIKING SUN

BUILT: *1988 by Wartsila Marine, Turku*
TONNAGE: *37 845 gross*
DIMENSIONS: *670 × 95 ft (204 × 28.9 m)*
SERVICE SPEED: *21 knots*
PROPULSION: *Sulzer diesels/twin screws*

It had been many years since a new passenger liner arrived in Australia on its maiden voyage, so when *Royal Viking Sun* entered Sydney Harbour on the afternoon of 1 February 1989, it was an occasion worth noting. Unfortunately, the weather was not in accord with the warm reception accorded the latest addition to the Royal Viking Line fleet as she proceeded slowly towards her berth at the Sydney Cove Passenger Terminal.

Royal Viking Sun was constructed in a covered graving dock, and floated out in late April 1988. Using this procedure, the vessel was in a very advanced state of construction, and only the internal fitting out remained, and this was completed in a few months. Then *Royal Viking Sun* left the cold waters of Finland for the California port of San Francisco, where Royal Viking Line have their headquarters, despite their Norwegian origins. It was here, on 8 January 1989, that famous actor James Stewart officially christened the new liner, which then departed on a 100-day round-the-world cruise.

This inaugural cruise visited 34 ports in 24 countries on five continents, starting with Honolulu, then Apia and Nuku'alofa en route to New Zealand. Here *Royal Viking Sun* called at Opua, Auckland and Picton, before proceeding to Sydney for a two day stopover. On 4 February, the new liner called at Brisbane, then spent a day at anchor in the Whitsunday Passage before continuing to Cairns, and finally Darwin, where she berthed on 11 February for ten hours. Leaving Australia behind, *Royal Viking Sun* went to ports in Asia, India and Europe, then crossed the Atlantic to finish her

maiden cruise in Port Everglades.

Royal Viking Sun is an outstanding liner, with great thought being given to passenger comfort. For the 768 passengers there are 384 cabins, over a third having private balconies, and all with private facilities. A wide range of public rooms are provided, the largest being the Show Lounge, seating 750. Smaller rooms include the Night Club, Observation Lounge, Card Room, Cinema, and numerous bars. All passengers can dine at one sitting, in three restaurants. Following the tradition started by the earlier Royal Viking ships, there are numerous open spaces, including a teak-covered promenade deck that wraps completely around the superstructure. There are three forward observation decks forward, with sports and sunbathing areas aft. Atop of the superstructure is another large open deck protected from the wind, ideal for sunbathing, or viewing passing scenery. Among the many "firsts" on this fine liner are the walk-in closets in all staterooms, an elegant a la carte restaurant, a "swim-up" bar in one of the swimming pools, an automatic window washing system, and air conditioned shore tenders.

To reduce vibration and noise, the engines are mounted on a thick cushion of rubber. This allows the machinery to vibrate independently from the ship, and to accommodate this movement, all hoses, pipes and cables, as well as the entire exhaust system attached to the engines must be flexible.

Following her maiden cruise, *Royal Viking Sun* joined the older units of the fleet in a schedule of cruises of varying lengths that took her to many parts of the world, including northern Europe and Scandinavia, Canada, the Caribbean, and back into the Pacific again. This type of wide-ranging cruising is what *Royal Viking Sun* was designed for, and in 1990 the liner returned to Australia again, on her second cruise around the world. Hopefully this liner will be a regular visitor to our shores for many years to come.

ROYAL VIKING SUN

VASCO DA GAMA

BUILT: *1961 by S.A. Cockerill-Ougree, Hoboken.*
TONNAGE: *24 562 gross*
DIMENSIONS: *641 × 80 ft (195.5 × 24.5 m)*
SERVICE SPEED: *21 knots.*
PROPULSION: *Geared turbines/twin screws*

Vasco Da Gama was the first Portuguese liner to visit Australia in many years when she made a world cruise in 1989. This liner was built for Cia. Colonial, of Lisbon, being named *Infante dom Henrique* when launched on 29 April 1960. Completed in September 1961, she entered service from Lisbon to West, South and East Africa, calling at Luanda, Lobito, Cape Town, Lourenco Marques and Beira, having cabins for 156 first class and 862 tourist class passengers.

As the Portuguese African colonies gained their independence, the demand for passages declined, and on 3 January 1976, *Infante Dom Henrique* was laid up in Lisbon. In July 1977 she was moved to Sines, on the Portuguese coast, and after both propellers were removed, assumed a role as an accommodation ship for construction workers, floating in a specially constructed basin.

For eleven years, *Infante Dom Henrique* served in her static role, during which she received very little maintenance. The vessel was in very poor condition when she was offered for sale in 1985, and it was thought she would only be of interest to shipbreakers. In 1987, she was purchased by Arcalia Shipping, of Lisbon. Surprisingly, the new owners wished to return the ship to active service, and she was towed to Greece in April 1988 for a major refit. This involved the complete rebuilding of the interior of the liner, with luxury accommodation for 660 passengers, and redesigned public rooms. Fortunately the attractive external lines of the vessel were not altered, and she was renamed *Vasco Da Gama*.

Chartered to a West German tourist organisation, *Vasco Da Gama* arrived in Lisbon on 4 December 1988 to commence her new career, but a few days later suffered an engine room fire, and had to be towed to Bremerhaven for repairs. The liner then departed Genoa on 7 January 1989 for her round-the-world cruise, which included visits to Auckland, Wellington, Picton and Milford Sound before arriving in Sydney on 7 March. Departing two days later, *Vasco Da Gama* went on to visit Hobart and Melbourne, then called at Albany on 17 March, berthing in Fremantle the following day. From there *Vasco Da Gama* continued her cruise back to Genoa. To date this is the only visit by this vessel to the South Pacific.

VASCO DA GAMA

INDEX

P&O presents 21 great cruises in 1968

Cruises from 5 days to 31 days. (from Sydney) Roam the South Seas. Explore the Orient.

Step aboard a big, white, P & O liner and head for the kind of holiday that takes you away from the humdrum into a gay, lively world of sunshine, blue skies, sparkling seas and exotic lands beyond the horizon.

Can you spare 5 days for a holiday? 10 days? 2 weeks? A month? Check the list of cruises below. Look what you get for your money: a complete holiday at Australia's fastest-growing resort—a P & O cruise liner—where you can play, swim, dine, dance away each fun-filled day with a group of happy people, out for a good time—just like yourself.

Your fare includes accommodation, all meals, recreation, entertainment and exciting foreign travel. Your only expenses on board will be personal items like drinks and cigarettes, which are mostly duty free.

See your P & O Travel Agent for literature and reservations. There's one right near you in your city, suburb or country centre.

Join the swing to gay, lively holidays – Choose one of these fabulous P&O cruises!

Sailing dates shown are from Sydney back to Sydney. Ask about connecting travel from other States. Allocation of a cabin at a particular rate depends on availability at date of application.

JAN. 6 – Orsova SOUTH SEA ISLES CRUISE to Suva and Nuku'alofa, 10 days. (Fully booked).

JAN. 18 – Orsova 8 day FIJI CRUISE to Suva. Fares from $181 First; $133 Tourist.

JAN. 20 – Arcadia HAPPY WANDERER CRUISE to Suva, Nuku'alofa, Auckland, 13 days. Fares from $322 First; wait list Tourist.

JAN. 27 – Orsova FIJI-N.Z. CRUISE to Suva, Auckland and Bay of Islands, 11 days. Fares from $250 First; $184 Tourist.

FEB. 3 – Arcadia CRUISE LA RONDE to Noumea, Fiji (Lautoka and Suva), Auckland, 13 days. Fares from $322 First; wait list Tourist.

FEB. 17 – Arcadia DOUBLE DATELINE CRUISE to Pago Pago, Suva, Auckland, 13 days. Fares from $322 First; $218 Tourist.

MAR. 31 – Himalaya CHERRY BLOSSOM CRUISE to Guam, Yokohama (Tokyo), Kobe, Hong Kong and Manila, 31 days. One Class fares from $700.

MAY 27 – Oriana CORAL SEA CRUISE to Hayman Island and Port Moresby, 8 days. Fares from $244 First; $152 Tourist.

HIMALAYA'S 8 ADVENTURE CRUISES —ONE CLASS

JULY 25 to Suva, Noumea and Melbourne, 13 days. Fares from $217.

AUG. 8 to Lautoka, Suva and Nuku'alofa, 11 days. Fares from $186.

AUG. 20 to Pago Pago, Suva and Melbourne, 14 days. Fares from $233.

SEPT. 5 to Hayman Island via the Great Barrier Reef and Whitsunday Passage, 5 days. Fares from $92.

SEPT. 14 to Suva and Noumea, 9 days. Fares from $151.

SEPT. 25 to Noumea, Suva and Auckland, 11 days. Fares from $186.

OCT. 7 to Suva, Lautoka and Brisbane, 10 days. Fares from $168.

OCT. 19 to Pago Pago, Suva and Brisbane, 13 days. Fares from $217.

OCT. 17 Canberra ORIENTAL CRUISE to Yokohama (Tokyo), Kobe, Nagasaki, Hong Kong, 28 days. Fares from $809 First; $435 Tourist.

DEC. 1 Orcades Cruise to Noumea, Suva and Auckland, 13 days. One Class from $204.

DEC. 15 Orcades CHRISTMAS CRUISE to Brisbane, Suva, Lautoka, Auckland, 14 days. One Class from $240.

DEC. 20 Iberia CHRISTMAS/NEW YEAR CRUISE to Noumea, Picton, Wellington, Bay of Islands, 12 days. Fares from $281 First; $205 Tourist.

Provisional Cruise

DEC. 30 Orsova to South Sea Island Ports.

Go gay - go Cruising with P&O in '68